# Analysis and Argumentation in Rabbinic Judaism

Jacob Neusner

BARD COLLEGE

Studies in Judaism

University Press of America,® Inc.
Lanham · New York · Oxford

Copyright © 2003 by
University Press of America,® Inc.
4501 Forbes Boulevard
Suite 200
Lanham, Maryland 20706

12 Hid's Copse Rd.
Cumnor Hill, Oxford OX2 9JJ

All rights reserved
Printed in the United States of America
British Library Cataloging in Publication Information Available

ISBN 0-7618-2527-4 (clothbound : alk. ppr.)

☉™ The paper used in this publication meets the minimum
requirements of American National Standard for Information
Sciences—Permanence of Paper for Printed Library Materials,
ANSI Z39.48—1984

# Studies in Judaism

EDITOR

Jacob Neusner
Bard College

EDITORIAL BOARD

Alan J. Avery-Peck
College of the Holy Cross

Herbert Basser
Queens University

Bruce D. Chilton
Bard College

José Faur
Bar Ilan University

William Scott Green
University of Rochester

Mayer Gruber
Ben-Gurion University of the Negev

Günter Stemberger
University of Vienna

James F. Strange
University of South Florida

## Table of Contents

Preface ............................................................................................................. xi

Introduction ................................................................................................... xiv

### Part One

#### A Preliminary Probe:
#### Types of Analysis in Tractate Moed Qatan

1. Moed Qatan, Chapter One ...................................................................... 3
   - i. Mishnah .......................................................................................... 3
   - ii. Tosefta ............................................................................................ 6
   - iii. Yerushalmi ...................................................................................... 8
   - iv. Bavli .............................................................................................. 12
   - v. Types of Analysis. An Initial Proposal ........................................ 19

2. Moed Qatan, Chapter Two .................................................................... 21
   - i. Language-Analysis: The close reading of the language of the rule, yielding insight based on the wording ............................... 21
   - ii. Category-Criticism: Taxonomic inquiry into category-formations of the law and the comparison and contrast thereof ....................... 23
   - iii. Rationality: The reason behind the rule, yielding the possibility of transcending the limits of the case ........................................ 26
   - iv. Analogy-Criticism: Finding the correct analogy for the identification of the governing rule ................................................................ 26
   - v. Types of Analysis ......................................................................... 26

### Part Two

#### A Secondary Probe:
#### Types of Analysis in Select Tractates:
#### Qiddushin, Abodah Zarah

3. Qiddushin ............................................................................................... 33
   - i. Language-Analysis ....................................................................... 33
     - a. Mishnah ................................................................................ 33
     - b. Tosefta ................................................................................. 33

|   |       | c.   | Yerushalmi ............................................................................... 33 |
|---|-------|------|---|
|   |       | d.   | Bavli ........................................................................................ 33 |
|   | ii.   | Category-Criticism .............................................................................. 40 |
|   |       | a.   | Mishnah .................................................................................. 40 |
|   |       | b.   | Tosefta .................................................................................... 40 |
|   |       | c.   | Yerushalmi ............................................................................... 40 |
|   |       | d.   | Bavli ........................................................................................ 43 |
|   | iii.  | Rationality ........................................................................................... 43 |
|   |       | a.   | Mishnah .................................................................................. 43 |
|   |       | b.   | Tosefta .................................................................................... 43 |
|   |       | c.   | Yerushalmi ............................................................................... 43 |
|   |       | d.   | Bavli ........................................................................................ 43 |
|   | iv.   | Analogy-Criticism ............................................................................... 43 |
|   |       | a.   | Mishnah .................................................................................. 43 |
|   |       | b.   | Tosefta .................................................................................... 43 |
|   |       | c.   | Yerushalmi ............................................................................... 43 |
|   |       | d.   | Bavli ........................................................................................ 45 |
|   | v.    | Scriptural Foundations of the Halakhah ............................................ 47 |
|   |       | a.   | Mishnah .................................................................................. 47 |
|   |       | b.   | Tosefta .................................................................................... 47 |
|   |       | c.   | Yerushalmi ............................................................................... 47 |
|   |       | d.   | Bavli ........................................................................................ 51 |
|   | vi.   | Types of Analysis ................................................................................ 56 |

4. ABODAH ZARAH ................................................................................................... 57

|   | i.    | Language-Analysis ............................................................................... 57 |
|---|-------|---|---|
|   |       | a.   | Mishnah .................................................................................. 57 |
|   |       | b.   | Tosefta .................................................................................... 57 |
|   |       | c.   | Yerushalmi ............................................................................... 57 |
|   |       | d.   | Bavli ........................................................................................ 57 |
|   | ii.   | Category-Criticism .............................................................................. 57 |
|   |       | a.   | Mishnah .................................................................................. 57 |
|   |       | b.   | Tosefta .................................................................................... 57 |
|   |       | c.   | Yerushalmi ............................................................................... 57 |
|   |       | d.   | Bavli ........................................................................................ 57 |
|   | iii.  | Rationality ........................................................................................... 57 |
|   |       | a.   | Mishnah .................................................................................. 57 |
|   |       | b.   | Tosefta .................................................................................... 58 |
|   |       | c.   | Yerushalmi ............................................................................... 58 |
|   |       | d.   | Bavli ........................................................................................ 59 |
|   | iv.   | Analogy-Criticism ............................................................................... 62 |

|  |  | a. | Mishnah | 62 |
|---|---|---|---|---|
|  |  | b. | Tosefta | 63 |
|  |  | c. | Yerushalmi | 63 |
|  |  | d. | Bavli | 63 |
|  | v. | Scriptural Foundations of the Halakhah | | 63 |
|  |  | a. | Mishnah | 63 |
|  |  | b. | Tosefta | 63 |
|  |  | c. | Yerushalmi | 63 |
|  |  | d. | Bavli | 64 |
|  | vi. | Types of Analysis | | 66 |

PART THREE

TYPES OF ANALYSIS IN SELECTED MIDRASH COMPILATIONS

5. GENESIS RABBAH ............................................................................. 69

 i. Language-Analysis ............................................................... 70
 ii. Analogy- and Category-Criticism ....................................... 71
 iii. Rationality ........................................................................... 76
 iv. Scriptural Foundations of the Halakhah ............................. 87
 v. The Types of Analysis in Genesis Rabbah ......................... 91

6. LEVITICUS RABBAH ........................................................................ 93

 i. Language-Analysis ............................................................... 94
 ii. Analogy- and Category-Criticism ....................................... 97
 iii. Rationality ......................................................................... 101
 iv. Scriptural Foundations of the Halakhah ........................... 105
 v. The Types of Analysis in Leviticus Rabbah ..................... 108

7. SIFRÉ TO NUMBERS ...................................................................... 111

 i. The Priority of Scripture over Analogical-Contrastive
  Reasoning ........................................................................... 111
 ii. Language-Analysis ............................................................. 114
 iii. Analogy- and Category-Criticism ..................................... 119
 iv. Rationality ......................................................................... 127
 v. Scriptural Foundations of the Halakhah ........................... 129
 vi. The Types of Analysis in Sifré to Numbers ...................... 135

vii. Conclusion: Types of Analysis of Rabbinic Judaism, Halakhic and Aggadic .................................................................................. 136

PART FOUR

A PRELIMINARY PROBE:
TYPES OF ARGUMENTATION IN TRACTATE MOED QATAN

8. MOED QATAN CHAPTER ONE .................................................................. 141

   i. Mishnah .................................................................................. 144
   ii. Tosefta .................................................................................. 144
   iii. Yerushalmi ............................................................................ 146
   iv. Bavli ..................................................................................... 147
   v. The Types of Argumentation ................................................. 150

9. MOED QATAN CHAPTER TWO ................................................................. 153

   i. Arguments Based on Tradition and Reason ......................... 153
   ii. Arguments Executed through Exegesis of Scripture ........... 155
   iii. The Types of Argumentation ................................................. 155

PART FIVE

A SECONDARY PROBE:
TYPES OF ARGUMENTATION IN SELECT TRACTATES:
QIDDUSHIN, ABODAH ZARAH

10. QIDDUSHIN .............................................................................................. 159

    i. Arguments Based on Tradition and Reason ......................... 159
       a. Mishnah ........................................................................... 159
       b. Tosefta ............................................................................. 159
       c. Yerushalmi ....................................................................... 159
       d. Bavli ................................................................................. 159
    ii. Arguments Executed through Exegesis of Scripture ........... 165
       a. Mishnah ........................................................................... 165
       b. Tosefta ............................................................................. 165
       c. Yerushalmi ....................................................................... 165
       d. Bavli ................................................................................. 166
    iii. Arguments Concerning the Governing Analogy ................... 168
       a. Mishnah ........................................................................... 168

|     |      | b.    | Tosefta ................................................................................. 168 |
| --- | ---- | ----- | --- |
|     |      | c.    | Yerushalmi .......................................................................... 168 |
|     |      | d.    | Bavli ................................................................................... 168 |
|     | iv.  | The Types of Argumentation ............................................................. 168 |

11. ABODAH ZARAH ................................................................................................ 169

    i. Arguments Based on Tradition and Reason ........................................ 169
        a. Mishnah ............................................................................. 169
        b. Tosefta ............................................................................... 170
        c. Yerushalmi ......................................................................... 171
        d. Bavli .................................................................................. 171
    ii. Arguments Executed through Exegesis of Scripture ........................... 173
        a. Mishnah ............................................................................. 173
        b. Tosefta ............................................................................... 174
        c. Yerushalmi ......................................................................... 175
        d. Bavli .................................................................................. 176
    iii. Arguments Concerning the Governing Analogy ................................. 176
        a. Mishnah ............................................................................. 176
        b. Tosefta ............................................................................... 176
        c. Yerushalmi ......................................................................... 176
        d. Bavli .................................................................................. 176
    iv. The Types of Argumentation ............................................................. 176

12. DIALECTICAL VERSUS NON-DIALECTICAL ARGUMENTS .................................. 177

    i. A Simple Typology of Argumentation: Dialectical versus Non-Dialectical Arguments ........................................................................ 177
    ii. Defining the Dialectical Argument and Two Instances of a Non-Dialectical Argument ..................................................................... 178
    iii. An Example of a Dialectical Argument ............................................. 184
    iv. A Contrasting Example of an Argument of an Other-than-Dialectical Character ........................................................................................... 190
    v. The Importance of the Dialectical Argument in the Halakhic Literature ........................................................................................... 202
    vi. The Law behind the Laws ................................................................. 205
    vii. The Unity of the Law ........................................................................ 208
    viii. Dialectics and the Intellectual Dynamics of the Halakhic Literature ........................................................................................... 212

PART SIX

TYPES OF ARGUMENT, AUTHENTIC AND INAUTHENTIC,
IN MIDRASH-COMPILATIONS

13. GENESIS RABBAH ................................................................................ 217

    i.   Dialectical Arguments ................................................................ 217
    ii.  Non-Dialectical Arguments ....................................................... 217
    iii. Types of Argumentation in Genesis Rabbah ........................... 225

14. LEVITICUS RABBAH ........................................................................... 227

    i.   Dialectical Arguments ................................................................ 227
    ii.  Non-Dialectical Arguments ....................................................... 227
    iii. Types of Argumentation in Leviticus Rabbah ........................ 235

15. SIFRÉ TO NUMBERS ............................................................................ 237

    i.   Dialectical Arguments ................................................................ 237
    ii.  Non-Dialectical Arguments ....................................................... 237
    iii. Types of Argumentation in Sifré to Numbers ......................... 259
    iv. Conclusion: Types of Argumentation of Rabbinic Judaism: Halakhic and
        Aggadic ....................................................................................... 262

# Preface

Do ubiquitous modes of thought — types of analysis, types of argumentation — pervade the entire corpus of the Rabbinic writings of late antiquity and impart coherence to those diverse documents? Here I report on the results of a systematic probe of representative Halakhic and Aggadic documents in search of the answer to that question. The result is limited but one-sided: the answer is yes, they do.

The inquiry proves urgent, because the bases for supposing the Rabbinic documents coalesce have diminished, and the differences between and among the respective documents have made their mark. For we now realize, each of the Rabbinic documents of the formative age, from the Mishnah through the Talmud of Babylonia, ca. 200-600, exhibits indicative traits that distinguish that document from all others in the Rabbinic canon. If we characterize a document by reference to its governing program of topic, rhetoric, and logic of coherent discourse, none recapitulates the definitive qualities of any other. Some share traits of common forms or rhetoric; others appeal to a logic of coherent discourse that pertains beyond their limits; and still other sets of documents may go over the same topics or propositions at some determinate points. But the particular combination of [1] rhetorical forms, [2] topical issues, and [3] the logical media of coherence that define one document prove unique to that document. The same is so of Rabbinic narrative: documents exhibit clear-cut preferences, and the types of narrative are not uniformly spread over the documents by any means. Rather, each document chooses a narrative type or form that serves its particular task and neglects those that do not.[1]

---

[1] I have shown this in a survey of eight documents, conducted both synchronically and diachronically, in the following work: *Rabbinic Narrative: A Documentary Perspective.* Volume One. *Forms, Types, and Distribution of Narratives in the Mishnah, Tractate Abot, and the Tosefta.* Leiden, 2003: E. J. . Brill. THE BRILL REFERENCE LIBRARY OF JUDAISM; *Rabbinic Narrative: A Documentary Perspective.* Volume Two. *Forms, Types, and Distribution of Narratives in Sifra, Sifré to Numbers, and Sifré to Deuteronomy.* Leiden, 2003: E. J. Brill. THE BRILL REFERENCE LIBRARY OF JUDAISM; *Rabbinic Narrative: A Documentary Perspective.* Volume Three. *Forms, Types, and Distribution of Narratives in Song of Songs Rabbah and Lamentations Rabbah. And a Reprise of Fathers According to Rabbi Nathan Text A.* Leiden, 2003: E. J. Brill. THE BRILL REFERENCE LIBRARY OF JUDAISM; *Rabbinic Narrative. A Documentary Perspective.* Volume Four. *The Precedent and the Parable in Diachronic View.* Leiden, 2003: E. J. Brill. THE BRILL REFERENCE LIBRARY OF JUDAISM.

Comparing one document to another yields a single result throughout. In one aspect or another, what distinguishes the set of indicative traits of one document does not characterize that of any other document. Not only so, but when we take up the propositions attributed to diverse named authorities of the Rabbinic writings, we find a mass of conflicting opinion, rich in controversy and dispute. Everyone understands that fact, which makes difficult the characterization of Rabbinic Judaism as a coherent religious system and structure. For if the parts do not cohere, of what can the whole consist? And how do the documents join together into a cogent whole? In terms familiar in the History of Religion, how do the diverse bits of evidence coalesce so that we may speak of a single Judaism — a coherent Judaic religious system — to which all the documents — Aggadic and Halakhic alike — attest?[2]

To answer that question, in this project I turn to issues of an intellectual character. I ask whether, however diverse, all of the documents conform to a single, determinate program of [1] analysis and [2] argumentation. Do they raise in common a set of questions that are ubiquitous, and do they pursue a uniform inquiry, whatever the data subject to study?

Further, does a single protocol of argumentation dictate the means by which analytical propositions are advanced and tested? If they do, then Rabbinic Judaism finds coherence in shared intellectual traits. These, then, would serve to define the foundations for the construction of all components into the Rabbinic system and structure. If not, then we shall have to look elsewhere for that inner coherence that forms into an intellectual canon the authoritative writings of Judaism in its formative stage. As matters now stand, those writings share some traits, not others, as we work our way from start to finish. Each document intersects with others, even with all others, in some ways but not in others.

---

[2] I have shown the shared language of the Rabbinic canon in *The Theological Grammar of the Oral Torah*. Binghamton, 1999: Dowling College Press/Global Publications of Binghamton University [SUNY]. I. *Vocabulary: Native Categories*; *The Theological Grammar of the Oral Torah*. Binghamton, 1999: Dowling College Press/Global Publications of Binghamton University [SUNY]. II. *Syntax: Connections and Constructions; The Theological Grammar of the Oral Torah*. Binghamton, 1999: Dowling College Press/Global Publications of Binghamton University [SUNY]. III. *Semantics: Models of Analysis, Explanation and Anticipation*. But the unity of Halakhic and Aggadic documents represents a more difficult problem. Identifying common modes of thought strikes me as a possible solution, hence the present project.

*Preface* *xiii*

The translation and reference system in this project derive from my academic commentaries to the two Talmuds and the Midrash-compilations,[3] which signal information not conveyed by the received reference systems. Since the work is widely available in libraries, those who wish to follow up and check on the results reported here can readily do so.

This book presents a condensation and revision of the following two volumes:

*The Modes of Thought of Rabbinic Judaism*. I. *Types of Analysis.* Binghamton 2000: Global Publications. ACADEMIC STUDIES IN THE HISTORY OF JUDAISM SERIES.

*The Modes of Thought of Rabbinic Judaism.* II. *Types of Argumentation.* Binghamton 2000: Global Publications. ACADEMIC STUDIES IN THE HISTORY OF JUDAISM SERIES.

I determined to bring out an abbreviated account of my results for those who want the main evidence and outcome but do not wish to plough through the considerable research report that sustains the results.

I began work on this project in my tenth and final year as Distinguished Research Professor of Religious Studies at the University of South Florida and completed it in my first year as Research Professor of Religion and Theology at Bard College. I express thanks to colleagues at both places for their on-going interest in, and interesting comments upon, my inquiries. I thank both University of South Florida and Bard College for the research support they have accorded to me, from 1990 through 2000 by USF, and from 1994 to the present day, by Bard.

I accomplished the revision and condensation at the beginning of my third year as full-time Research Professor at Bard College and express thanks for the opportunities afforded to me by that position. Bard College forms a delightful academic community, rich in talent and achievement, and I am proud to take part in it.

JACOB NEUSNER
BARD COLLEGE
ANNANDALE-ON-HUDSON, NEW YORK 12504
NEUSNER@WEBJOGGER.NET

---

[3] *The Talmud of Babylonia. An Academic Commentary.* Atlanta, 1994-1996, 1999: Scholars Press for *USF Academic Commentary Series*; *The Talmud of the Land of Israel. An Academic Commentary to the Second, Third, and Fourth Divisions.* Atlanta, 1998-1999: Scholars Press for *USF Academic Commentary Series. For Midrash: The Components of the Rabbinic Documents: From the Whole to the Parts.* Atlanta, 1997: Scholars Press for USF Academic Commentary Series. With the demise of Scholars Press, these titles are now published by University Press of America.

# Introduction

What, if anything, do all the canonical documents of Rabbinic Judaism have in common, and how do they all together attest to a common structure and system? The answer to that question allows us to characterize that Judaic religious system that encompasses all of the discrete, diverse writings of the Rabbinic canon — to speak of the Judaism, the Judaic religious structure and system, that animates them all. And to accomplish the goal of definition, that characterization would have to focus on profound, not superficial, traits: modes of thought everywhere in command. True, we should have no difficulty in formulating what the documents have in common, but whether the commonalities prove weighty and consequential is another matter. For, to permit using the entire corpus of writing to define the Judaism to which each document attests, more is needed. What requires identification is not the lowest common denominator, but the deeply embedded qualities of mind that permeate the whole, from the Mishnah through the Bavli, encompassing the entirety of both the Halakhic and the Aggadic corpus. We accordingly are led to ask how all of the documents, viewed all together and all at once, participate in a single religious system, form an intellectually coherent statement that we may call a "Judaism," a system of religious thought possessed of integrity and philosophical and theological coherence.

Answers come from the generalizing sciences: theology (philosophical thinking about religious ideas), and also, in this context, hermeneutics, and literature. The documents can be, and have been, shown to participate in a coherent theological system that defines the norms of belief animating each of the Aggadic compilations, a system that furthermore correlates with the counterpart theological system permeating the Halakhic ones.[1] The systemic myth and its logic, moreover, have been demonstrated in detail to permeate the whole. The corpus of writings can further be, and has been, demonstrated to invoke a single set of hermeneutical rules of category-formation throughout the Halakhic documents.[2] The two native literary genres of the canon, Halakhah and Aggadah, can be, and have been, shown to

---

[1] *The Theology of the Oral Torah. Revealing the Justice of God.* Kingston and Montreal, 1999: McGill-Queens University Press and Ithaca, 1999: Cornell University Press; *The Theology of the Halakhah* (Leiden. 2001: E. J. Brill).

[2] *The Comparative Hermeneutics of Rabbinic Judaism.* Binghamton, 2000: Global Publications. ACADEMIC STUDIES IN ANCIENT JUDAISM series. I-VIII.

exhibit, respectively, uniform traits of formulation and expression, transcending documentary lines.[3] So in works on theology and hermeneutics and Aggadic and Halakhic relationships — the substance of thought, the guiding principles of category-formation and interpretation, and the correlation of the genres of writing — I have taken up the problem of the cogency of the Rabbinic canon. In a variety of exercises I have asked how, having differentiated each document from all others, we may speak of the whole. The governing hypothesis has come to articulation in these terms. It holds that

[1] a system of thought unfolds in tight logic from start to finish and encompasses all the Rabbinic documents;

[2] a persistent hermeneutics dictates the definition of native category-formations;

[3] fixed rules of discourse affect one type of writing rather than another.

What awaits is probative: the demonstration of the intellectual cogency of the Rabbinic canon, particularly as concerns the Halakhah, where norms are defined. That work begins here.

How, then, to proceed? As usual, I conduct an initial probe to establish some guide-lines and frame a taxonomic hypothesis. Then I test that hypothesis against a larger corpus of data. I form the hypothesis of the taxonomy of modes of thought — analytical initiatives, conventions of argumentation. Then I turn to Aggadic documents to see whether the same types of analysis and argumentation occur. The results speak for themselves.

## II

Let me spell out the procedure of the project. In the present project, I turn to modes of thought. In a systematic, systematizing inquiry, I ask what rules of intellect governed the Rabbinic sages' encounter with any topic, any problem, and how the results of the encounter were to be signaled? Identifying modes of thought — [1] rules of analysis, [2] laws of argumentation — proves perhaps less concrete and more speculative than uncovering the generative logic of the documents of the Oral Torah or the hermeneutical rules of the Halakhic category-formations. But the modes of thought certainly are more telling in framing an argument for the fundamental unity of Rabbinic Judaism in its formative statement(s). That is because they are more pervasive, permeating every level of reflection and inquiry.

---

[3] *The Unity of Rabbinic Discourse.* Lanham, 2000: University Press of America. STUDIES IN ANCIENT JUDAISM SERIES. I-III; *Dual Discourse, Single Judaism. The Category-Formations of the Halakhah and of the Aggadah Defined, Compared, and Contrasted.* Lanham, 2000: University Press of America. STUDIES IN ANCIENT JUDAISM SERIES; *The Aggadic Role in Halakhic Discourse..* Lanham, 2000: University Press of America. Studies in Ancient Judaism Series. I-III.

*Introduction* xvii

About what, exactly, do I mean to inquire? By modes of thought I mean, the rules of intellect that guide

[1] how people identify problems and solve them and

[2] how they propose to convey the results in such as way as to persuade others of the cogency of those solutions.

I propose to lay out the types of inquiry that everywhere prevail. Analysis involves the scrutiny of a proposition or proposition, the identification of its constituent parts and how they fit together; to analyze is to divide a complex whole into its constituent parts, a dictionary definition that serves perfectly well here, with the provision that analysis demands a reconstructive effort as well.

What is at stake in the matter of argument in behalf of, or against, one proposition among a set of conflicting ones? It is whether the Rabbinic writings altogether cohere or whether they form a mere mass of conflicting opinions. Scripture for its part allows two or more versions of a story to stand side by side, e.g., in abiding two distinct stories of creation to flow in succession; two separate stories of the flood to intertwine; and other cases. But philosophical thought rarely abides contradictory propositions, in the theory that both cannot be right. And we owe to Greek philosophy that insistence upon the integrity of truth. Then at stake in whether or not coherent modes of thought govern intellectual endeavor in Rabbinic Judaism is whether or not that Judaism forms a system of philosophical coherence or a mere collection of conflicting data, with which one may prove pretty much anything and its opposite: a mess, a mass of contradictions. In asking about whether types of analysis and types of argumentation in the Rabbinic writings conform to a few set rules throughout, or whether the modes of thought in the Rabbinic writings prove contradictory and incoherent, I address that question head on.

Most Judaic religious systems, represented by their respective canonical writings, in antiquity refrain from rigorous thinking and accept as authoritative a variety of unanalyzed propositions. What I show here, for the Halakhic and the Aggadic writings alike, is that Rabbinic Judaism is exceptional in its commitment to coherent analytical inquiries that pertain everywhere and philosophically-rigorous types of argumentation that dictate the rules of engagement throughout. G. E. R. Lloyd describes this matter in language that serves equally well for the various Judaic systems, most of them capable of sustaining contradictory propositions, only one of them characterized by systematic articulation of, and argument about, conflicting viewpoints:

> The Egyptians...had various beliefs about the way the sky is held up. One idea was that it is supported on posts, another that it is held up by a god, a third that it rests on walls, a fourth that it is a cow or a goddess...But a story-teller recounting anyone such myth need pay no attention to other beliefs about the sky, and he would hardly have been troubled by any inconsistency between them. Nor, one may assume, did he feel that his own account was in competition with any other in the

sense that it might be more or less correct or have better or worse grounds for its support than some other belief.[4]

If, as I said a moment ago, we examine the two creation-myths of Genesis, or the two stories of the Flood, we see how readily conflicting stories might be joined together, and how little credence was placed on the possibility that one theory of matters, embodied in one version, might be correct, the other wrong. In search of dispute and debate, articulated and pursued, we simply look in vain through the entire heritage of Israelite Scriptures (with a stated exception given presently) and through all extra-scriptural writings of various Judaic systems. Greek philosophy and Rabbinic Judaism by contrast, articulately faced the possibility that differing opinion competed and that the thinker must advocate the claim that his theory was right, the other's wrong. Conflicting principles both cannot be right, and merely announcing an opinion without considering alternatives and proposing to falsify them does not suffice for intellectual endeavor. And with the recognition of that possibility of not only opinion but argument, Greek philosophy engaged in debate:

> When we turn to the early Greek philosophers, there is a fundamental difference. Many of them tackle the same problems and investigate the same natural phenomena [as Egyptian and other science], but it is tacitly assumed that the various theories and explanations they propose are directly competing with one another. The urge is towards finding the best explanation, the most adequate theory, and they are then forced to consider the grounds for their ideas, the evidence and arguments in their favor, as well as the weak points in their opponents' theories.[5]

And what was true of science pertained to civilization in all aspects:

> In their very different spheres of activity, the philosopher Thales and the law-giver Solon may be said to have had at least two things in common. First, both disclaimed any supernatural authority for their own ideas, and, secondly, both accepted the principles of free debate and of public access to the information on which a person or an idea should be judged. The essence of the Milesians' contribution was to introduce a new critical spirit into man's attitude to the world of nature, but this should be seen as a counterpart to, and offshoot of, the contemporary development of the practice of free debate and open discussion in the context of politics and law throughout the Greek world.[6]

---

[4] G. E. R. Lloyd, *Early Greek Science. Thales to Aristotle.* New York, 1970: W. W. Norton & Co., pp. 11-12. See also his *Greek Science after Aristotle.* N.Y., 1973: W. W. Norton Co., and his *Polarity and Analogy. Two Types of Argumentation in Early Greek Thought.* Cambridge, 1966: Cambridge University Press.
[5] Lloyd, *op. cit.,* p. 12.
[6] Lloyd, *op. cit.* p. 15.

*Introduction*                                                                                                                      xix

Now among all the Judaisms documented for antiquity, one of them has portrayed not only its conclusions but the arguments for and against those conclusions, not only positions but contrary positions and how the contradictions are to be resolved, and that is, Rabbinic Judaism. So it is quite reasonably to ask about the types of argumentation, however classified, that served in the working out of the Rabbinic structure and system.

### III

What we mean by "types of analysis" is clear, but what about types of argumentation? Argumentation is best defined by the German word, "Auseinandersetzung," the explicit confrontation of conflicting viewpoints in the medium of exchanges of opinion, fact, and reason, yielding the possibility of a rational resolution of conflict or a clear perception of the reasonable foundations for contradictory positions. By types of argumentation, then, I mean, the rules that govern authentic *Auseinandersetzungen* in Rabbinic literature. Some of these are blatant but uninstructive. For one example, Rabbinic literature everywhere requires a full exposition of the grounds for opposed views and the responses of both parties to a given challenge. So one rule of a valid *Auseinandersetzung* is that both parties be given a fair chance to spell out their respective positions. Another rule insists that each party address the substance of the opposed view, so that a direct confrontation of conflicting viewpoints and the reasons for them is provided for. But in this inquiry, I am concerned with classifying particular types of arguments, not defining the general rules.

To summarize: given a statement of fact, an active mind will engage with that fact, identify the problems provoked by that fact that demand solution. The vivid intellect will then conduct analyses, see how the parts break down and how they are put back together again, produce propositions, above all, pursue a program of speculation about said fact. As is clear, these modes of analytical, constructive thought break down into two classes, the theoretical and the practical. Theoretical modes of thought guide people in identifying what they wish to know about a given fact or subject: types of analysis. Practical ones lay out the rules of rhetoric, specifically, the kinds of argument, that dictate how the results of analysis are framed for persuasive interchange. Divorcing types of analysis from types of argumentation imposes a distinction between two stages of intellect — the formulation of a proposition, the expression in a persuasive way of that proposition — that do not sustain separation. It is only for the sake of clear expression that I treat the two media of intellect in isolation from one another.

### IV

I treat the Halakhah as normative, the Aggadah as the question-mark, because the Halakhah emerges in continuous documents, one flowing from its predecessor, while the Aggadah comes to us in diverse documents indeed. These questions, phrased in abstract language concerning how a system coalesces in its documentary statement, to begin with pertain to particular texts of the Halakhah and the Aggadah. The former are the Mishnah, Tosefta, Talmud of the Land of Israel, Talmud of Babylonia, and Tannaite Midrash-compilations of a Halakhic sort. The latter are comprised by the Rabbinic exegesis of the Pentateuch and books of the Hebrew Scriptures important in synagogue liturgy. The Halakhic compilations form the initial phase of the inquiry, because they supply articulate evidence for the description of an analytical program, on the one side, and of rhetorical requirements in the articulation of that program, on the other. The survey of the Halakhic documents yields a basic repertoire of analytical initiatives characteristic of Halakhic thinking. Then I examine representative documents of the Aggadah to see whether the Halakhic types of analysis pertain. Why do I privilege Halakhic discourse? The initial phase of the work concerns the Halakhah, because in form the documents present themselves as continuous, from the Mishnah, which is cited by the Tosefta, to the Yerushalmi, which rests upon the Mishnah and the Tosefta, and ending in the Bavli, which follows suit. Any inquiry into intellectual coherence should start at points of formal coherence. The results in hand, we then can turn to the Aggadic component of the canon.

For the work on this volume, devoted to types of analysis the question governs: having identified principal analytical initiatives of the Halakhic documents (though by no means claiming to catalogue them all), I ask whether these same initiatives play a role in Aggadic ones. For *Argument* the counterpart questions are clear: having sketched in a rough way an account of the types of arguments in the Halakhic documents and then limited the scope to dialectical versus not-dialectical, I turn to the Aggadic compilations in quest of counterparts.

V

The plan of inquiry, already alluded to, is simple and familiar. I work from a case to a hypothesis and then test the hypothesis against other cases, the whole in a systematic way. Whenever I have undertaken a major new initiative of systematization, I have begun with a tractate I deem representative: not too long, not to brief, not too complex, not too simple, not too Halakhic, not too Aggadic. That has ordinarily been Moed Qatan as laid out in the Mishnah-Tosefta-Yerushalmi-Bavli, though one may make a strong case for many other tractates in the Halakhic literature. What I seek in that tractate is a starting point: a repertoire of types of analysis and types of argument of a particular document. In the examination of Moed Qatan I produce a working hypothesis: types of analytical initiatives or questions, on the one side, a schematization of the types of argumentation, on the other.

Then, with a hypothetical range of categories of both in hand, I proceed to a systematic survey of the Mishnah, the Tosefta, the Yerushalmi, and the Bavli, in

Berakhot, Qiddushin, Abodah Zarah, and Niddah. Once I have validated the results of the initial probe by testing their serviceability in tractates from the several divisions of the Halakhah, I proceed to my systematic survey of three tractates of each the three divisions which intersect at the Mishnah-Tosefta-Yerushalmi-Bavli. That suffices for the present purpose. Then I test in important and representative Aggadic documents the results attained in the systematization of Halakhic documents within the present taxonomy. The outcome is one-sided.

The results are sketchy, because the premise of the survey, that analysis and argumentation form critical components of the documentary program, pertains only partially to the Rabbinic canon; much more of the canon is expository or narrative or exegetical than propositional, analytical, and argumentative. That is why, even at the very beginning of the work, an important caveat is in order. The documents of the Halakhah, all the more so those of the Aggadah, do not uniformly or ubiquitously yield ample evidence on the particular modes of thought that concern us: the types of analysis, the varieties of argument. Much of the Rabbinic canon is and descriptive. It sets forth expositions of theses that, as a matter of fact, cannot claim to undertake systematic analysis at all. Nor does argument, though formally prominent, dominate Rabbinic discourse. I have already shown that the single emblematic mode of argument, the dialectical one, in volume plays only a modest role in the unfolding of Halakhic discourse.[7] So if I were to represent as broadly characteristic of entire documents the modes of thought described and systematized in this project, that would mislead. I do not claim to characterize the documents seen in their entirety. As to representing them one by one, that is work I have already completed. Here I only inquire into the shared traits of mind that can be shown to pervade them all — the logic and the rhetoric that form a common foundation for those clearly differentiated compilations, the formally-distinct and internally-cogent statements of Rabbinic Judaism. What the documents share at their intellectual sources defines our inquiry; I have already identified their distinctive traits, respectively.

## VI

The actual conduct of the inquiry is readily explained. I pay only casual attention to the Mishnah's modes of thought. That is for two reasons. First, I have already dealt with the generative modes of thought in the Mishnah in my study of the category-formations and how (in my hypothetical reconstruction of the thought

---

[7] *Talmudic Dialectics: Types and Forms.* Atlanta, 1995: Scholars Press for South Florida Studies in the History of Judaism. I-II. And compare *Judaism as Philosophy. The Method and Message of the Mishnah.* Columbia, 1991: University of South Carolina Press and *Jerusalem and Athens: The Congruity of Talmudic and Classical Philosophy.* Leiden, 1997: E. J. Brill. *Supplements to the Journal for the Study of Judaism.*

processes) they take shape.⁸ I should argue that the Mishnah's framers work on the problem of the organization of data into consequential formations, constructions that impart to the data consequence and meaning. It is only occasionally that the Mishnah's writers articulately undertake an analytical task within the context of the data that they construct and structure.⁹ Hence I address the Mishnah only as the setting for the analytical discussions that constitute later documents' contribution to matters. In general I take the Mishnah to define the foundation on which analytical work is build, not the arena for self-aware inquiry into the why and wherefore and what-if of a matter. When it comes to the Tosefta, I find much refinement of the Mishnah's presentation of information, secondary exercises of reorganization, comparison and contrast and clarification and definition. But only occasionally do I identify evidence of a systematic analytical program. This I do find in the two Talmuds, which clearly stand apart from the received corpus of law that the Mishnah and the Tosefta (and the Baraita-corpus) have handed on and see that corpus as a set of problems awaiting discernment. And that is where we shall focus our attention.

Once the Halakhah has defined for us a sample of the types of analysis, I turn to three Aggadic documents, each representative of a type of Aggadic compilation. They are Genesis Rabbah, Leviticus Rabbah, and Sifré to Numbers. Genesis Rabbah stands for the type of Midrash-Aggadic compilation made up of verse-by-verse exegeses of base-texts. It holds together by reference to the sequence of verses of the book of Scripture subject to re-presentation. It does not effect the coherence of successive statements (sentences) through their composition into a coherent propositional exposition and argument. By contrast, Leviticus Rabbah is made up of thirty-seven large, sustained thematic expositions of propositions. These constitute syllogisms of a curious form. Sifré to Numbers investigates both Halakhic and Aggadic texts of Scripture in an exegetical form. So each choice represents its own type of Aggadic writing and indicates whether the Halakhic initiatives of analysis and principal types of argumentation serve. The probe serves, then, only to supply guide-lines for further inquiry into the possibilities of a common mode of thought that pervades both the Halakhic and the Aggadic documents by their types and forms.

---

⁸ That is in *The Comparative Hermeneutics* I-VIII, cited above.

⁹ They conduct their project through sequences of hierarchical classification of category-formations that have been identified through analogical-contrastive reasoning. The work of *Listenwissenschaft* takes place through the construction of series of cases. That leads to prolixity, which is systematically subjected to Talmudic criticism, which is precipitated by disdain for redundancy. So what makes the Mishnah work, the construction of series, supplies part of the Talmud's critical agendum, the differentiation of the items of a series into taxonomically distinct units — the deconstruction of series. Stated simply: the Mishnah's own traits dictated principal parts of the Talmud's mission.

*Introduction*

## VII

Let me briefly signal the outcome of the project, even though it is only tentative and suggestive. The question, then, is, do the Halakhic types of analysis and argument pertain in representative Aggadic compilations? The answer is, they do. That is not the result I anticipated, but it is what I found when I moved from the Halakhah and its norms of conduct and action, inductively defined, to the Aggadah and its rules of consciousness and attitude. At the outset I intuited that common modes of thought do not — should not — pervade both Halakhic and Aggadic writing. For each genre of writing undertakes its own distinct tasks and selects its distinctive kinds of writing, analytical and expository for the Halakhah, exegetical and narrative for the Aggadah. I did not imagine the outcome, which is that Aggadic modes of thought adapt for Aggadic purposes pertinent Halakhic modes of thought. This finding requires much further investigation. For people commonly suppose that Aggadah and Halakhah pursue distinct programs, so asking how common modes of thought and argument may pervade both ought to prove futile. Each devises a program of analytical questions and argumentation that serves its distinctive purpose. But accepting that the two genres of expression of Rabbinic Judaism in its formative canon, the two types of writing, address each its particular subject matter and information settles nothing about shared modes of thought, e.g., analytical or argumentative.

In its way, the Rabbinic documents of antiquity themselves answer the question, what would a composite that joined Halakhic and Aggadic modes of discourse actually look like? We have an explicit answer to that question, an answer predicated on the premise that Aggadah and Halakhah do undertake a common task. Here is evidence that, in the Rabbinic circles themselves, compositions circulated that presupposed the unity of the Halakhah and the Aggadah.

### B. TO M. BABA QAMMA 6:4G-H I.11-12/60B
#### LINKING LAW TO LORE: "IF FIRE BREAK OUT AND CATCH IN THORNS"

I.11  A.  *R. Ammi and R. Assi in session before R. Isaac Nappaha—*

B.  *One of them said to him, "May the master teach us some traditions of law [Halakhah]."*

C.  *The other of them said to him, "May the master teach us some traditions of lore [Aggadah]."*

D.  *So when he started to teach lore, the one would not let him go on, and when he started some traditions of law, the other would not let him go on.* He said to them, "I shall draw a parable for you: to what is the matter comparable? It is like the case of a man who had two wives, one a girl, the other an old lady. The girl plucked out the white hair, the old lady, the black, so he was made bald on both sides."

E.  He said to them, "Well, if that's the situation, let me say for you something that will please both sides: 'If fire break out and catch in thorns' — 'break out' on itself. '...He who kindled the fire shall surely make restitution' — said the Holy One, blessed be He, 'It is my obligation to pay for the fire which I kindled. I was the one who kindled a fire in Zion: "And he has kindled a fire in Zion which has devoured the foundations of thereof" (Lam. 4:11); I am the one who will build it again by fire: "For I will be unto her a wall of fire round about and I will be the glory in the midst of her" (Zech. 2:9).' And as to the side of law: the verse speaks first of all of damage done with chattel and then ends with damage done by the person, to show you that implied in the classification of damage done by fire is human agency."

I.12 A. "And David longed and said, Oh that one would give me water to drink of the well of Bethlehem which is by the gate. And the three mighty men broke through the host of the Philistines and drew water out of the well that was by the gate" (2 Sam. 23:15-16):

B. *What was the problem?*

C. *Said Raba said R. Nahman, "What he required was a ruling in connection with the status of hidden objects that are burned up, since he did not know whether the law accords with R. Judah or with rabbis, and they solved the problem for them in whatever way they solved it."*

D. *R. Huna said, "Well, this is the problem: there were near the battlefield stacks of barley that belonged to Israelites, and Philistines had concealed themselves in them, and he wanted to know the law as follows: Is it permitted to save one's own life at the cost of the property of someone else?"*

E. They sent him word: "It is forbidden to save one's own life at the cost of the property of someone else. But you are the king, **and the king [may exercise the right to] open a road for himself, and [others] may not stop him [M. San. 2:4B]."**

F. *Rabbis, and some say, Rabbah bar Mari, said, "There were near the battlefield stacks of barley that belonged to Israelites and stacks of lentils that belonged to Philistines. And this is the question that required an answer:* What is the law on taking the stacks of barley belonging to the Israelites to feed the beasts of the army on the stipulation that later on they would pay for them with the stacks of lentils that belonged to the Philistines? *They sent him word,* "'If the wicked restore the pledge, give again what was taken by the robber" (Ezek. 33:15) — even if the robber later on pays up for what he robbed, he is still wicked. But you are the king, **and the king [may exercise the right to] open a road for himself, and [others] may not stop him [M. San. 2:4B]."**

G. *Now from the viewpoint of him who has said that he wanted to make an exchange of barley and lentils, that is in line with the verse,* "Where was a plot of ground full of lentils" (2 Sam. 23:11) and also "where there was a plot of ground full of barley" (1 Chr. 11:13). *But from the*

*Introduction*                                                                                           xxv

        *perspective of him who says that at issue was whether or not he could burn them down, what need is there for these two verses?*

H.    *He may say to you, "There were also stacks of lentils there that belonged to Israelites, in which Philistines were concealed" [and had to be burned down].*

I.    *From the perspective of him who has said that he wanted to burn down the stacks of barley belonging to the Israelites and repay them later on, we can understand the verse, "But he stood in the midst of the ground and defended it" (1 Chr. 11:12). But from the perspective of the one who says he wanted to make a trade, what is the point of "...and defended it" (1 Chr. 11:12)?*

J.    *He did not allow them to make the exchange.*

K.    *Now in line with these two views, we can understand why the two verses are set forth.* **[61A]** *But from the angle of vision of him who has said that what he needed to know was the rule governing what is concealed but burned in a fire, what need is there for these two verses?*

L.    *He will say to you that besides the issue of the compensation for hidden goods in case of fire, he also had one of those other problems in mind as well.*

M.    *Now in line with the other two views, we can understand the meaning of, "But David would not drink thereof" (2 Sam. 23:16), for he said, "Since it is subject to a prohibition, I don't want it." But from the perspective of him who maintained that at issue was the status of hidden goods burned in a fire, didn't they send him a received, traditional teaching, so what would be the sense of "But David would not drink thereof" (2 Sam. 23:16)?*

N.    *He didn't want to quote the teaching in their names [those who broke through the lines], for he said, "This is what I have received as a tradition from the court of Samuel of Ramah: 'Whoever risks his life for teachings of the Torah — they never cite a legal teaching in his name.' [Whatever positions such a person takes would be authoritative and supported by the collegium of the masters, hence would not be marked as schismatic by being assigned only an individual's name.]"*

**I.13**  A.    "But he poured it out unto the Lord" (2 Sam. 23:16):

      B.    *Now from the perspective of him who has said one of these two things, it is because he acted for the sake of heaven. But from the perspective of him who said that at issue was the status of compensation for buried goods damaged in a fire, what is the meaning of the verse, "But he poured it out unto the Lord" (2 Sam. 23:16)?*

      C.    *He repeated the rule in the name of tradition [and not in a particular authority's name].*

We see at I.11E that the master explicitly proposes to ask the Halakhah and the Aggadah to join forces: propositional law and narrative to unit. The first exercise applies the law at hand to God himself, and that settles the issue of whether damage done by fire involves human agency. Then, I.12, David's statement, 2 Sam. 23:15-

16, is interpreted in the Halakhic framework at hand. Now the details of David's transaction intersect with the Halakhah, as formulated by Huna, D, and Rabbis, F. Then the two positions are measured against the Aggadic data, G, and again at I, K-L, M-N. The integration of the Halakhah into the Aggadic narrative is then solid and total. The Halakhah without the Aggadah is incomprehensible, since details of the Aggadah play a principal part in the exposition of the Halakhah. In this context, then, it is clear, the modes of thought of the one corpus of writing and thought work in partnership with those of the other, and it is not out of line to ask how the types of analysis of the Halakhah and the types of argumentation that play a part in the Halakhic exposition work in tandem with those of the Aggadah. But, I repeat, the exercise of the present volume and its companion represents only an initial effort at framing the question in the way I deem logical and necessary.

PART ONE

A PRELIMINARY PROBE

TYPES OF ANALYSIS IN
TRACTATE MOED QATAN

# 1

# MOED QATAN CHAPTER ONE

### I. MISHNAH

The probe commences with a short, coherent tractate, then extends the results to two others of greater size.

The topic of the tractate Moed Qatan is conduct on the intermediate days of the festivals of Passover and Tabernacle, that is, the days between the opening and closing festival days, on which servile labor is forbidden. In the interval certain forms of labor may be carried on, and the tractate through cases defines the principles that govern what may or may not be done in accord with the lower level of sanctity that applies between the first and the last days of the festival season. An analytical program distinct from the topical exposition of the Mishnah's laws is difficult to ferret out. The subject is restrictions imposed during the intermediate days of the Festivals, Passover and Tabernacles, on the ordinary conduct of work. The intermediate days, between the opening and closing Festival days of Passover and Tabernacles, define an interstitial category, not wholly holy, not wholly secular. They are like the Festival days, being part of the designated holy season, but they are not like the Festival days, in that the restrictions of the Festivals, e.g., not working, are not explicitly applied to them. So, likeness being the given, the Halakhah takes up the problem of how they are unlike. Analogical-contrastive inquiry here treats the intermediate days of a Festival (Passover, Tabernacles) as

[1] like the Festival, therefore subject to prohibitions as to labor that may be done, but also

[2] unlike the Festival, therefore subject to said prohibitions in a distinctive way.

But the premise, start to finish, never articulated but always required, is that the Temple and the household form a continuum on the occasion of sacred time. That defines the hermeneutical foundation of the category-formation.

Within the Mishnah's Halakhic exposition, we wish to know whether we can identify an analytical initiative, a point at which, out of a given set of facts, sages perceive a whole that they wish to dismantle and reconstruct — frame a problem for solution, a proposition for testing, an effort to generalize or to assess a hypothesis. For this initial probe, we consider the complete Mishnah-chapter. Beyond this point, we shall address only passages that convey the results of analysis of a topic into its components and reconstitute of the parts into a now-well-reconstructed whole: ask a penetrating question and answer it.

1:1   A.   They water an irrigated field on the intermediate days of a festival and in the Seventh Year,
     B.   whether from a spring which first flows at that time, or from a spring which does not first flow at that time.
     C.   But they do not water [an irrigated field] with (1) collected rainwater, or (2) water from a swape well.
     D.   And they do not dig channels around vines.

1:2   A.   R. Eleazar b. Azariah says, "They do not make a new water channel on the intermediate days of a festival or in the Seventh Year."
     B.   And sages say, "They make a new water channel in the Seventh Year, and they repair damaged ones on the intermediate days of a festival."
     C.   They repair damaged waterways in the public domain and dig them out.
     D.   They repair roads, streets, and water pools.
     E.   And they (1) do all public needs, (2) mark off graves, and (3) go forth [to give warning] against Diverse Kinds [ = M. Sheq. 1:11].

1:3   A.   R. Eliezer b. Jacob says, "They lead water from one tree to another,
     B.   "on condition that one not water the entire field.
     C.   "Seeds which have not been watered before the festival one should not water on the intermediate days of the festival."
     D.   And sages permit in this case and in that.

1:4   A.   They hunt moles and mice in a tree-planted field and in a field of grain,
     B   not in the usual manner,
     C.   on the intermediate days of a festival and in the Seventh year
     D.   And sages say [sic! B. M.Q. 7a: Judah], "[They do so] in a tree-planted field in the normal manner, and in a grain field not in the normal manner.
     E.   They block up a breach in the intermediate days of a festival.
     F.   And in the seventh year, one builds it in the normal way.

1:5   A.   R. Meir says, "They examine Nega-markings [to begin with] to provide a lenient ruling but not to provide a strict ruling."
     B.   And sages say, "Neither to provide a lenient ruling nor to provide a strict ruling."
     C.   And further did R. Meir say, "A man may go out and gather the bones of his father and his mother,

## One. Moed Qatan. Chapter One

|      | D. | "because it is a time of rejoicing for him." |
|------|----|--|
|      | E. | R. Yosé says, "It is a time of mourning for him." |
|      | F. | A person may not call for mourning for his deceased, |
|      | G. | or make a lamentation for him thirty days before a festival. |
| 1:6  | A. | They do not hew out a tomb niche or tombs on the intermediate days of a festival. |
|      | B. | But they refashion tomb niches on the intermediate days of a festival. |
|      | C. | They dig a grave on the intermediate days of a festival, |
|      | D. | and make a coffin, |
|      | E. | while the corpse is in the same courtyard. |
|      | F. | R. Judah prohibits, unless there were boards [already sawn and made ready in advance]. |
| 1:7  | A. | They do not take wives on the intermediate days of a festival, |
|      | B. | whether virgins or widows. |
|      | C. | Nor do they enter into levirate marriage, |
|      | D. | for it is an occasion of rejoicing. |
|      | E. | But one may remarry his divorced wife. |
|      | F. | And a woman may prepare her wedding adornments on the intermediate days of a festival. |
|      | G. | R. Judah says, "She should not use lime, since this makes her ugly." |
| 1:8  | A. | An unskilled person sews in the usual way. |
|      | B. | But an expert craftsman sews with irregular stitches. |
|      | C. | They weave the ropes for beds. |
|      | D. | R. Yosé says, "They [only] tighten them." |
| 1:9  | A. | They set up an oven or double stove or a hand mill on the intermediate days of a festival. |
|      | B. | R. Judah says, "They do not rough the millstones for the first time." |
| 1:10 | A. | They make a parapet for a roof or a porch in an unskilled manner, |
|      | B. | but not in the manner of a skilled craftsman. |
|      | C. | They plaster cracks and smooth them down with a roller, by hand, or by foot, but not with a trowel. |
|      | D. | A hinge, socket, roof beam, lock, or key, [any of] which broke |
|      | E. | do they repair on the intermediate days of the festival, |
|      | F. | so long as one had not had the intention to do work on it on the intermediate days of the festival. |
|      | G. | And all pickled foods which a man can eat during the intermediate days of a festival he also may pickle. |

Clearly, the Mishnah's Halakhah works out the tension between the two theories of the classification of the intermediate days of the Festival: like the holy days in some ways, like ordinary work-days in others. But at no particular ruling do I discern an analytical initiative, a point at which the components of the ruling are singled out and dismantled and then reconstructed; nor is there an effort at articulating the premises of a position and sustaining or challenging them. The presentation of conflicting opinions on various specific problems does not represent the same thing as a systematic analytical inquiry: an effort at generalization of a governing principle and at identifying the alternatives, the premises or the consequences of a ruling. Clearly, those who receive the chapter can and do undertake such initiatives. But the Mishnah only rarely forms the setting for that work. In the remainder of this project, the Mishnah's presentation of the Halakhah will require comment only when an analytical program that transcends the details of the Mishnah-law is articulated, or in the context of the Tosefta, the Yerushalmi, or the Bavli.

## II. TOSEFTA

With Tosefta we enter the main current of Rabbinic Mishnah- and Halakhah-exposition: clarification, extension, refinement, amplification. I cite only those compositions that undertake an articulated analytical exercise.

T. 1:2 E. To a matter which brings about loss do they attend on the intermediate days of a festival.
F. To a matter which does not bring about loss do they not attend on the intermediate days of a festival.
G. A person may sell his spring of water to a gentile or make a trade with him on the Sabbath to take effect at the end of the Sabbath,
H. and one need not scruple on that account [because the spring may falter, and the man lose out].

Note also the following:

T. 1:11 A. And they grind flour during the festival [for use on the festival week itself].
B. To a matter which brings about loss do they attend on the intermediate days of a festival.
C. To a matter which does not bring about loss do they not attend on the intermediate days of a festival.
D. Under what circumstances?
E. With reference to that which is plucked up from the ground [cf. M. M.Q. 2:1-2].
F. But with reference to that which is not yet plucked up from the ground, even to a matter which brings about loss they do not attend on the intermediate days of a festival.
G. [If] one does not have anything to eat, he cuts grain, stacks and threshes it,
H. on condition that he not thresh with cows.

The first, and most important analytical exercise in the modes of thought governing Halakhic formation and execution is before us: the interest in generalization from a case to a rule, and from a rule to an abstract principle affecting a variety of types of law. Here we have a generalization that turns the cases of the Mishnah into a fully-articulated principle, so T. 1:2E-F. That is then illustrated at G-H (and elsewhere, throughout the Halakhic exposition). The analytical interest,

## One. Moed Qatan. Chapter One

then, is in generalization and extension, transcending the topical limits and framing principles that shape the law at many distinct points. The Mishnah rarely contains such an analytical exercise, the Tosefta very commonly, often rather subtly, changes the presentation of the Halakhah, from a rule particular to a topic or situation, to an exemplification of a law.

But I do not see how the illustration constitutes an argument in behalf of the proposition. What we have is a governing principle that emerges from the (hypothetical) analysis of the interplay of the two principles identified at the outset. The same matter recurs at T. 1:11, now with a further distinction, T. 1:11E-F, G-H. Now the principle is refined in yet another way.

T. 1:7 A.   He whose wall was leaning into the public domain tears it down and rebuilds it,
     B.   because of the threat to life [cf. M. M.Q. 1:2].
     C.   A city wall which was breached — they stop it up.
     D.   [If] they stopped it up and it was breached [again], they do not stop it up.
     E.   But if the city was near the frontier, one [has the right to] tear it down and rebuild it in the proper way.

The key language is "because of the threat to life," which identifies at M. 1:2 the operative consideration, I assume behind the ruling that one may attend to the water channels, waterways, roads and streets, and the like. These then are explained by appeal to the priority of life-maintenance over the sanctity of the intermediate days of the festival. What the Mishnah implies the Tosefta articulates. The process of analysis of the law ("why may one rebuild the wall on the intermediate day of the festival") may be implicit in the Mishnah's statement, then made explicit later on; identifying the analytical initiative contained within the statement does not carry a judgment as to the occasion for the taking of the initiative.

Here is yet another exposition of not only the rule but the reason, which generates the possibility of further rules in the model of the one at hand:

T. 1:12 A.   [On the intermediate days of a festival] they purchase from gentiles fields, houses, vineyards, cattle, male slaves, and female slaves,
     B.   because it is as if one rescues [them] from their power [cf. M. Meg. 2:4A].
     C.   And one writes and registers the deeds in the archives.
     D.   And if one was a priest, he contracts corpse-uncleanness on their account [by going outside the Holy Land to regain [and held by gentiles].
     E.   And one may give evidence concerning such matters or enter into judgment about them [by going] abroad [and thus, contracting corpse-uncleanness].
     F.   And just as [a priest] contracts corpse-uncleanness [by going] abroad [for these purposes], so he contracts corpse-uncleanness by going into a cemetery for these purposes.

Here again, the generalization is articulated, yielding a broad policy indeed: what saves from idolaters' control property and persons and acreage in the Holy

Land overrides the sanctity of the intermediate days of the Festival. The Tosefta's way then is to treat the generalization in an abstract framework altogether. Here is yet another case in which we move beyond the limits of the cases and their immediate generalizations:

T. 1:12 G. And [a priest] contracts corpse-uncleanness for purposes of study of Torah and contracts corpse-uncleanness for purposes of marrying a woman.
H. R. Judah says, "If there is someone else who can teach, lo, this [priest] should not contract corpse-uncleanness.
I. "But if not, lo, he should contract corpse-uncleanness."
J. R. Yosé says, "Even though there is someone else there who can teach, lo, this one should contract corpse-uncleanness,
K. "for no one is so meritorious as to be able to learn from just anybody.
L. "[But he can learn only] from the particular person who has the merit to be his [teacher]."

We have now established that considerations of enhancing the sanctification of the Land of Israel override the sanctity of the intermediate days of the Festivals. That means that the sanctity of the priesthood, its obligation to avoid contracting corpse-contamination, is set aside by other public goods: procreation, Torah-study. These have nothing to do with the case at hand, the intermediate days; nor do they pertain to the matters just now addressed, the remission of the priest's particular restrictions. Rather, the principle implicit in the matter — the establishment of a hierarchy of concerns — is shown to extend far beyond the limits of the cases at hand and even the initial generalizations that those cases produced.

### III. YERUSHALMI

In discussing what I take to be analytical programs of Yerushalmi, I reproduce the relevant parts in my translation as shaped into a commentary in *The Talmud of the Land of Israel. An Academic Commentary to the Second, Third, and Fourth Divisions*. Atlanta, 1998-1999: Scholars Press for *USF Academic Commentary Series*. XII. *Yerushalmi. Tractate Moed Qatan*. At the margin I set what I take to be the principal parts of the Talmud's discourse on a given Mishnah-passage or in the context of such a passage. The indentations signal successive steps in the primary and secondary exposition of a given proposition, e.g., basic statements, interpolations are marked off from one another. This exposes in graphic form the components of the document. Bold face type signifies the citation of the Mishnah or the Tosefta, regular type, Hebrew, italics, Aramaic, I present the base-Mishnah and then only those parts of the Talmud that undertake analytical inquiries of one kind or another. That means I omit vast stretches of both Talmuds, specifically, those many and extensive composites that do not undertake an analytical program of any weight or depth.

## Yerushalmi Moed Qatan 1:1

[A]   [80a] **They water an irrigated field on the intermediate days of a festival and in the Seventh Year,**

[B]   **whether from a spring that first flows at that time, or from a spring that does not first flow at that time.**

[C]   **But they do not water [an irrigated field] with collected rain water, or water from a swape well.**

[D]   **And they do not dig channels around vines.**

[I:1 A]   *There is no difficulty understanding why* one may utilize a spring that does not first flow at that time. But in the case of a spring that first flows at that time, is this not a considerable amount of work [for the intermediate days of the festival]?

[B]   *The law accords with the view of R. Meir. For* **R. Meir has said, "From a spring that first flows on the intermediate days of a festival they irrigate [even] a field that depends upon the rain [and does not need this water]"** [T. Moed 1:1 A].

[C]   Said R. Yosé, "In the opinion of all parties, if the spring had a single flow and it divided into two, or if the water was spare and became abundant[, they may make use of such a spring on the festival]. [It does not fall into the category of a spring that first flows at that time.]"

[D]   *And so it has been taught:*

[E]   **"[From] a spring that first flows [on the intermediate days of a festival], they irrigate a field that depends upon the rain," the words of R. Meir.**

[F]   **And sages say, "They irrigate from it only a field that depends upon irrigation, [the spring of which] has gone dry"** [T. Moed 1:1 A-B].

[G]   *In the view of R. Meir* they may draw water from it for a crop that will not perish [if not watered on the intermediate days of the festival], and they may draw water from it even if it is much work.

[H]   *In the view of rabbis,* they may draw water from it only for a crop that otherwise will perish, and that is on condition that it is not much work.

[I]   In the case of a crop that will perish, but in which much labor is involved for drawing water, *what is the law in the view of rabbis?*

[J]   *Let us derive the answer from the following:*

[K]   Any field that progressively dries up — this falls into the category of an irrigated field [which may be watered on the intermediate days of a festival].

[L]   If the field stopped deteriorating, this field is in the category of a field that depends upon the rain, subject to the dispute of R. Meir and sages. [So the principal consideration, in answer to I, is the loss of the crop in the field rather than the amount of labor involved.]

The governing principle, it is taken for granted, is that light work is permitted on the intermediate days of the festival, but heavy labor is forbidden. Then the rules are tested against that principle, and one of the rules contradicts it. The solution is to invoke the schismatic view of Meir, who regards the utilization of newly-available water as so critical as to override all other considerations. So the Mishnah contains no contradiction, rather accords with a principle other than that presumed to govern to begin with. Sages' view, which we have correctly identified, is that the consideration of excessive labor prevails, H. A secondary development of that logic then completes the analysis.

The next pertinent items ask about interstitial classifications of water, rain-drippings that continue to flow from the hills, cascades of water, and the like; I abbreviate the presentation, since the mode of answering the question is of modest interest, the character of the question defining the focus:

[II:2 A] *R. Jeremiah asked,* "As to water of rain-drippings [80b] which has not ceased to flow from the hills, into what category does it fall?"
[B] *Let us derive the answer from the following:*
[C] **And what are rain-drippings? So long as the rains fall and the mountains trickle with water, lo, they are like the water of a spring. If they ceased to trickle, lo, they are like the water of pools [T. Miq. 1:13H-L].** [Y. continues:] **If they ceased to trickle, lo, they are like water in pools.** [So long as the flow continues, therefore, the water is not in the category of that in a swape well and may be used on the intermediate days of the festival.]
[II:3 A] *R. Eleazar b. R. Yosé asked,* "*As to cascades of water, how do you treat them?*
[B] "*Are they in the status of swape-well water or not?* [No answer is given.]

Questions of classification of interstitial categories represent no formidable analytical exercise but carry forward the Mishnah's own taxonomic program, which aims at the rational and systematic classification of data. We shall not log in as analytical initiatives further examples of a perfectly commonplace, well-established procedure, since I do not discern fresh questions, or new ways of asking questions, in context.

### Yerushalmi Moed Qatan 1:2

[A] R. Eleazar b. Azariah says, "They do not make a new water channel on the intermediate days of a festival or in the Seventh Year "
[B] And sages say, "They make a new water channel in the Seventh Year,
[C] "and they repair damaged ones on the intermediate days of a festival."
[D] They repair damaged waterways in the public domain and dig them out.
[E] They repair roads, streets, and water pools.
[F] And they do all public needs, mark off graves, and go forth [to give warning] against Diverse Kinds [= M. Sheq. 1:1].

[II:1 A] **And they repair damaged ones on the intermediate days of a festival [M. 1:2C].**
[B] That is the case for one that is necessary for the festival.
[C] But in the case of one that is not necessary for use on the festival, it is prohibited to do so.

*One. Moed Qatan. Chapter One*

[D]   That is the case in the instance of a channel belonging to an individual. But in the case of a channel available for public use, even in the instance of one that is not for use on the festival, it is permitted.

The qualification of the rule introduced at B-C is itself re-qualified at D. Repairing damaged water channels is permitted only within the principle that the work be essential under emergency conditions. But that is further qualified, D, by the condition that the channel be private property; but public property is not subject to such restrictions. What analytical initiative is before us? The Halakhah contains a variety of principles, which must be sorted out, each applying in its particular circumstance, and which must be shown to harmonize. So a basic analytical inquiry will concern the resolution of conflict among valid principles through distinctions restricting the possibility of disharmony.

### Yerushalmi Moed Qatan 1:7

[A]   **They do not take wives on the intermediate days of a festival,**
[B]   **whether virgins or widows.**
[C]   **Nor do they enter into levirate marriage,**
[D]   **for it is an occasion of rejoicing.**
[E]   **But one may remarry his divorced wife.**
[F]   **And a woman may prepare her wedding adornments on the intermediate days of a festival.**
[G]   **R. Judah says, "She could not use lime, since this makes her ugly."**

[I:1  A]   [With reference to M. 1:7A-D:] Simeon bar Abba in the name of R. Yohanan, "It is because [people will hold up weddings until the festival, and so have one meal for the two events, the festival and the wedding]. [Consequently, they will postpone marriages and so] nullify the act of procreation [for the interval]."

   [F]   R. Ila, R. Eleazar in the name of R. Hananiah: "It is because people must not confuse one cause of rejoicing with some other."

      [G]   R. La derived that lesson from the following verse of Scripture: "[And on the eighth day they held a solemn assembly;] for they had kept the dedication of the altar seven days and the feast seven days" (2 Chron. 7:9).

      [H]   R. Jacob bar Aha derived the rule from the following: "Complete the week of this one, and we will give you the other also in return for serving me another seven years" (Gen. 29:27).

   [I]   R. Abbahu in the name of R. Eleazar: "The prohibition is on account of the excessive work [involved in preparing for the wedding]."

      [J]   *It has been taught:* But one may decide to get married on the eve of the festival.

         [K]   *That lenient ruling, moreover, does not stand at variance with the view of R. Eleazar, R. Yohanan, or even R. Haninah.*

[L] Said R. Ba, "When the bride enters [the marriage canopy], the work is gone and done."

The analytical inquiry is blatant: what is the governing consideration behind the rule at hand? A single rule proves accessible of diverse explanation: [1] people will postpone weddings until the festival; [2] people must not confuse several distinct causes of rejoicing; [3] too much work is involved to justify preparing on the intermediate days of the festival. The opening response of the Yerushalmi is typical: what is the reason for the rule (I:1 A, F, I; II.1, IV:1)? Once the reason is proposed, secondary implications are identified (1.B-E). A further interest is in the low-level glossing of the language of the Mishnah or the Tosefta, as at III:1. The secondary amplifications of each primary entry do not require attention.

### IV. BAVLI

As before, italics signify the use of Aramaic, plain type, Hebrew, and bold face, a statement deriving from the Mishnah or the Tosefta.

#### BAVLI MOED QATAN 1:1-2
#### 1:1

A. **They water an irrigated field on the intermediate days of a festival and in the Sabbatical Year [when many forms of agricultural labor are forbidden],**
B. **whether from a spring that first flows at that time, or from a spring that does not first flow at that time.**
C. **But they do not water [an irrigated field] with (1) collected rainwater, or (2) water from a swape well.**
D. **And they do not dig channels around vines.**

#### 1:2

A. **R. Eleazar b. Azariah says, "They do not make a new water channel on the intermediate days of a festival or in the Sabbatical Year."**
B. **And sages say, "They make a new water channel in the Sabbatical Year, and they repair damaged ones on the intermediate days of a festival."**
C. **They repair damaged waterways in the public domain and dig them out.**
D. **They repair roads, streets, and water pools.**
E. **And they (1) do all public needs, (2) mark off graves, and (3) go forth [to give warning] against [maintaining a field that is planted with] Diverse Kinds [or species of crops].**

I.1 A. **[They water an irrigated field on the intermediate days of a festival and in the Sabbatical Year, whether from a spring that first flows at that time, or from a spring that does not first flow at that time:]** *since it is explicitly stated that they may water a field from a spring that flows for the first time, which*

*One. Moed Qatan. Chapter One* 13

       *may damage the soil by erosion [making necessary immediate repair of the damage during the intermediate days of the festival], is it necessary to specify that they may water from a spring that does not first flow at that time, which is not going to cause erosion?*

  B.  *One may say that it is necessary to include both the latter and the former, for if the Tannaite framer had given the rule only covering a spring that first flows on the intermediate days of the festival, it is in that case in particular in which it is permitted to work on an irrigated field, but not for a rain-watered field, because the water is going to cause erosion, but in the case of a spring that does not first flow on the intermediate days, which is unlikely to cause erosion, I might have said that even a rain-watered field may be watered. So by specifying both cases the framer of the Mishnah-paragraph informs us that there is no distinction between a spring that flows for the first time and one that does not flow for the first time. The rule is the same for both: an irrigated plot may be watered from it, but a rain-watered plot may not be watered from [either a new or an available spring].*

Mishnah-criticism presupposes that the document says only what is necessary, but does not set forth in so many words rules that one may infer on the basis of what is made explicit. The analytical initiative then is provoked by an interest in showing why it is necessary to articulate a rule accessible through close reading of an already-stated law. The solution demonstrates that without making the rule articulate, the Mishnah's formulation left room for misconstruction. Specifically, we can have concluded that a consideration present in one case but not in the other accounts for the lenient ruling accorded only that case. This is amply spelled out.

The next analytical point begins in premise of the Talmud that a rule that is anonymous stands for the consensus of sages and is the law, while one that bears a name is schismatic and is not the law. At stake, once we know the authority behind the law, is whether other rulings in the name of that same authority, intersecting if not in detail then in principle, are consistent with this one. If they are not, then the decided law shows flaws of coherence, and these have to be identified and worked out.

3.  A.  *Who is the Tannaite authority who takes the position that work on the intermediate days of a festival is permitted if it is to prevent loss, but if it is to add to gain it is not permitted, and, further, even to prevent loss, really heavy labor is forbidden?*

The premise of the Mishnah's rule is now made explicit. The cases yield the rule that on the intermediate days of a festival one may carry out those acts of labor that prevent loss but not those that produce gain. And that leniency is further limited by the consideration that even to prevent loss, heavy labor is forbidden.

B.  *Said R. Huna, "It is R. Eliezer b. Jacob, for we have learned in the Mishnah:* **R. Eliezer b. Jacob says, 'They lead water from one tree to another, on condition that one not water the entire field. Seeds which have not been watered before the festival one should not water on the intermediate days of the festival' [M. 1:3]."**

Watering the entire field is forbidden, since it merely hastens the maturing process. But seeds that have not begun their growth-processes may not be watered at all; that would be work not to prevent loss but to secure gain. Neither however concerns preventing loss. That question now arises.

C.  *Well, I might concede that there is a representation of R. Eliezer's position that he prohibits work to add to one's gain, but have you heard a tradition that he disallows work in a situation in which otherwise loss will result?*
D.  *Rather, said R. Pappa, "Who is the authority behind this rule? It is R. Judah, for it has been taught on Tannaite authority:* **'From a spring that first flows on the intermediate days of a festival they irrigate even a rain watered field,' the words of R. Meir. And sages [=Judah vis à vis Meir] say, 'They irrigate from it only a field that depends upon irrigation, which has gone dry.' R. Eleazar b. Azariah says, "Not this nor that, [[but they do not irrigate a field from it [namely, a field the spring of which has gone dry] even in the case of an irrigated field]' [T. Moed 1:1A-C].** Even further, said R. Judah, 'A person should not clean out a water channel and with the dredging on the intermediate days of a festival water his garden or seed bed.'"
E.  *Now what is the meaning of* "that has gone dry"? *If you say that it really has dried up, then what is going to be accomplished by watering it?*
F.  *Said Abbayye, "The point is that this former water source has gone dry and another has just emerged."*

Judah's ruling at D clearly pertains to preventing loss; the field depends on irrigation, so its crop is in danger. That reading is challenged at E: how does this prevent loss? The answer is, the earlier spring has gone dry, a new spring has begun to flow. Judah maintains the farmer may use that. We revert to our task, showing the authority behind the anonymous rule. Our interpretation of the cited passage has yielded the attribution to Judah. But another interpretation of the same passage, based on a different premise, produces a different result.

H.  *And how to you know [that it is Judah in particular who takes the position that work on the intermediate days of a festival is permitted if it is to prevent loss, but if it is to add to gain it is not permitted, and, further, even to prevent loss, really heavy labor is forbidden]? Perhaps R. Judah takes the position that he does, that is, that it is permitted to use the water for an irrigated field but not for a field that depends on rain, only in the case of a spring that has just now begun to flow,* **[2B]** *since it may cause erosion, [hence, that may cause damage, as stipulated], but in the case of a spring that has not just now begun to flow*

## One. Moed Qatan. Chapter One

and will not cause erosion, such a spring might be permitted for use even on a field that depends on rain?

Then Judaism will permit watering a field from a spring that has not just emerged, even in a field that depends on rain; but the Mishnah's anonymous rule says that in the case of a spring that has not emerged for the first time, the water may be used for irrigation only for a field that depends on irrigation but not for a field that depends on rain water, in which case Judah and the Mishnah's anonymous rule take contradictory positions.

> I. *If so, then in accord with which authority will you assign our Mishnah-paragraph? For in fact, in R. Judah's view, there is no distinction between a spring that has just now flowed and one that has not just now flowed; in either case, an irrigated field may be watered, while one that depends on rain may not. And the reason that the passage specifies the spring that has just now flowed is only to show the extend to which R. Meir was prepared to go, even a spring that has just now flowed may be used, and that is, even for a field that depends upon rain.*

The solution is to insist that Judah does not make the proposed distinction, and that yields a rule in his name that is consistent with the Mishnah's. The language that is supposed to have yielded the distinction for Judah is to be read in the context of Meir's position, which is still more lenient than Judah's, as the language before us explains.

**II.1** **A. But they do not water [an irrigated field] with (1) collected rain water, or (2) water from a swape well [1:1C]:**
  B. *There is no trouble in understanding why water from a swape well should not be used, since watering in that way involves heavy labor. But what objection can there be to using collected rain water, since what heavy labor can possibly be involved in irrigating with rain water?*
  C. *Said R. Ilaa said R. Yohanan, "It is a precautionary decree, on account of the possibility of the farmer's going on to make use of water from a swape well."*
  D. *R. Ashi said, "Rain water itself can be as hard to draw as the water of a swape well."*
  E. *At issue between them is what R. Zira said. For* said R. Zira said Rabbah bar Jeremiah said Samuel, "From irrigation streams that draw water from ponds it is permitted to irrigate on the intermediate days of the festival." *One authority [Ashi] concurs with the position of R. Zira, and the other authority does not concur with the position of R. Zira.*

We do not understand why the same rule applies to two distinct classes of water-sources, so B. The answer, C, takes the form of a dispute: Yohanan concedes the premise of the question, Ashi does not, but insists upon commensurability. But the dispute is situated on a shared premise, so shown to be rational. The dispute rests upon whether or not it is permitted to draw water from ponds, as Zira maintains is the case; so the problem is whether or not the rain water is in the same classification as standing water.

**IV.1 A. R. Eleazar b. Azariah says, "They do not make a new water channel on the intermediate days of a festival or in the Sabbatical Year." And sages say, "They make a new water channel in the Sabbatical Year, and they repair damaged ones on the intermediate days of a festival:"**

The analysis of the rule involves the comparison and contrast of species of a single genus. That is, we find ourselves thrust once more into the comparison of different spells that are at a lower level of sanctification than the Sabbath or the Festival, namely, the intermediate days of the festival and the Sabbatical Year. Consequently, we resume the task we began earlier, and, specifically, we want to know why the Sabbatical Year is subject to the prohibition at hand, which obviously pertains to the intermediate days of the festival. Here, the Mishnah-rule has dictated its own exegetical problem.

B. *There is no problem with respect to the prohibition concerning the intermediate days of a festival, since the operative consideration is that this is heavy labor, but why ever not make a channel in the Sabbatical Year?*
C. *R. Zira and R. Abba b. Mamel differ on the matter —*
D. One said, "The reason is that the one who digs appears to be hoeing."
E. And the other said, "The reason is that he looks as though he is preparing the banks for sowing."
F. *So what's at stake?*
G. *At issue is a case in which the water comes along immediately. From the perspective of him who has said,* "The reason is that he looks as though he is preparing the banks for sowing," *it is still objectionable. But from the perspective of him who has said,* "The reason is that the one who digs appears to be hoeing," *there is no objection.*
H. *But should not the one who objects for the reason that it looks as though he is spading also object that he looks as though he is preparing the bank for seed?*
I. *Rather, this is what's at stake between the two explanations: it would involve a case in which he takes what is in the trench and tosses it out. From the perspective of him who says,* "The reason is that he looks as though he is preparing the banks for sowing," *there is no objection; but from the perspective of him who says,* "The reason is that the one who digs appears to be hoeing," *it is still subject to an objection.*
J. *But from the perspective of him who says that he appears to be preparing the sides for seed, would he not also admit that he seems to be hoeing?*
K. *Not really, for one who hoes, as soon as he takes up a spadeful, he puts it down again in place.*

*One. Moed Qatan. Chapter One*

What makes the exposition satisfying is that each side is given an opportunity to apply its reasoning at every stage in the argument, hence a full account, through the dialectic of back-and-forth exchange of positions and reasoning, is set forth. We proceed to a secondary analysis of the matter just now spelled out; the whole is continuous and cogent. The next step in the exposition raises the possibility that a given authority has taken two positions that contradict one another in principle.

### MISHNAH-TRACTATE MOED QATAN 1:3

A. R. Eliezer b. Jacob says, "They lead water from one tree to another,
B. "on condition that one not water the entire field.
C. "Seeds which have not been watered before the festival one should not water on the intermediate days of the festival."
D. And sages permit in this case and in that.

The Talmud's special interest in the comparison of the two distinct types of spells of time that possess diminished sanctity, the intermediate days of the festival and the Sabbatical Year, generates what follows. The Mishnah at hand has omitted reference to the latter, so it is the Talmud's framers' interest, not the Mishnah's rule, that accounts for the selection and introduction of what follows, No. 2.

2. A. *Our rabbis have taught on Tannaite authority:*
   B. They sprinkle water on a field of grain in the Sabbatical Year but not during the intermediate days of a festival.
   C. *But lo, it has been taught on Tannaite authority:*
   D. It is permitted to sprinkle a grain field both in the Sabbatical Year and in the intermediate days of the festival?
   E. *Said R. Huna, "There is no contradiction, the one speaks for R. Eliezer b. Jacob* [**R. Eliezer b. Jacob says, "They lead water from one tree to another, on condition that one not water the entire field. Seeds which have not been watered before the festival one should not water on the intermediate days of the festival"**], *the other, rabbis."*
3. A. *It has been further taught on Tannaite authority:*
   B. A field of grain may be sprinkled on the even of the Sabbatical Year so that the greens may sprout in the Sabbatical Year; and not only so, but they may sprinkle a field of grain in the Sabbatical Year so that the greens may sprout in the year after the Sabbatical Year.

The secondary expansion of the Tannaite rules of No. 2 then explicitly links our topic's problem, conduct on the intermediate days of the festival, with the comparison of the rule governing that span of time with the one that covers the Sabbatical Year.

## Bavli-tractate Moed Qatan 1:7-8

### 1:7

A. They do not take wives on the intermediate days of a festival,
B. whether virgins or widows.
C. Nor do they enter into levirate marriage,
D. for it is an occasion of rejoicing for the groom.
E. But one may remarry his divorced wife.
F. And a woman may prepare her wedding adornments on the intermediate days of a festival.
G. R. Judah says, "She should not use lime, since this makes her ugly."

### 1:8

A. An unskilled person sews in the usual way.
B. But an expert craftsman sews with irregular stitches.
C. They weave the ropes for beds.
D. R. Yosé says, "They [only] tighten them."

The opening clause is immediately challenged at its vulnerable point: is this not a form of celebration of the festival, so that there should be no such prohibition?

I.1 A. *So if it's* **an occasion of rejoicing for the groom***, what's so bad about that?*
B. Said R. Judah said Samuel, and so said R. Eleazar said R. Oshaia, and some say, said R. Eleazar said R. Hanina, "The consideration is that one occasion of rejoicing should not be joined with another such occasion."
C. Rabbah bar R. Huna said, "It is because he neglects the rejoicing of the festival to engage in rejoicing over his wife."
E. Ulla said, "It is because it is excess trouble."
F. R. Isaac Nappaha said, "It is because one will neglect the requirement of being fruitful and multiplying" [if people postponed weddings until festivals, they might somehow diminish the occasion for procreation, which is the first obligation]."
G. *An objection was raised:* All those of whom they have said that they are forbidden to wed on the festival **[9A]** are permitted to wed on the eve of the festival. *Now this poses a problem to the explanations of all the cited authorities!*
H. *There is no problem from the perspective of him who has said,* "The consideration is that one occasion of rejoicing should not be joined with another such occasion," *for the main rejoicing of the wedding is only a single day.*
I. *And from the perspective of him who has said,* "It is because it is excess trouble," *the principal bother lasts only one day.*
J. *And from the perspective of him who has said,* "It is because one will neglect the requirement of being fruitful and multiplying," *for merely one day someone will not postpone the obligation for any considerable length of time.*

*One. Moed Qatan. Chapter One*

The most interesting point, also the most abstract, concerns not confusing two occasions for rejoicing but allowing each its own integrity, hence not celebrating two religious duties at one and the same time.

### v. Types of Analysis. An Initial Proposal

Now to generalize upon the chosen materials of Mishnah-Tosefta-Yerushalmi-Bavli Moed Qatan Chapter One.

#### 1. How Cases Exemplify a Rule: Generalization, Extension

> T. 1:2/1:11: explaining the rule of the Mishnah: to a matter that brings about loss, they attend, to one that does not, they do not attend. I see no formalization of language that pertains to the exercise at hand,
> T. 1:7: …because of the threat to life: the operative consideration behind the Mishnah's detailed rule
> T. 1:12: …because it is as if one rescues them from their power; other instances in which a greater good overrides the restrictions of the intermediate days of the festival

The Tosefta contributes the category, transforming a case into a rule, a rule into a principle, a principle pertinent here into one that applies there and everywhere. This movement toward abstract consideration of concrete instances represents a thought process of considerable interest. The sequence of question is, [1] is the case unique, or is there a rule that is exemplified? [2] if there is a generative rule (exemplified in the case), then how does it apply to other cases of the same classification of the law? [3] Can we transcend the limits of our classification and treat the generative rule in abstract form, as a principle applicable in many areas of the Halakhah?

#### 2. What Is the Reason behind the Rule? What are the implications in play, and what is the range of possible explanation for a single case

> T. 1:12 As before, the analysis identifies the governing consideration that generates the rule, and then shows that that same consideration pertains to other Halakhic topics altogether.
> Y. to M. M. Q. 1:7 I:1: The several reasons adduced to explain a single rule, each with its own implications on other areas of law altogether.
> B. to M. 1:7-8 I.1/8b-9a: Same as the foregoing

#### 3. Once the governing principle is identified, the several rules are tested against it for contradictions, and when these emerge, they are ironed out

Y. to M. M.Q. 1:1 I:1: The anomaly in the law, identified when the principle is articulated, is ironed out by showing that diverse authorities take each his own view of the matter.

**4. SORTING OUT THE OPERATIVE PRINCIPLES BEHIND A GIVEN RULING OF THE LAW: HOW DOES EACH PRINCIPLE APPLY IN A PARTICULAR CIRCUMSTANCE, AND HOW TO THE WHOLE HARMONIZE?**

Y. to M. Q. 2:1 II:1, as explained above.

**5. SINCE IT IS EXPLICITLY STATED THAT..., WHY IS IT NECESSARY TO SPECIFY...**

B. to M.Q 1:1-2 I:1/2a: The language of the Mishnah is subjected to a close reading to identify any redundant formulations.

**6. HOW CAN THE SAME RULE APPLY TO TWO DISTINCT CLASSES**

B. to M. Q. 1:1-2 II.1, the dispute is situated on a shared premise, so is rational

**7. THE COMPARISON OF THE SPECIES OF A SINGLE GENUS, A VARIATION ON THE FOREGOING**

B. to M. Q. 1:1-2 IV.1

The Talmuds analytical inquiries define a broad program. I see three large categories of analysis:

- A. The close reading of the language of the rule, yielding insight based on the wording: No. 5
- B. Taxonomic inquiry into category-formations of the law and the comparison and contrast thereof: Nos. 6, 7
- C. The reason behind the rule, yielding the possibility of transcending the limits of the case: Nos. 2, 3, 4

So far as I am able to discern, the Talmudic analyses of the Halakhah all fit into one of these three classifications. We now continue our survey of Moed Qatan, with the hypothesis in hand that Moed Qatan Chapter One has yielded. It is simple: the analytical program that transforms the Halakhah into a large and encompassing system, capable of almost unlimited extension and variation, is comprised by at least these three types of thought, in logical order: [1] analysis of language, [2] analysis of category-formations and their relationships, [3] analysis of the implications of the law of one category-formation for some other.

# 2

# Moed Qatan Chapter Two

I now utilize the established classification of types of analytical inquiry, adding new types as called for.

### I. LANGUAGE: THE CLOSE READING OF THE LANGUAGE OF THE RULE, YIELDING INSIGHT BASED ON THE WORDING

    A.    MISHNAH: —
    B.    TOSEFTA: —
    C.    YERUSHALMI

#### YERUSHALMI TO MISHNAH-TRACTATE MOED QATAN 2:1

[A] He who [prior to the festival] had turned his olives, and then an occasion for mourning or some accident befell him,
[B] or whose workers proved unreliable [so that he could not complete the processing prior to the festival],
[C] "[during the intermediate days of the festival] applies the pressing beam [to the olives] for the first time, but [then] leaves it until after the festival," the words of R. Judah.
[D] R. Yosé says, "He squeezes out the oil entirely and seals it in jar. in the usual way."

[I:1 A] *We have learned:* **He who had turned his olives [one time].**
    [B] *And R. Hiyya taught: "He who had his olives turned over once and yet a second time...."*
    [C] *The law of the Mishnah requires the clarification of the saying of R. Hiyya, and the saying of R. Hiyya requires the clarification of the law of the Mishnah.*
    [D] *If we had learned what the Mishnah had to say, and not that which R. Hiyya taught, we should have ruled that* the dispute applies only if someone had

turned over his olives one time alone. But if he had done so once and again a second time, all parties concur that it is permitted [but now we see that the dispute of M. applies to this case as well].

[E] *So it was necessary to learn the teaching of R. Hiyya.*
[F] *If, further, we had in hand what R. Hiyya taught but had not learned what the Mishnah says, we should have ruled that the dispute applies only in the case of one who had turned over the olives once and then done so a second time. But if one had done so only one time, then in the opinion of all parties, it is forbidden [to do so on the festival].*
[G] *Accordingly, there was need to provide that which the Mishnah has stated as well as that which R. Hiyya has taught.*

The contradictory formulations of the law are required and fit will together. The close reading of the Mishnah's formulation yields an ambiguity, settled by the variant tradition of Hiyya. The analytical inquiry aims at finding how diverse wordings of the same law contribute to a common enterprise.

### YERUSHALMI TO MISHNAH-TRACTATE MOED QATAN 2:2

[A] **And so: He who had his wine in the cistern, and then an occasion for mourning or some accident befell him,**
[B] **or workers proved unreliable,**
[C] **"empties out the wine completely and seals it in jars in the usual way," the words of R. Yosé.**
[D] **R. Judah says, "He [only] makes a cover for it of shingles, so that it not turn sour."**

[I:1 A] Said R. Zeira, "The text states only, **'And so: He who had his wine in the cistern'** [M. 2:2A] [already]. [That is, the farmer had begun the vintage prior to the festival.] Lo, to begin with it is forbidden [on the festival itself, if the work had not been begun already, to carry out the procedures specified by M. 2:2C or D].

[B] *"For how shall we [81b] interpret the case before us?* If we deal with a situation in which the time came to cut the grapes and he did not do so, then the farmer has injured himself [and has caused the loss himself].

[C] "If we deal with a case in which the time for cutting the grapes had not yet come, he could have left the grapes in place.

[D] *"But we must deal with a case in which* the time came to cut the grapes. He thought that he could leave the grapes in place [not hastening the grape-cutting], and he found that he could not do so. [Nonetheless, he bears the responsibility for his own loss, and that is M.'s point.]"

A close reading of the formulation of the law clarifies what is at stake.

D. BAVLI: —

*Two. Moed Qatan. Chapter Two*

## II. CATEGORY-CRITICISM: TAXONOMIC INQUIRY INTO CATEGORY-FORMATIONS OF THE LAW AND THE COMPARISON AND CONTRAST THEREOF

    A.    MISHNAH: —
    B.    TOSEFTA: —
    C.    YERUSHALMI

### YERUSHALMI TO MISHNAH-TRACTATE MOED QATAN 2:5

[A] They cover up fig cakes [left to dry] with straw.
[B] R. Judah says, "They also pile them up in heaps."
[C] Those who sell produce, clothing, and utensils sell them discretely, for the purposes of the festival.
[D] Hunters, groats makers, and grist-millers do their work discretely, for the purposes of the festival.
[E] R. Yosé says, "They have adopted a strict ruling for themselves."

[I:2 A] Kahana said, "There are rules concerning the intermediate days of a festival that are more difficult than the rules governing the transfer of uncleanness through overshadowing, and the rules governing Negas. [Here is an example.]
   [B] "There R. Jeremiah said in the name of Rab, '[If it should rain,] they spread mats on top of shavings that cover the bricks on the Sabbath.' *And here the law has said this* [that one may not make use of something to cover the figs if it is a source of much work to utilize it]."
   [C] Rabbis of Caesarea in the name of R. Jacob bar Aha: "At issue among the conflicting sayings [about hard work being permitted for protecting bricks from rain and, in M., about covering fig cakes only in the most convenient way], is whether or not one may pull straw from the ground.
   [D] "Rabbis maintain that one may cut the straw and make a covering with it.
   [E] "R. Judah says, 'One may not cut it, but one may make a covering with it.'"

The comparison of the laws governing the several category-formations yields a clarification of the practical rule.

    D.    BAVLI

### BAVLI TO MISHNAH-TRACTATE MOED QATAN 2:1

A. [11B] He who had turned his olives, and then an occasion for mourning or some accident befell him,
B. or workers proved unreliable [so that he could not complete the processing prior to the festival],

C. "[during the intermediate days of the festival] applies the pressing beam [to the olives] for the first time, but [then] leaves [the oil] until after the festival," the words of R. Judah.
D. R. Yosé says, "He squeezes out the oil entirely and seals it in jars in the usual way."

I.1 A. While the passage commences by discussing mourning, it concludes solely with advice on how to press oil!
B. Said R. Shisha b. R. Idi, "That bears the implication that what one may do during the intermediate days of a festival one may not do during the week of mourning." [Lazarus: one may do these things now only in the intermediate days of the festival but not during the mourning week].
C. [Rejecting this thesis,] R. Ashi said, *"The formulation is meant to yield the reading, 'it goes without saying,' in this way: it is not necessary to give the rule governing the time of mourning, which is in any event based on the authority of rabbis and so such acts of labor are permitted, but even during the intermediate days of a festival, during which, on the authority of the Torah, acts of supererogatory labor are forbidden, still, where there may be a great loss, rabbis have permitted such an act of labor."* [Ashi thus reads the present rule as consistent with the one yielded by M. 1:1.]

The Bavli's Mishnah-criticism turns to the stylistic problem involved in changing the subject from a question of mourning, A — meaning, on ordinary days — to conduct on the intermediate days of the festival, B. The substantive point of interest presented by the analogy opens the way to the discussion of the rules of conduct during the week of mourning for the death of a close relative. Here is where the comparison and contrast of kindred category-formations come into play. Once we treat as comparable the rules governing the mourning week and the festival week, a variety of relevant cases arises. The analogy is perceived at I.1.A and exploited at I.1.B, C.

### BAVLI TO MISHNAH-TRACTATE MOED QATAN 2:2 I:1

A. And so: he who had his wine in the cistern, and then an occasion for mourning or some accident befell him,
B. or whose workers proved unreliable,
C. "empties out the wine completely and seals it in jars in the usual way," the words of R. Yosé.
D. R. Judah says, "He [may do no such thing, but he only] makes a cover of shingles for it, so that it not turn sour."

I.1 A. *It was necessary to give us the cases of both olives and wine, for had the first case alone been given to us, we might have supposed that it is in that case in particular that R. Yosé took the position that he did, because in the case of the loss of oil, the monetary penalty would be considerable, but in the case of the*

*Two. Moed Qatan. Chapter Two*

> loss of the wine, the monetary penalty of which would not be so substantial, I might say that he concurs with R. Judah.
>
> B. And had we been given only the second case, it would have been in that case in particular that R. Judah took the position that he did, but as to the other, I might have said that he concurs with R. Yosé. So both cases had to be set forth.

The mode of analysis is to distinguish one case from another, e.g., showing how a principle operative here may not pertain there. The larger issue concerns performing on the intermediate days of the festival work that will prove beneficial after the festival. The issue in M. 2:2C vs. D is whether one may perform work necessary for the emergency — not incurring severe loss on the intermediate days of the festival — that also has bearing upon the situation once the festival is over. Yosé holds that one may do so, and Judah says one may perform on the intermediate days of the festival only work that is absolutely necessary to prevent loss thereon, but work that produces benefit later on may not be carried out on the intermediate days of the festival. Identifying the principle subject to dispute in the case of Yosé and Judah permits us to see whether a rule is uniformly imposed, or whether within the law are case-rules that contain contradictions in principle. We now take up a further exercise of the same classification.

### BAVLI TO MISHNAH-TRACTATE MOED QATAN 2:2 I:4

A. And so: he who had his wine in the cistern, and then an occasion for mourning or some accident befell him,

B. or whose workers proved unreliable,

C. "empties out the wine completely and seals it in jars in the usual way," the words of R. Yosé.

D. R. Judah says, "He [may do no such thing, but he only] makes a cover of shingles for it, so that it not turn sour."

I.4  A. Said R. Hama bar Guria said Rab, "The laws governing the intermediate days of the festival are in the same classification as the laws governing relationships with the Kutim [Samaritans]."

B. *For what concrete legal purpose is such a statement set forth?*

C. Said R. Daniel bar Qattina, "That is to say that they are all episodic and do not provide analogies, one for the other."

D. *For said Samuel, "They may coat a jug with pitch, but they may not coat a cask," and R. Dimi of Nehardea said, "They may coat a cask with pitch, but not a jug." The one master concerned himself with the question of loss* [there is more loss involved in neglecting a cask than a jug], *and the other was concerned about not undertaking heavy labor on the intermediate days of the festival."*

E. Said Abbayye, "*We hold the tradition:* The laws governing the intermediate days of the festival are analogous to the laws governing the Sabbath. [12B] There are among them actions that are exempt from sanctions but nonetheless forbidden, and there are among them actions that are permitted to begin with."

Our interest is in finding analogies to the present category of law, which will then deepen our grasp of the principles that are in play. In general, two analogies present themselves, the one to the Sabbatical Year, based on the comparison of spells of time of diminished levels of sanctification, the other to the situation of the mourner during a week during which activities are restricted, as they are during the intermediate days of the festival. Reverting to the conception of interstitial occasions or situations, we turn to the comparison of the laws governing the intermediate days of the festival, of diminished sanctification, to the laws governing relationships with Samaritans. They are neither gentiles nor Israelites, but form an interstitial category; they keep the laws of the Torah, but not the oral laws that accompany them. They are not wholly sanctified but also not entirely common. But why in the world draw such an analogy? Abbayye proposes another analogy, now to the laws governing the Sabbath, because in both the laws of the intermediate days of the festival and in those of the Sabbath, there are actions that are interstitial, neither permitted nor penalized, as well as those that are permitted to begin with.

### III. RATIONALITY: THE REASON BEHIND THE RULE, YIELDING THE POSSIBILITY OF TRANSCENDING THE LIMITS OF THE CASE:

- A. MISHNAH: —
- B. TOSEFTA: —
- C. YERUSHALMI: —
- D. BAVLI: —

### IV. ANALOGY-CRITICISM: FINDING THE CORRECT ANALOGY FOR THE IDENTIFICATION OF THE GOVERNING RULE

We now come to a further category of analysis, as the Bavli shows us. It has to do with the consequences of identifying the governing analogy, and forms a development of the preceding. That is, once we know to what a matter is comparable, we also know the law that pertains, which is the law that decides the case of that to which the item subject to doubt is analogous.

- A. MISHNAH: —
- B. TOSEFTA: —
- C. YERUSHALMI: —
- D. BAVLI

#### BAVLI TO MISHNAH-TRACTATE MOED QATAN 2:4A

A. They buy houses, slaves, and cattle, only for the needs of the festival or for the needs of a seller who has nothing to eat.

*Two. Moed Qatan. Chapter Two* 27

**I.1** A. *Raba raised this question to R. Nahman:* "As to hiring for make-work jobs someone who has not got food — what is the law?"

The issue requires that we identify the governing analogy. If the case of the poor person is comparable to the case of anyone who does not have food to eat, then the rule is explicit in the matter of the seller. If the primary component of the case is, make-work, as against the work, e.g., of scribes, then a different consideration emerges, F. Yet other analogies produce absurdities.

B. *He said to him, "We have learned in the Mishnah,* **or for the needs of a seller who has nothing to eat.** *Now what does* **who has nothing to eat** *encompass? It is surely make-work for starving workers."*

C. *He said to him, "No, it serves to amplify the clause."*

D. Objected Abbayye, "**They do not write writs of indebtedness on the intermediate days of a festival. But if one does not trust him, or if he had nothing to eat, lo, this one should write [a writ of indebtedness]** [M. 3:4A-D]. *Now what does* **if he had nothing to eat** *encompass? It is surely make-work for starving workers."*

E. *That is decisive proof.*

F. *Objected R. Sheshet,* "**And sages say, 'Three sorts of craftsmen perform work on the eve of Passover up to noon, and these are they: tailors, barbers, and laundry-men.' R. Yosé b. R. Judah says, 'Also: shoemakers'** [M. Pes. 4:6D-F]. tailors, barbers, and laundry-men — for the same reason that an individual may do some sewing in the ordinary way during the intermediate days of the festival; hairdressers and fullers, for the same reason that persons coming home from abroad or coming out of prison may have a hair cut and wash their clothes during the intermediate days of the festival. *Now if you assume that it is permitted to hire for make-work jobs starving people, then all other work should have been permitted hear, since, if make-work jobs are permitted where one is starving, anything else should also be permitted on the same principle."*

G. *Objected R. Pappa, "Then how about the following [equally plausible objection, leading to an absurd result]: building too should be permitted, for the following rule applies:* **As to a wall that is hanging over into public domain, they may tear it down and rebuild it in the usual way, because it is a public nuisance** [T. 1:7A-B]."

H. Objected Rabina, "Then how about the following: a scribe should be permitted to do his work, since in any event, **And these do they write on the intermediate days of a festival: (1) writs of betrothal for women, (2) writs of divorce, (3) receipts [for payment of the marriage settlement], (4) testaments, (5) deeds of gift, (6) prosbols [assigning to the court writs of indebtedness, so that the writs will not be nullified by the advent of the Sabbatical Year], (7) deeds of valuation, (8) deeds of alimony, (9) writs of the rite of removing the shoe and of the exercise of the rite of refusal, (10) deeds of arbitration, (11) court decrees, and (12) official decrees** [M. Moed Qatan 3:3]."

I. [The premises throughout invoke an analogy that is inappropriate, namely, the intermediate days of the festival and the conduct of ordinary people on the fourteenth of Nisan, prior to the advent of Passover; but that day is not the counterpart to a festival day at all.] *Rather, said R. Ashi, "How can you compare the rules governing the intermediate days of the festival week and the rules concerning the fourteenth of Nisan? Those governing the intermediate days of the festival week are so as to avoid heavy labor, but where there is the possibility of severe loss, rabbis have permitted work; rules governing the fourteenth of Nisan are based on the requirements of the festival of Passover, so that whatever is needed for the observance of the festival of Passover have our rabbis permitted, but anything that is not needed for the observance of the festival of Passover have our rabbis not permitted."*

Abbayye's principle is that on the intermediate days, one takes account of the needs of those without food, hiring them to do make-work, inessential jobs to make sure they earn money to buy provisions. But Sheshet cites a rule bearing the opposite implication. To that Pappa, then Rabina, object with a reductio ad absurdum. All of these cases rest on the analogy of the intermediate days of the festival to the fourteenth of Nisan, prior to the festival altogether. That is inappropriate, it is no counterpart. Each occasion has its own governing consideration. The reasoning is then quite articulate: find the correct analogy. To generalize: the basic mode of analysis concerns the identification of the appropriate analogy to the case at hand, to reason from the known to the unknown via analogical thinking. The task now is to discover the valid analogy, and criticize a position on grounds of the appropriate or inappropriate character of said analogy.

### V. TYPES OF ANALYSIS

We have identified a fourth classification of analytical inquiry, as indicated.

i.. Language: Y. to M. M.Q. 2:1, diverse wordings of the same law; Y. to M. Q. 2:2 I:1 clarifies what is at issue in diverse wordings
ii. Category: Y. to M.Q. 2:5 I:2: comparing the classifications, the rules governing the intermediate days of the festival and the rules governing the transfer of uncleanness through overshadowing; B. to M. M.Q. 2:1: comparing the rules of conduct in the week of mourning with those pertaining to the festival week; B. to M.Q. 2:2 I:1: comparing the category of wine and olives; I:4: explicit comparison of the laws governing the intermediate days of the festival and those governing relationships with Samaritans, both constituting interstitial categories
iii. Rationality: —
iv. Analogy-Criticism: B. to M. M.Q. 2:1 I:1: we conduct an operation of not comparison but analogical inquiry: can a comparison be made at all?

As we noted, the issue of analogy-criticism flows from the interest in category-criticism and forms a development of it. More to the point, the initial hypothesis, that the types of analytical inquiry divide into language, category, and rationality, continues to serve, with the refinement just now observed.

PART TWO

A SECONDARY PROBE:
TYPES OF ANALYSIS IN SELECT TRACTATES:
QIDDUSHIN, ABODAH ZARAH

# 3

## Qiddushin

I. **Language-Analysis**

    A.   Mishnah: —
    B.   Tosefta: —
    C.   Yerushalmi: —
    D.   Bavli

**Bavli to Qiddushin 1:9**

A. **Every commandment which is dependent upon the Land applies only in the Land,**

B. **and which does not depend upon the Land applies both in the Land and outside the Land,**

C. **[37A] except for 'Orlah [produce of a fruit tree in the first three years of its growth] and mixed seeds [Lev. 19:23, 19:19].**

D. **R. Eliezer says, "Also: Except for [the prohibition against eating] new [produce before the omer is waved on the sixteenth of Nisan] [Lev. 23:14]."**

I.1   A.   *What is the meaning of,* **which is dependent upon,** *and what is the meaning of,* **which does not depend upon***? If I say that the sense of* **which is dependent upon** *pertains where the language,* "entering the Land" *is used, and the sense of* **which does not depend upon** *pertains where the language,* "entering the Land" *is not used, then what about the matters of* phylacteries and the disposition of the firstling of an ass, which pertain both in the Land of Israel and abroad, *even though the language* "entering the Land" *is used in their connection?*

    B.   *Said R. Judah, "This is the sense of the statement:* Every religious duty that is an obligation of the person applies whether in the Land or abroad, but if it is an obligation that is incumbent upon the soil, it applies only in the Land."

The "clarification" of the meaning of the language is precipitated by a theory that requires testing: does this mean thus-and-so, because, if it does, then what about such-and-such? So language-analysis involves a very specific problem, the implications of a given formulation for a legal problem that is deemed to intersect. The solution, B, is to side-step the question altogether and propose a different reading of the ambiguous language. The upshot is, the question is provoked by an extrinsic problem of law, not an intrinsic problem in the wording of matters.

### BAVLI TO MISHNAH QIDDUSHIN 1:10A-D

A. Whoever does a single commandment — they do well for him and lengthen his days.
B. And he inherits the Land.
C. And whoever does not do a single commandment — they do not do well for him and do not lengthen his days.
D. And he does not inherit the Land.

I.1 A. *By way of contradiction:* **These are things the benefit of which a person enjoys in this world, while the principal remains for him in the world to come: [Deeds in] honor of father and mother, [performance of] righteous deeds, and [acts which] bring peace between a man and his fellow. But the study of Torah is as important as all of them together** [M. Peah 1:1C-E]. [Freedman. *Qiddushin, ad loc.:* Thus only for these is one reward in this world, while the Mishnah says that that is so of any precept.]

B. *Said R. Judah, "This is the sense of the matter:* **Whoever does a single commandment** — over and above the advantage deriving from his inherited merits — **they do well for him,** and he is as though he had carried out the entire Torah."

C. *Then does it follow that for these other deeds, one is rewarded even for a single one [with no other deeds to one's credit]?*

D. Said R. Shemaiah, "It is to say that if there is an equal balance, then that one deed tips the scale in his favor."

The ambiguity of the Mishnah's formulation of intersecting statements, M. Qid. 1:10 and M. Pe. 1:1, is identified and resolved. The pattern identified at the earlier entry recurs: the Halakhic context — the legal hermeneutics — dictates the linguistic exegesis.

### BAVLI TO MISHNAH QIDDUSHIN 2:1A-C

A. A man effects betrothal on his own or through his agent.
B. A woman becomes betrothed on her own or through her agent.
C. A man betroths his daughter when she is a girl on his own or through his agent.

*Three. Qiddushin*

I.1 A. [**A man effects betrothal on his own or through his agent:**] *If it is clearly stated that* **a man effects betrothal through his agent,** *can there be any question that* **a man effects betrothal on his own?**
B. Said R. Joseph, "The formulation bears the sense that it is a religious duty better carried out by him than by his agent."

The question is, how can the Mishnah articulate what is redundant, A? The answer, B, is, a fresh point is contained within the formulation. This is a form of language-criticism that is very common in the Bavli's reading of the Mishnah and other received legal formulations: the quest for redundancy and inconsistency in language. The premise is, the Mishnah is a perfect piece of writing, and imperfections such as redundancy or inconsistency cannot occur. That same premise intervenes in the reading of Scripture as well, we see many times over.

### BAVLI TO MISHNAH QIDDUSHIN 3:10-11
#### 3:10

A. He who says to a woman, "I have betrothed you,"
B. and she says, "You did not betroth me" –
C. he is prohibited to marry her relatives, but she is permitted to marry his relatives.
D. [If] she says, "You betrothed me," and he says, "I did not betroth you" –
E. he is permitted to marry her relatives, and she is prohibited from marrying his relatives.
F. "I betrothed you,"
G. and she says, "You betrothed only my daughter,"
H. he is prohibited from marrying the relatives of the older woman, and the older woman is permitted to marry his relatives.
I. He is permitted to marry the relatives of the young girl, and the young girl is permitted to marry his relatives.

#### 3:11

A. "I have betrothed your daughter,"
B. and she says, "You betrothed only me,"
C. he is prohibited to marry the relatives of the girl, and the girl is permitted to marry his relatives.
D. He is permitted to marry the relatives of the older woman, but the older woman is prohibited from marrying his relatives.

I.1 A. He who says to a woman, "I have betrothed you," and she says, "You did not betroth me" — he is prohibited to marry her relatives, but she is permitted to marry his relatives:
B. *It was necessary to list all of these situations. For had we been informed of the rule with respect to his statement [that if he said, I betrothed you, his relatives*

*are not forbidden to her,]* since to a man such a situation makes no difference, so that is how he talks; but as to her, I might suppose, if she were not sure of herself, she would not have made such a statement, so her relatives would be forbidden to him. So we are informed that that is not the case.

As in the foregoing, so here, we want to account for what appears to be, if not redundant, then at least, prolix. Why is it necessary to cover so many situations? The premise of the framer of the Mishnah, to establish a general rule, present a series, meaning a minimum of three cases, is sidestepped. Rather, each case is made to make its own point. In this way the formal, rhetorical program of the Mishnah is made to respond to an altogether different set of considerations; establishing a series is less valued, identifying refinements and clarifications, more. Then the Mishnah's very mode of thought generates the Talmud's exegetical program — in a negative way. What makes the Mishnah possible — its presentation of series in a sustained exercise of *Listenwissenschaft* — makes necessary the Talmudic critique of prolixity.

### BAVLI TO MISHNAH QIDDUSHIN 4:1

A. **Ten castes came up from Babylonia: (1) priests, (2) Levites, (3) Israelites, (4) impaired priests, (5) converts, and (6) freed slaves, (7) Mamzers, (8) Netins, (9) "silenced ones" [shetuqi], and (10) foundlings.**

I.1 A. **Ten castes came up from Babylonia:** *How come the Tannaite formulation prefers the language,* **came up from Babylonia**, *rather than saying,* came to the Land of Israel?

B. *En passant he informs us of another matter, as has been taught on Tannaite authority:* "Then you shall arise and ascend to the place which the Lord your God shall choose" (Deut. 17:8) — this teaches that the house of the sanctuary is higher than the whole of the Land of Israel, and the Land of Israel is higher than all other lands.

C. *Well, there is no problem with the claim that* the house of the sanctuary is higher than the whole of the Land of Israel, *for that is in line with what has been written:* **[69B]** "If there arise...matters of controversy in your gates, then you shall arise and go up" (Deut. 17:9). *But as to the allegation that* the Land of Israel is higher than all other lands, *how on the basis of Scripture do we know that fact?*

D. "Therefore behold, the days come, says the Lord, that they shall no more say, As the Lord lives, which brought up the children of Israel out of the land of Egypt; but, as the Lord lives, which brought up and which led the seed of the house of Israel out of the north country and from all the countries whither I had driven them" (Jer. 23:7-8).

I.2 A. *How come the Tannaite formulation prefers the language,* **came up from Babylonia**, *rather than saying,* came up to the Land of Israel?

*Three. Qiddushin*

B. *That formulation sustains the position of R. Eleazar, for* said R. Eleazar, "Ezra did not go up from Babylonia until he had made it pure as sifted flour; then he went up" [Freedman: taking those of inferior genealogy, so that they should not remain in Babylonia].

The formulation of the law is taken to be purposive, and the choice of one wording over another, equally serviceable one, yields a lesson on an extraneous issue. The premise that every word has a bearing on all others makes possible the present manner of reading.

### BAVLI TO MISHNAH QIDDUSHIN 4:3

A. All those who are forbidden from entering into the congregation are permitted to marry one another.
B. R. Judah prohibits [their marrying one another].
C R. Eliezer says, "Those who are of certain status are permitted to intermarry with others who are of certain status.
D. "Those who are of certain status and those who are of doubtful status, those who are of doubtful status and those who are of certain status, those who are of doubtful status and those who are of doubtful status –
E. "[intermarriage among persons in such classifications] is prohibited."
F. And who are those who are of doubtful status?
G. The "silenced one," the foundling, and the Samaritan.

I.1 A. All those who are forbidden from entering into the congregation:
B. *What is the meaning of,* **all those who are forbidden from entering into the congregation?** *Should I say this refers to Mamzers, Netins, silenced ones, and foundlings? Lo, the opening clause states explicitly:* **Converts, freed slaves, Mamzers, Netins, "silenced ones," and foundlings are permitted to marry among one another.** *And furthermore, with reference to the statement,* **R. Judah prohibits [their marrying one another],** *to which clause does R. Judah's statement pertain? Should I say, it refers to the marriage of persons whose status is certain and persons whose status is subject to doubt? Now, since the concluding clause states,* **R. Eliezer says, "Those who are of certain status are permitted to intermarry with others who are of certain status. Those who are of certain status and those who are of doubtful status, those who are of doubtful status and those who are of certain status, those who are of doubtful status and those who are of doubtful status — [intermarriage among persons in such classifications] is prohibited,"** *it must follow that R. Judah does not take that position. And should you say* **R. Judah forbids** *pertains to the marriage of a proselyte and a mamzer girl, then does the language at hand state,* a proselyte with a mamzer girl? *What it states is,* **All those who are forbidden from entering into the congregation!**
C. Said R. Judah, **[74B]** *"This is the sense of the statement at hand:* **All those who are forbidden from entering into the congregation** *of the priesthood — and who might that be? It is a proselyte girl who converted at less than three*

years and a day old, thus not in accord with R. Simeon b. Yohai [as will be explained presently] — **are permitted to marry one another**." [Then the statement, **R. Judah prohibits** their marrying one another refers to the marriage of a proselyte and a mamzer girl (Freedman).]

D. *Well, why not assign the rule to a girl three years and a day old, in accord also with R. Simeon b. Yohai?*

E. *If that were the case, the refutation would stand right along side, in the following argument: So the operative consideration is that it is a girl three years and a day old; lo, in the case of one less than that age, since she may enter the congregation of the priests, she is forbidden to intermarry with the others [Mamzers and the like]. Then what about the one who is less than three years and a day old from the perspective of R. Simeon b. Yohai, who, though she may enter into the assembly of priests, nonetheless may intermarry with the others?* [Freedman: For since she may marry a mamzer, it follows that the assembly of proselytes does not fall into the category of an assembly, so the same would hold good if she is a proselyte prior to that age as well.]

I.2 A. *And is it an encompassing generalization that* **all those who are forbidden from entering into the congregation are permitted to marry one another?** What about a widow, a divorcée, a woman of impaired priestly genealogy, and a whore [Lev. 21:7], all of whom are prohibited from entering into the congregation of the priesthood, but who also are forbidden to marry with these others? *Furthermore,* then is one who is permitted to marry into the priesthood forbidden to marry with these? But what about a proselyte, who is permitted to marry a priest's daughter but also is permitted to marry a mamzer girl?

B. *Rather, said R. Nathan bar Hoshayya, "This is the sense of the statement:* Anyone whose daughter a priest is forbidden to marry — and who might that be? it is a proselyte man who married a proselyte women, and that is in accord with the position of R. Eliezer b. Jacob — is permitted to marry with one another.

C. *And is it an encompassing generalization that* anyone whose daughter a priest is forbidden to marry is permitted to marry with one another? *What about the case of* a priest of impaired genealogical status who married a daughter of Israelite status, in which case, a priest is forbidden to marry his daughter, but, nonetheless, he may not intermarry with these others [the mamzer and the like]?

D. *No problem, the rule accords with R. Dosetai b. Judah* ["Israelite women constitute an immersion pool for the purpose of purification of priests who have been profaned"].

E. *What about the case of* a priest of impaired genealogical status who married a priest girl of impaired genealogical status? Here, though a priest may not marry his daughter, yet such a one may intermarry with those others! *And furthermore,* the formulation implies, but one whose daughter is permitted to marry a priest is forbidden to intermarry with these — then what about the case of a proselyte who married an Israelite woman, in which case a priest is permitted to marry his daughter, but he may intermarry with these others!

F. *Rather, said R. Nahman said Rabbah bar Abbuha, "Here at issue between them is the case of a mamzer born of a sister and a mamzer born of a married*

*Three. Qiddushin* 39

woman. *The first Tannaite position is that even a mamzer born of his sister is classified as a mamzer. And R. Judah takes the view that a mamzer born of a married woman is a mamzer, but one born of a sister is not."* [Freedman: The rule does not refer to a proselyte at all, but to the question of whether these two mamzer children may intermarry. A sister is forbidden on pain of extirpation, adultery with a married woman is forbidden on pain of the death penalty. The first authority treats the offspring of both unions as a mamzer and holds those who are forbidden to enter the assembly as Mamzerim may nonetheless intermarry; Judah holds that only the latter, forbidden on pain of death, is a mamzer, but not the former, so they may not intermarry.]

G. *Well, if that's the case, then what does the framer of our Mishnah paragraph propose to tell us that is fresh and interesting, when we have already learned the same point in the Mishnah elsewhere:* **What is the definition of a "mamzer"?** "[The offspring of] any [marriage of near of kin — the rubric, 'He shall not come into the congregation of the Lord' (Deut. 23:3)," the words of R. Aqiba. Simeon of Teman says, "[The offspring of] any [marriage] for which the participants are liable to extirpation by Heaven." And the law follows his opinion. R. Joshua says, "[The offspring of] any [marriage] for which the participants are liable to be put to death by a court" [M. Yeb. 4:13]*?*

H. *Rather, said Raba, "Here at issue between them is the case of an Ammonite and Moabite proselyte, and this is the sense of the statement:* **All those who are forbidden from entering into the congregation** — *and who might that be? an Ammonite and a Moabite proselyte* — **are permitted to intermarry**."

I. *If so, what is the meaning of,* **R. Judah prohibits [their marrying one another]***?*

J. *This is the sense of his statement,* "Even though **R. Judah prohibits** a proselyte to marry a mamzer girl, that is a proselyte who is eligible to enter into the assembly; but it does not apply to Ammonite and Moabite proselytes, who are not eligible to enter into the assembly."

The clarification of the wording of the law, I.1, permits consideration of special problems, not explicitly introduced, as I.1C indicates. The close reading of the Mishnah's formulation is standard for the Bavli, in particular. I.2 raises a second analytical question of language-interpretation, asking about the exceptions to the rule that the Mishnah so confidently announces. The clarification, B, yields its own problem, C. Then E raises a complicating question that upsets the proposed solution. But the answer, F, contains its own difficulty, that of redundancy, G. I.2H-J then provide a final solution, the other possibilities having been systematically addressed and dismissed.

### Bavli to Mishnah Qiddushin 4:9

A. He who gave the power to his agent to accept tokens of betrothal for his daughter, but then he himself betrothed her —
B. if his came first, his act of betrothal is valid.

C. And if those of his agent came first, his act of betrothal is valid.
D. And if it is not known [which came first], [79A] both parties give a writ of divorce.
E. But if they wanted, one of them gives a writ of divorce, and one consummates the marriage.
F. And so: A woman who gave the power to her agent to accept tokens of betrothal in her behalf, and then she herself went and accepted tokens of betrothal in her own behalf —
G. if hers came first, her act of betrothal is valid.
H. And if those of her agent came first, his act of betrothal is valid.
I. And if it is not known [which of them came first], both parties give a writ of divorce.
J. But if they wanted, one of them gives a writ of divorce and one of them consummates the marriage.

I.1 A. *Both cases given in the Mishnah paragraph [A-E, F-J], are required. For if we had been informed of the rule in respect to the father, that might have been because a man is solid in his knowledge of genealogy, but as to a woman, who is not solid in her knowledge of genealogy, I might say that that her act of betrothal is invalid. And if we were told that that is the case of the woman, it is because before a woman accepts a betrothal, she carefully investigates the situation, but as for the father, I might have supposed he doesn't really care [about pure genealogy, in which case he didn't cancel the agent's authority but made a provisional act of betrothal on his own]. So both formulations are required.*

The issue of redundancy arises because the Mishnah's two cases seem to go over the same ground, and the analytical approach then finds a need to state both matters.

## II. CATEGORY-CRITICISM

Category-criticism and analogy-criticism go hand in hand, but clearly are to be differentiated. The former involves the comparison and contrast of species of a common genus. The latter concerns the identification of the analogy that governs in the solution of a problem of applied law: to what is the case comparable dictates the rule for said case. While striking media of analytical thinking, however, neither mode of criticism preoccupies the Rabbinic thinkers, playing an important role principally in the Talmuds, and then rarely.

A. MISHNAH: —
B. TOSEFTA: —
C. YERUSHALMI

*Three. Qiddushin*

## Yerushalmi Qiddushin 1:2

- [A] A Hebrew slave is acquired through money or a writ.
- [B] And acquires himself through the passage of years, by the Jubilee year, or by deduction from the purchase price [redeeming himself at his outstanding value (Lev. 25:50-51)].
- [C] The Hebrew slave girl has an advantage over him.
- [D] For she acquires herself [in addition through the appearance of tokens [of puberty].
- [E] The slave whose ear is pierced is acquired through an act of piercing the ear (Ex. 21:5).
- [F] And he acquires himself by the Jubilee or by the death of the master.

[I.1 A] [A Hebrew slave is acquired through money or a writ:] It is written, "If your brother, a Hebrew man, or a Hebrew woman, is sold to you, he shall serve you six years, and in the seventh year you shall let him go free from you" (Deut. 15:12). Scripture treats in the same context a Hebrew man and woman. Just as the Hebrew woman is acquired through money or a writ, so a Hebrew man is acquired through money or a writ.

[B] *The proposition that that is through money poses no problems, for it is said,* "she shall go out for nothing, without payment of money" (Ex. 21:11). But whence do we know that that applies also to a writ?

[C] We derive the rule for the Hebrew woman servant from a free woman, and the rule for a Hebrew man servant derives from that for a Hebrew woman servant.

[D] It turns out that what derives from one proposition serves to teach the rule for another.

[E] *To this point we have proved the proposition in accord with R. Aqiba, who indeed concurs that* what derives from one proposition may then serve to teach the rule for another. *But as to R. Ishmael, who does not concur that* what derives from one proposition may then serve to teach the rule for another, [how do we prove that a Hebrew manservant is acquired through a writ]?

[F] *The following Tannaite teaching is available:* R. Ishmael teaches in regard to this statement, "freedom has not been given to her" (Lev. 19:20), "You shall let him go free from you" (Deut. 15:12). [The latter is interpreted in the light of the former.]

[G] *Now in all [other] contexts R. Ishmael does not concur that what derives from one proposition may then serve to teach the rule for another, and yet here [at J] he does indeed hold that view.*

[H] *It was taught in the name of a sage,* "How does R. Ishmael prove [that a writ is applicable to the Hebrew manservant]? "'Sending forth' is stated at Deut. 15:2, and also 'sending' is stated at Deut. 24:1. Just as 'sending forth' stated in regard to a divorce means that it is done through a writ, so the 'sending forth' stated in regard to the slave means that it is done through a writ."

[I] *[But the issue is not the same.] The two cases are dissimilar. For in the case of the divorce of the woman, the writ serves to give her full possession of herself. But here the writ serves to give possession of the Hebrew slave to others. [The proposition is to prove that a Hebrew man is acquired through a writ, and that has not been proved.]*

[J] Said R. Matteniah, "The use of the language of sale will prove the case. ['If your brother... is sold to you' (Deut. 15:12); 'If your brother becomes poor and sells part of his property' (Lev. 25:25).] Just as 'sale' stated in the latter case involves use of a Writ, so the language of 'sale' used here involves use of a writ."

[K] Or, perhaps may one argue, just as in the case of a field acquisition may be made through usucaption, so in the case of the slave, it may be through usucaption?

[L] [There is a better mode of proof of the besought proposition.] Said R. Hiyya bar Ada, "A Hebrew man and a Hebrew woman are subject to one and the same law."

The key language for the categorical analysis is this: We derive the rule for the Hebrew woman servant from a free woman, and the rule for a Hebrew man servant derives from that for a Hebrew woman servant. It turns out that what derives from one proposition serves to teach the rule for another. Then we proceed in a two-stage analysis, compare A to X, then B to A to X. Category-criticism involves comparison and contrast of species of a genus. Here Scripture is asked to supply the facts of whether, and how, Hebrew male and female slaves are comparable. Scripture treats as belonging to the same genus both the woman and the man, so A. The issue, B, is the writ, which is not covered by the proof-text, B. So a reciprocal process of proof is in play, C-D. But a problem of logic intervenes, E. If we hold that once we establish comparability, it is reciprocal, then the proposed proof pertains. But if we do not take that logic as fact, then how do we accomplish the same proof? The first effort, F, does not work, I. The next effort proves dubious, K, and the final demonstration simply brings us back to our starting point.

### YERUSHALMI TO MISHNAH QIDDUSHIN 1:3

[A] **A Canaanite slave [that is, any non-Israelite slave] is acquired through money, through a writ, and through usucaption. And he acquires himself through money paid by others or through a writ [of indebtedness] taken on by himself, " the words of R. Meir.**

[B] **And sages say, "Also: by money paid by himself or by a writ taken on by others, on condition that the money belongs to others."**

[I.1 A] It is written, "[As to Canaanite slaves] you may bequeath them to your sons after you, to inherit as a possession forever; you may make slaves of them" (Lev. 25:46).

[B] Acquisition of slaves thereby is treated under the same rubric as inherited real estate.

[C] Just as inherited real estate is acquired through money, writ, or usucaption, so a Canaanite slave is acquired through money, writ, or usucaption.

[D] How do we know that inherited real estate itself is acquired through money, writ, or usucaption?

*Three. Qiddushin* 43

[E] It is written, "Fields will be bought for money, deeds will be signed and sealed and witnessed" (Jer. 32:44) —

[F] "And signed and sealed and witnessed"— "signed and sealed" refers to witnesses to a writ; "witnessed" refers to witnesses to usucaption.

[G] Or perhaps these latter serve as witnesses to the writ?

[H] Since it already is written, "And signed and sealed," [which must mean a writ, the other witnesses are to usucaption].

What makes the passage important is the demonstration of how Scripture guides the work of category-criticism. Canaanite slaves are now classified as real estate, so I.1A-C. The secondary proof is conventional.

D. BAVLI: —

## III. RATIONALITY

A. MISHNAH: —
B. TOSEFTA: —
C. YERUSHALMI: —
D. BAVLI: —

My failure to identify pertinent instances in which the analytical inquiry concerns the rationality of conflicting positions indicates only the paucity of striking, fully articulated cases. In fact, every instance of the dispute form in every Halakhic document bears the intent of showing how opposed positions rest upon reasonable, if conflicting, grounds.

## IV. ANALOGY-CRITICISM

As we saw earlier, so here too, the distinction between category- and analogy-criticism is not always blatant. But the main point is clear: the comparison of categories to one another, in the supposition that if X is like Y, then X follows the rule of Y. But which categories truly compare to which others occasionally presents an occasion for rich analytical inquiry, of which, here, we have a striking instance.

A. MISHNAH: —
B. TOSEFTA: —
C. YERUSHALMI

YERUSHALMI TO MISHNAH QIDDUSHIN 1:3 I:3

[I:3 A] [**A Canaanite slave is acquired through money, through a writ, and through usucaption**:] *There are Mishnah rules that maintain* slaves are equivalent to real estate; *there are Mishnah passages that maintain* they are equivalent to movables; *and there are Mishnah passages that maintain* they are neither like real estate nor like movables.

[B]  *A Mishnah passage that treats slaves as equivalent to real estate is what we have learned there:* **Title by usucaption to houses, cisterns, trenches, vaults, dovecotes, bathhouses, olive presses, irrigated field, and slaves, [and whatever brings a regular return, is gained by usucaption during three complete years] [M. B.B, 3:1]** .

[C]  *A Mishnah passage that treats slaves as not equivalent to real estate is in line with what we have learned there* (following QE): **How is usucaption [established in the case of] slaves? [If] he [the slave] tied on his [the master's] sandal, or loosened his sandal, or carried clothes after him to the bathhouse, lo, this is usucaption. [If] he lifted him up [the slave lifted the master up] — R. Simeon says, 'You have no act of usucaption more effective than that!"** [T. Qid. 1:5].

[D]  *What rabbis have stated implies that slaves are equivalent to movables. For R. Yosé said in the name of rabbis,* "No lien applies to one who makes a gift [unless it is made explicit]. They do not exact payment from a debtor's slaves as they do from his real estate. [That is, slaves cannot be treated as mortgaged for payment of a debt.]

[E]  Said R. Mana to R. Shimi, "Who are these rabbis?"

[F]  He said to him, "They are R. Isaac and R. Immi."

[G]  *[The following case shows that fact:] A widow seized a slave girl as payment for her marriage settlement.* R. Isaac ruled, "Since she has seized her, she is properly seized, [and the action is valid]. [But that is not the case at the outset, and hence, in general, the slave is not equivalent to real estate.]"

[I]  *R. Immi took the slave away from her, for she thought that the slave belonged to her, and she was not hers [for the collection of her outstanding marriage settlement]. [The slave is in the status of movables, not real estate.]*

[J]  *Slaves are not equivalent to real estate, for it has been taught:* [If one sold] real estate and slaves to someone, when he has taken possession of the real estate, [he has not taken possession of the slaves]. Now if you maintain that slaves are in the status of real estate, once the purchaser has taken possession of the real estate, he should be deemed to have taken possession of the slaves.

[K]  For R. Yosa in the name of R. Yohanan has said, "If someone had two fields, one in Judah and one in Galilee, and the purchaser took possession of this one in Judah, intending also to acquire ownership of that one in Galilee, or if he took possession of that one in Galilee, [60a] intending to take possession of this one in Judah, he has acquired possession thereof. [Consequently, by taking possession of one piece of real estate, one may take possession of all the real estate. But in the cited case, taking possession of real estate has no effect upon ownership of the slaves, which therefore are not equivalent to real estate.]"

*Three. Qiddushin* 45

[L]  They are not equivalent to movables: If you say that slaves are equivalent to movables, once the purchaser has acquired possession of real estate, he should have acquired possession of the slaves .

[M]  *For we have learned there:* If one has to take an oath in regard to movables, the oath may be extended to real estate as well, [and movables are acquired along with real estate].

Here is a classic case of analogy-criticism: to what is the (Canaanite) slave deemed comparable, as articulated at I:3A+B-C. The matter is resolved at J, L, and slaves are left a category unto themselves, not analogous to the supposedly-comparable categories.

### D. BAVLI

#### BAVLI TO MISHNAH QIDDUSHIN 3:1

A.  He who says to his fellow, "Go and betroth Miss So-and-so for me," and he went and betrothed her for himself —
B.  she is betrothed.
C.  And so:
D.  He who says to a woman, "Lo, you are betrothed to me after thirty days [have passed]," and someone else came along and betrothed her during the thirty days —
E.  she is betrothed to the second party.
F.  [If] it is an Israelite girl betrothed to a priest, she may eat heave-offering.
G.  [If he said,] "...as of now and after thirty days," and someone else came along and betrothed her during the thirty days,
H.  she is betrothed and not betrothed.
I.  [If it is either] an Israelite girl betrothed to a priest, or a priest girl betrothed to an Israelite, she should not eat heave-offering.

II.2 A.  If no one else came along to betroth her, but she retracted her agreement in the interim, what is the law?
B.  R. Yohanan said, "She may retract: Words can come and wipe out words."
C.  R. Simeon b. Laqish said, "She may not retract: Words can't come and wipe out words."
D.  *R. Yohanan objected to R. Simeon b. Laqish:* "**[In a case in which one] gave permission to a member of his household, to his slave, or to his maidservant to separate heave-offering — that which that individual separates is [valid] heave-offering. [If he] retracted [the permission] — if he retracted [it] before [the other individual] separated heave-offering — that which [that individual] has separated is not [valid] heave-offering. But if he retracted [it] after [the other individual] separated heave-offering — that which [that individual] has separated is [valid] heave-offering [M. Ter. 3:4D-H].** *Now here is a case in which it is merely a matter of one act of speech as against another, and yet here* words can come and wipe out words."

E. *Handing over money into a woman's hand is exceptional, because it is tantamount to an action, and obviously* words can come and wipe out actions.
F. *An objection was raised:* **He who sends a writ of divorce to his wife, and overtakes the messenger, or who sent a messenger after him, and said to him, "The writ of divorce which I gave you is null" — lo, this is null [M. Git. 4:1A-D].** *Handing over a writ of divorce into the agent's hand is tantamount to an action, and the Tannaite formulation is* **lo, this is null,** *[so here, obviously, words can come and wipe out actions].*
G. *In that case too, so long as the writ of divorce has not reached the woman's hand, it is simply an act of speech, so* words can come and wipe out words.
H. *R. Simeon b. Laqish objected to R. Yohanan,* **"All utensils descend into the power of their uncleanness with thought but do not ascend from the power of their uncleanness except by an act which changes them. [59B] For the act cancels both an act and intention, but intention does not cancel either an act or intention [M. Kel. 25:8C-D].** *Now there is no problem understanding that intention cannot nullify a deed, for* words can't come and wipe out words. *But why shouldn't it nullify another intention!"*
I. *Intentionality in the context of uncleanness is exceptional, because in that case, it is tantamount to action, in line with R. Papa's view. For R. Pappa contrasted verses of Scripture:* "'It is written, 'and if one put water,' while we read, 'and if water be put' [at Lev. 11:38, in the context of rendering food susceptible to uncleanness by putting water on it]. *How so?* 'If it be put' *must be equivalent to* 'if one put,' *namely, just as when puts the water because he wants it, so when it is put, it must be because he wants it [so thought is tantamount here to action].*"

Here is the best illustration of the type of analysis set forth in analogy-criticism. At the simplest level, analogy-criticism involves the disposition of a proposed case deemed comparable to the case at hand: if it is like, then the principle that operates in the proposed case pertains, if not, then not. To resolve the conflict in principle — can words nullify words — a variety of analogous cases are introduced: [1] the designation of a portion of the crop as heave-offering; [2] the nullification of a writ of divorce; [3] the immersion of utensils. How these quite distinct classifications pertain to the issue at hand, the way in which each party disposes of the analogy proposed by his opponent — these form the foundations of the analogy-criticism. While the present mode of analytical thought appears only occasional, in fact every time a decision is required for a case lacking in obvious precedents, what is required is an assessment of the valid analogy: to what is the case comparable? Then the decision follows: if that is like this, then the case of that is decided in the model of this.

*Three. Qiddushin*

## V. Scriptural Foundations of the Halakhah

In sheer volume, the analysis of the scriptural foundations of the Halakhah matches all the other analytical initiatives combined. In most cases, the analytical program is contained within the formula, "how do we know [on the basis of Scripture] that such-and-such is the case?" I comment only on exceptional cases. More of the entries are formally standard.

    A.    Mishnah: —
    B.    Tosefta: —
    C.    Yerushalmi

### Yerushalmi to Mishnah Qiddushin 1:1

[A] [58b] **A woman is acquired [as a wife] in three ways, and acquires [freedom for] herself [as a free agent] in two ways.**
[B] **She is acquired through money, a writ, or sexual intercourse.**

[I:2 A] **She is acquired through money [writ, or sexual intercourse}:** How do we know [on the basis of Scripture the rule that one of the three media suffices]?
[B] "If any man takes a wife" (Deut. 22:13) tells us that a woman is acquired through money.
[C] Through sexual relations: How do we know [that item on the basis of Scripture]?
[D] "And goes in to her [having sexual relations with her]" (Deut. 22:13) tells us that a woman is acquired through sexual relations.
[E] I should then have reached the conclusion that the transaction is effected both through this means and through that [together].
[F] How do we know that money effects acquisition without sexual relations, or that sexual relations effect acquisition without money?
[G] R. Abbahu in the name of R. Yohanan: "It is written, 'If a man is found lying with a woman who has had sexual relations with her husband' (Deut. 22:22).
[H] "Now take note: Even if the man has acquired her only through sexual relations, the Torah has decreed that he who has sexual relations thereafter is [guilty of having sexual relations with a married woman and is subject to the death penalty through] strangling."

The verbs, "take," "goes in," bear the burden of proving the relevant proposition.

### Yerushalmi to Mishnah Qiddushin 1:2

[III.1 A] **[The Hebrew slave girl has an advantage over him. For she acquires herself in addition through the appearance of tokens of puberty (M. 1:1C-D:]** "She shall go out for nothing, without payment of money" (Ex. 21:11).
[B] "For nothing"— refers to the time of pubescence.

[C] "Without payment of money"— refers to the tokens of maturity.

[D] And why should the law not refer to only one of them?

[E] If it had referred to only one of them, I might have maintained, "If she goes forth through the appearance of the signs of puberty, all the more so will she go forth at the time of pubescence."

[F] If so, I would have maintained, the time of pubescence is the only time at which she goes forth, and not the time at which she produces signs of puberty.

[G] Now logic would suggest as follows: Since she leaves the domain of the father and leaves the domain of the master, just as from the domain of the father she goes forth only when she has produced the signs of puberty, also from the domain of the master she should go forth only when she produces signs of puberty.

[H] *On that account it was necessary to state:*

[I] "For nothing"— refers to the time of pubescence.

[J] "Without a payment of money"— refers to the signs of puberty.

[K] And perhaps matters are just the opposite [so that "she will go forth for nothing" refers to the period of twelve and a bit more in which she is a girl, and "without a payment" refers to the time at which she has reached puberty]?

[L] R. Tanhuma in the name of R. Huna: "'Without money'— In any context in which the father receives money, the master does not receive money."

The analytical inquiry, D-J, K-L, conducts its own criticism of the proposed demonstration, B-C. Here again, the issue is the framing of matters: why both proofs are required to make the point. This is elegantly articulated, E—G.

### YERUSHALMI TO MISHNAH QIDDUSHIN 1:2

[IV:1 A] [Supply: **The slave whose ear is pierced is acquired through an act of piercing the ear (Ex. 21:5). And he acquires himself by the Jubilee or by the death of the master:**] R. Judah b. R. Bun interpreted this word: "The lobe of the ear is pierced so that, should the slave be a priest, he is not invalidated for service."

[B] R. Meir says, "He was pierced at the gristle [cartilage forming the ear]."

[IV:2 A] "With an awl" (Ex. 21:6): I know that one may use only an awl. How do I know that it may be done with a wooden prick. thorn, or shard of glass?

[B] Scripture says, "And he will pierce" [by whatever means].

[C] Up to this point [we have answered the question] in accord with R. Aqiba['s mode of exegesis]. How does R. Ishmael answer the same question?

[D] *R. Ishmael taught as a Tannaite formulation:* "In three places the practical law supersedes the biblical text. and in one the legitimate interpretation of the text [ignoring the rules of interpretation]. The Torah has said, 'in a book' (Deut. 24 :1), and the practical law says that on anything that is uprooted from the ground [a writ of divorce may be written]. The Torah has said, 'With dirt' [the blood is to be covered up] (Lev. 17:13), but the

*Three. Qiddushin* 49

practical law requires that it be done with anything in which seeds will grow. The Torah has said, 'With an awl,' but the practical law permits use of a wooden prick, thorn, or shard of glass. And in one place the legitimate interpretation of the text: [R. Ishmael taught] 'And it shall be on the seventh day he shall shave all his hair (Lev. 14:9)'— a generalization; 'of his head and his beard and his eyebrows'— a particularization; 'even all his hair he shall shave off'— generalization. Where there is a general proposition followed by a particular specification and again followed by a general proposition, only what is like the particulars is included. This then tells you, 'Just as the particularization refers explicitly to a place on the body on which hair is gathered together and is visible, so I know only that every place on the body where hair is gathered together and is visible is to be shaved off. But the law rules: 'He should shave him as [smooth as] a gourd."

[IV:3 A] "With an awl": Just as an awl is made of metal so anything made of metal [will serve].
[B] Rabbi says, "This refers to a large spit."
[C] R. Yosé b. R. Judah says, "This refers to a chisel."
[D] "And he shall bring him to the door" (Ex. 21:6). Is it possible to suppose that that is the case even if the door is lying [on the ground]?
[E] "Scripture says, 'Or to the doorpost' (Ex. 21:6).
[F] "Just as the doorpost is standing, so the door must be standing. It is a matter of shame to the slave and a matter of shame to a family."

The pertinent passage is IV.2. Two proofs are offered, each in accord with its exegetical rule. IV:3 completes the exposition of the pertinent verses, and the law is shown well-grounded in Scripture.

### Yerushalmi to Mishnah Qiddushin 1:7

[A] **For every commandment concerning the son to which the father is subject— men are liable, and women are exempt.**
[B] **And for every commandment concerning the father to which the son is subject, men and women are equally liable.**
[C] **For every positive commandment dependent upon time, men are liable, and women are exempt.**
[D] **And for every positive commandment not dependent upon time, men and women are equally liable.**
[E] **For every negative commandment, whether dependent upon time or not dependent upon time, men and women are equally liable.**
[F] **except for "not marring the corners of the beard, not rounding the corners of the head " (Lev. 19:27, "and not becoming unclean because of the dead " (Lev. 21:1).**

[G] [The cultic rules of] laving on of hands, waving, drawing near, taking the handful, burning the incense, breaking the neck of a bird, sprinkling, and receiving [the blood]

[H] apply to men and not to women,

[I] except in the case of a meal offering of an accused wife and of a Nazirite girl, which they wave.

[I.A] What is a commandment pertaining to the father concerning the son [M. 1:7A]?

[B] To circumcise him, to redeem him, and to teach him Torah, and to teach him a trade, and to marry him off to a girl.

[C] And R. Aqiba says, "Also to teach him how to swim" [T. Qid. 1:1 1E-G].

[D] To circumcise him, in line with the following verse of Scripture: "And on the eighth day the flesh of his foreskin shall be circumcised" (Lev. 12:3).

[E] To redeem him, in line with the following verse of Scripture: "Every first born of man among your sons you shall redeem" (Ex. 13:13).

[F] To teach him Torah, in line with the following verse of Scripture: "And you shall teach them to your children [talking of them when you are sitting in your house, and when you are walking by the way, and when you lie down, and when you rise]" (Deut. 11:19).

[G] To teach him a trade: R. Ishmael taught, "[I call heaven and earth to witness against you this day, that I have set before you life and death, blessing and curse;] therefore choose life, [that you and your descendants may live]" (Deut. 30:19).

[H] "This [refers to] learning a trade."

[I] To marry him off to a girl, in line with the following verse of Scripture: "[Only take heed, and keep your soul diligently, lest you forget the things which your eyes have seen, and lest they depart from your heart all the days of your life;] make them known to your children and your children's children" (Deut. 4:9).

[J] In what circumstances do you have the merit [of seeing] children and grandchildren? When you marry your children off when they are young.

[K] R. Aqiba says, "Also to teach him how to swim," in line with the following verse of Scripture: "[I call heaven and earth to witness against you this day, that I have set before you life and death, blessing and curse; therefore choose life,] that you and your descendants may live" (Deut. 30:19).

The exercise is conventional: x — in line with the following verse of Scripture. There is no secondary expansion of any one of the proofs, e.g., a challenge to its effect and a response to the challenge. That is what gives the whole its rather formal quality. We have already seen far more complex executions of the analytical mode of proof-texting.

### YERUSHALMI TO MISHNAH QIDDUSHIN 2:1

[A] [62a] A man effects betrothal on his own or through his agent.

[B] A woman becomes betrothed on her own or through her agent.

*Three. Qiddushin*

[C] A man betroths his daughter when she is a girl on his own or through his agent.

[D] He who says to a woman, "Be betrothed to me for this date, be betrothed to me with this," if [either] one of them is of the value of a perutah, she is betrothed, and if not, she is not betrothed.

[E] "By this, and by this, and by this" — if all of them together are worth a perutah, she is betrothed, and if not, she is not betrothed.

[F] [If] she was eating them one by one, she is not betrothed unless one of them is worth a perutah.

[I:1 A] How on the basis of Scripture do we know that a man's agent is equivalent to himself?

[B] Said R. Eleazar, "'Then the whole assembly of the congregation of Israel shall kill it [the Passover lamb] at dusk' (Ex. 12:6). Now do all of them slaughter it? And is it not so that only one actually slaughters it in behalf of all of them? But on this basis we learn that a man's agent is equivalent to himself [so that what the agent does is as if the man himself did it]."

[C] *And from which [verse] do you know this?* "They shall take every man a lamb according to their fathers' houses, a lamb for a household" (Ex. 12:3). Now did all of them take a lamb? And is it not so that only one of them takes it in behalf of all of them? But on this basis we learn that a man's agent is equivalent to himself.

[D] Said R. Yosé, "[A second proof text, Ex. 12:3, is necessary, for the first proof text given above, Ex. 12:6, is not acceptable, since] that case is different. For a man may slaughter the Passover offering of his fellow without the latter's knowledge or consent."

[E] If you say that a man may designate a lamb as a Passover offering for his fellow without the latter's knowledge and consent, [that is not so, for] he may not do this (I.E-J follows Pené Moshe and QE).

[F] For R. Zeira said in the name of R. Eleazar, "A man may slaughter the Passover offering of his fellow without his knowledge and consent, but he may not designate it without his knowledge and consent."

Here is the contrast to the foregoing. The exercise of demonstrating scriptural foundations now shades over into an analytical inquiry into the comparison and contrast of various cases, D-E+F. Otherwise the instance is standard.

D. BAVLI

BAVLI TO MISHNAH QIDDUSHIN 1:1

A. A woman is acquired [as a wife] in three ways, and acquires [freedom for] herself [to be a free agent] in two ways.

B. She is acquired through money, a writ, or sexual intercourse.

II.1 A. She is acquired through money:

B. What is the scriptural source of this rule?
C. And furthermore, we have learned in the Mishnah: **The father retains control of his daughter [younger than twelve and a half] as to effecting any of the tokens of betrothal: money, document, or sexual intercourse [M. Ket. 4:4A]** — *how on the basis of Scripture do we know that fact?*
D. Said R. Judah said Rab, "Said Scripture, 'Then shall she [the Hebrew slave girl] go out for nothing, without money' (Ex. 21:11). No money is paid to this master, but money is paid to another master, and who would that be? It is the father."
E. *But might one say that it goes to her?*
F. *But how can you suppose so? Since the father has the power to contract her betrothal, as it is written,* "I gave my daughter to this man" (Deut. 22:16), *can she collect the money? [Obviously she cannot, so the father gets the money.]*
G. *But maybe that is the case only for a minor, who has no domain ["hand," with which to effect acquisition], but in the case of a girl, who has a domain for the stated purpose, she may contract the betrothal and also get the money paid for the betrothal?*
H. Said Scripture, "Being in her youth, in her father's house" (Num. 30:17) — every advantage accruing to her in her youth belongs to her father.
I. *Then what about what R. Huna said Rab said,* "How on the basis of Scripture do we know that the proceeds of a daughter's labor go to the father? 'And if a man sell his daughter to be a maidservant' (Ex. 21:7) — just as the proceeds of the labor of a maidservant go to the master, so the proceeds of the labor of a daughter go to the father"? *What need do I have for such a proof, when the same proposition may be deduced from the phrase,* "Being in her youth, in her father's house" (Num. 30:17)?
J. *Rather, that verse refers to releasing her vows [and not to the matter at hand, as the context at Num. 30:17 makes clear].*
K. *And, furthermore, should you say, so let us derive the rule covering money from the rule covering other propositions, in fact, we do not ever derive the rule covering money from the rule covering other propositions!*
L. *And, furthermore, should you propose, so let us derive the rule governing the disposition of monetary payments from the rule governing fines, it is the simple fact that the rule governing monetary payments is not to be derived from the rule governing the disposition of fines.*
M. *Then here is the reason that compensation for humiliation and damages is assigned to the father:* [add: *if he wanted, he could hand her over [for marriage] to an ugly man or to a man afflicted with boils].* [Since he himself could subject her to indignity and benefit from it, he gets the compensation from someone who does that to her (Slotki).]
N. *Rather, it is more reasonable that, when the All-Merciful excluded another "exodus" [from the household],* **[4A]** *it was meant to be like the original.* [Slotki, *Qiddushin*, ad loc.: As in the original, it is the master, not the slave girl, who would have received the money for her redemption, but a specific text states to the contrary, so in the implication it must be the father, corresponding to the master, who gets the money when she leaves his control at betrothal.]

*Three. Qiddushin* 53

    O.  *Yes, but the one "exodus" is not really comparable to the other. For in the case of the master, the slave girl entirely exits from his control, while in the exodus from the domain of the father, the exit to the bridal canopy has not yet been completed.*

    P.  *Nonetheless, so far as it concerns his power to remit her vows, she does entirely exit his domain, for we have learned in the Mishnah:* **A betrothed girl — her father and her husband annul her vows [M. Ned. 10:1A-B].**

The interesting point comes at I: having a proof, for what reason is another proof-text required? But the quest for scriptural foundations is integrated into the larger study of the law, e.g., II.1.E-H broadens the matter from exegesis to legal theory encompassing exegesis.

### BAVLI TO MISHNAH QIDDUSHIN 1:1

VIII.1 A.  **The deceased childless brother's widow is acquired through an act of sexual relations:**

    B.  *How on the basis of Scripture do we know that she is acquired by an act of sexual relations?*

    C.  Said Scripture, **[14A]** "Her husband's brother shall go in to her and take her to him as a wife" (Deut. 25:5).

    D.  *Might I say that she is his wife in every regard [so that she can be acquired by money or a deed]?*

    E.  *Don't let it enter your mind, for it has been taught on Tannaite authority:* Might one suppose that a money payment or a writ serve to complete the bond to her, as much as sexual relations does? Scripture says, "Her husband's brother shall go in to her and take her to him as a wife" (Deut. 25:5) — sexual relations complete the relationship to her, but a money payment or a writ do not do so.

    F.  *Might I say, what is the meaning of* take her to him as a wife? *Even against her will he enters into levirate marriage with her?*

    G.  *If so, Scripture should have said,* "and take her...." *Why say,* "and take her to wife"? *It bears both meanings just now under discussion.*

IX.1 A.  **And acquires [freedom for] herself through a rite of removing the shoe:**

    B.  *How on the basis of Scripture do we know it?*

    C.  Said Scripture, "And his name shall be called in Israel, the house of him who has had his shoe removed" (Deut. 25:12) — once his shoe has been removed by her, she is permitted for all Israel.

    D.  *Is this the purpose of the word "Israel" in this context? Isn't it required in line with that which R. Samuel bar Judah taught as a Tannaite statement:* "'In Israel' (Deut. 25:7) means that the rite of removing the shoe must be done in front of a court of Israelites by birth, not a court of proselytes"?

    E.  *There are two references in context to* "in Israel."

    F.  *Nonetheless, it is required in line with that which has been taught on Tannaite authority:* Said R. Judah, "Once we were in session before R. Tarfon, and a levirate woman came to perform the rite of removing the shoe, and he said to us, 'All of you respond: "The man who has had his shoe removed"' (Deut. 25:10)."

G. *That is derived from the formulation,* "and his name shall be called" [with "in Israel" free for its own purpose].

Once more, we see the analytical potential of the simple mode of thought involved in proof-texting. It is not a matter of simply joining a verse to a kindred proposition but of criticizing and defending the demonstration. VIII.1 is a classic progression: how do we know + text; might I say + refutation (2x). The refutations are based on a clear premise that rules of common speech apply to Scripture, thus VIII.1G finds in the formulation the solution to the problem, and IV.1D does the same.

### Bavli to Mishnah Qiddushin 1:5

A. **Property for which there is security is acquired through money, writ, and usucaption.**
B. **And that for which there is no security is acquired only by an act of drawing [from one place to another].**
C. **Property for which there is no security is acquired along with property for which there is security through money, writ, and usucaption.**
D. **And property for which there is no security imposes the need for an oath on property for which there is security.**

I.1 A. **Property for which there is security is acquired through money:**
 B. *How on the basis of Scripture do we know that fact?*
 C. Said Hezekiah, "Said Scripture, 'people will acquire fields with money' (Jer. 32:44)."
 D. *But might one say, that is valid only unless there is a deed, since the verse goes on,* "And subscribe the deeds and attest them and call witnesses" (Jer. 32:44)?
 E. *If the order of the language were such that* "acquire" *came at the end, it would be as you maintain; but since* "acquire" *appears at the beginning, the meaning is, money transfers title, the deed merely attests to that fact.*

III.1 A. **And usucaption:**
 B. *How on the basis of Scripture do we know that fact?*
 C. Because it is written, "And dwell in the cities that you have taken" (Jer. 40:10) — how did you take them? By dwelling in them.
 D. *A Tannaite authority of the household of R. Ishmael:* "And you shall possess it and dwell therein" (Deut. 11:31) — how shall you possess it? By dwelling therein.

IV.1 A. **And that for which there is no security [= movables] is acquired only by an act of drawing [from one place to another]:**
 B. *How on the basis of Scripture do we know that fact?*
 C. It is written, "And if you sell anything to your neighbor or buy anything of your neighbor's hand" (Lev. 25:14) — this speaks of something that is acquired by passing from hand to hand [by drawing, that is, only movables].

*Three. Qiddushin* 55

        D.   *And from the viewpoint of R. Yohanan, who has said,* "By the law of the Torah, the transfer of cash serves to transfer title," *what is to be said?*
        E.   *The Tannaite authority here repeats the rule governing an ordinance deriving from rabbis.*

V.1    A.   **Property for which there is no security is acquired along with property for which there is security through money, writ, and usucaption:**
        B.   *How on the basis of Scripture do we know that fact?*
        C.   Said Hezekiah, "Said Scripture, 'And their father gave them gifts...with walled cities in Judah' (2 Chr. 21:3)." [Thus they acquired the gifts, which were movables, in conjunction with the walled cities, that is, real estate.]

The contrast between the simple and the complex mode of scriptural demonstration is sharply drawn in the juxtaposition of the present item to the foregoing. Here we have an unchallenged, utterly formal exercise.

### BAVLI TO MISHNAH QIDDUSHIN 1:8

    A.   **[The cultic rites of] laying on of hands, waving, drawing near, taking the handful, burning the fat, breaking the neck of a bird, sprinkling, and receiving [the blood] apply to men and not to women,**
    B.   **except in the case of a meal-offering of an accused wife and of a Nazirite girl, which they wave.**

I.1    A.   **Laying on of hands:**
        B.   *For it is written,* "Speak to the sons of Israel...and he shall lay his hand upon the head of the burnt-offering" (Lev. 7:29-30) —
        C.   The sons of Israel, not the daughters of Israel do it.
II.1   A.   **Waving:**
        B.   *For it is written,* "Speak to the sons of Israel...the fat...may be waved" (Lev. 6:7).
        C.   The sons of Israel, not the daughters of Israel do it.
III.1  A.   **Drawing near:**
        B.   *For it is written,* "And this is the law of the meal-offering: The sons of Aaron shall offer it –
        C.   The sons of Aaron, not the daughters of Aaron do it.
IV.1  A.   **Taking the handful:**
        B.   *For it is written,* "And he shall bring it to Aaron's sons, the priests, and he shall take out of it his handful of the fine flour" (Lev. 2:2) –
        C.   The sons of Aaron, not the daughters of Aaron do it.
V.1    A.   **Burning the fat:**
        B.   *For it is written,* "And Aaron's sons shall burn it" (Lev. 2:2).
        C.   The sons of Aaron, not the daughters of Aaron do it.
VI.1  A.   **Breaking the neck of a bird, sprinkling:**
        B.   *For it is written,* "And he shall wring off his head and burn it on the altar" –
        C.   *Treating as comparable wringing the neck and burning the fat.*
VII.1 A.   **And receiving [the blood]:**

B. *For it is written,* "And the priests, the sons of Aaron," and a master has said, **[36B]** "'And they shall bring' refers to receiving the blood."

The sequence of proofs follows a fixed form and is standard, presenting no surprises, formal or otherwise.

## VI. TYPES OF ANALYSIS

I do not identify any instance of an analysis of the rational basis for disputes, though I am certain that the tractate, in the Talmuds, contains that type of inquiry. The analysis of the language of the law of the Mishnah derives from the Bavli alone. But both Talmuds provide ample evidence of following an analytical program along familiar lines. Along with the Bavli, the Yerushalmi contributes the category- and analogy-criticism (distinguishing them proves uncertain) and the quest for scriptural foundations. So the entire representation of analytical inquiry in Qiddushin derives from the two Talmuds.

# 4

# Abodah Zarah

I. **LANGUAGE-ANALYSIS**

    A. **MISHNAH:** —
    B. **TOSEFTA:** —
    C. **YERUSHALMI:** —
    D. **BAVLI:** —

II. **CATEGORY-CRITICISM**

    A. **MISHNAH:** —
    B. **TOSEFTA:** —
    C. **YERUSHALMI:** —
    D. **BAVLI:** —

III. **RATIONALITY**

    A. **MISHNAH**

**MISHNAH ABODAH ZARAH 2:5**

A. Said R. Judah, "R. Ishmael asked R. Joshua as they were going along the road.
B. "He said to him, 'On what account did they prohibit cheese made by gentiles?'
C. "He said to him, 'Because they curdle it with rennet from carrion.'

D. "He said to him, 'And is not the rennet from a whole offering subject to a more stringent rule than rennet from carrion, and yet they have said, 'A priest who is not squeamish sucks it out raw'?

E. (But they did not concur with him and ruled, "It is not available for [the priests'] benefit, while it also is not subject to the laws of sacrilege.")

F. "He went and said to him, 'Because they curdle it with rennet of calves sacrificed to idols.,

G. "He said to him, 'If so, then why have they not also extended the prohibition affecting it to the matter of deriving benefit from it?'

At issue is the consistency of the ruling: if the cheese is prohibited because it is curdled with rennet of calves deriving from sacrifices to idols, then it should also be prohibited from benefit, not only Israelite use. So Ishmael does not find consistent the reasoning behind the rule.

B. TOSEFTA: —
C. YERUSHALMI

### YERUSHALMI TO MISHNAH ABODAH ZARAH 1:1

[III:1 A] [R. Ishmael says, "Three days before them and three days after them it is prohibited for Israelites to do business with gentiles"] [M. A.Z. 1:1G]. *Associates state the reasoning of R. Ishmael. It is because of the [continuing celebration of] the meal associated with the festival [so, as the eating and carousing continue, Israelites should have no part of the matter, even after the festival day itself].*

[B] Said R. Ba, "Since [the pagan] knows that it is prohibited for you to do business with him, it diminishes the celebration of his festival" [and that is the basis of Ishmael's reasoning that even after the festival one may not do business, for even on the festival the pagan will be concerned that later on he will be deprived of the benefit of Israelite trade]."

[C] *What is the practical difference between the two [explanations of R. Ishmael's position]?*

[D] Selling [to a gentile even prior to the festival] things that do not last.

[E] *In accord with the position of associates,* it is prohibited to do so, *and in accord with the position of R. Ba* it is permitted to do so, [for in the former case, the fact that the articles will not last is immaterial, whereas in Ba's reasoning it is crucial. Associates will regard selling things that do not last as contributory to the pleasure of the festival, while Ba will not regard that as critical issue.]

At issue is the reason behind the rule of Ishmael, stated at A vs. B, and then the practical difference between the two reasons is articulated, C-E. The rationality of the ruling is taken for granted, the only question being the identification of the governing consideration.

Four. Abodah Zarah

### Yerushalmi to Mishnah Abodah Zarah 3:1

- [A] "All images are prohibited,
- [B] "because they are worshipped once a year," the words of R. Meir.
- [C] And sages say, "Prohibited is only one that has in its hand a staff, bird, or sphere."
- [D] Rabban Simeon b. Gamaliel says, "Any which has anything at all in its hand."

[I.1 A] *If the idols are worshipped once a year,* then how come rabbis permit?
- [B] Said R. Hiyya bar Ba, "[The reason all images are prohibited] is that in the great city of Rome they are worshiped twice in a septennate."
- [C] If that is the operative reasoning, then in a locale in which they are worshiped they should be forbidden, while in a locale in which they are not worshiped they should be permitted [for Israelite commerce].
- [D] Said R. Yosé, "Once they are prohibited in a single locale, the prohibition applies in every locale."
- [E] *How shall we explain [the dispute between Meir and the sages]?*
- [F] [Here is the problem:] If it is a matter of certainty that [statues are] of kings [and hence made for worship], then all will have to concur that they are forbidden.
- [G] If it is a matter of certainty [that the statues are] of local authorities [and hence not for worship], then all will have to concur that they are [made merely for decoration and hence] permitted.
- [H] *But thus we must interpret the dispute:* in the case of a statue lacking all specification [as to its clear-cut purpose].
- [I] R. Meir says, "When they lack all specification, they are of kings."
- [J] And rabbis maintain, "When they lack all specification, they are of local rulers."

Once more, the governing consideration behind the ruling is articulated, the issue being raised at I.1A, consistency once more defines the problem. The outcome, H-J, identifies a narrow area of disagreement.

### D. Bavli

### Bavli to Mishnah Abodah Zarah 3:5

- A. [45A] Gentiles who worship hills and valleys —
- B. these [hills or valleys] are permitted, but what is on them is forbidden [for Israelite use],
- C. as it is said, "You shall not covet the silver or gold that is upon them not take it."
- D. R. Yosé says, "Their gods are on the mountains, and the mountains are not their gods. Their gods are in the valleys, and the valleys are not their gods."

E. On what account is an *asherah* prohibited? Because it has been subject to manual labor, and whatever has been subject to manual labor is prohibited.
F. Said R. Aqiba, "I shall explain and interpret the matter before you:
G. "In any place in which you find a high mountain, a lofty hill, or a green tree, you may take for granted that there is an idol there."

I.4 A. *It has been stated:*
B. *As to boulders of a mountain, which had rolled off —*
C. *the sons of R. Hiyya and R. Yohanan:*
D. *one said, "They are forbidden."*
E. *And the other said, "They are permitted."*
F. *What is the logic behind the position of him who has said that* they are permitted?
G. *They are comparable to the mountain itself.* Just as the mountain has not been subject to manual labor and is permitted, *so these* have not been subjected to manual labor and are permitted.
H. But the distinguishing trait of the mountain is that it is attached to the ground [which does not, by definition, apply to the rolling stones]!
I. A beast will prove the contrary [since it is not attached to the ground, but if it had been worshipped for idolatry, still it may be used for secular purposes].
J. But the distinguishing trait of a beast is that it is animate.
K. A mountain will prove to the contrary.
L. Now we are going around in circles, but the upshot is that the indicative trait of the one is not the same as the indicative trait of the other, and the indicative trait of the other is not the same as the indicative trait of the one, but what the two have in common is that neither one has been subjected to manual labor, and so is permitted. So anything that has not been subjected to manual labor [but has been worshipped] will be permitted.
M. The indicative trait of them both, to the contrary, is that neither one of them has been changed from their original, natural condition.
N. *[Then derive the rule that a boulder is permitted by drawing] an analogy from the case of a beast that has been blemished, or from the case of a mountain; or from the case of a beast that has not been blemished and from that of a withered tree.* [Cohen, *Abodah Zarah,* ad loc.: The animal while unblemished was worshipped; it may be used later if it was blemished; so the criterion of not having changed its form cannot apply to the boulder. The withered tree is changed from its original condition but is permitted because its existence is not due to human action.]
O. *One who prohibits the boulders derives the rule from Scripture's statement,* "You shall utterly detest it and you shall utterly abhor it" — *on which account, even though through reason one might conclude that they are permitted, yet do not draw that conclusion.* [Cohen: Allow only what the Torah expressly permits.]
P. *In point of fact, it is the sons of R. Hiyya who permitted [use of the boulders], for Hezekiah [Hiyya's son] raised the question,* "If one set up an egg to bow down to it, what is the law?"
Q. *The premise of the question is that one set up the egg to bow down to it and then bowed down to it. And this is the basis of the question: Is this act of setting up the egg classified as an action or not classified*

as an action? But if he had not set up the egg, the egg would not have been forbidden. And that yields the inference that it was the sons of R. Hiyya who permitted use of the boulders [for no human action was involved].

R. Not at all, for I might say to you that the sons of R. Hiyya are the ones who forbade use of the boulders, on the premise that the question involves the man's actually having bowed down to the egg, even though he had not set it up, in which case it is forbidden, and here with what sort of case do we deal? It is with a man who set up the egg to worship it but did not do so.

S. But in accord with whom is the question raised? If it were in accord with the position of him who maintains that in the case of an idol that belongs to an Israelite, it is forbidden forthwith, obviously the egg would be forbidden. If it is in accord with the position of him who has said that it is forbidden only once it will have been worshipped, lo, one has not worshipped it.

T. In point of fact, the case must involve a situation in which one set up an egg to worship it but did not worship it, and then a gentile came along and worshipped it. That is in line with what R. Judah said Samuel said, "An Israelite who set up a brick to worship but did not worship it, and a gentile came along and worshipped it, — the brick is forbidden. And when Hezekiah framed his question, it was this: "Did he specify 'a brick' because setting it up is clearly to be discerned, but the law as to an egg would be different, or perhaps there is no difference between a brick and an egg?" And that question stands.

The rationality between the position of I.4E is simply stated: the boulders are comparable to the mountain, G, and so not deemed to have been turned into idols for worship, any more than the mountain is subject to classification in that way. That solution is challenged: the indicative traits of the mountain and the boulder are not the same, so the rule governing the one cannot apply to the other, H. This is challenged by another appropriate analogy. The three analogies — mountain, boulder, beast — then are shown to form a polythetic set, bearing some traits in common, some not, and that suffices, L. But then a different indicative trait is adduced, M. O then finds a scriptural basis for the rule. Then at P, we shift the grounds of inquiry entirely.

## IV. ANALOGY-CRITICISM

### A.  MISHNAH

#### YERUSHALMI TO MISHNAH ABODAH ZARAH 3:6

[A] He [the wall of] whose house was adjacent to [and also served as the wall of the temple of] an idol, and [whose house] fell down —
[B] it is forbidden to rebuild it.
[C] What should he then do?
[D] He pulls back within four cubits inside his own property and then rebuilds his house.
[E] [If there was a wall belonging] both to him and to [the temple of an] idol, it is judged to be divided half and half.
[F] The stones, wood, and mortar deriving from it impart uncleanness in the status of a dead creeping thing, for it is said, "You will utterly detest it" (Dt. 7:26).
[G] R. 'Aqiba says, "In the status of a menstruant['s uncleanness], as it is said, 'You shall cast them away as a menstrual thing; you shall say unto it, Get you hence (Is. 30:22).
[H] "Just as a menstruating woman imparts uncleanness to one who carries her [or objects that she carries], so also an idol imparts uncleanness to one who carries it."

[I:1 A] "Abomination" is written in connection with the menstruating woman, "abomination is written in connection with dead creeping things, and "abomination" is written in connection with an idol.
[B] In connection with the menstruating woman: ". . . for whoever shall do any of these abominations — [the persons] that do them shall be cut off . . ." (Lev. 18:29). [Lev. 18:19 explicitly includes under the stated curse one who has sexual relations with a menstruating woman.]
[C] In connection with dead creeping things: "You shall not eat any abominable thing" (Deut. 14:3).
[D] In connection with idolatry: "And you shall not bring an abominable thing into your house and become accursed like it; you shall utterly detest and abhor it; for it is an accursed thing" (Deut. 7:26).
[E] But I do not know to which matter an analogy is to be drawn.
[F] R. Aqiba said, "It is to be compared to the abomination stated with reference to the menstruating woman:
[G] "Just as a menstruating woman imparts uncleanness to the one who carries her, so an idol imparts uncleanness to the one who carries it."
[H] Or perhaps: Just as a menstruating woman imparts uncleanness [by the pressure of her weight when she is seated] on top of a large stone [to objects located beneath said stone], so an idol imparts uncleanness when located on top of a large stone [and not in direct contact with objects underneath the stone].

Four. Abodah Zarah 63

- [I] R. Zeriqa in the name of R. Haninah, *and there is he who holds he said it in the name of R. Hisda*, "R. Aqiba concurs with the sages that an idol does not impart uncleanness to [what is beneath] a large stone."
- [J] And the rabbis state [that an idol is analogous] to the "abomination" stated with regard to dead creeping things.
- [K] Just as a dead creeping thing imparts uncleanness to the one who merely shifts its position [without bearing its weight], so the idol imparts uncleanness to the one who merely shifts its position.

The governing analogy for the stones, wood and mortar of a wall shared with a temple of idolatry dictates the pertinent rule of uncleanness: that of the menstruating woman or that of the dead creeping thing, so M. A.Z. 3:6 F vs. G-H. The consequence of choosing the right analogy is, how is the uncleanness transmitted? The Talmud then articulates the details of the Mishnah's analogical exegesis.

- B. TOSEFTA: —
- C. YERUSHALMI: —
- D. BAVLI: —

## V. SCRIPTURAL FOUNDATIONS OF THE HALAKHAH

- A. MISHNAH: —
- B. TOSEFTA: —
- C. YERUSHALMI

### YERUSHALMI TO MISHNAH ABODAH ZARAH 1:1

- [A] **[39a] Before the festivals of gentiles for three days it is forbidden to do business with them...**

- [I:1 A] *R. Hama bar Uqba derived scriptural support for all of those [statements about the interval of three days during which it is prohibited to do business with gentiles prior to a festival of theirs] from the following verse:* "[Come to Bethel and transgress; to Gilgal and multiply transgression;] bring your sacrifices every morning, your tithes on the third day" (Amos 4:4).
- [B] *Said to him R. Yosé, "If so, then even in the exilic communities [the rule should be the same].*
- [C] *"Yet it has been taught in a Tannaitic tradition:* **'Nahum the Mede says, "One day in the exilic communities [before their festival] it is prohibited [to do business with gentiles, and not the three days specified by M. A.Z. 1:1, which apply only to the Holy Land]"** [T. A.Z. 1:1 A]."
- [D] *Why so?*
- [E] *There* [in Babylonia] *they looked into the matter and found out that [the pagans] prepare their requirements [for celebrating a festival] in only a single day, so*

they forbade business dealings with them for a single day. *But here* [in the Holy Land] they looked into the matter and found out that they prepare their requirements [for celebrating a festival] in a full three days, so they forbade business dealings with them for a full three days.

[F] *How then does R. Yosé interpret the cited verse of Scripture,* "Bring your sacrifices every morning [etc.]"?

[G] Concerning the reign of Jeroboam does Scripture speak.

[H] Once Jeroboam took up the reign over Israel, he began to entice Israel [toward idolatry], saying to them, "Come and let us practice idolatrous worship. Idolatry is permissible."

[I] *That is the meaning of the following verse of Scripture:* "[Because Syria with Ephraim and the son of Remaliah has devised evil against you, saying,] 'Let us go up against Judah and terrify it, and let us conquer it for ourselves and set up the son of Tabeel as king in the midst of it'" (Is. 7:5-6).

The dispute concerns the pertinent scriptural foundation for the stated law, proposed at I:1.A, then shown impertinent at B-C, F-I.

### YERUSHALMI TO MISHNAH ABODAH ZARAH 1:2

[A] These are the festivals of gentiles:
[B] [1] Calends, [2] Saturnalia, [3] Kratesis [the commemoration of the empire],
[C] and [4] the emperor's anniversary, [5] his birthday,
[D] "and [6] the day of his death," the words of R. Meir.
[E] And sages say, "In any case of death rites in which there is a burning, there is idolatry, and in which there is no burning, there is no idolatry."

[I:1 A] Rab said, "Their testimonies [spelling the word for festivals at M. 1:2A with an 'ayin]."

[B] And Samuel said, "Their calamity [with an 'alef]."

[C] He who claims that the word is spelled with an 'ayin [as "their testimonies,"] draws evidence from the following verse: "Let them bring their witnesses to justify them" (Is. 43:9).

[D] And he who claims that the word is spelled with an 'alef, as "their festivals," draws evidence from the following verse: "For the day of their calamity ('YDM) is at hand" (Dt. 32:35).

The difference in spelling, as indicated by the cited verses, accounts for the disputes between Rab and Samuel.

### D. BAVLI

### BAVLI TO MISHNAH ABODAH ZARAH 1:1

A. [2A] **Before the festivals of gentiles for three days it is forbidden to do business with them.**

Four. Abodah Zarah

**I.1** A. Rab and Samuel [in dealing with the reading of the key word of the Mishnah, translated festival, the letters of which are 'aleph daled, rather than 'ayin daled, which means, calamity]:
B. *one repeated the formulation of the Mishnah as, "their festivals."*
C. *And the other repeated the formulation of the Mishnah as "their calamities."*
D. *The one who repeated the formulation of the Mishnah as "their festivals" made no mistake, and the one who repeated the formulation of the Mishnah as "their calamities" made no mistake.*
E. *For it is written, "For the day of their calamity is at hand" (Dt. 32:15).*
   F. *The one who repeated the formulation of the Mishnah as "their festivals" made no mistake, for it is written, "Let them bring their testimonies that they may be justified" (Is. 43:9).*
   G. *And as to the position of him who repeats the formulation of the Mishnah as "their festivals," on what account does he not repeat the formulation of the Mishnah to yield, "their calamities"?*
   H. *He will say to you, "'Calamity' is preferable [as the word choice when speaking of idolatry]."*
   I. *And as to the position of him who repeats the formulation of the Mishnah as "their calamities," on what account does he not repeat the formulation of the Mishnah to yield "their festivals"?*
   J. *He will say to you, "What causes the calamity that befalls them if not their testimony, so testimony is preferable!"*

The important side is F-J, both parties have solid foundations not only in Scripture but in reason for the positions that they take, as articulated at G-H, I-J.

### BAVLI TO MISHNAH ABODAH ZARAH 1:8A-F

A. **And they do not make ornaments for an idol:**
B. **(1) necklaces, (2) earrings, or (3) finger rings.**
C. **R. Eliezer says, "For a wage it is permitted [to do so]."**
D. **They do not sell them produce as yet unplucked.**
E. **But one may sell it once it has been harvested.**
F. **R. Judah says, "One may sell it to him with the stipulation that he will harvest it."**

**I.1** A. *What is the scriptural basis for this rule?*
B. Said R. Yosé bar Hanina, **[20A]** "It is because Scripture has said, '...nor be gracious to them,' [the letters of which can yield the phrase,] 'you shall not give them a place to settle on the ground.'"
   C. *But that clause is required to make this point, which the All-Merciful wishes to set forth:* "You shall not admire their grace."
   D. *If that were the case, then Scripture could as well have used the passive tense. Why use the active? That yields two points [the ones of B and C].*

|      | E. | *Still, the phrase is required to make this point, which the All-Merciful wishes to set forth:* "You shall not give them gratuitous gifts." |
|      | F. | *If that were the case, then Scripture could as well have used different vowels [which would have yielded that other meaning]. Why use the form we have? That yields three points.* |

The proof from Scripture, B, is then challenged and shown to cohere, C-F.

### BAVLI TO MISHNAH ABODAH ZARAH 4:5

|      | A. | How does one nullify it? |
|------|----|--------------------------|
| I.   | B. | [If] he has cut off the tip of its ear, the tip of its nose, the tip of its finger, |
|      | C. | [if] he battered it, even though he did not break off [any part of] it, |
|      | D. | he has nullified it. |
| II.  | E. | [If] he spit in its face, urinated in front of it, scraped it, threw shit at it, lo, this does not constitute an act of nullification. |
| III. | F. | [If] he sold it or gave it as a pledge on a loan — |
|      | G. | Rabbi says, "He has nullified it." |
|      | H. | And sages say, "He has not nullified it." |

| II.1 | A. | [If] he spit in its face, urinated in front of it, scraped it, threw shit at it, lo, this does not constitute an act of nullification: |
|------|----|----|
|      | B. | *What is the scriptural source for this rule [that these gestures of disrespect do not constitute acts of nullification of the idol?* |
|      | C. | Said Hezekiah, "It is that Scripture has said, 'And when they shall be angry, they shall fret themselves and curse their king and their god and turn their faces upward' (Is. 8:21), and then, 'they shall look to the earth and behold distress and darkness' (Is. 8:22). Even though he may curse his king and his god and turn his face upward, still he looks to the earth [Cohen: and resumes his idolatry; his repudiation of the idol is only the effect of momentary exasperation]." |

Scripture itself specifies the ineffective modes of nullification that are specified: gestures of transient disrespect as indicated.

## VI. TYPES OF ANALYSIS

The Yerushalmi identifies reasons behind rules, so Y. to M. A.Z. 1:1 III.1; the basis for disputes also is shown rational at Y. to M. A.Z. 3:1 I:1, B. to M. A.Z. 3:5 I.4.

Analogy-criticism is made explicit at M. A.Z. 3:6 and further spelled out in the accompanying Talmud, Y. to M. A.Z. 3:6.

Not only are scriptural foundations for the law set forth but the foundations of disputes resting on conflicting readings of the cited verses are laid out, Y. to M. A.Z. 1:1, Y. to M. A.Z. 1:2, B. to M. A.Z. 1:1 I:1, B. to M. A.Z. 1:8A-F I:1.

# Part Three

# Types of Analysis in
# Selected Midrash Compilations

# 5

# Genesis Rabbah

Midrash, exegesis, encompasses Midrash-Aggadah and Midrash-Halakhah, that is, exegesis for theological or narrative purposes and exegesis for legal purposes. We address three Midrash-compilations, that is, documents of a principally-exegetical character. These are both Aggadic and Halakhic in character. With Genesis Rabbah we begin with a document of systematic, verse-by-verse exegesis, representative of the exegetical reading of mostly Aggadic passages of Scripture; when we come to Leviticus Rabbah we proceed to a document that forms of Scripture a set of syllogistic propositions, with a mixed focus on Aggadic and Halakhic topics with stress on the former; and at Sifré to Numbers we conclude with a document of exegesis that is heavily Halakhic, not Aggadic at all.

In Genesis Rabbah the entire narrative of Genesis is so formed as to point toward the sacred history of Israel, the Jewish people: its slavery and redemption; its coming Temple in Jerusalem; its exile and salvation at the end of time — the whole a paradigm of exile and return. In the rereading by the authorship of Genesis Rabbah, Genesis proclaims the prophetic message that the world's creation commenced a single, straight line of significant events, that is to say, history, leading in the end to the salvation of Israel and, through Israel, of all humanity. The single most important proposition of Genesis Rabbah is that, in the story of the beginnings of creation, humanity, and Israel, we find the message of the meaning and end of the life of the Jewish people in the here and now of the fifth century. The deeds of the founders supply signals for the children about what is going to come in the future. So the biography of Abraham, Isaac, and Jacob also constitutes a protracted account of the history of Israel later on.

Genesis Rabbah is a composite document. As with the Talmud that it accompanies, so in Genesis Rabbah, some of the material in the compilation can be shown to have been put together before that material was used for the purposes of the compilers. Many times a comment entirely apposite to a verse of Genesis has been joined to a set of comments in no way pertinent to the verse at hand. Proof for a given syllogism, furthermore, will derive from a verse of Genesis as well as from numerous verses of other books of the Bible. Such a syllogistic argument therefore has not been written for exegetical purposes particular to the verse at hand. On the contrary, the particular verse subject to attention serves that other, propositional plan; it is not the focus of discourse; it has not generated the comment but merely provided a proof for a syllogism. That is what it means to say that a proposition yields an exegesis. That fundamental proposition, displayed throughout Genesis Rabbah, which yields the specific exegeses of many of the verses of the book of Genesis and even whole stories, is that the beginnings point toward the endings, and the meaning of Israel's past points toward the message that lies in Israel's future. The things that happened to the fathers and mothers of the family, Israel, provide a sign for the things that will happen to the children later on. What is at stake is the discovery, among the facts provided by the written Torah, of the social rules that govern Israel's history. At stake is the search for the order yielded by the chaos of uninterpreted data.

## I. Language-Analysis

Aggadic exercises in Scriptural interpretation routinely examine the meanings of words and phrases in quest of new meanings. But these inquiries bear slight resemblance to their counterparts in the Halakhic compilations. I give a few examples to show the quality of the former in each of the documents under consideration.

## XXX:VIII.
2.  A.  R. Yohanan said, "Whoever is described with the verb to be, [as in 'Noah was....,'] remained just as he was, beginning to end."

B.  The following objection was raised: "And lo, it is written, 'Abraham was one, and he inherited the earth' (Ez. 33:24). On the basis of the use of the word 'one' do we know that he was one, beginning to end? [Surely he changed in the course of his life.]"

C.  He said to him, "Indeed, this item does not contradict my proposition." [We shall now carry forward this statement.]

E.  [Continuing the former proposition:] "The use of the word 'was' in the case of 'Man was...,' (Gen. 3:22) means that the first man was designated for death.

F.  "The use of the word 'was' in the case of the snake (Gen. 3:1) means that the snake was designated as the vehicle of punishment.

G.  "The use of the word 'was' in the case of Cain (Gen. 4:2) means that Cain was designated to go into exile.

H.  "The use of the word 'was' in the case of Job ["Job was...," (Job 1:1)] means that Job was designated for suffering.

I.  "The use of the word 'was' in the case of Noah means that Noah was designated for the performance of a miracle.

J.  "The use of the word 'was' in the case of Moses [at Ex. 3:1] means that Moses was designated to serve as the redeemer.

*Five. Genesis Rabbah*

    K.    "The use of the word 'was' in the case of Mordecai [Est. 2:5] means that he was designated for redemption."

The exegetical proposition, A, treats the verb "to be" as attributive of permanent qualities, that is, "was through all time." That proposition is tested and shown by the evidence to stand. The examples serve for negative and positive instances of the same phenomenon. I cannot discern any Halakhic counterpart to this mode of reading language, which serves to synthesize data, while the Halakhic interest is in analyzing and differentiating them.

### XXXVIII:VI.
1.  A.    "Now the whole earth had one language and few words" (Gen. 11:1):
    B.    R. Eleazar said, "'Few words' means that while the deeds of the generation of the Flood were spelled out, the deeds of the generation of the Dispersion were not spelled out [and hence were covered by only a few words]."
2.  A.    "Few words:" That phrase means that they addressed words against the two who are singular [using the same word as is translated few], against the one of whom it is said, "Abraham was one" (Ez. 33:24), and against, "The Lord, our God, the Lord is one" (Deut. 6:4).
    B.    [They thus spoke against Abraham and against God.] They said, "This man Abraham is a barren mule, who will never have offspring."
    C.    "Against 'The Lord our God, the Lord is one:'" "He does not have the power to select the heavenly spheres for himself and hand over to us merely the lower world. So come, let us make a tower for ourselves and put an idol on top of it, and put a sword in its hand, so that it will appear as if it carries on warfare with him."
3.  A.    Another explanation for the phrase, "Few words [now in the sense of things]:" property held in common.
    B.    What this one held in his possession was held in the possession of the other.

The linguistic interest is in identifying the range of meanings a given formula conveys, not in discerning within that usage fresh lessons, implications, e.g., for norms of belief, in the model of the counterpart in the Halakhic framework.

## II. ANALOGY- AND CATEGORY-CRITICISM

We found that the Halakhic documents, built as they are on a hermeneutics of analogy and contrast, find in criticism of proposed analogies and their hierarchical classification and relationship a critical dynamic of analytical thought. Once more, we find in the Aggadic compilation a counterpart, which hardly compares in character and function but does relate. Since analogy and contrast to begin with rest on the alleged likeness of a classification of data to some other classification of data, the comparison of the aptness of parables, which surfaces from time to time in the Aggadic compilation, serves as a counterpart. That is to say, once an analytical proposition is set forth by appeal to an analogy from the known to the unknown, the counter-argument will call into question the aptness of the analogy. That same process of comparison and objection to the comparison takes place, when an analogy is proposed and rejected in favor of another analogy: this parable instead of that. Then, as we see, a dispute over the appropriate parable functions, for Aggadic discourse, as a counterpart to a dispute over the appropriate category-formations: are they alike, or are they not alike?

II:II.1. A. "And the earth was unformed"(Gen. 1:2):
B. R. Abbahu and R. Judah b. R. Simon:
C. R. Abbahu said, "The matter is to be compared to a king who bought himself two slaves on a single bill of sale and with a single price [for the two]. In regard to one [of the two slaves] he gave orders that he should be fed on the public charge, and with regard to the other he gave orders that he should work for his keep. The latter sat unformed and void [in total confusion]. He said, 'The two of us were purchased for the same price, and now one of the two is fed on the public charge, while I have to work for my keep!'
D. "So did the earth sit unformed and void [in total confusion]. The earth said, 'The creatures of the upper world and those of the lower were created at the same instant. The creatures of the upper world draw sustenance from the splendor of the Presence of God, while as to the lower realm of creation, if the created ones do not work, they will not eat!'"
E. R. Judah b. R. Simon said, "The matter may be compared to a king who purchased two servant-girls, both on the same bill of sale and for the same price. In regard to one he gave orders that she should not move from the palace, and in regard to the other he gave orders that she should be banished. The one who had been banished sat unformed and void [in total confusion]. She said, 'Both of us were on the same bill of sale and for the same price. This one does not move out of the palace, while in my regard he gave orders that I should be banished!'
F. "So the earth sat unformed and void [in total confusion]. The earth said, 'The creatures of the upper world and those of the lower world were created at the same instant. Why is it the case, then, that the upper world['s creatures] live [and never taste death] while the lower world's creatures are subject to death. Therefore: 'The earth was unformed and void [in total confusion].'"
2. A. Said R. Tanhuma, "The matter may be compared to a prince who was sleeping in his cradle, and his nurse-maid was unformed and void [in total confusion]. Why? Because she knew that she was destined to receive her fate on account of the prince. So the earth foresaw that it was destined to receive her fate on account of man: 'Cursed be the earth on your account' (Gen. 3:17).
B. "Therefore: The earth was unformed and void [Freedman: desolate and anxious]."

These proposed parables, C, E, are comparable, but differ at the key point. Then the upshot is spelled out at D, F. The dispute is worked out in the framework

*Five. Genesis Rabbah*

of the conflict of parables, therefore, just as disputes in the Halakhah will play themselves out in the issue of identifying the right, the appropriate analogy and establishing a contrast thereto. We note that Tanhuma, No. 2, goes his own way and is not party to the dispute.

## IX:IV.
1. A. R. Hama bar Hanina and R. Jonathan:
   B. R. Hama bar Hanina said, "The matter may be compared to the case of a king who built a palace. He saw it and it pleased him. He said, 'O palace, palace! May you always charm me as you charm me at this hour!' So said the Holy One, blessed be he, to his world, 'O my world, my world! May you always charm me as you charm me at this hour!'"
   C. R. Jonathan said, "The matter may be compared to the case of a king who married off his daughter and arrayed for her a marriage-canopy, a house, which he plastered, paneled, and painted. He saw [what he had made] and it pleased him. He said, 'O my daughter, my daughter, may this marriage canopy always charm me as it charms me at this hour. So said the Holy One, blessed be he, to his world, 'O my world, my world! May you always charm me as you charm me at this hour.'"

The conflict concerns the comparison of creation: a palace, a daughter in her marriage canopy. Is God's relationship to the world comparable to the king or the father? The answer within the system is, both metaphors prevail.

## XXVIII:VI.
1. A. "Man and beast and creeping things and birds of the air" (Gen. 6:7):
   B. R. Yudan said, "The matter [of destroying the beasts and fowl] may be compared to the case of a king who handed his son over to a tutor, who misguided the boy and led him into bad ways. The king grew angry with his son and put him to death. Said the king, 'Is it not so that this one alone is responsible for leading my son into bad ways? My son has perished and should this one survive?' Therefore: 'Man *and beast* ' (Gen. 6:7). [How the beasts are responsible for man's sin is not specified. This will come up shortly. The beasts contributed to an excess of prosperity, on which the sin is blamed. But the passage as a whole would better explain wiping out a generation accused of bestiality.]"
   C. R. Phineas said, "The matter may be compared to the case of a king who was marrying his son off and made a marriage-canopy for him, which he plastered, painted, and decorated. The king grew angry with his son and killed him. He went into the marriage canopy and began to break down the rods, destroy the partitions, and tear the hangings. He said, 'My son has perished and should these remain?' Therefore: 'Man *and beast*' (Gen. 6:7). [But here why the king killed the son is not specified at all. Following is an attempted explanation of the destruction of the beasts, but that does not help us with the killing of the son in the present parable.]

>    D. "That [verse, concerning destroying the beasts and fowl too] is in line with this verse of Scripture: 'I will consume man and beast, and the stumbling blocks with the wicked' (Zeph. 1:3). [The beasts] were the ones that served as stumbling blocks for the wicked, for one would hunt a bird and say, 'Go, get fat, and then come back' which the bird did. [There was abundant prosperity, which led to evil.]"

The issue focuses on the valid parable to explain the destruction of beasts on account of man's sins. Is there a rational basis for God's doing that? So the theological dispute works itself out in the choice of parables: is it a rational decision or one based on temper?

### XXX:IX.
1. 
   A. "[Noah was a righteous man, blameless] in his generation" (Gen. 6:9):
   B. R. Judah and R. Nehemiah:
   C. R. Judah said, "By the standard of his generation, he was indeed righteous. But had he been in the generation of Moses or in the generation of Samuel, he would hardly have been regarded as a righteous.
   D. "In the market of the blind, they call a one eyed man far-sighted, and the baby is a scholar.
   E. "The matter may be compared to the case of a man who had a wine cellar. He opened the first keg and found it vinegar, the second and found it vinegar. When he came to the third, he found it turning. They said to him, 'It is turning.' He said to them, 'Is there anything better here?' They told him, 'No.'
   F. "So too by the standard of his generation, he was a righteous man. [But that is only by that standard.]"
   G. R. Nehemiah said, "Now if in the generation in which he lived, he was righteous, in the generation of Moses, all the more so!
   H. "The matter may be compared to the case of a vial of perfume lying tightly sealed in a cemetery, giving out a wonderful odor. If it were located outside of the cemetery, how much the more so!"

The pertinent parable dictates the assessment of the righteousness of Noah: relative (as in the parable of the wine) or absolute (as in the parable of the perfume). I cannot point to a clearer case of the utilization of parables to sustain positions in contested Aggadic issues, comparable to the process of finding the right comparison and contrast in the case of contested Halakhic issues.

### XXXII:III.
1. 
   A. "The Lord tries the righteous, but the wicked and him who loves violence his soul hates" (Ps. 11:5):
   B. Said R. Jonathan, "A potter does not test a weak utensil, for if he hits it just once, he will break it. So the Holy One, blessed be he, does not try the wicked but the righteous: 'The Lord tries the righteous' (Ps. 11:5)."

## Five. Genesis Rabbah

C. Said R. Yosé bar Haninah, "When a flax maker knows that the flax is in good shape, then the more he beats it, the more it will improve and glisten. When it is not of good quality, if he beats it just once, he will split it. So the Holy One, blessed be he, does not try the wicked but the righteous: 'The Lord tries the righteous' (Ps. 11:5)."

D. Said R. Eleazar, "The matter may be compared to a householder who has two heifers, one strong, one weak. On whom does he place the yoke? It is on the one that is strong. So the Holy One, blessed be he, does not try the wicked but the righteous: 'The Lord tries the righteous' (Ps. 11:5).

Why the three parables — potter, flax maker, householder —yield a conflict is not clear to me.

### XLIX:II.
2. A. "The Lord said, 'Shall I hide from Abraham [what I am about to do, seeing that Abraham shall become a great and mighty nation and all the nations of the earth shall bless themselves by him? No, for I have chosen him that he may charge his children and his household after him to keep the way of the Lord by doing righteousness and justice...']" (Gen. 17:17-19).

   B. Said R. Joshua b. Levi, "The matter may be compared to the case of a king who gave an estate to his ally and then later on the king wanted to cut down from the property five barren trees [for use as wood]. The king said, 'If I had wanted to cut down trees from his inherited property [and not from the property I gave him], he would not stop me. So what difference does it make.' He nonetheless [paid him respect and so] took counsel with him.

   C. "So said the Holy One, blessed be he, 'Now I have already given the land as a gift to Abraham: "To your seed have I given this land" (Gen. 15:18). These towns fall within my property. But if they belonged to his inheritance, he would not object. So what difference does it make to me if I ask his permission?'"

3. A. Said R. Judah bar Simon, "The matter may be compared to the case of a king who had three allies and who would do nothing without their knowledge and consent. One time, however, the king wanted to do something without their knowledge and content. He took the first and drove him out and put him away from the palace. He took the second and put him in prison. He put his seal on the prison door. As to the third, who was a special favorite, he said, 'I simply shall do nothing without his knowledge and consent.'

   B. "So in the case of the first man: 'So he drove out the man' (Gen. 3:23).

   C. "As to Noah: 'The Lord shut him in the ark' (Gen. 7:5).

   D. "But when it came to Abraham, who was the special favorite, he said, 'I simply shall do nothing without his knowledge and consent.'"

4. A. Said R. Samuel b. Nahman, "The matter may be compared to the case of a king who had an adviser, without whose knowledge and consent he would do absolutely nothing. One time he considered doing something without his knowledge and consent. Said the king, 'Did I not make him my counselor only so as not to do anything without his knowledge and consent?'"

B. Said R. Yudan, "So said the Holy One, blessed be he, 'Did I not call him a man of my own counsel only so as not to do anything outside of his knowledge and consent? Lot, his brother's son is with [the Sodomites], and should I not let him know?'"

The comparisons invoke a king who takes back a gift as against a king who acknowledged his allies. Is God's discussion of Sodom with Abraham an act of grace, which he is not coerced to do, or an act of obligation, respect for an alley? No. 4 goes over the latter position as well.

### III. RATIONALITY

Showing the rationality of both sides of a dispute is important in the Halakhic exposition, showing as it does the equally valid claims of both parties to normativity. This may be demonstrated by assigning to each party a valid scriptural foundation or a compelling rational consideration or a overriding tradition. The Aggadic counterpart is shown in what follows

### IX:III.
1. A. ["And God saw all that he had made, and behold, it was very good" (Gen. 1:31):] R. Yohanan and R. Simeon b. Laqish:
   B. R. Yohanan said, "A mortal king builds a palace, then examining the upper floors in one inspection and the lower ones in another, but the Holy One, blessed be he, could take in both the upper floors and the lower floors in a single look."
   C. Said R. Simeon b. Laqish, "'Lo, it was very good' refers to this world. '*And* lo, it was very good' [with the addition of *and* ] encompasses the world to come. The Holy One, blessed be he, encompassed both of them with a single look."

The intersection of the two opinions on "lo, it was very good," contains no argument on a common point but two complementary readings.

### XIV:V.
1. A. "And the Lord God formed" (Gen. 2:7): The word is written with two Y's, representing two acts of creation,
   B. creation in this world and creation in the world to come.
   2. A. The House of Shammai and the House of Hillel:
      B. The House of Shammai say, "The act of creation of man in this world is not the same as the act of creation of man in the world to come. In this world the act of creation begins with the skin and the flesh and is completed with the sinews and bones. But in the world to come the act of creation begins with the sinews and bones and is completed with the skin and flesh. For so does Scripture say with reference to the dead to whom Ezekiel preached: 'And I beheld and lo, there were sinews upon them and flesh came up and skin covered them above [in that order]' (Ez. 37:8)."

## Five. Genesis Rabbah

C. Said R. Jonathan, "One may not derive the facts from the case of the dead of whom Ezekiel spoke. For to what may the dead to whom Ezekiel spoke be compared? To one who entered the bath house [who leaves his clothes in a pile]. What he takes off first he puts on last."

D. The House of Hillel say, "Just as the act of creation of man is done in this world, so is the act of creation of man done in the world to come. In this world the act begins with the skin and the flesh and is completed with the sinews and bones. So too in the age to come the act begins with the skin and the flesh and ends with the sinews and the bones. For so does Job say, 'Will you [in the age to come] not pour me out as milk and curdle me like cheese? You will clothe me with skin and flesh and knit me together with bones and sinews' (Job 10:10-11).

E. "'You poured me out and curdled me' is not what is says, but rather, 'you *will* pour me out and *will* curdle me.' 'You have clothed me with skin and flesh' is not what it says, but rather, 'You *will* cloth me. 'And with bones and sinews you have knit me together' is not what it says but rather, 'You *will* knit me together.'

F. "The matter may be compared to a bowl that is filled with milk. Until one puts rennet into the milk, the milk is flowing. Once one puts rennet into the milk, the milk congeals and becomes firm. That is in line with what Job said, 'Will you not pour me out as milk...skin and flesh...you have granted me life and favor' (Job 10:12)."

The dispute is head-on: whether the act of creation in the beginning is the same as the counterpart act at the resurrection. Each position is well-grounded in scriptural support, and the one corresponds with the other.

### XX:V.
**2.** A. R. Yudan and R. Huna:

B. One of them said, "You are the one who caused my creatures to walk along bent over [in grief caused by the advent into the world of death], so you too: 'Upon your belly you shall go' (Gen. 3:14)."

C. Said R. Eleazar, "Even the curse of the Holy One, blessed be he, contains a blessing. If God had not said to him, 'On your belly you shall go' (Gen. 3:14), how could the snake flee to the wall to find refuge, or to a hole to be saved?"

The form signals a dispute: X/Y — one said...the other said...But the former is broken, and Eleazar's statement does not intersect with what is, theoretically at least, at issue in the unstated position contrary to B.

### XXII:IV.
**1.** A. ."And at the end of days it came to pass" (Gen. 4:3) [RSV: In the course of time"]:

B. R. Eliezer and R. Joshua:

C. R. Eliezer says, "In Tishré [the fall] the world was created."
D. R. Joshua says, "In Nisan [the spring]."
E. He who says that it was in Tishré treats Abel as having lived from Tabernacles to Hanukkah.
F. He who says that it was in Nisan treats Abel as having lived from Passover to Pentecost.
G. Whether in accord with this party or in accord with that party, all concur that Abel did not remain alive for more than fifty days.

The importance of the composition occurs at E-J, which allows each party to deal with the issue at hand: the lifetime of Abel. The parties then concur, G, on the length of his life. So the dispute is played out within a limited framework.

## XXIII:I.
1. A. "And Cain knew his wife [and she conceived and bore Enoch, and he built a city and called the name of the city after the name of his son, Enoch]" (Gen. 4:17):
   B. "Their inward thought is that their houses shall continue for ever" (Ps. 49:12)
   C. R. Yudan and R. Phineas:
   D. R. Yudan said, "What do the wicked people think? It is: 'Their inward thought is that their houses shall continue for ever, and their dwelling places shall exist to all generations, and they will call their lands after their own names' (Ps. 49:12).
   E. "For example, Tiberias after the Tiberian dynasty, Alexandria after the Alexandrians, Antiochia after Antiochus."
   F. R. Phineas said, "'Their inward thought is that their houses shall continue for ever,' but tomorrow their houses will turn into their graves [a play on their consonants QRB and QBR].
   G. "'Their dwelling places shall exist to all generations' means that they will not be resurrected or subjected to judgment,
   H. "and not only so, but: 'they have called their lands after their own names:' 'And he built a city and called the name of the city after the name of his son, Enoch' (Gen. 4:17)."

Here the dispute form as worked out in Genesis Rabbi — X/Y, X said/Y said — is well-realized. The two parties concur that the wicked want their houses to continue, but the proof-text does not yield the conclusion for Phineas that Yudan derives from it. Here again, the dispute concerns restricted matters.

## XXVI:II.
3. A. Said R. Hanina, "In the age to come death will apply only to the children of Noah [but not to Israel]."
   B. R. Joshua b. Levi said, "It will apply neither to Israel nor to the nations: 'And the Lord God will wipe away tears from off *all* faces' (Is. 25:8)."
   C. How does R. Hanina deal with the cited verse? "From off all faces" speaks only of Israel.

## Five. Genesis Rabbah

D. And lo, it is written, "For the youngest shall die at the age of a hundred years" (Is. 65:20). [Surely that speaks not of everyone, but just Israelites.] And that verse supports the view of R. Hanina.

E. How does R. Joshua deal with the cited verse? It speaks of one who at that time becomes liable to punishment.

F. And lo, it is written, "Like sheep they are appointed for the nether-world; death shall be their shepherd" (Ps. 49:15). Now that verse supports the view of R. Hanina.

G. How does R. Joshua deal with the cited verse? Now in this age, each was punished in his time: Pharaoh in his time, Sisera in his time. But in the age to come, the angel of death will be appointed their superior [to make sure their punishment is eternal, not only for the time in which they lived]. That is in line with this verse: "And the upright shall have dominion over them in the morning, and their form shall be for the wearing away of the nether-world on account of his habitation" (Ps. 49:15). This teaches that while Sheol will wear away, their bodies will never wear away [but will continue to suffer].

H. All this why? "On account of his habitation," meaning, because they stretched forth their hands against his habitation [the Temple]. That is in line with this verse: "I have surely built you a house of habitation" (1 Kgs. 8:13).

The dispute is rationally-grounded, for the one party takes up the proof-texts of the other, an equal opportunity being accorded to them both. The balance is fully maintained throughout.

### LIV:I.

1. A. "At that time Abimelech and Phicol the commander of his army said to Abraham, 'God is with you in all that you do'" (Gen. 21:22).

   B. "When a man's ways please the Lord, even his enemies are at peace with him" (Prov. 16:7).

   C. R. Yohanan said, "The reference to one's enemies speaks, in fact, of one's wife: 'A man's enemies are the people of his own house' (Mic. 7:6)."

   D. There was the case of a woman who complained against her husband to the government, and they cut off his head.

   E. And some say that they also cut off her head.

   F. R. Samuel bar Nahman said, "The cited verse refers to the snake."

   G. A Tannaite authority of the house of Halapta bar Saul taught, "The snake lusts for garlic."

   H. Said R. Samuel bar Nahman, "There was the case of a snake that went down into a house and found a bowl of garlic and ate it and vomited up into the bowl. There was a [second] snake in the house, and it could not withstand the intruder [and keep it out, being too weak]. But when the first snake left, the second snake went and filled the bowl with dirt [saving the life of the people of the house, who otherwise would have eaten the venom]."

I. R. Joshua b. Levi said, "The cited verse refers to the impulse to do evil."

J. "Under ordinary circumstances if someone grows up with a fellow for two or three years, he develops a close tie to him. But the impulse to do evil grows with someone from youth to old age, and, if one can, someone strikes down the impulse to do evil even when he is seventy or eighty."

K. "So did David say, 'All my bones shall say, "Lord, who is like unto you, who delivers the poor from him who is too strong for him, yes, the poor and the needy from him who spoils him"' (Ps. 35:10)."

The dispute is worked out at B, C, F, I+J-K. The form of the dispute governs, with some interpolations and a secondary development, leaving no ambiguity on what is at issue, which is a relatively minor matter.

## LXXIII:V.

2. A. "'God has taken away my reproach:" in the incident of the concubine of Gibeah.

B. "Cursed is he who gives a wife to Benjamin" (Judges 21:18).

C. 'God has taken away my reproach:'

D. In the days of Jeroboam: "Neither did Jeroboam recover strength again in the days of Abijah, and the Lord smote him and he died" (2 Chr. 13:20).

E. Said R. Samuel bar Nahman, "Do you think that Jeroboam was smitten? But in fact Abijah was smitten."

F. Why was Abijah smitten?

G. Said R. Abba b. Kahana, "Because he removed the identifying marks of the faces of the Israelites, as it is written, 'The show of their countenance does witness for them' (Is. 3:9)."

H. Said R. Assi, "Because he set up guards over them for three days until the features of their faces were disfigured.

I. "For so we have learned in the Mishnah: **People give testimony to the identity of a corpse only through the features of the face together with the nose, and that is the case even if there are other marks of identification on the body and the garments; and one may give testimony only within three days of death [beyond which point the face is disfigured] [M. Yeb. 16:3].**

J. "And it says, 'The widows are increased to me above the sands of the seas' (Jer. 15:8)."

K. R. Yohanan said, "It was because he treated with contempt Ahijah the Shilonite: 'And there were gathered to him vain men, base fellows' (2 Chr. 13:7). So he treated Ahijah as worthless."

L. R. Simeon b. Laqish said, "It was because he humiliated them in public: 'And you are a great multitude and there are with you the golden calves' (2 Chr. 13:7)."

M. Rabbis said, "It was because an idol came into his possession and he did not nullify it: 'And Abijah pursued after Jeroboam and took cities from him, Bethel and the towns thereof, and Jeshanah and the towns thereof' (2 Chr. 13:19), and further: 'And he set the one [golden calf] in Bethel and the other in Dan' (1 Kgs. 12:29).

*Five. Genesis Rabbah*

N. "Now is it not an argument *a fortiori* : If, in the account of Scripture, because a king insulted a king like himself and therefore was smitten, if an ordinary person insults an ordinary person, how much the more so!"

Once more the dispute concerns a subordinate detail, F, with a variety of opinions, G, H-J, K, L, M. The balance is acute, and the issue restricted.

## LXXVIII:VI.
1. A. "Therefore to this day the Israelites do not eat the sinew of the hip, which is upon the hollow of the thigh, because he touched the hollow of Jacob's thigh on the sinew of the hip" (Gen. 32:32):
   B. Said R. Haninah, "Why is it called 'the thigh vein' [Hebrew: *gid hannasheh* ] ? Because it slipped [*nashah* ] out of its place."
2. A. R. Huna said, "The secondary parts of the thigh vein are permitted, but the Israelites, being holy, treat those parts as forbidden as well."
   B. R. Judah says, "He touched only one of the veins, and that particular one of the veins is the one alone that is forbidden."
   C. R. Yosé says, "He touched only one of the veins, but two of them were forbidden."
      D. There is a Tannaite authority who repeats, "Reason points to the conclusion that it was the one on the right, in accord with the view of R. Judah."
      E. There is a Tannaite authority who repeats, "Reason points to the conclusion that it was the one on the left, in accord with the view of R. Yosé."
      F. He who maintains that it was on the right cites this verse: "And he touched the hollow of his thigh" (Gen. 32:26), and the one who thinks it was on the left cites this verse, "Because he touched the hollow of Jacob's thigh" (Gen. 32:33).

Here is a fine example of a balanced dispute, D-E+F. The several parties are given balanced opinions and proof-texts.

## C:III.
1. A. "Then Joseph fell on his father's face and wept over him and kissed him. And Joseph commanded his servants the physicians to embalm his father. So the physicians embalmed Israel" (Gen. 50:1-2):
   B. Why did Joseph die before his brothers [as at Ex. 1:6]?
   C. Rabbi and rabbis:
   D. Rabbi said, "Because he had his father embalmed. Said the Holy One, blessed be he, 'Am I not able to watch out for my righteous? Did I not say to him, "Do not fear the worm, O Jacob" (Is. 41:14), which is to say, Jacob, do not be afraid of the worm.'"
   E. Rabbis say, "But he was the one who gave orders that they embalm him. For it is said, 'And his sons did to him as he had ordered them' (Gen. 50:12)."
   F. Rabbi's view presents no problems, but in the view of rabbis, [he died first for this reason:]

G. Nearly five times Judah said, "Your servant, my father," "Your servant, my father," and he heard that and said not a word. [So he permitted Judah to refer to his father as "his servant."]

The dispute form distinctive to Genesis Rabbah, X/Y, X said/Y said/say, is augmented at F-G with a challenge and response for one of the parties.

## C:VII.
**1.** A. "When they came to the threshing floor of Atad, which is beyond the Jordan, they lamented there with a very great and sorrowful lamentation, and he made a mourning for his father seven days" (Gen. 50:10):

B. How on the basis of Scripture do we know that mourning lasts for seven days?

C. R. Aha derives proof from the following: "...and he made a mourning for his father seven days" (Gen. 50:10).

D. But does proof derive from a matter pertaining to the age prior to the giving of the Torah?

E. R. Simeon b. Laqish in the name of Bar Qappara derives proof from the following: "And you shall not go out from the door of the tent of meeting for seven days' (Lev. 8:13). Just as you are anointed with anointing oil for seven days, so you will observe for your brothers seven days [of mourning]."

F. R. Hoshaiah derives proof from the following: "'And at the door of the tent of meeting you shall dwell day and night for seven days and keep the observance of the Lord' (Lev. 8:35). Just as the Holy One, blessed be he, kept an observance for his world for seven days, so you must observe seven days of mourning for your brothers."

G. For R. Joshua b. Levi said, "For seven days the Holy One, blessed be he, went into mourning for his world [before he brought the flood, as it is said, 'And it grieved him in his heart' (Gen. 6:5), and further it says, 'For the king grieved for his son' (2 Sam. 19:3)]."

H. R. Yohanan derives proof from the following: "'Let her not, I pray you, be as one dead,' but rather: 'let her be shut up seven days' (Num. 12:12, 14). Just as the days of shutting up last for a week, so the mourning lasts for seven days."

I. One of the masters told this statement of R. Yohanan to R. Simeon b. Laqish, who did not accept it. Why did he not accept it? He said, "[Freedman:] There the rule treats the case as a matter of shutting up, while here it is treated as a matter of decided and definite illness."

J. R. Abbahu in the name of R. Yohanan came and said, ""Let her not, I pray you, be as one dead,' (Num. 12:12, 14). Just as the days of mourning for the deceased last for a week, so the period of probationary waiting lasts for seven days."

K. Said R. Jeremiah and R. Hiyya bar Abba in the name of R. Simeon b. Laqish, "'And I will turn your feasts into mourning' (Amos 8:10).

## Five. Genesis Rabbah

- L. "Just as the days of the Festival [of Tabernacles] are seven, so the period of mourning should be seven days."
- M. Said R. Hiyya, "The eighth day [of Solemn Assembly, observed at the end of Tabernacles] is an independent festival day. Hence, one may argue, just as the Eighth Day of Solemn Assembly is a single day, so the period of mourning is a single day."
  - N. They said to him, "On this basis we learn the rule governing conduct when the news of a death comes after some time. For so it has been taught on Tannaite authority: In the case of the news of a death that comes close to the event, a period of thirty days of mourning and of seven days of intense mourning is to be observed. But in the case of a report of a bereavement that comes long after the event, there is no question of observing thirty days of mourning and seven days of intense mourning."
    - O. There are those who repeat the Tannaite tradition: The rule of a long-postponed report applies after twelve months, and one that is close to the event is one that is within twelve months of the death, and there are Tannaite authorities who repeat, the rule of a long-postponed report of a bereavement applies after thirty days of the death and of a prompt report, within thirty days of the death.
    - P. R. Abbahu in the name of R. Yohanan said, "The law accords with the position of him who says the following: 'The rule of a long-postponed report of a bereavement applies after thirty days of the death and of a prompt report, within thirty days of the death.'"
- Q. [Reverting to the question with which we began:] R. Berekhiah and R. Jonah in the name of R. Simeon b. Laqish in the name of R. Judah the Patriarch: "It is written, 'So the days of weeping in the mourning for Moses were ended' (Deut. 34:8).
- R. "'Days' stands for two, 'weeping' stands for seven, and 'mourning' stands for thirty."
- S. There are those who reverse matters: "Days" stands for seven, "weeping" stands for two, and "mourning" stands for thirty.
  - T. Now we understand the references to seven and to thirty days [respectively, since these are known periods involved in the mourning procedure]. But what is the point of a reference to two days?
  - U. It deals with the case of a poor person, who cannot afford to take off time from work. If such a person is very poor, he does not do any work on the first and second days of the bereavement, on the third he works in private. But a curse be on the heads of his neighbors, who made it necessary [by their neglect] for him to conduct himself in that way.

V. Bar Qappara said, "Even on the third day he should not do anything at all, because that is the time when the grief is at its strongest."

W. Bar Qappara taught, "The entire depth of grief comes only on the third day."

X. Up to the third day the soul keeps returning to the body, thinking that it will go back in. When it sees that the features of the face have crumbled, it goes its way and leaves the body. That is in line with this verse: "But his flesh grieves for him, and his soul mourns over him" (Job 14:22).

Y. In the age to come the mouth and the belly will have a quarrel with one another. The mouth will say to the belly, "Whatever I stole and grabbed I gave you." After three days the body bursts and says to the mouth, "Here is what is everything you stole and grabbed."

Z. "And the pitcher is broken at the fountain" (Qoh. 12:6).

AA. What is the rule on the mourner's putting on *Tefillin*?

BB. R. Eliezer and R. Joshua:

CC. R. Eliezer said, "On the first day he does not do so, and on the second day he does so. And if new people make an appearance [coming to express condolences], he takes them off."

DD. R. Joshua says, "On the first day and on the second, he does not put them on, and on the third day, he puts them on, and if new people come, he does not take them off."

EE. If he does not put them on even on the second day, must one specify in the law [at M. Ber. 3:1]: **One whose deceased relative is yet unburied does not have to recite the Prayer and put on Tefillin**? [Surely that is an argument *a fortiori* ! Why bother to specify what is self-evident?]

FF. But since the Tannaite author made one statement, he made the other as well.

GG. R. Zeira, R. Jeremiah in the name of Rab, R. Zeira and Mar Uqba in the name of Samuel: "The decided law follows the view of R. Eliezer as to putting on the *Tefillin* , and accords with the view of ,R. Joshua as regards the law of removing them."

HH. R. Zeira asked, "What is the law as to putting them on the second day in accord with the view of R. Eliezer, and further, in accord with the view of R. Joshua in regard to not removing them?" [This question is not answered.]

II. How on the basis of Scripture we do know that the laws of mourning do not apply on the Sabbath?

JJ. R. Joshua of Sikhnin in the name of R. Levi derives proof from the following: "'The blessing of the Lord makes rich and grief adds nothing thereto' (Prov. 10:22).

## Five. Genesis Rabbah

KK. "'The blessing of the Lord makes rich' refers to the Sabbath: 'And God blessed the seventh day' (Gen. 2:3).
LL. "'...and grief adds nothing thereto' refers to mourning, in line with this verse: 'The king grieves for his son' (2 Sam. 19:3)."
MM. Said Rab, "Turning around and putting up are required, uncovering and putting on shoes are optional. That is, turning around the tear in the garment and putting up the bed are obligatory, but uncovering the head and putting on shoes are optional."
NN. Samuel said, "Uncovering, turning around, and putting up are required, but putting on, the prohibition of intercourse, and not washing, are optional. That is to say, uncovering the head, turning around the tear in the garment, and putting up the bed are required; not putting on shoes, not having sexual relations, and not washing, are optional."
OO. One disciple of Samuel had sexual relations and then went and bathed [during a period of mourning]. He said to him, "It was as a matter of legal theory that I made that statement to you, but did I tell it to you as a law governing actual practice?"
PP. He grew angry with the student, who died.
QQ. R. Yosé bar Halapta repeated praise of R. Meir before the people of Sepphoris. He said to him, "He is a great man, a holy man." One time he found them standing in a line to comfort the mourners on the Sabbath. He said to them, "Peace to you."
RR. They said to him, "Is this the one whom you have praised? [It is not customary to greet mourners in this way.]"
SS. He said to them, "Know the true praise of this man. He came to inform us that the rules of mourning do not apply on the Sabbath [and he did so by the simple act of giving a greeting]."
TT. R. Hoshaiah went to a certain place and on the Sabbath found the people standing in line to express sympathy to mourners.
UU. He said to them, "I really do not know what your custom is. But [I shall say,] 'Peace be to you.' For doing so is in accord with the custom of our place."
VV. Of the two sons of Rabbi, one of them went out with his head covered and wearing sandals, and

the other went out with his head not covered and barefooted.
WW. R. Jonah went to great the brother of R. Gurion, who came out to receive him wearing sandals.
XX. He said to him, "Tell your brother, R. Gurion: 'We do not derive the rule governing actual practice on the basis of what common folk do.'" [Freedman, p. 997, n. 8: Jonah understood that the mourner had acted on his brother's instructions. He further held that the wearing of sandals on the Sabbath of mourning is voluntary, and so his only purpose in wearing sandals was to show that there is no mourning on the Sabbath. Therefore he told him that one deduces a law from the act of a great man, but not from that of an ordinary person, and so he need not have worn them.]
YY. R. Haninah bar Papa went to greet R. Tanhum bar Hiyya of Kefar Agin. He came out to receive him, wearing his best clothes [as a mourner].
ZZ. What are these "best clothes"? They are clothing without tears.
AAA. He said to him, "Is this what people do here?"
BBB. He said to him, "This is what R. Yohanan did."
CCC. He said to him, "Pray for me."
DDD. He said to him, "May your breach go away."
EEE. He said to him, "This is not what you should say, but rather: 'May your breach be fixed.'"
FFF. It has been taught on Tannaite authority: An association [formed for the practice of a religious duty] or a natural family are comparable to a pile of stones. If you take away one the whole is loosened, and if you put back one, the whole is strengthened. So for the entire period of seven days a sword is stretched out, and up to the end of the period of thirty days, the sword is hovering, and it returns to its sheath only at the end of twelve months.
GGG. Said R. Eleazar, "If a male child is born into that family, the family forthwith is healed."
HHH. If [there is no mourning on the Sabbath], why do people greet the mourner on the Sabbath?
III. Said R. Joshua of Sikhnin, "It is so as not to arouse wrath [that the mourner will feel if his bereavement is ignored]."

*Five. Genesis Rabbah*

The dispute of interest in C:VII concerns the proof-texts for the shared proposition, B plus C, E, F, H, J, K-L, M. The secondary expansion, I, glosses H. The rest of the material wanders off in its own direction, not continuing the dispute, which is self-contained. I have indented what I regard as secondary to the basic dispute.

### IV. SCRIPTURAL FOUNDATIONS OF THE HALAKHAH

The invocation of proof-texts for Halakhic propositions finds a counterpart in the Aggadic compilations, not only when Halakhah is at issue, but also when Aggadah yields generalizations that sustain disputes. So I encompass in the present rubric not only the exact parallel to the Halakhic utilization of verses of Scripture as proof-texts for propositions, but also the Aggadic counterpart to that same procedure. It is more common in Genesis Rabbah than my probe suggests, but I preferred to choose only the more probative instances. The fact is, every point at which a proposition is joined to a cited verse of Scripture would correspond, and that would, loosely indicated, encompass the whole of the document.

### I:XV.
1. A. ["...the heaven and the earth" (Gen. 1:1):] The House of Shammai say, "The heaven was created first."
   B. The House of Hillel say, "The earth was created first."
   C. In the view of the House of Shammai the matter may be compared to the case of a king who first made a throne for himself and afterward the footstool for the throne, as it is said, "The heaven is my throne, and the earth the dust of my feet" (Is. 66:1).
   D. In the view of the House of Hillel the matter is to be compared to the case of a king who built a first palace for himself. Only after he had built the bottom floor did he build the upper floor, for so it is written, "On the day on which the Lord God made earth and [only then] heaven" (Gen. 2:4).
      E. Said R. Judah bar Ilai, "The following verse of Scripture supports the view of the House of Hillel: 'Of old you laid out the foundations of the earth..., ' and afterward, '...and the heavens are the work of your hands' (Ps. 102:25).
      F. Said R. Hanin, "On the basis of the verse of Scripture that supports the position of the House of Shammai the House of Hillel find evidence to reject that same view: 'The earth was...' (Gen. 1:2), meaning that it had already come into being."
         G. R. Yohanan [said] in the name of sages, "As to the act of creation, heaven came first. As to the process of finishing off creation, the earth came first."
         H. Said R. Tanhuma, "I shall supply a verse of Scripture to support that statement. As to creation, the heaven came first: 'In the beginning God created [the heaven, then the earth]'

(Gen. 1:1). But as to the process of finishing off creation, the earth came first: 'On the day on which the Lord God made heaven and earth' (Gen. 2:4)."

I. Said R. Simeon, "I should be surprised if the fathers of the world disputed concerning this matter. For both of them were created only as are the pot and its lid [which is to say, in a single act]. In this regard I recite the following verse of Scripture: '[My hand established the earth, and my right hand spread out the heaven.] When I call them, they stand up together' (Is. 48:13)."

J. Said R. Eleazar b. R. Simeon, "According to this opinion of my father, why is it that sometimes heaven comes before earth, sometimes earth comes before heaven. But what it teaches is that the two of them are equal [having been created at the same instant]."

In an Aggadic compilation, we need not anticipate a rich corpus of proofs for a Halakhic proposition. What is interesting is that, on occasion, Aggadic propositions are offered sustaining support in the manner of Halakhic ones, as in the exchange of proof-texts joined to parables in the present composition. Then, Eff., the position of the House of Hillel is one-sidedly advanced. The simple fact is, just as Halakhic propositions are offered proof-texts, so too are Aggadic ones sustained in a similar manner.

VI.VI.3.A. R. Yannai and R. Simeon b. Laqish say, "Gehenna in point of fact is nothing other than a day which will burn up the wicked. What is the scriptural evidence? 'For lo, a day comes, it burns as a furnace' (Mal. 3:19)."

B. Rabbis say, "In point of fact there is really such a thing as Gehenna, as it is said, 'Whose fire is in Zion, and his furnace in Jerusalem' (Is. 31:9)."

C. R. Judah b. R. Ilai: "Gehenna is neither a day nor a real place. But it is a fire that goes forth from the body of a wicked person and consumes him. What is the scriptural evidence for that proposition? 'You conceive chaff, you shall bring forth stubble, your breath is a fire that shall devour you' (Is. 33:11). "

D. R. Joshua bar Bun said, "'The heavens declare his righteousness' (Ps. 50:6). In the age to come heaven will declare the righteous act that the Holy One, blessed be he, performed, in that he did not put the sun in the first firmament. For if it had been placed in the first firmament, no creature could have withstood the heat by day."

The four positions are assigned proof-texts in the Halakhic manner. The positions do not exactly intersect, as we see in the indentation, so that we cannot

*Five. Genesis Rabbah*

claim that a classic debate is at hand, even though the extension in proof-texts signals the presence of exactly that.

### XII:II.
1.   A.   "For all these things has my hand made" (Is. 66:2):
   B.   R. Berekhiah in the name of R. Judah bar Simon: "It was not with hard work or heavy labor that the Holy One, blessed be he, created his world, and yet you say, 'All these things has my *hand* made' (Is. 66:2)?"
   C.   R. Yudan said, "It was on account of the merit of the Torah, to which reference is made in the verse, 'These are the laws, the judgments, and the torahs' (Lev. 26:46), that the world was made."
   D.   R. Joshua b. R. Nehemiah says, "It was on account of the merit of the tribes: 'And these are the names of the tribes' (Ez. 48:1). 'And so all these things came to be, says the Lord' (Is. 66:2)."
   E.   "Thus: 'These are the generations of heaven...' (Gen. 2:4)."

Here again, the proof-text suggests the presence of disputed propositions, each with its own support from Scripture. But only C, D represent a dispute on a common point.

### LVIII:VIII.
2.   A.   "...the field with the grave which was in it, and all the trees that were in the field, throughout its whole area:"
   B.   Said Rabbi, "How do we know on the basis of Scripture the rule that we have learned in the Mishnah: **He who sells a field has to write in the deed marks that characterize the field [M. B.B. 4:5]**?
   C.   "It is from this verse: '...the field with the grave which was in it, and all the trees that were in the field, throughout its whole area.'"

Here is a standard citation of a proof-text in support of a Halakhic proposition, 2.A.

### LX:V.
1.   A.   "The maiden was very fair to look upon, a virgin, whom no man had known" (Gen. 24:16):
   B.   We have learned in the Mishnah:
   C.   **"The marriage-settlement owing to a girl who had lost her virginity by the blow of a piece of wood is two hundred," the words of R. Meir.**
   D.   **And sages say, "As to a girl who had lost her virginity by the blow of a piece of wood, it is a maneh [one hundred]" [M. Ket. 1:3].**
   E.   R. Abbahu in the name of R. Eleazar: "The scriptural basis for the position of R. Meir is as follows: '... whom no man had known.' Lo, if she had lost her virginity by the blow of a piece of wood, she remains a virgin."
   F.   "The scriptural basis for the position of sages is as follows: '... a virgin.' Lo, if she had lost her virginity by the blow of a piece of wood, she would not have been regarded as a virgin."

Here is another instance in which a passage of the Mishnah is given scriptural support in the Aggadic compilation.

## LXXII:IV.
1. A. "[Rachel said, 'Then he may lie with you tonight for your son's mandrakes.'] When Jacob came from the field in the evening, [Leah went out to meet him and said, 'You must come in to me, for I have hired you with my son's mandrakes.' So he lay with her that night]" (Gen. 30:15-17):
   B. We have learned in the Mishnah: **He who hires workers and made an agreement with them to get up for work earlier than is the norm or to work later in the evening than is the norm — in a place in which it is not customary to get up early or to stay late, he cannot force them to do so [M. B.M. 7:1].**
   C. Said R. Mana, "In a place in which there is no customary practice, the rule is covered by the generally applicable stipulation of the court. This requires that going forth to work is on the householder's time, and coming home from work is on the worker's time, as it is said, 'The sun rises, they [animals] slink away and couch in their dens,' and then: 'Man goes forth to his work, and to his labor until the evening' (Ps. 104:22-23)."
   D. Said R. Ammi in the name of R. Simeon b. Laqish, "If it is a Friday afternoon, they have placed on the householder the burden, so that the return from work is on his time.
   E. "To what extent [must the householder allow the workers on Friday to come home early]? To such an extent that each one has the time to fill a jug of water and to roast a fish for himself and to light a candle."

It is hard to point to C as proof for the Halakhic proposition of B, and the rest amplifies the matter.

## LXXII:VI.
1. A. "[And Leah conceived again and she bore Jacob a sixth son.] Then Leah said, 'God has endowed me with a good dowry; now my husband will honor me, [because I have borne him six sons,' so she called his name Zebulun]" (Gen. 30:20):
   B. As to a field, so long as you manure it and hoe it, it produces fruit. [The name of Zebulun and of the verb, "endowed with a good dowry" are connected to the word for "manure," which shares the same consonants. Hence (Freedman, p. 666, n.1:) "The more children I bear the more he will love me."]
2. A. "Afterwards she bore him a daughter and called her name Dinah" (Gen. 30:21):
   B. **If a man's wife was pregnant and he said, "May it please God that my wife give birth to a male child," lo, this is a vain prayer [M. Ber. 9:3].**
   C. A member of the house of R. Yannai said, "The cited paragraph of the Mishnah treats a case in which the wife is already sitting on the labor stool [by which point the matter is decided, one way or the other, anyhow]."

*Five. Genesis Rabbah*

D. Said R. Judah bar Pazzi, "Even if the wife is already sitting on the labor stool, the sex of the child can change, in line with this verse: 'O house of Israel, cannot I do with you as this potter? says the Lord. Behold, as the clay in the potter's hand, so are you in my hand, O House of Israel' (Jer. 18:6)."

E. An objection was raised from the following verse: "Afterwards she bore him a daughter and called her name Dinah." [There was no issue of changing the birth of that child at the last minute.]

F. He said to them, "In point of fact, while Dinah was taking shape, in the main she was to be male, but on account of the prayer of Rachel, who had said, 'May the Lord add to me another son!' (Gen. 30:24), she was turned into a girl-child.. [Freedman, p. 666, n. 7: Since Jacob was only destined to beget twelve sons, this one had to be a daughter.]"

As before, so here too, the role of Scripture in sustaining the Halakhic role is marginal.

### LXXXI:III.

1. A. "So Jacob said to his household and to all who were with him, 'Put away the foreign gods that are among you and purify yourselves and change your garments. [Then let us arise and go up to Bethel, that I may make there an altar to the God who answered me in the day of my distress and has been with me wherever I have gone]'" (Gen. 25:2-3):

   B. R. Keruspedai in the name of R. Yohanan: "We are not so expert in the details of the rules of idolatry as Jacob was. For we have learned in the Mishnah: **He who finds garments with the figure of the sun or moon or a dragon incised upon them should take them to the Salt Sea [M. A.Z. 3:3]**."

   C. Said R. Yohanan, "All forms of clothing are affected by the prohibition against idolatry." [Freedman, p. 748, n. 2: "All figures that such clothing may bear subjects the clothing to the prohibition. Jacob therefore had his children change all their garments, which the text understands to mean those which they had taken as spoil in Shechem and which had been used there in the service of idolatry. That is a mark of how well informed he was about idolatry. The verse that follows justifies this rather acute observation.]

The allusion to the statement of Jacob, B, hardly represents an invocation of scriptural support for the cited law of the Mishnah.

## v. The Types of Analysis in Genesis Rabbah

The upshot is unanticipated. Having drawn so rigid a distinction between Aggadic and Halakhic discourse, I had expected that the types of analysis characteristic of the former would not correspond in any significant manner with those typical of the latter. I had supposed that I should find either of the analytical modes of inquiry or no serious analytical interest at all. But the first Aggadic compilation to come under scrutiny yields counterparts to all four of the Halakhic types of analysis. When we control for the difference in the kind of material under study, allowing the Aggadah to pursue its interests, we find that the Aggadic types of analysis represent effective adaptations, for the Aggadic setting, of the Halakhic types. Thus the careful scrutiny of words and phrases, characteristic of the Halakhah in its reading of the Mishnah, finds a counterpart, for theological or exegetical purposes to be sure, in the Aggadic corpus of Genesis Rabbah.

Indeed, the representation of linguistic analysis proves so remarkably rich that a mere fraction of the available cases sufficed. The Halakhic interest in establishing the rationality of conflicting rulings on a shared agendum finds its counterpart in the Aggadic care to balance opinions on the same subject, so that each position enjoys plausibility and ample scriptural support. There are few cases in which one part is set up as a straw man for the other to demolish, and many in which exact balance marks the representation of conflicting opinions. Further, we found exactly that same interest in adducing proof in Scripture for Halakhic propositions that the Halakhic documents evince, and not only so, but an equivalent commitment to finding Scriptural support for Aggadic propositions manifested itself in a rich way.

Since the generative hermeneutics of the Halakhah derives its force from analogical-contrastive argument and analysis, indeed since the definitive category-formations of the Mishnah and therefore of the Halakhah derive from analogy- and category-criticism, I took for granted that in the Aggadic documents I would find no counterpart to that mode of thought, so integral as it is of the Halakhah. I could not have been more wrong. The Aggadah adapts for its own purposes that very same mode of analytical inquiry. As we have seen, the comparison and contrast of parables turns out to function in the Aggadah as does the comparison and contrast of category-formations and their components in the Halakhah. Drawing an analogy permits the parable, whether or not in narrative form, to sustain a position classifying the unknown by comparison and contrast to the known, as much as does the Halakhic argument on whether the comparison between the known classification to the unknown one is apt or not.

The unanticipated result is, the Halakhic and the Aggadic modes of thought meet in the types of analysis characteristic of each kind of writing and corpus of data of a particular order. In the companion volume to this one, furthermore, we shall see that, when it comes to types of argument, one of the two types (admittedly a compendious category) serves for the Halakhic and the Aggadic dispute equally well.

Now we shall see whether the same category-formations of types of analysis serve other Aggadic documents.

# 6

# Leviticus Rabbah

The framers of Leviticus Rabbah, closed in the mid-fifth century, set forth, in the thirty-seven *parashiyyot* or chapters into which their document is divided, thirty-seven well-crafted propositions. They made no pretense at a systematic exegesis of sequences of verses of Scripture, abandoning the verse by verse mode of organizing discourse They struck out on their own to compose a means of expressing their propositions in a more systematic and cogent way. Each of the thirty-seven chapters proves cogent, and all of them spell out their respective statements in an intellectually economical, if rich, manner. Each *parashah* makes its own point, but all of them furthermore form a single statement. The message of Leviticus Rabbah — congruent with that of Genesis Rabbah — is that the laws of history may be known, and that these laws, so far as Israel is concerned, focus upon the holy life of the community. If Israel then obeys the laws of society aimed at Israel's sanctification, then the foreordained history, resting on the merit of the ancestors, will unfold as Israel hopes. So there is no secret to the meaning of the events of the day, and Israel, for its part, can affect its destiny and effect salvation.

The authorship of Leviticus Rabbah has thus joined the two great motifs, sanctification and salvation, by reading a biblical book, Leviticus, that is devoted to the former in the light of the requirements of the latter. In this way they made their fundamental point, which is that salvation at the end of history depends upon sanctification in the here and now. To prove these points, the authors of the compositions make lists of facts that bear the same traits and show the working of rules of history. It follows that the mode of thought brought to bear upon the theme of history remains exactly the same as in the Mishnah: list-making, with data exhibiting similar taxonomic traits drawn together into lists based on common monothetic traits or definitions. These lists then through the power of repetition make a single enormous point or prove a social law of history. The catalogues of exemplary heroes and historical events serve a further purpose. They provide a model of how contemporary events are to be absorbed into the biblical paradigm.

Since biblical events exemplify recurrent happenings, sin and redemption, forgiveness and atonement, they lose their one-time character. At the same time and in the same way, current events find a place within the ancient, but eternally present, paradigmatic scheme. So no new historical events, other than exemplary episodes in lives of heroes, demand narration because, through what is said about the past, what was happening in the times of the framers of Leviticus Rabbah would also come under consideration.

## I. LANGUAGE-ANALYSIS

Language-analysis in Halakhic texts yields insight into the law, and, in the Aggadic ones equivalent interest in meanings of words and phrases bears theological results.

### I:IX
1. A. "And (the Lord) called to Moses" (Lev. 1:1) (bearing the implication, to Moses in particular).
   B. Now did he not call Adam? (But surely he did:) "And the Lord God called Adam" (Gen. 3:9).
   C. (He may have called him, but he did not speak with him, while at Lev. 1:1, the Lord "called Moses and spoke to him"), for is it not undignified for a king to speak with his tenant farmer (which Adam, in the Garden of Eden, was)?
   D. "... and the Lord spoke to him" (Lev. 1:1) (to him in particular).
   E. Did he not speak also with Noah? (But surely he did:) "And God speak to Noah" (Gen. 8:15).
   F. (He may have spoken to him, but he did not call him,) for is it not undignified for a king to speak with (better: call) his ship's captain (herding the beasts into the ark)?
   G. "And (the Lord) called to Moses" (Lev. 1:1) (in particular).
   H. Now did he not call Abraham? (But surely he did:) "And the angel of the Lord called Abraham a second time from heaven" (Gen. 22:15).
   I. (He may have called him, but he did not speak with him,) for is it not undignified for a king to speak with his host (Gen. 18:1)?
   J. "And the Lord spoke with him" (Lev. 1:1) (in particular).
   K. And did he not speak with Abraham? (Surely he did:) "And Abram fell on his face, and (God) spoke with him" (Gen. 17:3).
   L. But is it not undignified for a king to speak with his host?

The formulation, "call... spoke...," yields the specified lessons of a theological character. At interest is the particular lesson yielded by the language, specifically the unique standing of Moses, when compared with Adam and with Noah and with Abraham. In a Halakhic setting, the proposition that is yielded by the peculiarities of language is articulated; here it is left for us to identify the point, which is, Moses is unique in the setting of both antediluvian Man, the Noachides, and even Israel.

## Six. Leviticus Rabbah

### IX:I

1. A. "This is the law governing the sacrifice of peace offerings ( . . . If he offers it for a thanksgiving)" (Lev. 7:11-12).
   B. "He who brings thanksgiving as his sacrifice honors me; (to him who orders his way aright I will show the salvation of God)" (Ps. 50:23).
   C. R. Huna in the name of R. Aha said, "'He who brings a sin offering as his sacrifice,' (or) 'he who brings a guilt offering as his sacrifice' is not written here, rather, 'He who brings thanksgiving as his sacrifice honors me.'"
2. A. R. Yudan in the name of R. Abba bar Kahana: "'Honors me' (with a single N, YKBDNY) is not written here, but rather, 'honors me' (with two Ns, thus YKBDNNY). (The doubling of the N) means that such a one has honored me in this world and honored me in the world to come.
   B. "Another interpretation: 'Honors me' (with two Ns) means one expression of honor after another."
   3. A. Another interpretation: "'Honors me' refers to Achan, who sacrificed his impulse to do evil as a thanksgiving offering."
      B. That is in line with the following verse of Scripture: "Then Joshua said to Achan, 'My son, give honor to the Lord God of Israel and render a thanksgiving offering (RSV: praise) to him; and tell me now what you have done; do not hide it from me'" (Josh. 7:19).

The manner of spelling the pertinent word, duplicating the consonant, yields the stated lesson, 2.A, B. The word-choice, "honors," resonates with the specific case of Achan, who made a thanksgiving offering. So the intersecting verse, 1.B, illuminates the base-verse, 1.A, by supplying a concrete context in which the thanksgiving offering is presented. No. 2 then introduces another dimension altogether, this world and the world to come. Honoring God by thanksgiving offerings represent honor in this world and the next. We should not miss the particular relevance of No. 3 to No. 2. By telling the truth, Achan incurred the death penalty, but he also won a place for himself in the world to come, a matter made explicit at M. San. 6:2:

A. (When) he was ten cubits from the place of stoning, they say to him, "Confess," for it is usual for those about to be put to death to confess.
B. For whoever confesses has a share in the world to come.
C. For so we find concerning Achan, to whom Joshua said, "My son, I pray you, give glory to the Lord, the God of Israel, and confess to him, (and tell me now what you have done; hide it not from me.) And Achan answered Joshua and said, Truly have I sinned against the Lord, the God of Israel, and thus and thus I have done" (Josh. 7:19). And how do we know that his confession achieved atonement for him? For it is said, "And Joshua said, Why have you troubled us? The Lord will trouble you this day" (Josh. 7:25) — This day you will be troubled, but you will not be troubled in the world to come.

So Achan embodies those who atone for their sins in this world and so win the world to come, and that reading means, the thanksgiving offering effects atonement, which is the proposition of the composite. This represents a particularly subtle form of linguistic analysis, highly characteristic of Midrash-Aggadah in general. Just as linguistic analysis of Mishnah- or Tosefta- formulations of the Halakhah yields insight into the Halakhah that transcend the case at hand and propose a governing proposition, so the same type of analysis yields theological propositions of considerable, general interest.

## XIX:V

5. A. "For many days Israel (was without the true God and without a teaching priest and without the Torah)" (2 Chron. 15:3).
   B. Now was it really a matter of many days? (No,) but because they were days of anguish, the author calls them many.
      C. Along these same lines: "And it came to pass after many days, and the word of the Lord came to Elijah" (1 Kgs. 18:1).
      D. R. Berekhiah and R. Helbo in the name of R. Yohanan: "It was a matter of three months at the outset and three months at the end and twelve in the middle, so in all, eighteen months."
      E. And were they so many? (No.)
      F. But because they were days of anguish, therefore the author calls them many.
      G. And along these same lines: "And it came to pass in the course of those many days (that the king of Egypt died)" (Ex. 2:23).
      H. Now were they many? (No.) But because they were days of anguish, therefore the author calls them many.
      I. And along these same lines: "Many days, one hundred eighty days" (Est. 1:4).
      J. Now were they many days? (No.) But because (they were days of anguish, the author therefore calls them many).
      6. A. And there is the following verse: "If a woman has a discharge of blood for many days" (Lev. 15:25).
         B. R. Hiyya taught (Y. Yoma 2:4), "The reference to 'days' is to two days, and to 'many' means that three days in all (are under discussion).
         C. "From that time onward (if a woman continues to produce blood), the woman is not regarded as a menstruant but as a 'sick' woman (that is, afflicted by flux in line with Lev. 15:25)."
         D. "And a menstruating woman in her menstrual period" is not written here but rather, "And a sick woman in her menstrual period" (Lev. 15:33).

The point is, "many days" are many by reason of misery. That point is announced at A-B, then instantiated at C-F, G-H, I-J. A Halakhic case serves equally well, as No. 6, inserted whole, indicates. The Aggadic demonstration of the meanings

*Six. Leviticus Rabbah* 97

and implications of particular language forms the counterpart to the Halakhic process of linguistic analysis. Here the proposition is theological, there, legal, but the type of analysis is the same.

## II. ANALOGY- AND CATEGORY-CRITICISM

Just as Halakhic problems are solved by identifying the governing legal model or analogy, so Aggadic ones invite the invocation of appropriate parables. If a case is likened to one sort of situation, it will yield one set of implications, to another, a different set.

### II:I
1. A. "Speak to the children of Israel (and say to them, when any man of you brings an offering to the Lord, you shall bring your offering of cattle from the herd or from the flock)" (Lev. 1:2).
   B. "Is Ephraim a precious son to me? (Is he a child that is dandled? For as often as I speak of him, I still keep mentioning him)" (Jer. 31:20).

### II:V
1. A. Said R. Simeon b. Yohai, "(The matter may be compared) to a king who had an only son. Every day he would give instructions to his steward, saying to him, 'Make sure my son eats, make sure my son drinks, make sure my son goes to school, make sure my son comes home from school.'
   B. "So every day the Holy One, blessed be he, gave instructions to Moses, saying, 'Command the children of Israel,' 'Say to the children of Israel,' 'Speak to the children of Israel.'"
2. A. Said R. Judah b. R. Simon, "(The matter may be compared) to a person who was sitting and making a crown for the king. Someone passed by and said to him, 'What are you doing?'
   B. "He replied, 'Making a crown for the king.'
   C. "He said to him, 'Whatever (precious stones) that you can affix (to the crown) you should affix, put on emeralds, put on jewels, put on pearls. For that crown is going to be put on the head of the king.'
   D. "So too did the Holy One, blessed be he, say to Moses, 'In whatever way you can praise Israel, give that praise, if you can magnify them, do it, if you can adorn them, do it. Why? Because through (Israel) I am going to be glorified.' (That is) in line with the following verse of Scripture: 'And he said to me, You are my servant, Israel, in whom I will be glorified'" (Is. 49:3).

At issue are the instructions of Lev. 1:2: God's telling Moses to speak to Israel. That generates the criticism of the correct analogy: To what is God's relationship with Israel likened? Is the relationship like that of a king to his son via his steward, representing Moses? Or is it like a passerby to a craftsman, making a crown for the king? The theological issue is explicit in the first parable: Moses is God's steward in relationship to Israel, carrying out God's instruction for his children.

In the second, Moses is called upon to glorify Israel; he is not the steward and intermediary, but a servant. Framed in theological language, these parables yield different theories of the person and role of Moses. But the correspondence to Halakhic analogy-criticism is only formal.

## V:VII

1. A. "(If the whole congregation of Israel commits a sin unwittingly and the thing is hidden from the eyes of the assembly, and they do any one of the things which the Lord has commanded not to be done and are guilty, when the sin which they have committed becomes known, the assembly shall offer a young bull for a sin offering and bring it before the tent of meeting;) and the elders of the congregation shall lay their hands (upon the head of the bull before the Lord)" (Lev. 4:13-15).
   B. (Since, in laying their hands (SMK) on the head of the bull, the elders sustain (SMK) the community by adding to it the merit they enjoy,) said R. Isaac, "The nations of the world have none to sustain them, for it is written, 'And those who sustain Egypt will fall' (Ez. 30:6).
   C. "But Israel has those who sustain it, as it is written: 'And the elders of the congregation shall lay their hands (and so sustain Israel)'" (Lev. 4:15).

### TOPICAL COMPOSITE ON ISRAEL AS A COLLECTIVITY VS. THE NATIONS OF THE WORLD AS A COLLECTIVITY

2. A. Said R. Eleazar, "The nations of the world are called a congregation, and Israel is called a congregation.
   B. "The nations of the world are called a congregation: 'For the congregation of the godless shall be desolate' (Job 15:34).
   C. "And Israel is called a congregation: 'And the elders of the congregation shall lay their hands' (Lev. 4:15).
   D. "The nations of the world are called sturdy bulls and Israel is called sturdy bulls.
   E. "The nations of the world are called sturdy bulls: 'The congregation of (sturdy) bulls with the calves of the peoples' (Ps. 68:31).
   F. "Israel is called sturdy bulls, as it is said, 'Listen to me, you sturdy (bullish) of heart' (Is. 46:13).
   G. "The nations of the world are called excellent, and Israel is called excellent.
   H. "The nations of the world are called excellent: 'You and the daughters of excellent nations' (Ex. 32:18).
   I. "Israel is called excellent: 'They are the excellent, in whom is all my delight' (Ps. 16:4).
   J. "The nations of the world are called sages, and Israel is called sages.
   K. "The nations of the world are called sages: 'And I shall wipe out sages from Edom' (Ob. 1:8).
   L. "And Israel is called sages: 'Sages store up knowledge' (Prov. 10:14).
   M. "The nations of the world are called unblemished, and Israel is called unblemished.

## Six. Leviticus Rabbah

- N. "The nations of the world are called unblemished: 'Unblemished as are those that go down to the pit' (Prov. 1:12).
- O. "And Israel is called unblemished: 'The unblemished will inherit goodness' (Prov. 28:10).
- P. "The nations of the world are called men, and Israel is called men.
- Q. "The nations of the world are called men: 'And you men who work iniquity' (Ps. 141:4).
- R. "And Israel is called men: 'To you who are men I call' (Prov. 8:4).
- S. "The nations of the world are called righteous, and Israel is called righteous.
- T. "The nations of the world are called righteous: 'And righteous men shall judge them' (Ez. 23:45).
- U. "And Israel is called righteous: 'And your people — all of them are righteous' (Is. 60:21).
- V. "The nations of the world are called mighty, and Israel is called mighty.
- W. "The nations of the world are called mighty: 'Why do you boast of evil, O mighty man' (Ps. 52:3).
- X. "And Israel is called mighty: 'Mighty in power, those who do his word' (Ps. 103:20).

Here is a exercise in category-criticism. The category is "humanity," divided into Israel and "the nations of the world.," species of the common genus. Then the speciation is systematic. The same traits that characterize Israel mark the nations of the world. They differ on the matter announced at the outset: The nations of the world have none to sustain them. But Israel has those who sustain it, and these are the sages. That outcome of the category-criticism leaves the striking proposition that the sages are what make Israel Israel.

### XXVI:IV

1. A. "(The heavens recount the glory of God; and the firmament proclaims his handiwork.) Day to day pours forth speech, (and night to night declares knowledge. There is no speech, nor are there words; their voice is not heard; yet their line goes out through all the earth and their words to the end of the world)" (Ps. 19:1-4).
    - B. It has been taught (y. Ber. 1:1): On the first day of the spring season in Nisan, and on the first day of the fall season of Tishré, the day and the night are equal above.
    - C. From that time onward, the day borrows from the night, or the night borrows from the day.
    - D. "Day to day pours forth speech" (without elaborate provision for recompense).
    - E. But (that is not how things are here) down on earth, for how many deeds and decrees there are (to secure compensation).
    - F. "Their line goes out through all the earth" (Ps. 19:4).
    - G. R. Shalom in the name of R. Ahbah son of R. Zira: "(The matter may be compared) to the case of one who received dominion from the king.

H. "Before he reaches the borders of his province, he walks along like an ordinary person. But once he reaches the borders of his province, he walks about like a nobleman.
  I. "So before they go forth to the world: 'There is no speech, there are no words' (Ps. 19:3).
  J. "But once they go forth to the world, how many deeds and decrees there are! 'Their line goes out through all the earth'" (Ps. 19:4).

**XXVI:V**

1. A. R. Berekhiah in the name of R. Levi: "The matter may be compared to an Israelite and a priest who were smitten with epilepsy.
   B. "The physician prescribed for them a well-tested amulet and gave orders to the Israelite (that he avoid cemeteries), but ignored the priest.
   C. "Said the priest to him, 'My lord, physician, did you not give the amulet to both of us simultaneously? Why then do you give orders to the Israelite but you leave me alone?'
   D. "He said to him, 'This is an Israelite, who ordinarily will walk among graves. (He should not do so wearing the amulet.) But you are a priest, and you do not ordinarily walk among graves. Therefore I gave orders to the Israelite, but I left you alone.'
   E. "Thus, because the passion to do evil is not found among the creatures of the upper world, a single act of speech suffices for them,
   F. "as it is said, 'The matter is by the decree of the watcher, and the sentence is by the word of the holy ones' (Dan. 4:14). (Thus there is only a single reference to 'word.')
   G. "But as to the creatures of the lower world, among whom the passion to do evil is commonplace, would that they could stand through two acts of speech!
   H. "That is in line with the following verse of Scripture: 'The Lord <u>said</u> to Moses, "<u>Speak</u> to the priests the sons of Aaron and say to them"' (Lev. 21:1) (thus two acts of speaking)."

The conflict of parables, XXVI:IV1.G-J vs. XXVI:V.1 A-H, focuses on how to explain why God has a great deal more to say to the lower beings, on earth, than to the upper beings, in Heaven. The issue is articulated, in so many words, in the second of the two parables, at E, G. The creatures of the lower world need more instructions. The former suffice with a single act of divine speech, the latter need two. So much for Berekhiah-Levi. The alternative parable has a king who behaves like others within his realm, but when he goes beyond the limits of his kingdom — thus from Heaven to earth — he conducts himself in a more assertive way. The first of the two parables then explains God's conduct in Heaven, where there is no speech and there are not words, but his change in demeanor on earth, "their line goes out through all the earth." The second of the two parables differentiates man on earth from angels in Heaven, and, by the way, Israel from the priesthood. Man on earth requires ample instruction by reason of the inclination to do evil, thus the Torah with its numerous requirements. The conflict between the two parables then yields

*Six. Leviticus Rabbah* 101

two quite distinct theological positions in respect to God's relationship to the upper and the lower beings: with or without the torah. The first of the two parables underscores the difference between God in Heaven and God's presence on earth through the commandments of the Torah. The second of them contrasts angels, who do not require the Torah, and men, who do.

### III. RATIONALITY

The demonstration that disputes are comprised by two (occasionally: three) equally plausible and reasonable positions constitutes a continuing project of Leviticus Rabbah. A few cases suffice to make the point. Ordinarily, what is subject to dispute is minor. But where significant propositions collide, the balance in the orderly presentation of each position and its proofs is maintained throughout. In most cases for Leviticus Rabbah, the rationality of the dispute is exposed with great clarity, and only a few comments are required.

**I:IV**
3.   A.   (Abin continues,) "'I have exalted one chosen from the people' (Ps. 89:20).
    B.   "'It is you, Lord, God, who chose Abram and took him out of Ur in Chaldea'" (Neh. 9:7).
4.   A.   ("I have exalted one chosen from the people" [Ps. 89:20]) speaks of David, with whom God spoke both in speech and in vision.
    D.   " . . . saying, 'I have set the crown upon one who is mighty,'" (Ps. 89:20) —
        E.   R. Abba bar Kahana and rabbis:
        F.   R. Abba bar Kahana said, "David made thirteen wars."
        G.   And rabbis say, "Eighteen."
        H.   But they do not really differ. The party who said thirteen wars (refers only to those that were fought) in behalf of the need of Israel (overall), while the one who held that (he fought) eighteen includes five (more, that David fought) for his own need, along with the thirteen (that he fought) for the need of Israel (at large).

The rationality of the dispute, E-H, is shown in the claim that, while the parties reach different conclusions, they do not really differ at all. That is one way of dealing with the dispute.

**VIII:I**
1.   A.   "The Lord said to Moses, "This is the offering which Aaron and his sons shall offer to the Lord on the day when he is anointed'" (Lev. 6:13 [RSV: 6:19]).
    B.   R. Levi bar Hita opened (discourse with the following verse:) "'For God is judge. This one he humbles, and that one he lifts up'" (Ps. 75:6).
3.   A.   R. Jonah of Bosrah and rabbis:
    B.   R. Jonah of Bosrah interpreted (Ps. 75:6) to speak of Israel: "With the word, 'this,' they were humbled, and with the word, 'this,' they were lifted up.

102                                    *Analysis and Argumentation in Rabbinic Judaism*

    C.    "With the word, 'this,' they were lifted up: 'This they shall give, every one that passes among them that are numbered, (a half a shekel for an offering to the Lord)' (Ex. 30:13).

    D.    "With the word, 'this,' they were humbled: 'As for this man, Moses, the man that brought us up out of Egypt, we do not know what has become of him'" (Ex. 32:1).

    E.    And rabbis interpreted the verse to speak (not of the people of Israel) but of Aaron: "With the word, 'this,' he was humbled, and with the word, 'this,' he was lifted up.

    F.    "With the word, 'this,' he was humbled: 'And I threw it into the fire and this [the gold calf] just came out' (Ex. 32:24).

    G.    "With the word, 'this,' he was lifted up: 'This is the offering which Aaron and his sons shall offer to the Lord on the day when he is anointed)'" (Lev. 6:13).

The issue is that to which "this" pertains, as B vs. E articulate matters. B has the matter refer to the people of Israel, exalted, then humbled by the word "this," and E says it pertains to Aaron, humbled and exalted with the same word. The close match of opposites contributes to the picture of a rational, not an arbitrary, dispute.

## XVI:I

1.    A.    "This shall be the law of the leper (for the day of his cleansing)" (Lev. 14:2).

    B.    "There are six things which the Lord hates, and seven which are an abomination to him: (haughty eyes, a lying tongue, hands that shed innocent blood, a heart that devises wicked plans, feet that make haste to run to do evil, a false witness who breathes out lies, and a man who sows discord among brothers)" (Prov. 6:16-19).

    C.    R. Meir and rabbis:

    D.    R. Meir said, "Six and seven add up to thirteen."

    E.    And rabbis say, "Seven (is the number of abominations)."

    F.    How do rabbis interpret the use of "And" ["And seven" (Prov. 6:16]?

    G.    This refers to the seventh on the list (gossiping), which is the worst of the lot.

    H.    And which one is it? It is "he who sows discord among brothers."

    I.    And what are the others? "Haughty eyes, a lying tongue, hands that shed innocent blood, a heart that devises wicked plans, feet that make haste to run to do evil, a false witness who breathes out lies, and a man who sows discord among brothers" (Prov. 6:17-19).

What makes the dispute rational is the effort to account for the difference of opinion ("how do rabbis interpret..."). The dispute takes place within the framework of concurrence on basic matters.

## XXII:I

1.    A.    "If any man of the house of Israel kills (an ox or a lamb or a goat in the camp, or kills outside the camp, and does not bring it to the door of the tent of meeting, to offer it as a gift to the Lord before the tabernacle of the Lord, blood-guilt shall be imputed to that man; he has shed blood; and that man shall

## Six. Leviticus Rabbah

be cut off from among his people. This is to the end that the people of Israel may bring their sacrifices which they slay in the open field, that they may bring them to the Lord, to the priest at the door of the tent of meeting, and slay them as sacrifices of peace offerings to the Lord)" (Lev. 17:3-5).

B. "For the superfluities of the land are among all of them (and a king makes himself servant to the field)" (Qoh. 5:8).

C. R. Judah and R. Nehemiah:

D. R. Judah said, "Even things that you regard as superfluous (are 'for a profit') for the world, for example, bast for making ropes, twigs for a hedge for a vineyard. So even they serve for the benefit of the world.

E. "'A king makes himself servant to a field.' Even a king who rules from one end of the world to the other 'makes himself servant to a field.' If the earth yields a crop, he can do something, but if the earth does not yield a crop, he cannot do anything.

F. "Therefore: 'He who loves silver will not be satisfied with silver' (Qoh. 5:9). If one loves money, he will not find satisfaction in money. For whoever covets and is greedy for money but has no real estate — what enjoyment does he have (in his capital)?"

3. A. R. Nehemiah said, "'For the superfluities of the land are among all of them.' Even things that you may regard as superfluities in the revelation of the Torah, for example, show fringes, phylacteries, and amulets for the doorpost, even they fall into the category of the revelation of the Torah [although laws concerning them are not spelled out]."

The dispute, 1.D vs. 3A, lacks the formal balance that is common in Halakhic disputes and, more often than not, in Aggadic ones as well. Judah expounds the verse in its entirety, but E-F make no impact on the dispute. Judah deems superfluities" to pertain to bast, twigs, and the like: all useful. Nehemiah has the word pertain to show fringes, phylacteries, and amulets, which are revealed by the Torah even though not spelled out. It is difficult to define much subject to dispute; each party reads the verse in his own framework, and neither opinion excludes the other or needs to intersect with the other. Here the dispute is formal, not substantive. Then issues of rationality do not arise.

### XXXII:IV

1. A. "Whose father was an Egyptian" (Lev. 24:10). — "He looked this way and that" (Ex. 2:12).

   L. Forthwith: "He saw that there was no man" (Ex. 2:12).

   M. What did he see? R. Judah, R. Nehemiah, and rabbis:

   N. R. Judah said, "He saw that there was no one else who would rise up and act zealously for the sake of the Holy One, blessed be he, by killing him, so he went and acted zealously for the sake of the Holy One, blessed be he, and killed him."

   O. R. Nehemiah said, "He saw that there was no one who would rise up and make mention in his regard of the name (of God) and kill him, so he went and made mention of the name of God and killed him."

|   | P. | Rabbis say, "He saw that nothing of value would ever come forth from that man, from his children, or from his descendants for all generations." |
|---|---|---|
| Q. | | Forthwith: "He smote the Egyptian" (Ex. 2:12). |
|   | R. | With what did he kill him? |
|   | S. | R. Isaac said, "He killed him with his fist. That is in line with the following verse of Scripture: 'And to smite with the fist of wickedness'" (Is. 58:4). |
|   | T. | R. Levi said, "He smote him with the Mystery of Israel (by stating the Ineffable Name)." |
|   | U. | (Supply: That is in line with the following verse of Scripture: "'Is it to kill me that you intend?' And he hid him in the sand" (Ex. 2:12). He hid him on account of Israel, who are compared to sand.) That is in line with the following verse of Scripture: "And the number of the people of Israel will be like the number of grains of sand on the seashore" (Hos. 2:2). |

The two disputes, M-P, R-T, represent minor glosses. The first present a reasonable difference: he saw no one else who would act, so Judah, or who would act by invoking God's name, so Nehemiah; rabbis change the frame of reference altogether. They see nothing coming from the man. The dispute, S, T, involves whether Moses killed the man by a physical action or by invoking God's name.

## XXXVI:I

1. A. "Of old you laid out the foundation of the earth, and the heavens are the work of your hands" (Ps. 102:25).

### TOPICAL COMPOSITE ON PRECEDENCE

B. The House of Shammai and the House of Hillel:
C. The House of Shammai say, "The heaven was created first, and then the earth."
D. The House of Hillel say, "The earth was created first, then the heaven."
E. This party brings a proof text for its opinion, and that party brings a proof text for its view.
F. In the view of the House of Shammai, who maintain that the heaven was created first and then the earth, we may make a comparison. To what is the matter comparable?
G. To the case of a king who made a throne. Only after he made the throne did he make its footstool. Thus: "So says the Lord, 'The heaven is my throne, and the earth the dust at my feet'" (Is. 66:1).
H. In the view of the House of Hillel, who maintain that the earth was created first and then the heaven, we may make a comparison. (To what is the matter comparable?)
I. To the case of a king who built himself a palace. Only after he builds the lower floors does he build the upper floors.
J. So it is written, "My hand laid the foundation of the earth, and my right hand (then) spread out the heaven" (Is. 48:13).

K. Said R. Haninah, "Also the following verse of Scripture supports the position of the House of Hillel: 'Of old you laid out the foundations of the earth,' and afterward: 'and the heavens are the work of your hands'" (Ps. 102:25).
L. Said R. Judah, "From the very passage of Scripture which is adduced in support of the position of the House of Shammai, the House of Hillel find proof to dismiss that same position.
M. "In the view of the House of Shammai, who maintain that the heaven was created first and then the earth, (the following proof text confirms their position:) 'In the beginning God created the heaven and the earth' (Gen. 1:1).
N. "In the view of the House of Hillel, who say that the earth was created first, then the heaven: 'And the earth was unformed and void' (Gen. 1:2), indicating that the earth already was in being."

Here is the model of the rational dispute, with each party assigned pertinent proof texts in balance with the other, and then with each party given a chance to introduce its own parable. So the dispute covers reasonable positions on both sides, each position closely balanced against the other.

## IV. SCRIPTURAL FOUNDATIONS OF THE HALAKHAH

We cannot expect to find a rich trove of compositions in which Aggadic documents attempt to support Halakhic rulings.

## XV:VIII

1. A. It has been taught (Sifra Negaim Pereq 4:3:) **How do (priests) examine a leprosy spot?**
   B. A man is examined as one who hoes or one who harvests olives, as one who hoes in respect to the private parts, and as one who harvests olives in regard to the armpit.
   C. And a woman (is examined) as one who weaves (Sifra: who rolls out dough) and as one who suckles her infant, as one who weaves (Sifra: rolls out dough) with respect to the private parts, and as one who suckles her infant with regard to the area under the breast. As one who weaves at a loom with regard to the armpit of the right hand.
   D. R. Judah says, "Also as one who spins flax with regard to the left."
   E. Just as one is examined with respect to a leprosy sign, so he is examined with respect to shaving himself (after the leprosy sign has been declared clean, during the rite of purification).
2. A. It has been taught (M. Neg. 2:5:) **All leprosy signs does a person examine, except for his own.**
   B. R. Meir says, "Also not those of his relatives."
3. A. Who inspected the leprosy sign of Miriam?

B. If you claim that it was Moses who examined it, can one who is not a priest examine leprosy signs? If you say that it was Aaron who did so, (we know that) a relative may not examine leprosy signs.
C. Said the Holy One, blessed be he, "I shall serve as priest to her. I shall shut her up, I am the one who will declare her clean."
D. That is in line with the following verse of Scripture: "And the people did not undertake a journey until Miriam was brought in again (having been declared clean)" (Num. 12:14).
E. Said R. Simon, "The people were with the Indwelling Presence of God, and God's presence was waiting on her."

4. A. R. Levi in the name of R. Hama b. R. Haninah, "Moses was greatly pained by this matter: 'Is it appropriate to the standing of my brother, Aaron, that he should examine leprosy signs?'
B. "Said to him the Holy One, blessed be he, 'Now does the priest not enjoy the benefit of the twenty-four gifts (that are given to the priests)?'"
C. In a proverb people say, "He who eats palm's heart will be flogged by a stick of a dried-up palm.'"

The first entry cites the indicated Halakhic passage, and then we find a gloss at No. 3, amplifying the cited rule for the case of Miriam. The point here is, the Halakhah makes a general rule that relatives may not inspect one another's leprosy-signs. The Aggadah then makes the matter concrete and places it within the scriptural narrative. Here is a case in which the Aggadah serves the Halakhic setting with great effect.

## XXVII:III

1. A. R. Jacob b. R. Zabedi in the name of R. Abbahu opened (discourse by citing the following verse:) "'And it shall never again be the reliance of the house of Israel, recalling their iniquity, (when they turn to them for aid. Then they will know that I am the Lord God)' (Ez. 29:16).
B. "It is written, 'Above him stood the seraphim: (each had six wings, with two he covered his face, and with two he covered his feet, and with two he flew)' (Is. 6:2).
C. "'With two he flew' — singing praises.
D. "'With two he covered his face' — so as not to gaze upon the Presence of God.
E. "'And with two he covered his feet' — so as not to let them be seen by the face of the Presence of God.
F. "For it is written, 'And the soles of their feet were like the sole of a calf's foot' (Ez. 1:6).
G. "And it is written, 'They made for themselves a molten calf' (Ex. 32:8).
H. "So (in covering their feet, they avoided calling to mind the molten calf,) in accord with the verse, 'And it shall never again be the reliance of the house of Israel, recalling their iniquity'" (Ez. 29:16).

2. A. There we have learned in the Mishnah (M. R.H. 3:2): **"All (horns) are suitable except for that of a cow."**

## Six. Leviticus Rabbah

    B.    Why except for that of the cow? Because it is the horn of a calf.
    C.    And it is written, "They made for themselves a molten calf" (Ex. 32:8).
    D.    So (in not using the horn of a cow, they avoid calling to mind the molten calf, in accord with the verse), "And it shall never again be the reliance of the house of Israel, recalling their iniquity" (Ez. 29:16).

5.    A.    And so too here: "When a bull or a sheep or a goat is born" (Lev. 22:27).
    B.    Now is it born as a bull and not as a calf? But because it is said, "They made for themselves a molten calf," therefore the Scripture refers to it as a bull and not as a calf: "A bull, a sheep, a goat."

What the Aggadic composition contributes at No. 2 is a moral lesson to account for the Halakhic rule. Why not use the specified horn? Because it calls to mind the sin of the golden calf. The entire cult, then, is represented as the antidote to Israel's sin at Sinai. The Halakhic lesson, No. 2, is repeated at No. 5's Aggadic formulation. Here again the contribution of the Aggadah is to realize, within the scriptural narrative, the Halakhic generalization. The Aggadic response to the Halakhah makes the rule an embodiment of a lesson in Israel's sacred history.

## XXVII:X

1.    A.    "(When a bull or sheep or goat is born,) it shall remain seven days with its mother; (from the eighth day on it shall be acceptable as an offering by fire to the Lord)" (Lev. 22:27).
    B.    Why for seven days?
    C.    So that the beast may be inspected, for if the dam should have gored it, or if some disqualifying blemish should turn up on it, lo, it will be invalid and not be suitable for an offering.
    D.    For we have learned (M. Nid. 5:1): **"That which goes forth from the side (delivered by Caesarian section) — they do not sit out the days of uncleanness and the days of cleanness (Lev. 12:1ff.) on its account, and they are not liable on its account for an offering.**
    E.    **"R. Simeon says, 'Lo, this is like one that is born (naturally) (so that the rules of Lev. 12:1ff. do apply).'"**

2.    A.    Another interpretation: "It shall remain seven days with its mother" (Lev. 22:27).
    B.    Why for seven days?
    C.    R. Joshua of Sikhnin in the name of R. Levi said, "The matter may be compared to the case of a king who came into a town and made decrees, saying, 'None of the residents who are here will see me before they first see my lady.'
    D.    "Said the Holy One, blessed be he, 'You will not make an offering before me until a Sabbath shall have passed over (the animal that is to be offered), for seven days cannot pass without a Sabbath, and (for the same reason) the rite of circumcision (takes place on the eighth day) so that it cannot take place without the advent of a Sabbath.
    E.    "'And from the eighth day on it shall be acceptable (as an offering by fire to the Lord)'" (Lev. 22:27).

The Aggadah finds a reason for the Halakhic rule, so No. 1. No. 2 goes over the matter from another perspective altogether. The Halakhah requires keeping the offspring for a week, and requires explanation. D-E illustrate the rule and account for it, showing that the governing consideration is as specified at B-C. The other interpretation supplies a narrative-Aggadic reason for the rule, complete with a parable and its concretization. This is a fine case of an Aggadic foundation for a Halakhic ruling.

## v. The Types of Analysis in Leviticus Rabbah

The Aggadic document presents counterparts to each of the Halakhic analytical initiatives, some corresponding precisely, some only approximately. Language-analysis yields insight bearing theological implications, which are not articulated but readily identified. I:IX.1 in a detail manages to examine the standing of Moses in comparison with Adam, Noah, and Abraham. IX:I.1-3 invoke the theme of atonement here for entry into the world to come later on. XIX:V finds in the language at hand that "many days" may refer to only a few, miserable days, which seem long. The upshot is simply stated: linguistic analysis serves theological as much as legal inquiry, and the results are equivalently formidable in the issues that they raise.

The counterpart to Halakhic critique of category-formations, inclusive of the Halakhic interest in identifying the correct analogy, is the Aggadic exchange of parables in a dispute. Here too, the character of the parable, comparable to the Halakhic analogy or category-formation, dictates the outcome of a dispute. II:IV, V works on the appropriate comparison to define God's relationship with Israel. The counterpart to a dispute on the correct category-formation is contained in the comparison of Israel with the nations of the world, V:VII; the two are shown to be completely comparable, point by point, with the one difference imposed from on high: Israel has those who sustain it, but the nations do not, and these are the sages. The exchange of parables at XXVI:IV-V produces an equivalent result. So, in all, the analytical initiatives of the Aggadah form a counterpart to those of the Halakhah, controlling for the difference in the assignments of each genre of writing, respectively.

Demonstrating the rationality of disputes — the effort to expose the reasonable basis for both sides of a dispute, so underscoring the logical coherence of the system as a whole — requires little comment. Both Halakhic and Aggadic disputes are rendered in balance, with each side given both a reasonable position based on premises shared with the other, and also ample opportunity to adduce evidence in the form of proof-texts for its chosen position. In our examination of *Types of Argumentation* (Chapter Fourteen, below) we shall further note that each party is ordinarily given the opportunity to dispose of the proofs presented by the other. XXXVI:I.1 is a fine example of such a meticulous balance between positions and arguments therefor, inclusive, here, of both proof-texts and parables. All of this is

## Six. Leviticus Rabbah

in exact comparison with the Halakhic disputes and the sustained interest in their rationality.

We cannot claim that the Aggadah, in the nature of things, is going to form a rich source of demonstrations of the scriptural foundations of the Halakhah. But we do note at XV:VIII an Aggadic amplification of a Halakhic rule, which is cited and then translated into a concrete, narrative case of Scripture.

We once more find ourselves able to match the principal Halakhic types of analysis with Aggadic counterparts. A single program of analytical inquiry, natural to the Halakhah, is adapted for Aggadic discourse as well and yields modest but irrefutable evidence of a single mode of thought governing throughout the Rabbinic writings, Aggadic and Halakhic alike.

So much for Midrash-Aggadah, the exegetical genre as applied to the exposition of Aggadic narrative and theological discourse. Now, with Sifré to Numbers, we shall ask whether the exegetical genre obscures the established analytical program of the Halakhah in the setting of Midrash-Halakhah, the exegetical genre as applied to the exposition of Halakhic passages of Scripture. This is the final step in establishing that the modes of thought embodied in the types of analysis under consideration here govern throughout the genres of Rabbinic writing. We shall now see that they do.

# 7

# Sifré to Numbers

Sifré to Numbers provides a miscellaneous reading of most of the book of Numbers, but examining the implicit propositions of the recurrent forms of the document yields a clear-cut purpose. While the document follows no topical program, it makes recurrent efforts to prove a few fundamental points. The document as a whole through its fixed and recurrent formal preferences or literary structures makes two complementary points. [1] Reason unaided by Scripture produces uncertain propositions. [2] Reason operating within the limits of Scripture produces truth. These two complementary principles are never articulated but left implicit in the systematic reading of most of the book of Numbers, verse by verse. The exegetical forms stand for a single proposition: the human mind joins God's mind when humanity receives and sets forth the Torah. The Torah opens the road into the mind of God, and our minds can lead us on that road, because our mind and God's mind are comparable. We share a common rationality.

Only when we examine the rhetorical plan and then in search of the topical program reconsider the forms of the document does this propositional program emerge. Sifré to Numbers follows no topical program distinct from that of Scripture, which is systematically clarified. What we shall now see is that Midrash-Halakhah, amply represented in Sifré to Numbers, though exegetical in character, sets forth types of analysis such as govern in the expository-Halakhic documents, Mishnah-Tosefta-Yerushalmi-Bavli.

### I. THE PRIORITY OF SCRIPTURE OVER ANALOGICAL-CONTRASTIVE REASONING

The principal analytical initiative characteristic of Sifré to Numbers — as of Sifra (Leviticus) and Sifré to Deuteronomy — concerns whether or not reason of a particular sort can attain the same reliable results as revelation. The question nearly always produces a negative answer. Scripture on its own suffices. Reason on its own does not. The sort of reason that is subject to criticism involves analogical-contrastive reasoning. A category-formation is like another, therefore follows the rule governing the other; or it is not like the other, and follows the opposite. Then confronted by a category-formation the rule of which is unknown, we ask to what it is comparable? Finding the answer, we can determine the rule that pertains. Then all depends upon the power of the selected analogy. Now what if we can produce more than the proposed analogy, so that X is comparable not only to Y but also to Z? Then the result proves indeterminate. Now the question is raised, time and again, in the context of Scripture's declaring, via exegesis, that the law is such and so. Then the exegete asks, could not have produced the same result by means of an analogy to a known category, which case Scripture's demonstration is redundant. In most, though not all, instances, the answer is negative, because analogical-contrastive reasoning cannot provide a final answer to the question; only Scripture can. Here is a representative statement of the analytical initiative yielding an answer to the question of whether Scripture is required in the formation of the Halakhah.

## XXIII:I
1.   A.   "'...he shall separate himself from wine and strong drink; he shall drink no vinegar made from wine or strong drink, [and he shall not drink any juice of grapes or eat grapes, fresh or dried. All the days of his separation he shall eat nothing that is produced by the grapevine, not even the seeds or the skins]'" (Num. 6:1-4).
    B.   [The reference to strong drink] serves to treat wine drunk as a matter of religious duty as equivalent to wine drunk for mere pleasure.
    C.   For one might have argued as follows: just as one who has suffered a bereavement but not yet buried his dead is forbidden to drink wine, and a Nazirite is forbidden to drink wine, if I draw an analogy from the case of the bereaved, in which case the law has not treated wine drunk as a matter of religious duty as equivalent to wine drunk as a matter of mere pleasure [for the bereaved may drink the former but not the latter], so in the case of the Nazirite we should not treat wine drunk as a matter of religious duty as equivalent to wine drunk as a matter of mere pleasure.
    D.   And the view contrary to this one would be on the basis of an argument *a fortiori:*
    E.   now if in the case of one who has not yet buried his deceased, in which instance the law has placed in the same classification a religiously required meal and the drinking of wine as a religious duty, the law still has not placed in the same classification wine drunk as a religious duty and wine drunk as mere pleasure,
    F.   a Nazirite, in which case the law has *not* placed in the same classification the eating of a meal as a religious duty and the drinking of wine as a religious duty [since the latter is forbidden under all circumstances, even as a religious duty], is it not a matter of logic that the drinking of wine as a religious duty should not fall into the same classification as the drinking of wine as a matter of sheer

*Seven. Sifré to Numbers* 113

enjoyment? [Hence on this basis we should not treat wine drunk as a matter of religious duty as equivalent to wine drunk as a matter of mere pleasure.]

G. But lo, the one who carries out an act of cultic service to an idol will prove the contrary. For in that matter the law has not placed in the same classification the eating of a meal as a religious duty and the drinking of wine as a religious duty, but the law has treated in his case the drinking of wine as a religious duty and the drinking of wine as a matter of sheer pleasure. [One who drinks wine used for a libation is guilty, no matter the purpose of drinking the wine.] So that case will prove in the case of the Nazir, that even though the law has not treated the eating of a meal as a religious duty as belonging to the same classification as the drinking of wine as a religious duty, nonetheless the drinking of wine as a religious duty should be treated as equivalent to the drinking of wine as a matter of sheer pleasure.

H. Now lo, there is this argument *a fortiori* : now if in the case of one who performs an act of service to an idol, in which the law has not treated the refuse of food as equivalent to food, eating is equivalent to drinking and eating grapes is equivalent to drinking wine, and, in such a case wine drunk as a matter of religious duty is equivalent to wine drunk as a matter of sheer pleasure, in the case of a Nazirite, in which instance the refuse of food is treated as equivalent to food [since the Nazirite cannot eat grape pits as much as he cannot eat the grapes themselves], and eating is treated as equivalent to drinking, and eating grapes is treated as equivalent to drinking wine, is it not a matter of logic that we should treat the drinking of wine as a matter of religious duty to be equivalent to drinking wine as a matter of sheer pleasure?

I. No, at not at all. If you have made that rule in connection with the one who performs an act of service to an idol, such a one is subject to the death penalty, and it is for that reason that the law has treated the drinking of wine as a matter of religious duty as equivalent to the drinking of wine for sheer pleasure. But will you make the same rule in connection with the Nazirite, in which case violation of the law is not penalized by death? Since the death penalty does not apply, therefore wine drunk as a matter of religious duty is not to be treated as equivalent to wine drunk for sheer pleasure.

J. [We are left with a mass of contradictory propositions, all of them yielded by reason unguided by Scripture.] Accordingly, Scripture states, "...he shall separate himself from wine and strong drink; he shall drink no vinegar made from wine or strong drink, and he shall not drink any juice of grapes or eat grapes, fresh or dried. All the days of his separation he shall eat nothing that is produced by the grapevine, not even the seeds or the skins]'" (Num. 6:1-4).

K. [The reference to strong drink] serves to treat wine drunk as a matter of religious duty as equivalent to wine drunk for mere pleasure.

C states the null-hypothesis, that is, reason leads to a conclusion based on comparability of the Nazirite and the one who has suffered a bereavement but not yet buried his dead; and the contrary view derives, E-F, from an argument a fortiori. But the comparison competes with another. We have a category that is comparable, where the pertinent distinction does not register, G-H. I differentiates between the proposed analogy and the case at hand. Then, J-K, we recognize that analogical-contrastive thinking produces contradictory results and cannot be relied upon to settle the question. The upshot is, Scripture is necessary to define the rule for the category-formation under discussion.

The analytical issue before us forms the systematic program of Sifra and plays a considerable role in Halakhic parts of Sifré to Numbers as well. In *Types of Argumentation*, I have assembled a sizable sample of compositions of the present category. For the present purpose, it suffices to consider just one, which represents all of them. What we have is a type of analysis distinctive to Halakhic compilations of Midrash-exegesis; it never plays a role in purely-Aggadic exposition. Composites of the present type in the Talmuds nearly always occur, also, in the Tannaite Midrash-collections devoted to Halakhic exegesis.

## II. LANGUAGE-ANALYSIS

The analysis of language serves both Halakhic and Aggadic purposes in Sifré to Numbers. In the former case, the issue is how the law applies, and in the latter, how Scripture makes sense. The mode of analysis is to propose a hypothesis as to the meaning of a passage, then to find a comparable passage where matters are clear. Then, by analogy, the question is settled for the matter at hand as well.

### I:VI

1. A. "['The Lord said to Moses, 'Command the people of Israel that they put out of the camp every leper and every one having a discharge, and] every one [that is unclean through contact with the dead]'" (Num. 5:1-2).
   B. Concerning everyone Scripture speaks.
   C. Or is it possible that Scripture speaks only of the Levites, who bear the ark?
   D. Scripture states, "[You shall put out] both male and female, putting them outside the camp."
   E. [Referring both to male and to female means that not only Levites are subject to the commandment at hand, since women do not carry the ark. Accordingly,] it is with reference to everyone that Scripture here speaks.
2. A. All the same are adults and minors.
   B. You maintain that all the same are adults and minors.
   C. But perhaps in the present case the rule is the same as that is made explicit in connection with the penalty for violating the law at hand. Specifically, just as in the case of one who imparts uncleanness to the sanctuary, in which instance the penalty applies only to adults, as it is said, "But *the man* [not the minor] who is unclean and does not cleanse himself, that person shall be cut off from the midst of the assembly, since he has defiled the sanctuary of the Lord" (Num. 19:20), so here too, the admonition applies only to adults. [Accordingly, one can construct an argument to show that the rule is not the same for both adults and minors.]

*Seven. Sifré to Numbers* 115

    D.    Scripture states, "...You shall put out both male and female, putting them outside the camp."
    E.    Encompassed within the statement are both adults and minors.

Scripture contains its own clarification of its meanings, so that if we find the appropriate passage in which a formulation subject to doubt also occurs, we shall discover by analogy the meaning of the passage that is unclear. This is a form of analogical inquiry as well. Thus at No. 1, we find evidence that answers the question at hand by analogy, and the same is so at 2.A, D-E. The null hypothesis is expressed at 2.C, which produces a familiar result: logical argument can produce a result contrary to Scripture's clear intent.

### I:VII
**1.**    A.    "[The Lord said to Moses, 'Command the people of Israel that they put out of the camp every leper and every one having a discharge, and every one that is unclean through contact with the dead.] You shall put out both male and female, putting them outside the camp, that they may not defile their camp, in the midst of which I dwell'" (Gen. 5:1-4)
    B.    I know, on the basis of the stated verse, that the law applies only to male and female [persons who are suffering from the specified forms of cultic uncleanness]. How do I know that the law pertains also to one lacking clearly defined sexual traits or to one possessed of the sexual traits of both genders?
    C.    Scripture states, "...putting *them* outside the camp." [This is taken to constitute an encompassing formulation, extending beyond the male and female of the prior clause.]
    D.    I know, on the basis of the stated verse, that the law applies only to those who can be sent forth. How do I know that the law pertains also to those who cannot be sent forth?
    E.    Scripture states, "...putting them outside the camp." [This is taken to constitute an encompassing formulation, as before.]
    F.    I know on the basis of the stated verse that the law applies only to persons. How do I know that the law pertains also to utensils?
    G.    Scripture states, "...putting *them* outside the camp." [This is taken to constitute an encompassing formulation.]

How does Scripture encompass category-formations other than those to which it makes explicit reference? Once it refers to male and female, Scripture also refers to "them," and this is taken to encompass those that are neither male nor female. The process of inclusion continues at D-G.

### II:II
**1.**    A.    R. Josiah says, "'...a man or a woman....' Why are matters formulated so as to refer to both man and woman?
    B.    "Since it is said, 'When a man leaves a pit open, or when a man digs a pit...' (Ex. 21:33).

C. "I know only that a man is covered by the law. How do I know that a woman is equally culpable?

D. "Scripture states, '....a man or a woman....'

E. "That statement serves to encompass both a woman and a man in respect to all actions subject to sin-offerings and to all torts that are listed in the Torah."

F. R. Jonathan says, "It is hardly necessary to supply such a proof, for, in that same context, it is stated in any event: 'the *owner* of the pit shall make it good,' and it says, '*the one* that kindled the fire shall make full restitution' (Ex. 22:6). [These formulations encompass both genders.]

G. "Why then does Scripture state, '...a man or a woman...'? Merely to provide yet another occasion for the exercise of learning."

At issue in the clarification of Scripture's formulation is the mode of proving the besought proposition. Josiah finds the governing analogy at the cited verse, which treats a man or a woman as equivalent, and he finds therefore that when Scripture refers to "a man," it encompasses women as well. Jonathan concurs on the proposition but rejects the mode of proof. He finds neutral language, F, which indicates that the law pertains equally to both sexes. At issue then is not the outcome but the correct mode of attaining that outcome.

## XXIV:V

1. A. "...not even the seeds or the skins" (Num. 6:1-4).

   B. Why is this phrase added?

   C. Because it is said, "...he shall eat nothing that is produced by the grapevine," we have a generalization. Then the phrase, "...he shall separate himself from wine and strong drink; he shall drink no vinegar made from wine or strong drink," forms a particularization of the former.

   D. So we have a generalization followed by a particularization, which means that covered by the generalization are only those matters specified in the particularization.

   E. Just as the particular detail is spelled out to encompass the fruit and the refuse of the fruit, so I know only that the fruit and the refuse of the fruit are encompassed, thus encompassing the seeds and the skins, which constitute the fruit and the refuse of the fruit.

   F. Or may one argue that just as the produce is a fully formed piece of fruit, so encompassed under the rule is only fully formed fruit.

   G. You may argue in this way: What sort of fully ripe fruit have they not included?

   H. Lo, you should work the matter out not in accord with the latter, but in accord with the former mode of analysis:

   I. Just as the particular detail is spelled out to encompass the fruit and the refuse of the fruit, so I know only that the fruit and the refuse of the fruit are encompassed, thus including the seeds and the skins, which constitute the fruit and the refuse of the fruit.

   J. If I have gained the point through reason, what purpose does Scripture serve in specifying, "...not even the seeds or the skins"?

*Seven. Sifré to Numbers* 117

- K. It serves to teach you that in the case of a generalization which serves to augment the detailed specification, you may not construct an argument based on the detail in such wise as to exempt it from the encompassing generalization.
- L. The exception to that rule would be a case in which Scripture has served to spell out for you the rule at hand, as Scripture has spelled matters out in detail in the case of the Nazirite's law.

The formulation of Scripture serves to embody the exegetical principle that is articulated, K. Why does Scripture add the superfluous language, A-B? Because without it we should have missed the full coverage of the law. The language of the verse's formulation, "he shall eat nothing produced by the grapevine" generalizes; then that rule is particularized in terms of wine, strong drink, vinegar made from wine or string drink. That particularization limits the application of the generalization, D. Then E proceeds, what about seeds and skins? By the proposed reading, seeds and skins are encompassed under the prohibition. But logic — the logic of comparison and contrast — suggests otherwise, F. These are not fully formed, and the prohibition refers to fully formed fruit. I then invokes the former mode of analysis: the particularization encompasses the fruit and the refuse of the fruit. That leaves the question with which we started, A-B: the superfluous detail. It then yields the exegetical rule, C/K-L. The whole, then, is triggered by an interest in the analysis of Scripture's language, within the principle that Scripture contains nothing superfluous. Here, we note, logic does stand firm and yields a solid result: I-J.

## LXXVI:II

1. A. "[And when you go to war in your land] against the adversary who oppresses you, [then you shall sound an alarm with the trumpets]" (Num. 10:1-10):
   B. Scripture speaks of the [eschatological] war of Gog and Magog.
   C. You maintain that Scripture speaks of the [eschatological] war of Gog and Magog.
   D. But perhaps it speaks only of any wars that are mentioned in the Torah?
   E. Scripture says, "...that you may be remembered before the Lord your God, and you shall be saved from your enemies."
   F. Thus you may argue: go and find a war in which Israel is saved, but after which there is no period of subjugation?
   G. You can find only the war of Gog and Magog.
      H. And so Scripture says, "And the Lord will go forth and make war against those nations" (Zech. 14:3).

Language-analysis produces Aggadic, not only Halakhic, results in Sifré to Numbers. The procedure for Aggadah is comparable: a citation and a proposition, A-B. The proposition is challenged, C-D. The response is to revert to Scripture's own formulation, E, which yields the besought result, F-G.

**CVII:II**
1. A. "...and you offer to the Lord from the herd or from the flock an offering by fire [or a burnt offering or a sacrifice, to fulfil a vow or as a free will offering, or at your appointed feasts]:"
   B. May I infer that whatever is offered as an offering by fire requires a drink offering?
   C. Scripture refers specifically to a burnt-offering.
   D. I know only that that is the case of a burnt-offering.
   E. How do I know that the same rule applies to peace-offerings?
   F. Scripture alludes to a sacrifice.
   G. How about a thank-offering?
   H. Scripture refers to a sacrifice.
   I. Is the implication that one bring drink-offerings with these and likewise with a sin-offering or a guilt offering?
   J. Scripture states, "...to fulfil a vow or as a free will offering:" I have therefore encompassed within the rule [that drink offerings are required] only Holy Things that are brought on account of a vow or a free will offering.
   K. Then the inference is that I exclude these [a sin-offering or a guilt offering, which do not require drink offerings], but then I should further exclude a burnt-offering brought in fulfillment of an obligation on the pilgrim festivals [since that would be excluded by the rule that what is brought on one's own option requires the drink-offerings].
   L. When Scripture makes explicit reference to "at your appointed feasts," Scripture encompasses the obligatory burnt-offering brought on festivals. [That sort of offerings requires drink-offerings as well.]
   M. Then the inference is that one encompasses in the requirement of bringing drink offerings a burnt offering brought as a matter of obligation on pilgrim festivals and likewise a sin-offering that also is brought as a matter of obligations on festivals.
   N. Scripture says, "... you offer to the Lord from the herd or from the flock." An animal "from the herd" was encompassed by the general rule but singled out from the general rule to teach you a trait of the encompassing rule itself.
   O. That is, specifically, just as an animal of the herd is brought on account of a vow or as a free will offering and requires drink offerings, so whatever is brought on account of a vow or as a free will offering requires drink-offerings.
   P. Then a sin-offering and a guilt offering are excluded, for these do not come on account of keeping a vow or as a thank-offering [but only when the obligation is imposed on account of an inadvertent violation of the law], and so these do not require drink-offerings.

The language of Scripture is inclusive, so B-H. Each of the proposed categories qualifies: all require drink offerings, so burnt-offering is made explicit, peace offerings and thank-offerings are covered by the general reference to "sacrifice." Then we proceed to underscore the exclusive language, I-J. K-L take up one subordinated consideration, M-N-O another. The analytical initiative, then, involves systematically reading the verse at hand for its inclusions, then its exclusions. The

*Seven. Sifré to Numbers*

program of inquiry, it goes without saying, starts not with the verse but with the established facts, which are shown to cohere with the verse.

### III. ANALOGY- AND CATEGORY-CRITICISM

Arguments concerning the priority of Scripture over reason repeatedly focus upon issues of the correct analogy and how that is determined. It follows that analogy-criticism encompasses that quite particular mode of analysis. But as a general classification, it goes beyond the limits of that mode.

I begin with an exemplary case of category-criticism: the analysis of the indicative traits that define a category, the comparison and contrast of one category with another bearing comparable traits, thus analogical-contrastive thinking. I can offer no finer or better articulated account of matters than what follows.

### XXIV:I
1. A. "[And the Lord said to Moses, 'Say to the people of Israel, When either a man or a woman makes a special vow, the vow of a Nazirite, to separate himself to the Lord, he shall separate himself from wine and strong drink; he shall drink no vinegar made from wine or strong drink, and he shall not drink any juice of grapes or eat grapes, fresh or dried.] All the days of his separation he shall eat nothing that is produced by the grapevine, not even the seeds or the skins'" (Num. 6:1-4):
   B   The verse of Scripture teaches the lesson that if a Nazirite ate in all the bulk of an olive deriving, in toto, from each of the [specific varieties of forbidden species], he incurs a flogging of forty stripes.
   C. On the basis of the present case, moreover, one may draw an analogy to all other matters of prohibited substances listed in the Torah.
   D. Now if what exudes from the vine, the prohibition of which does not last forever [but only for the spell of the vow], and the prohibition of which does not extend to deriving benefit [but only eating], and the prohibition of which, moreover, is subject to a remission after the spell in which the substance is prohibited — lo, diverse substances join together to form the requisite minimum volume of an olive's bulk,
   E. as to all other substances, the prohibition of which does last forever, the prohibition of which does extend to deriving benefit [e.g., in commerce], and the prohibition of which is *not* subject to a remission after the spell in which the substance is prohibited — lo, is it not an argument all the more so that diverse substances join together to form the requisite minimum volume of an olive's bulk.

Here is a fine example of the analytical procedures of analogical-contrastive thinking: generalizing from a case. We treat the case at hand, A-B, as the foundation for an entire category of like things, C. An argument a fortiori follows, D-E. So once we establish categories, we are able to produce new knowledge from the relationships between and among those categories.

Now let us proceed more systematically to take up the way in which analogical- and categorical-criticism take place in Sifré to Numbers.

### II:V
1. A. ["And the Lord said to Moses, 'Say to the people of Israel, When a man or woman commits any of the sins that men commit [by breaking faith with the Lord,] and that person is guilty..." (Num. 5:5-10).
   B. Why is the verse so formulated as to refer to *that person* [rather than a man or a woman]?
   C. Since it is said, "...a man or woman," I know that the law applies only to a man or a woman. How do I know that one lacking clearly defined sexual traits or one who has he traits of both sexes is subject to the law?
   D. Scripture is so formulated as to indicate it, when it says, "...and that person is guilty..." (Num. 5:5-10).

### II:VI
1. A. ["And the Lord said to Moses, 'Say to the people of Israel, When a man or woman commits any of the sins that men commit by breaking faith with the Lord,] and that person is guilty..." (Num. 5:5-10).
   B. All classifications of persons are subject to the same rule [formulated with reference to *that person* ]: men, women, proselytes fall into the single classification before us.
   C. Accordingly, we cover all those listed. But does Scripture thereby intend also to include the minor?
   D. You may construct the following argument to the contrary:
   E. If in the case of idolatry, a most severe infraction of the law, the Torah has exempted the minor, all the more so [will the Torah exempt the minor from punishment [in the case of all of the other religious duties enjoined by the Torah.

Unlike the issues of analogical-contrastive criticism, which also involve the comparison and contrast of category-formations, here the category-criticism involves a simpler question of definition. It requires defining who is covered by, or excluded from, a given category. Here it concerns "person," and wishes to find out whether the category encompasses both women and men. The first issue is, what about those who are neither man nor woman but fall into an interstitial category. In the second case, we wish to know whether "person" includes both adults and minors. The mode of criticism is common in this document: finding a pertinent formulation, the close reading of which answers the question.

### VI:III
1. A. "'...every man's holy thing shall be his; whatever any man gives to the priest shall be his' (Num. 5:10).
   B. "Why does Scripture make this statement?
   C. "Because, with reference to the fruit of an orchard in the fourth year after its planting, it is said, 'And in the fourth year all their fruit shall be holy, an offering of praise to the Lord' (Lev. 19:24), [I do not know whether the sense is that] it

## Seven. Sifré to Numbers

is holy for the farmer or holy for the priesthood. Accordingly, Scripture says, '...every man's holy thing shall be his; whatever any man gives to the priest shall be his,' Scripture thereby speaks of produce of an orchard in the fourth year after its planting, indicating that it should belong to the farmer," the words of R. Meir.

D. R. Ishmael says, "It is holy to the farmer.

E. "You maintain that it is holy for the farmer.. Or is it holy for the priesthood? Lo, this is how you may logically [rather than by reference to the exegesis, B-C, based on Scripture] deal with the problem:

F. "Produce in the status of second tithe is called holy, and the fruit of an orchard in the fourth year after its planting is called holy. If I draw the analogy to produce in the status of second tithe, which belongs only to the farmer, then likewise produce of an orchard in the fourth year after its planting should belong only to the farmer."

G. No, produce separated as heave-offering [for priestly use] proves to the contrary, for it too is called Holy, but it belongs only to the priest. And that furthermore demonstrates for produce of an orchard in the fourth year after its planting that even though it is called holy, it should belong only to the priesthood.

H. "You may then offer [the following argument to the contrary, [showing the correct analogy is to be drawn not to heave-offering but to produce in the status of second tithe, as follows:] the correct separation of produce in the status of second tithe involves bringing the produce to the holy place [of Jerusalem, where it is to be eaten], and, along these same lines, produce of an orchard in the fourth year after its planning likewise involves bringing that produce to the holy place. If, therefore, I draw the rule for produce in the status of second tithe, maintaining that it belongs to the owner, so produce of an orchard in the fourth year after its planting likewise should belong only to the owner."

I. [No, that argument can be disproved from another variety of produce entirely:] lo, produce designated as first fruits will prove to the contrary, for such produce likewise has to be brought to the holy place, but it belongs only to the priest. So produce in that classification will prove for produce of an orchard in the fourth year after its planting, showing that even though it has to be brought to the holy place, it also should belong only to the priests. [So the labor of classification continues.]

J. "You may compose [the following argument to reply to the foregoing:] The [result of the] separation of produce in the status of second tithe falls into the classification of holy and has to be brought to the holy place, but further is subject to redemption [in that one can redeem the actual fruit and replace it with ready cash, and one may then bring that cash to Jerusalem and buy for it produce to be eaten in Jerusalem under the rules governing second tithe]. Produce of an orchard in the fourth year after its planting likewise is called holy, has to be brought to the holy place, and is subject to the rules of redemption. But let the matter of heave offering not come into the picture, for even though it is called holy, it does not have to be brought to the holy place [but is eaten wherever it is located], and let the matter of first fruit likewise not enter the picture, for even though it is produce that has to be brought to the holy place, it is not called holy."

K. Lo, there is the case of the firstling, which *is* called holy, and which has to be brought to the holy place, but which belongs only to the priesthood. [So we can now provide an appropriate analogy.] And that case will prove [the rule for other sorts of produce subject to the same traits, specifically] produce of an orchard in the fourth year after its planting, for, even though it is called holy, and even though it has to be brought to the holy place, it should belong only to the priesthood.

L. "You may invoke the consideration of separating [the produce into one of its several classifications]. Let me call to account three distinct considerations in a single exercise:

M. "[1] Food in the status of second tithe is called holy, requires delivery to the holy place, and is subject to the rules of redemption.

N. "[2] Produce of an orchard in the fourth year after its planting is called holy, requires delivery to the holy place, and is subject to the rules of redemption.

O. "[1] But let not food that has been designated as heave-offering enter into consideration. For even though it is called holy, it does not require delivery to the holy place.

P. "And [2] let not first fruits enter into consideration. For even though it requires delivery to the holy place, it is not called holy.

Q. "Nor should [3] the firstling enter into consideration. For even though it is called holy and requires delivery to the holy place, it is not subject to the rules of redemption.

R. "Let me then draw the appropriate analogy from the correct source, and let me then compose a logical argument on the basis of the correct traits of definition.

S. "I shall draw an analogy on the basis of three shared traits from one matter to another, but I shall not drawn an analogy from something which exhibits three traits to something which does not share these same traits, but only one or two of them.

T. "If then I draw an analogy to produce in the status of second tithe, which belongs only to the owner, so too in the case of produce of an orchard in the fourth year after its planting, it should belong only to the owner."

2. A. R. Joshua says, "What is called holy belongs to the owner.
   B. "You maintain that what is called holy belongs to the owner. But perhaps it belongs only to the priesthood?
   C. "Scripture states, 'But in the fifth year you may eat of their fruit that they may yield more richly for you' (Lev. 19:25). To whom does the increase go? To him to whom the produce already has been assigned [that is to say, the farmer, not the priesthood]."

The formulation, "shall be his," yields an ambiguity: whose? Is the holy thing assigned to the farmer or to the priest? Meir, C, identifies a relevant category-

*Seven. Sifré to Numbers*

formation, produce in the fourth year after planting, and finds equivalent language, justifying the comparison. Then, since the unknown has been established as comparable to the known, the rule of the known prevails; it belongs to the farmer. Ishmael concurs, D, on the comparison. But he prefers a different analogy, based on a different case of the governing usage, "holy." He concurs with Meir but provides his own proof. The secondary development, the exercise of comparison and contrast, then pertains to both Meir's and Ishmael's demonstrations, for in both cases the language "holy" occurs. I have signaled the challenge, involving the secondary expansion, from G onward through indentation. G finds produce called holy that belongs to the priest, which shows that the category-formation identified by Ishmael/Meir does not yield the result they propose. H allows Ishmael (as I have punctuated the matter, it could as well be Meir) to differentiate between his proposed analogy and the analogy drawn from heave-offering by G. I then proposes another anomalous analogy, this one involving produce that like that under discussion has to be brought to Jerusalem, and yet that belongs to the priest, not to the farmer; and since produce in the fourth year after planting has to be brought to Jerusalem, it belongs in the same category, with the same result. Then, J, we differentiate among classifications of produce that have to be brought to the holy place, Jerusalem. That permits us to exclude heave offering from the picture, so too firstfruits, each for its own reason based on its indicative trait. Then we find another analogical category, the firstling: holy, brought to the holy place, but belonging to the farmer, K. Then other classifications bearing the same indicative qualities follow suit. At L-T, the polythetic taxonomy is reconstructed, M, N vs., O, P, Q. That leads to R-T, a recapitulation of the whole, rejecting polythetic taxonomy in favor of monothetic (if complex) taxonomy. No. 2 then resorts to analogy based on common language. I do not think the Rabbinic literature contains a finer example of the exercise of analogical-contrastive reasoning than the present case.

We shall meet this important composition again in our consideration of *Types of Argumentation*.

**VIII:IV**
1. A. "...a tenth of an ephah of barley meal...:"
   B. Why is this matter made explicit?
   C. Because one might have argued to the contrary:
   D. Since the meal-offering brought by a sinner [accompanying a sin-offering] has to be brought on account of a sin, and this one too is brought on account of sin, if I draw an analogy to the meal-offering of a sinner, which is brought only as fine flour, so this one also should bring only meal of fine flour.
   E. Accordingly, Scripture makes explicit the contrary fact, that this meal-offering derives from barley-meal [and not fine flour].

**VIII:V**
1. A. "...barley....:"
   B. Why is this matter made explicit?

*124*  *Analysis and Argumentation in Rabbinic Judaism*

    C.    Because one might have argued to the contrary:
    D.    Since the meal-offering brought by a sinner [accompanying a sin-offering] comes on account of a sin, and this one is brought on account of sin, if I draw an analogy to the meal-offering of a sinner, which is brought only as wheat, so this one also should bring only a meal-offering of wheat.
    E.    Accordingly, Scripture makes explicit the contrary fact, that this meal-offering derives from barley [and not wheat].

Here the category-criticism is intended to show that categories that appear to look alike are not alike. The meal offering brought by a sinner is on account of sin, so too the matter under discussion, so they look alike. But not all offerings brought on account of sin are treated in the same way by Scripture, which is required, then, to correct the results of category-comparison.

## XXIII:I

1.    A.    "...he shall separate himself from wine and strong drink; he shall drink no vinegar made from wine or strong drink, [and he shall not drink any juice of grapes or eat grapes, fresh or dried. All the days of his separation he shall eat nothing that is produced by the grapevine, not even the seeds or the skins]'" (Num. 6:1-4).
    B.    [The reference to strong drink] serves to treat wine drunk as a matter of religious duty as equivalent to wine drunk for mere pleasure.
    C.    For one might have argued as follows: just as one who has suffered a bereavement but not yet buried his dead is forbidden to drink wine, and a Nazirite is forbidden to drink wine, if I draw an analogy from the case of the bereaved, in which case the law has not treated wine drunk as a matter of religious duty as equivalent to wine drunk as a matter of mere pleasure [for the bereaved may drink the former but not the latter], so in the case of the Nazirite we should not treat wine drunk as a matter of religious duty as equivalent to wine drunk as a matter of mere pleasure.
    D.    And the view contrary to this one would be on the basis of an argument *a fortiori:*
    E.    now if in the case of one who has not yet buried his deceased, in which instance the law has placed in the same classification a religiously required meal and the drinking of wine as a religious duty, the law still has not placed in the same classification wine drunk as a religious duty and wine drunk as mere pleasure,
    F.    a Nazirite, in which case the law has *not* placed in the same classification the eating of a meal as a religious duty and the drinking of wine as a religious duty [since the latter is forbidden under all circumstances, even as a religious duty], is it not a matter of logic that the drinking of wine as a religious duty should not fall into the same classification as the drinking of wine as a matter of sheer enjoyment? [Hence on this basis we should not treat wine drunk as a matter of religious duty as equivalent to wine drunk as a matter of mere pleasure.]
    G.    But lo, the one who carries out an act of cultic service to an idol will prove the contrary. For in that matter the law has not placed in the same classification the eating of a meal as a religious duty and the drinking of wine as a religious duty,

## Seven. Sifré to Numbers 125

but the law has treated in his case the drinking of wine as a religious duty and the drinking of wine as a matter of sheer pleasure. [One who drinks wine used for a libation is guilty, no matter the purpose of drinking the wine.] So that case will prove in the case of the Nazir, that even though the law has not treated the eating of a meal as a religious duty as belonging to the same classification as the drinking of wine as a religious duty, nonetheless the drinking of wine as a religious duty should be treated as equivalent to the drinking of wine as a matter of sheer pleasure.

H. Now lo, there is this argument *a fortiori* : now if in the case of one who performs an act of service to an idol, in which the law has not treated the refuse of food as equivalent to food, eating is equivalent to drinking and eating grapes is equivalent to drinking wine, and, in such a case wine drunk as a matter of religious duty is equivalent to wine drunk as a matter of sheer pleasure, in the case of a Nazirite, in which instance the refuse of food is treated as equivalent to food [since the Nazirite cannot eat grape pits as much as he cannot eat the grapes themselves], and eating is treated as equivalent to drinking, and eating grapes is treated as equivalent to drinking wine, is it not a matter of logic that we should treat the drinking of wine as a matter of religious duty to be equivalent to drinking wine as a matter of sheer pleasure?

I. No, at not at all. If you have made that rule in connection with the one who performs an act of service to an idol, such a one is subject to the death penalty, and it is for that reason that the law has treated the drinking of wine as a matter of religious duty as equivalent to the drinking of wine for sheer pleasure. But will you make the same rule in connection with the Nazirite, in which case violation of the law is not penalized by death? Since the death penalty does not apply, therefore wine drunk as a matter of religious duty is not to be treated as equivalent to wine drunk for sheer pleasure.

J. [We are left with a mass of contradictory propositions, all of them yielded by reason unguided by Scripture.] Accordingly, Scripture states, "...he shall separate himself from wine and strong drink; he shall drink no vinegar made from wine or strong drink, and he shall not drink any juice of grapes or eat grapes, fresh or dried. All the days of his separation he shall eat nothing that is produced by the grapevine, not even the seeds or the skins]'" (Num. 6:1-4).

K. [The reference to strong drink] serves to treat wine drunk as a matter of religious duty as equivalent to wine drunk for mere pleasure.

The category-comparison involves wine drunk as a matter of religious duty as against wine drunk for mere pleasure. Are these subject to the same rule, treated as forming the same common category? Logic would have suggested otherwise, C. But, D-F, once we introduce the analogy of the person who has suffered a bereavement but not yet buried his dead, we find grounds for making such a distinction. But such a distinction, between drinking wine for religious duty and drinking wine for pleasure, does not always register; we find in the case of one who carries out an act of cultic service to an idol that the distinction does not hold. And that reflects on the case at hand, H. But I differentiates between the category-formations that are treated here. That leaves matters in confusion, which only

*126* *Analysis and Argumentation in Rabbinic Judaism*

Scripture can sort out, J-K. So, we see, the exercise in category-criticism — comparison and contrast of category-formations — once more produces the demonstration of the priority of Scripture in the definition of category-formations and their relationships.

We meet this important composition in *Types of Argumentation*, since it not only shows the workings of category-criticism but also articulates the type of argument employed here.

### XXVIII:I
**1.** A. "And if any man dies very suddenly beside him, [and he defiles his consecrated head, then he shall shave his head on the day of his cleansing, on the seventh day he shall shave it]" (Num. 6:9):
   B. This statement serves to exclude from consideration in the imparting of corpse uncleanness a case of doubt. [If we do not know for sure that a Nazirite has had contact with a corpse, he is not regarded as having contracted corpse uncleanness and does not have to shave his head and start observing the vow afresh.]
   C. For one might have argued to the contrary: if in a case in which the law has not treated what happens under constraint as equivalent to what happens willingly [e.g., if someone produces flux under conditions of constraint, he is not unclean], the law nonetheless has treated as equivalent matters of doubt and matters of certainty [for in the private domain contamination that is subject to doubt is regarded as certain],
   D. in a classification in which the law has treated what happens under constraint as equivalent to what happens willingly ["if any man dies suddenly...."], should we not treat as equivalent matters of doubt and matters of certainty?
   E. Accordingly, Scripture makes the contrary clear:
   F. "And if any man dies very suddenly beside him, and he defiles his consecrated head, then he shall shave his head on the day of his cleansing, on the seventh day he shall shave it" (Num. 6:9):
   G. This statement serves to exclude from consideration in the imparting of corpse uncleanness a case of doubt.

The argument a fortiori rests on the comparison and contrast of the stated category-formations: what happens under constraint is equivalent to what happens willingly, matters of doubt, matters of certainty. The two dimensional grid then yields an anomalous result, and Scripture is required to set aside the consequences of analogical-contrasting reasoning.

### XII:I
**1.** A. "Then the priest shall make her take an oath, [saying to the woman, 'If no man has lain with you and if you have not turned aside to uncleanness, while you were under your husband's authority, be free from this water of bitterness that brings the curse. But if you have gone astray though you are under your husband's authority, and if you have defiled yourself and some man other than your husband has lain with you, then (let the priest make the woman take the

*Seven. Sifré to Numbers* *127*

oath of the curse and say to the woman), 'the Lord make you an execration and an oath among your people, when the Lord makes your thigh fall away and your body swell; and may this water that brings the curse pass into your bowels and make your body swell and your thigh fall away.' And the woman shall say, 'Amen, Amen.']" (Num. 5:16-22).

B. "Then the priest shall make her take an oath:"
C. The priest imposes the oath, and the woman does not take the oath on her own volition.
D. For logic might have dictated otherwise: the word "oath" appears in the present context, and the word "oath" is used presently [in another connection entirely, namely, that of the Nazirite, an oath a woman takes on her own account]. Just as the oath stated elsewhere requires that the person take the oath on her own volition, so the oath subject to discussion here may be taken on the woman's own initiative.
E. Accordingly, Scripture states, "Then the priest shall make her take an oath."
F. The priest imposes the oath, and the woman does not take the oath on her own volition.

"Oath" occurs in two contexts, establishing a link between distinct category-formations, the oath of the female Nazirite, the oath of the woman accused of adultery. That is why Scripture must explicitly differentiate between those category-formations and so correct the false results of category-analysis of the comparative type.

## IV. RATIONALITY

The demonstration that disputes rest on rational, not arbitrary, bases, so that both parties to a dispute have solid foundations for their views, takes place in Sifré to Numbers and forms one of the analytical initiatives characteristic of that document. One representative instance suffices. Here is a single example of the routine procedure.

### CLX:XIII

1. A. "But if the manslayer shall at any time go beyond the bounds of his city of refuge to which he fled:"
   B. Said R. Eleazar b. Azariah, "Now if in the case of the measure of punishment, which is the lesser, he who takes a single step [in this case], lo, he is liable for his life, all the more so in the case of the measure of goodness, which is the greater [will one who takes a single step gain a great reward]."
2. A. "and the avenger of blood finds him outside the bounds of his city of refuge, and the avenger of blood slays the manslayer, he shall not be guilty of blood:"
   B. This applies to anybody.
3. A. "For the man must remain in his city of refuge until the death of the high priest:"

|     | B. | On this basis you say: if he committed manslaughter in that same city, he goes into exile from one neighborhood to another, and a Levite goes into exile from town to town." |
| --- | --- | --- |
| 4.  | A. | "but after the death of the high priest the manslayer may return to the land of his possession:" |
|     | B. | **"And he may return to the office which he had held before," the words of R. Meir.** |
|     | C. | **R. Judah says, "He did not return to the office which he had held before"** [M. Mak. 2:8]. |

The dispute on the meaning of Scripture at No. 4 allows for the two possible positions: he may, or he may not, return to office, though he may return to his estate — a secondary issue, generated by the primary law of Scripture. So the dispute concerns what is peripheral, and what is central is subject to common agreement.

## LXV:I

|     |    |    |
| --- | --- | --- |
| 1.  | A. | "'Let the people of Israel keep the Passover at its appointed time. [On the fourteenth day of this month, in the evening, you shall keep it at its appointed time; according to all its statutes and all its ordinances you shall keep it.' So Moses told the people of Israel that they should keep the Passover. And they kept the Passover in the first month, on the fourteenth day of the month, in the evening, in the wilderness of Sinai; according to all that the Lord commanded Moses, so the people of Israel did]" (Num. 9:1-14): |
|     | B. | "Why is this statement made [emphasizing that they did so in the proper season]? |
|     | C. | "Because Scripture says, 'And the entire congregation of the community of Israel will slaughter it' (Ex. 12:6), I might draw the inference that this is to be done whether it is a weekday or the Sabbath, in which case, how shall I carry out the rule, 'Those who profane it [the Sabbath] will surely die'? [How keep the Passover at its appointed time and also keep the Sabbath?] |
|     | D. | "Does this pertain to all other forbidden forms of labor, except for the slaughtering of the lamb set aside as a Passover offering, or does it apply even to the slaughtering of the lamb set aside as a Passover offering? |
|     | E. | "And how am I to carry out the rule, 'And they shall slaughter it'? |
|     | F. | "Is this to be done on all the other days of the year, except for the Sabbath day, or is it to be done even on the Sabbath? |
|     | G. | "Accordingly, Scripture says, 'Let the people of Israel keep the Passover at its appointed time [even on the Sabbath, responding to F],'" the words of R. Josiah. |
|     | H. | Observed R. Jonathan to him, "On the basis of the inferences at hand we have not yet derived the rule [for the other questions listed above have not been answered]." |
|     | I. | Observed R. Josiah to him, "Scripture says, 'Command the children of Israel and say to them, "My offering, my food for my offerings by fire, my pleasing odor, you shall take heed to offer to me in its due season"' (Num. 28:2). Does this serve to teach you the rule for the daily whole-offering, specifically, that it overrides the prohibitions of the Sabbath. |

*Seven. Sifré to Numbers*

J.  "It is not necessary to maintain that view, for in any event Scripture says, 'And on the Sabbath two lambs a year old' (Num. 28:9) [so the rule is made explicit].
K.  "So why does Scripture stress, '... in its due season'?
L.  "The word remains available to provide grounds for an analogy, generating the following argument of comparison: in the one passage, 'in its due season' is mentioned, and the same words appear elsewhere. Just as in the latter passage the words indicate that the prohibitions of the Sabbath do not apply [that is, with reference to the daily whole offering], so when the words appear here, they indicate that the prohibitions of the Sabbath do not apply."

Josiah, A-G, lays out a set of questions and responds to one of them, F-G. Jonathan does not differ but points out that other questions require attention. Josiah responds that the daily whole offering overrides the restrictions of the Sabbath, and this is made articulate, Num. 28:2, even though it is also explicitly stated at Num. 28:9. So the language of the former is redundant and functions as spelled out at L. There is, then, no dispute at all, only an exchange in demonstrating law that both parties affirm as Scripturally-founded. And this leads us to the final analytical unit: the Scriptural foundations of the Halakhah, a critical issue in the present document.

## v. Scriptural Foundations of the Halakhah

The Halakhic passages of the book of Numbers are systematically expounded in Sifré to Numbers, it goes without saying, and it is not necessary to include them all. A single Halakhic exposition suffices for our purpose, and from that point, I catalogue only those items that intersect with the Halakhah of the Mishnah and the Tosefta. Here is the one case, representative of them all, that suffices to show how the document reads the Halakhic passages of Scripture in its own exegetical framework:

**IV:IV**
1.  A.  "...to the priest:"
    B.  Scripture speaks of the priestly watch on duty that week. [The priests on duty get the restitution brought in their week in charge of the cult.]
    C.  You maintain that Scripture speaks of the priestly watch on duty that week.
    D.  But perhaps the sense is that the man may make the restitution payment to any priest of his choice.
    E.  Scripture states, "...in addition to the ram of atonement with which atonement is made for him."
    F.  It is with the ones with which they make atonement [that the restitution is worked out]. And who are they? They are the men of that particular priestly watch on duty.
    G.  [But there is this exception:] Lo, in the case of one who robs from a priest — [the priest personally] makes acquisition [of the restitution that is paid]. [The priestly watch on duty that week does not get the restitution.]

H. Now [proving that Scripture speaks of the priestly watch on duty that week,] logic dictates: if such a priest effects acquisition of restitution paid on the account of others, should he not effect acquisition of what is paid for restitution on his own account. [So the fact stated at G proves the proposition at hand, by making possible the argument *a fortiori* just now given.]
    I. R. Nathan expressed the matter in a different formulation, "If in the case of something of which I could not effect acquisition before the object reached my possession, once the object reached my possession, no one else can remove it from my possession, something for which I have effected acquisition even before it entered my possession [namely, the restitution paid in the present case] — it is surely reasonable that no one else should effect acquisition of it and remove it from my possession."
    J. They said to him, "No, that is not necessarily so. [For you may construct a contrary argument as follows:] You may state the rule in the case of this one, in which instance other people have no share in what comes to his possession. But will you make the same statement of someone who has to share a portion of what he gets with others [namely, priests]?
    K. "Since others have a share in the matter, it is a matter of logic that the object should be taken away from him and divided up by the priests of the priestly watch on duty that week."

The rule is, the priests in charge of the cult in a given week gain possession of restitution made during their week in charge; they represent the priesthood in their persons, so A-B. What about other possibilities, D? Scripture, E-F, explicitly states to the contrary: the priestly watch on duty gets what is presented as atonement for what has been misappropriated from the property of the priesthood. The exception, G, is dealt with at H. The secondary exercise, I, is refuted at J-K, leaving the same result: Scripture is the source of reliable law.

We proceed to a sequence of compositions in which a verse of Scripture is cited, followed by a citation of the Halakhah as formulated by the Mishnah or the Tosefta, given in bold face type:

## I:IX

**1.** A. "[You shall put out both male and female, putting them outside the camp,] that they may not defile their camp, [in the midst of which I dwell]:"
    B. On the basis of this verse, the rule has been formulated:
    C. **There are three camps, the camp of Israel, the camp of the Levitical priests, and the camp of the Presence of God. From the gate of Jerusalem to the Temple mount is the camp of Israel, from the gate of the Temple mount to the Temple courtyard is the camp of the Levitical priesthood, and from the gate of the courtyard and inward is the camp of the Presence of God [T. Kelim 1:12].**

*Seven. Sifré to Numbers*

The Halakhah of the Tosefta is represented as a recapitulation of the cited verse.

## VI:II

1. A. "...every man's holy thing shall be his; whatever any man gives to the priest shall be his" (Num. 5:10).
   B. On the basis of this statement you draw the following rule:
   C. **If a priest on his own account makes a sacrificial offering, even though it falls into the week [during which] another priestly watch than his own [is in charge of the actual cult, making the offerings and receiving the dues], lo, that priest owns the priestly portions of the offering, and the right of offering it up belongs to him [and not to the priest ordinarily on duty at that time, who otherwise would retain the rights to certain portions of the animal] [T. Men. 13:17].**

The same procedure prevails.

## VII:III

1. A. "[And the Lord said to Moses, 'Say to the people of Israel, If any man's] wife goes astray and acts unfaithfully against him:"
   B. Scripture speaks of a case in which the woman is suitable for marriage to the husband, thereby excluding cases in which the woman should not have been married to that man to begin with, such as a widow married to a high priest, a divorcee or a woman who has carried out the rite of removing the shoe married to an ordinary priest.
   C. **And in accord with the position of Aqabiah b. Mehalalel, also [covered by B] is a freed bondwoman or the wife of a proselyte [to whom valid marital bonds do not extend].**
   D. **They said to him, "Now is it not the case that Karkemit was a freed bondwoman in Jerusalem, and Shemaiah and Abtalion imposed on her the rite of drinking the bitter water [contrary to view at C]."**
   E. **He said to them the following statement: "When they administered the water to her, it was merely to set an example [and not because the law required it]."**
   F. **[The other sages thereupon] placed him in ostracism and he died in that state, so when he died, the court stoned his bier [M. Ed. 5:6].**

The Mishnah's case is very special, the exegesis having attended to both the fundamental situation contemplated by Scripture and the special cases that are then excluded, A-B. The Mishnah's problem, the freed bondwoman, is then tacked on, but she would certainly fall under the exclusion of B.

## VII:X

1. A. "...and she is undetected [though she has defiled herself, and there is no witness against her, since she was not taken in the act]:"

132    *Analysis and Argumentation in Rabbinic Judaism*

  B. Now, as a matter of fact, we are not told the length of time that the woman's being in secret with another man involves.
  C. Scripture says, "... and she is undetected though she has defiled herself...."
  D. It is a span of being alone with the man sufficient to produce "contamination."
  E. **"It is sufficient time to 'walk around the palm tree," the words of R. Ishmael.**
  F. R. Eliezer says, "Sufficient time to 'mix the cup.'"
  G. R. Joshua says, "Sufficient time to 'drink the cup.'"
  H. Ben Azzai says, "Sufficient time to 'roast an egg.'"
  I. R. Aqiba says, "Sufficient time to 'swallow it.'"
  J. R. Judah b. Beterah says, "Sufficient time to 'drink three eggs,' one after the other" [T. Sot. 2:20].

Here the Halakhic formulation at T. Sot. serves as a gloss to the gloss of Scripture, C, at D.

### IX:I

**1.** A. "And the priest shall bring her near [and set her before the Lord; and the priest shall take holy water in an earthen vessel and take some of the dust that is on the floor of the tabernacle and put it into the water. And the priest shall set the woman before the Lord, and unbind the hair of the woman's head, and place in her hands the cereal offering of remembrance, which is the cereal offering of jealousy. And in his hand the priest shall have the water of bitterness that brings the curse. Then the priest shall make her take an oath, saying, 'If no man has lain with you and if you have not turned aside to uncleanness, while you were under your husband's authority, be free from this water of bitterness that brings the curse. But if you have gone astray though you are under your husband's authority, and if you have defiled yourself and some man other than your husband has lain with you, then (let the priest make the woman take the oath of the curse and say to the woman), 'the Lord make you an execration and an oath among your people, when the Lord makes your thigh fall away and your body swell; and may this water that brings the curse pass into your bowels and make your body swell and your thigh fall away." And the woman shall say, 'Amen, Amen.']" (Num. 5:16-22).
  B. On the basis of the cited phrase sages have ruled:
  C. **The bitter water is not administered to two accused wife at the same time [T. Sot. 1:6].**

### IX:II

**1.** A. "...and set her before the Lord:"
  B. **[The stress on setting her indicates] that one should not set up with her neither her bondmen nor her bond women, because her heart relies on them [and she will not feel ashamed] [M. Sot. 1:6].**

### IX:III

**1.** A. "...and set her before the Lord:"
  B. It is before Nicanor's gate.
  C. On the basis of this verse sages have ruled:

Seven. Sifré to Numbers

D. The head of the priestly watch of a given week sets unclean people at Nicanor's gate, for at that location they administer the bitter water to accused wives [M. Sot. 1:5, T. Sot. 1:4].

## XXIV:III
1.  A. "All the days of his separation he shall eat nothing that is produced by the grapevine, not even the seeds or the skins" (Num. 6:1-4).
    B. "The minimum number of seeds is two, and the skins, one," the words of R., Eleazar b. Azariah.
    C. What are grape pits and what are grape skins?
    D. "The former are what is outside and the latter are what is inside," the words of R. Judah.
    E. R. Yosé says, "That you not err: it is like the bell of cattle: what is outside is the hood, and what is inside is the clapper" (M. Naz. 6:2).

## CXXVI:VII
1.  A. "And every open vessel, which has no cover fastened upon it, is unclean:"
    B. On this basis, sages have said, **Utensils afford protection when tightly sealed in the tent of a corpse, and tents do so by covering objects over** [M. Oh. 5:3].

In these instances and the like, the foundations of the Halakhah in Scripture are deemed self-evident and not to require amplification.

## XXV:II
1.  A. "...until the time is completed for which he separates himself to the Lord:"
    B. How do we know the rule that **if one has said, "Lo, I shall be a Nazirite," without further specification, he shaves his head on the thirty-first day after the oath, but if he shaved on the thirtieth day, he has carried out his obligation?** [M. Naz. 3:1A-B].
    C. [We know that the thirty-first day is not essential] since it is written, "...*until* the time is completed," and lo, the days of Naziriteship have now been completed [on the thirtieth day].
    D. But can it be the case that if he said, "Lo, I shall be a Nazirite for one hundred days," then if he shaved on the thirty-first day, he has completed his obligation?
    E. Scripture says, "...until the time is completed," and the days he has taken on his Nazirite vow have not yet been completed.
    F. I know that the law covers only him who reaches a completion of his Nazirite vow. How do I know the rule covering the perpetual Nazirite [who has not specified a time-limit to his vow]?
    G. Scripture states, "All the days of his vow of separation no razor shall come upon his head; until the time is completed for which he separates himself to the Lord, he shall be holy" (Num. 6:5), encompassing the one who is a perpetual Nazir.

Here the inquiry into Scripture's source for the Halakhic rule is made explicit, B, and responded to at C, D-E, F-G.

**LX:I**

3. A. "He set up its lamps:"
   B. He made steps for the candelabrum.
   C. On this basis sages have ruled:
   D. **There was a stone before the candelabrum, with three steps, on which the priest would stand and dress the lamps. He left the cruse of oil on the second step and left [M. Tam. 3:9].**

D. The provision of steps for the candelabrum, B, yields the specific procedure, D.

3. A. "All who are native shall do these things:"
   B. This means that one may not give less.
   C. But is it the law that if one wants to give more, he may do so?
   D. Scripture says, "according to their number."
   E. Or if one wants to give double, may he give double?
   F. Scripture says, "so shall you do with every one" — in accord with the number applying to each of them.
   G. On this basis sages have ruled:
   H. **The priests may mix together [and offer as one] the drink offerings brought with oxen with those brought with other oxen, the ones brought with rams with those brought with other rams, those brought with lambs with those brought with other lambs, those brought with an animal brought by an individual and those brought with an animal offered by the community, those brought on a given day with those brought on the preceding day. But they may not mix the drink offerings brought with lambs and those brought with oxen or those brought with rams [M. Men. 9:4].**
   I. They have further ruled:
   J. **He who says, "Lo, incumbent on me is a gift of wine," a log of wine he may not bring, two he may not bring, three he may bring. If he said four, five he may not bring, six he may bring. From that point, he may bring [any volume]. Just as the community brings wine as a matter of obligation, so an individual is permitted to make a voluntary gift of wine. [M. Men. 12:4J: They do not volunteer as a free will offering a single log of wine, two or five. But they volunteer as a free will offering three, four, or six, and any number more than six.].**
   K. "...so shall you do with every one:" this serves to encompass the eleventh [beast designated as tithe of the flock].

Scripture specifies the rules that governing mixing the drink offerings for various classes of offerings. Essentially, the rule is, drink offerings for sacrifices of a single category may be mixed together, but not those for animals of a different category, and the species of beast dictates the category that governs.

*Seven. Sifré to Numbers* 135

## CX:IV
1. A. "Of the first of your coarse meal [you shall present a cake as an offering; as an offering from the threshing floor, so shall you present it. Of the first of your coarse meal you shall give to the Lord an offering throughout your generations]" (Num. 15:17-21):
   B. Why is this statement made?
   C. Because Scripture says, "...you shall present an offering to the Lord," I might infer that [unkneaded] flour is also covered by this requirement.
   D. Scripture says, "Of the first of your coarse meal," meaning, once the dough has congealed [become a compact mass].
      E. On this basis sages have ruled:
      F. **People may snack on dough without first separating dough offering from it until the woman preparing the dough rolls the dough out, in the case of dough made from wheat, or until she forms it into a solid mass, in the case of dough made from barley. Once she has rolled the dough out in the case of dough made from wheat, or formed it into a solid mass in the case of dough made from barley, one who eats from it without first separating dough offering is liable to death. As soon as she puts water into the flour, she must remove her portion of dough offering, so long as there is not five fourths of a qab of flour left unmixed with water [M. Hal. 3:1],**
      G. and, further, so long as the volume of dough has the appropriate measure.
      H. For people do not separate dough offering from uncongealed flour.
         I. What marks the completion of the work of preparing the dough?
         J. **R. Aqiba says, "Liability is determined [not by the status of the dough at the point at which one rolls it out, but] by its status at the point at which the crust forms on the bread in the oven' [M. Hal. 3:6]** [at which point the yeast has died].
         K. R. Yohanan b. Nuri says, "In the case of dough made from wheat, once one has formed it into balls, and in the case of dough made of barley, once one has formed it into a solid mass."

Scripture, D, states the rule, which the Mishnah then amplifies and instantiates.

## VI. THE TYPES OF ANALYSIS IN SIFRÉ TO NUMBERS

What we now have learned is that the usual types of analysis characteristic of Halakhic discourse apply to Halakhic discourse. I did not find in Sifré to Numbers a corpus of Aggadic exercises in which the pertinent types of analysis figure, only Halakhic ones. But that is an important finding. For it removes from consideration the proposition that the literary genre, exegesis of Scripture, differentiates between Halakhah and Aggadah. We might have supposed that where Halakhah is expounded in the usual, discursive-analytical manner of the Mishnah-Tosefta-Yerushalmi-Bavli, there the modes of thought characteristic of Halakhic discourse pertain. Then, we should expect, the types of analysis identified in the Halakhic documents to predominate. But where Halakhah is expounded in the framework of Midrash, there the modes of thought dominant in the exegetical genre — citation, gloss, types of analysis dictated by the requirements of a close reading of a given text in its own terms and framework — to prevail. That is not what Sifré to Numbers has shown us. Quite the opposite: the document has decisively proven that the types of analysis of the Halakhic-expository documents govern even when the exegesis of Scripture, not of the law in the abstract, defines the task at hand. The modes of thought of the Halakhah prevail not only when the Halakhah is systematically expounded but even in the genre of Midrash, where the systematic exposition concerns Scripture in its own order and context.

## VII. Conclusion: Types of Analysis of Rabbinic Judaism: Halakhic and Aggadic

The same types of analysis serve, though not in the same proportions nor invariably in the same manner, for both the Halakhic and the Aggadic writings. Once we have established the types of analysis characteristic of the Halakhah and turned to the Aggadah to ask whether these same types of analysis play a part in Aggadic exposition, the important evidence derives from Genesis Rabbah, Leviticus Rabbah, and Sifré to Numbers — two documents of Midrash-Aggadah (Aggadah expounded in the exegetical mode) and one of Midrash-Halakhah (Halakhah expounded exegetically). The sample suffices, since the generative question of this study is: does a single corpus of modes of thought govern in Aggadic as much as in Halakhic discourse?

Genesis Rabbah settled the question: it does. There we found effective adaptations for Aggadic purposes of the four Halakhic types of analysis identified after so much labor. Linguistic analysis of words and phrases, an interest in establishing the rationality of both positions in a dispute, discovery of proof in Scripture for Halakhic propositions (all the more so, theological propositions), and even analogy- and category-criticism — all find their place in the document. It was that fourth item. The comparison and contrast of categories defined in the narrative of parables forms the counterpart to the comparison and contrast of categories formed by common indicative qualities. What in the Halakhah is stated in abstract, expository terms comes out in the Aggadah in concrete, narrative ones. But the respective exercises of category-criticism of the Halakhah and of the Aggadah correspond. Leviticus Rabbah produced a comparable result.

The upshot of this protracted study may be set forth in very few words. The modes of thought embodied by the types of analysis of Halakhic discourse govern in Aggadic discourse as well. The same analytical initiatives occur in both parts of the Rabbinic corpus, which, therefore, exhibits qualities of intellectual integrity. The canon is characterized throughout its principal parts by the unity of analytical methods and interests. Much labor has produced a modest result — but a consequential one.

PART FOUR

A PRELIMINARY PROBE:
TYPES OF ARGUMENTATION
IN TRACTATE MOED QATAN

# 8

# MOED QATAN CHAPTER ONE

Let me give a single concrete example of what I conceive to represent a type of argument subject to definition and classification. It is valuable because not only the positions and reasons for them are adduced in evidence, but there is a clear articulation of the character of the argument that is mounted by each party. The issue is self-explanatory: how we deal with a case of doubt? The issue is, how do we select the governing metaphor? The argument by analogy then determines the outcome. The details are not difficult to master. An immersion-pool, to accomplish its work of raising objects or persons from the condition of cultic uncleanness to the condition of cultic cleanness, must contain a minimum volume of valid water. If such a pool is measured and found wanting, then what is the status of persons or objects immersed therein between the time of the discovery of its invalidity and the last time that the measure was taken and found sufficient?

### Tosefta Miqvaot 1:16-20

1:16 A. An immersion-pool which was measured and found lacking — all the acts requiring cleanness which were carried out depending upon it
 B. whether this immersion-pool is in the private domain, or whether this immersion-pool is in the public domain — [Supply: are unclean.]
 C. R. Simeon says, "[If the pool is situated] in the private domain, it is unclean. In the public domain, it is clean."'

1:17 A. Said R. Simeon, "M'SH B: The water-reservoir of Disqus in Yabneh was measured and found lacking.
 B. "And R. Tarfon did declare clean, and R. Aqiba unclean.
 C. "Said R. Tarfon, 'Since this immersion-pool is in the assumption of being clean, it remains perpetually in this presumption of cleanness until it will be known for sure that it is made unclean.'

|       |    |                                                                                                                                                                                                                                                                                      |
|-------|----|--------------------------------------------------------------------------------------------------------------------------------------------------------------------------------------------------------------------------------------------------------------------------------------|
|       | D. | "Said R. Aqiba, 'Since this immersion-pool is in the assumption of being unclean, it perpetually remains in the presumption of uncleanness until it will be known for sure that it is clean.' |
| 1:18  | A. | "Said R. Tarfon, "To what is the matter to be likened? To one who was standing and offering [a sacrifice] at the altar, and it became known that he is a son of a divorcee or the son of a *Halusah* [a woman who has executed the rite of removing the shoe and is in the classification of a divorcee]— for his service is valid." |
|       | B. | "Said R. Aqiba, 'To what is the matter to be likened? To one who was standing and offering [a sacrifice] at the altar, and it became known that he is disqualified by reason of a blemish — for his service is invalid.' |
| 1:19  | A. | "Said R. Tarfon to him, 'You draw an analogy to one who is blemished. I draw an analogy to the son of a divorcee or to the son of a Halusah. |
|       | B. | "'Let us now see to what the matter is appropriately likened. it is analogous to a blemished priest, let us learn the law from the case of the blemished priest. If it is analogous to the son of a divorcée or to the son of a Halusah, let us learn the law from the case of the son of the divorcee or the son of a *Halusah.*' |
| 1:20  | A. | "R. Aqiba says, 'The unfitness affecting an immersion-pool affects the immersion-pool itself, and the unfit aspect of the blemished priest affects the blemished priest himself. |
|       | B. | "'But let not the case of the son of a divorcee or the son of a *Halusah* prove the matter, for his matter of unfitness depends upon others. |
|       | C. | "'A ritual pool's unfitness [depends] on one only, and the unfitness af a blemished priest [depends] on an individual only, but let not the son of a divorcee or the son of a *Halusah* prove the matter, for the unfitness of this one depends upon ancestry.' |
|       | D. | "They took a vote concerning the case and declared it unclean. |
|       | E. | "Said R. Tarfon to R. Aqiba, 'He who departs from you is like one who perishes.'" |

Now the unusually lucid articulation of the logic of the argument makes it possible to classify the argument without ambiguity. The basic logic is, when confronted with an unknown, we identify the governing analogy. If we do not know the ruling for a given case, we translate the case into its general terms, and then identify a comparable case where the ruling is known. So the argument rests on the validity of the proposed analogies, and the rest follows. What makes the presentation lapidary is the provision of reasons for the validity of the proposed analogy, with the consequent distinctions proposed by the contesting party between the analogy that serves his case and the one that does not. Now, it is clear, the Rabbinic literature contains not only disputes about rulings, but debates between contesting parties, with the result that we have access to a variety of types of argumentation and the modes of thought that animate them. That is what is under study in the second part of this project: the collection and classification of arguments by their types.

Let me state matters in more general terms. Argumentation is best defined by the German word, "Auseinandersetzung," the explicit confrontation of conflicting viewpoints in the medium of exchanges of opinion, fact, and reason, yielding the

*Eight. Moed Qatan. Chapter One*

possibility of a rational resolution of conflict or a clear perception of the reasonable foundations for contradictory positions. By types of argumentation, then, I mean, the rules that govern authentic *Auseinandersetzungen* in Rabbinic literature. Some of these are blatant but instructive. For one example, Rabbinic literature everywhere requires a full exposition of the grounds for opposed views and the responses of both parties to a given challenge. So one rule of a valid *Auseinandersetzung* is that both parties be given a fair chance to spell out their respective positions. Another rule insists that each party address the substance of the opposed view, so that a direct confrontation of conflicting viewpoints and the reasons for them is provided for.

Let me now give an example of the kind of composition that I do *not* introduce as evidence for types of argumentation in the Rabbinic Halakhic documents.

### YERUSHALMI MOED QATAN 1:7

[A] **They do not take wives on the intermediate days of a festival,**
[B] **whether virgins or widows.**
[C] **Nor do they enter into levirate marriage,**
[D] **for it is an occasion of rejoicing.**

[I:1 A] [With reference to M. 1:7A-D:] Simeon bar Abba in the name of R. Yohanan, "It is because [people will hold up weddings until the festival, and so have one meal for the two events, the festival and the wedding]. [Consequently, they will postpone marriages and so] nullify the act of procreation [for the interval]."

[B] *They asked before R. Yosé,* "As to a slave, what is the law about his marrying a woman on the festival['s intermediate days]?"

[C] *He said to him, "Let us derive the answer from the following:* **Shall he refrain? But was not the world made only for procreation [M. Git. 4:5E-F]?** [Consequently, he too must not postpone his wedding until the intermediate days of a festival.]"

[D] And Simeon bar Abba said in the name of R. Yohanan, "[Anyone who is subject to] the religious duty of procreation [is prohibited from marrying a wife on the intermediate days of a festival]."

[E] That is to say that a slave is subject to the religious duty of procreation, and whoever is subject to the religious duty of procreation is prohibited from marrying on the intermediate days of a festival.

[F] R. Ila, R. Eleazar in the name of R. Hananiah: "It is because people must not confuse one cause of rejoicing with some other."

[G] R. La derived that lesson from the following verse of Scripture: "[And on the eighth day they held a solemn assembly;] for they had kept the dedication of the altar seven days and the feast seven days" (2 Chron. 7:9).

[H] R. Jacob bar Aha derived the rule from the following: "Complete the week of this one, and we will give you the other also in return for serving me another seven years" (Gen. 29:27).

[I] R. Abbahu in the name of R. Eleazar: "The prohibition is on account of the excessive work [involved in preparing for the wedding]."
  [J] *It has been taught:* But one may decide to get married on the eve of the festival.
  [K] *That lenient ruling, moreover, does not stand at variance with the view of R. Eleazar, R. Yohanan, or even R. Haninah.*
  [L] *Said R. Ba, "When the bride enters [the marriage canopy], the work is gone and done."*

What we do not see is an explicit *Auseinandersetzung*, a confrontation of the three conflicting reasons and the rationality that sustains each, together with an account of the reasons that the participants choose their explanation and not the other(s) in context. We have three explanations for the cited rule, A, F, and I. Each is given the support of a secondary amplification. B-E simply takes the stated rule with its reason and asks its own question, G-H finds scriptural support for the proposed explanation's factual basis, and J-L qualify the rule in line with the stated reasoning. So while we have the formal requirements of a dispute — three conflicting opinions about the same matter, in this case, exclusive explanations of the same phenomenon — the components of the dispute never intersect. No one asks how A can be right if F is also right, and no effort is made to sort out the cases in which one or another consideration supposedly predominates.

So we have the form of a dispute, but no engagement; and that means, we have no argument. These are the kinds of composites that I do not introduce in this account of types of argumentation and their forms. Now let us turn to the ones — and they are not many — that do register.

## i. Mishnah

I find neither analytical proposals nor attendant argumentation in the Mishnah. When we have examined cases of articulated arguments as these occur in Tosefta and the Talmuds, we shall have a clearer notion of what the Mishnah lacks. That is not to suggest that the Mishnah is comprised by inert data, lacking all construction into propositions of a compelling character. The opposite is the fact. The Mishnah's modes of argumentation, however, are implicit and have to be discerned and articulated by its heirs and continuators. In the Tosefta, Yerushalmi, and Bavli they do exactly that.

## ii. Tosefta

Begin with an example of the kind of evidence not pertinent to this inquiry: analysis without articulated argumentation. Here is an analytical exercise, but I see no detailed argumentation to support the proposed generalization. It would not be

## Eight. Moed Qatan. Chapter One

difficult hypothetically to reconstruct the argumentation attendant upon the analysis, but no material purpose would be served by so doing.

T. 1:2 E. To a matter which brings about loss do they attend on the intermediate days of a festival.
F. To a matter which does not bring about loss do they not attend on the intermediate days of a festival.
G. A person may sell his spring of water to a gentile or make a trade with him on the Sabbath to take effect at the end of the Sabbath,
H. and one need not scruple on that account [because the spring may falter, and the man lose out].

T. 1:11 A. And they grind flour during the festival [for use on the festival week itself].
B. To a matter which brings about loss do they attend on the intermediate days of a festival.
C. To a matter which does not bring about loss do they not attend on the intermediate days of a festival.
D. Under what circumstances?
E. With reference to that which is plucked up from the ground [cf. M. M.Q. 2:1-2].
F. But with reference to that which is not yet plucked up from the ground, even to a matter which brings about loss they do not attend on the intermediate days of a festival.
G. [If] one does not have anything to eat, he cuts grain, stacks and threshes it,
H. on condition that he not thresh with cows.

T. 1:7 A. He whose wall was leaning into the public domain tears it down and rebuilds it,
B. because of the threat to life [cf. M. M.Q. 1:2].
C. A city wall which was breached — they stop it up.
D. [If] they stopped it up and it was breached [again], they do not stop it up.
E. But if the city was near the frontier, one [has the right to] tear it down and rebuild it in the proper way.

I do not see how the illustrative materials constitute an argument in behalf of the principle, whether saving life or protecting property (as the case requires). The question, "why," clearly has an answer, but no one articulates it. Rather, there is the statement of the general rule (To a matter which...) with its governing criterion (...bring about a loss). No further need to spell out an argument is deemed necessary. The key language is "because of the threat to life," which identifies at M. 1:2 the operative consideration. It is not necessary to do more than invoke the principle; it is self-evident and prevails. In the substrate of established truths is preserved a sizable body of principles such as these.

### III. YERUSHALMI

#### YERUSHALMI MOED QATAN 1:1

[A]  [80a] **They water an irrigated field on the intermediate days of a festival and in the Seventh Year,**
[B]  **whether from a spring that first flows at that time, or from a spring that does not first flow at that time.**
[C]  **But they do not water [an irrigated field] with collected rain water, or water from a swape well.**
[D]  **And they do not dig channels around vines.**

[I:1  A]  *There is no difficulty understanding why* one may utilize a spring that does not first flow at that time. But in the case of a spring that first flows at that time, is this not a considerable amount of work [for the intermediate days of the festival]?
   [B]  *The law accords with the view of R. Meir. For* **R. Meir has said, "From a spring that first flows on the intermediate days of a festival they irrigate [even] a field that depends upon the rain [and does not need this water]" [T. Moed 1:1 A].**

If I find a contradiction between two versions of a rule on the same matter, I may resolve the contradiction if I can argue that one rule represents a given, named authority, another represents a different authority. The implicit argument is that the law contains no disharmonies, though individual sages take contrary positions on a given law. The law can accommodate the presence of schismatic opinion without itself being irreparably flawed. But we cannot build our systematization of matters on arguments that are merely implicit.

[II:3  A]  R. Eleazar b. R. Yosé asked, "As to cascades of water, how do you treat them?
   [B]  "Are they in the status of swape-well water or not? [No answer is given.]
   [C]  "As to a pool that was filled with spring water, the flow of which then ceased, what is the law as to watering a field from [such a pool]?"
   [D]  *Let us derive the answer from the following:* **But they do not water [an irrigated field] with collected rainwater or water from a swape well [M. 1:1 C].**
   [E]  *Now how shall we interpret that rule?* If we deal with a time in which the rain is falling, then [why should there be such a prohibition]? Is it not like irrigating the Great Sea? *But we must interpret the passage to speak* of the time in which the rain has ceased.

The implicit argument at E maintains that if we can set forth two possible explanations and dismiss one of them for good and sufficient reasons, then the other must stand. And its implication (in the present instance) suffices to answer the question at hand. But, as I said, this account of the argumentation found plausible, even compelling, in the Rabbinic Judaism surveys only the articulated statements thereof.

## IV. BAVLI

### BAVLI TO MISHNAH-TRACTATE MOED QATAN 1:1-2

IV.1 A.  R. Eleazar b. Azariah says, "They do not make a new water channel on the intermediate days of a festival or in the Sabbatical Year." And sages say, "They make a new water channel in the Sabbatical Year, and they repair damaged ones on the intermediate days of a festival:"

We find ourselves thrust once more into the comparison of different spells that are at a lower level of sanctification than the Sabbath or the Festival, namely, the intermediate days of the festival and the Sabbatical Year. Consequently, we resume the task we began earlier, and, specifically, we want to know why the Sabbatical Year is subject to the prohibition at hand, which obviously pertains to the intermediate days of the festival. Here, the Mishnah-rule has dictated its own exegetical problem. The matter is spelled out in so many words in the terms I introduced earlier:

B.  *There is no problem with respect to the prohibition concerning the intermediate days of a festival, since the operative consideration is that this is heavy labor, but why ever not make a channel in the Sabbatical Year?*
C.  R. Zira and R. Abba b. Mamel differ on the matter —
D.  One said, "The reason is that the one who digs appears to be hoeing."
E.  And the other said, "The reason is that he looks as though he is preparing the banks for sowing."
F.  So what's at stake?
G.  *At issue is a case in which the water comes along immediately. From the perspective of him who has said,* "The reason is that he looks as though he is preparing the banks for sowing," *it is still objectionable. But from the perspective of him who has said,* "The reason is that the one who digs appears to be hoeing," *there is no objection.*
H.  *But should not the one who objects for the reason that it looks as though he is spading also object that he looks as though he is preparing the bank for seed?*
I.  *Rather, this is what's at stake between the two explanations: it would involve a case in which he takes what is in the trench and tosses it out. From the perspective of him who says,* "The reason is that he looks as though he is preparing the banks for sowing," *there is no objection; but from the perspective of him who says,* "The reason is that the one who digs appears to be hoeing," *it is still subject to an objection.*
J.  *But from the perspective of him who says that he appears to be preparing the sides for seed, would he not also admit that he seems to be hoeing?*
K.  *Not really, for one who hoes, as soon as he takes up a spadeful, he puts it down again in place.*

What makes the exposition satisfying is that each side is given an opportunity to apply its reasoning at every stage in the argument, hence a full account, through the dialectic of back-and-forth exchange of positions and reasoning, is set forth. What is critical is the systematic character of the exposition of the argumentation. The argumentation works because each party is shown to address precisely the issue raised by the other party.

### BAVLI TO MISHNAH-TRACTATE MOED QATAN 1:5A-B

A. [On the intermediate days of the festival,] R. Meir says, "They examine marks of the presence of the skin ailment [to begin with] to provide a lenient ruling but not to provide a strict ruling."
B. And sages say, "Neither to provide a lenient ruling nor to provide a strict ruling."

5. A. *The master has said:* "And on the day" (Lev. 13:14) — there is a day on which you inspect him, and there is a day on which you do not inspect him. *How does the cited verse yield this conclusion?*
B. *Said Abbayye, "If the verse yielded no such conclusion, the All-Merciful could as well have written,* 'on the day.' *Why say,* 'and on the day'? *That yields the conclusion that* there is a day on which you inspect him, and there is a day on which you do not inspect him."
C. *Raba said, "The whole of the verse is redundant, for otherwise Scripture could have said,* 'and when raw flesh is seen in him.' *Why add,* 'and on a day'? *That yields the conclusion that* there is a day on which you inspect him, and there is a day on which you do not inspect him."
D. *And Abbayye?*
E. *That is required to indicate,* by day and not by night.
F. *And how does Raba know that it is to be* by day and not by night?
G. *He derives that fact from the following:* "According to everything that the priest sees" (Lev. 13:12) [which is to say, by day, when people can see properly].
H. *And Abbayye?*
I. *That is required to exclude from the inspection process a priest who is blind in one eye.*
J. *And does not Raba require the verse to make this point as well?*
K. *True enough.*
L. *Then how does he know that it is to be* by day but not by night?
M. *He derives it from the verse,* "Like as a plague was seen by me in the house" (Lev. 14:35) — by me, not with the help of a lamp.
N. *And Abbayye?*
O. *If the rule derived from there, I might have supposed that the restriction applies when the uncleanness does not affect a person's body, but where uncleanness affects the body, I might have supposed that one may inspect it by a lamp. So the original proof-text is the better one.*

Abbayye makes explicit his parsing of the proof-text, and Raba joins the issue at precisely the same point: the redundancy of the formulation, bearing the

*Eight. Moed Qatan. Chapter One*

alleged implication. Then Abbayye addresses the particular clause adduced in evidence by Raba, and Raba is asked to show that what he deems redundant is redundant. Each party is given a full exposition of his views, and the exposition is systematic and balanced, each one answering the argument adduced by the other. This is a remarkably successful exposition of an argument and its premises and implications, how the argument spins itself out, and why, in the end, each party has a solid and reasonable position. I cannot imagine a more satisfying exercise in rational *Auseinandersetzungen*.

### BAVLI-TRACTATE MOED QATAN 1:7-8

#### 1:7

- A. They do not take wives on the intermediate days of a festival,
- B. whether virgins or widows.
- C. Nor do they enter into levirate marriage,
- D. for it is an occasion of rejoicing for the groom.
- E. But one may remarry his divorced wife.
- F. And a woman may prepare her wedding adornments on the intermediate days of a festival.
- G. R. Judah says, "She should not use lime, since this makes her ugly."

#### 1:8

- A. An unskilled person sews in the usual way.
- B. But an expert craftsman sews with irregular stitches.
- C. They weave the ropes for beds.
- D. R. Yosé says, "They [only] tighten them."

I.1   A.   *So if it's* **an occasion of rejoicing for the groom,** *what's so bad about that?*
     B.   Said R. Judah said Samuel, and so said R. Eleazar said R. Oshaia, and some say, said R. Eleazar said R. Hanina, "The consideration is that one occasion of rejoicing should not be joined with another such occasion."
     C.   Rabbah bar R. Huna said, "It is because he neglects the rejoicing of the festival to engage in rejoicing over his wife."
     E.   Ulla said, "It is because it is excess trouble."
     F.   R. Isaac Nappaha said, "It is because one will neglect the requirement of being fruitful and multiplying" [if people postponed weddings until festivals, they might somehow diminish the occasion for procreation, which is the first obligation]."
         G.   *An objection was raised:* All those of whom they have said that they are forbidden to wed on the festival **[9A]** are permitted to wed on the eve of the festival. *Now this poses a problem to the explanations of all the cited authorities!*
         H.   *There is no problem from the perspective of him who has said,* "The consideration is that one occasion of rejoicing should not be joined with

another such occasion," *for the main rejoicing of the wedding is only a single day.*

I. *And from the perspective of him who has said,* "It is because it is excess trouble," *the principal bother lasts only one day.*

J. *And from the perspective of him who has said,* "It is because one will neglect the requirement of being fruitful and multiplying," *for merely one day someone will not postpone the obligation for any considerable length of time.*

Each of the four positions, B, C, E, F, is asked to address the same objection, and each solves the problem by giving a reason consistent with his ruling. The argument is, there is a sound position that sustains each one. The objection, G, is addressed to each party, and all are given the opportunity reasonably to respond. The result is an equally satisfying account of the rationality of the four conflicting views.

## V. ARGUMENT: THE TYPES AND THEIR FORMS. AN INITIAL RESULT

Once we eliminate from consideration implicit arguments, these are what we find on this initial probe:

### 1. CONFLICTING POSITIONS REST ON SHARED PREMISES: ARGUMENTS BASED ON COMPARISON AND CONTRAST OF VERSIONS OF THE LAW OR ON REASONING ABOUT THEM

Bavli to M. M.Q. 1:1-2 IV.1: each party to the dispute has a reason for his position, based on his view of the impression that a given activity creates; and both parties address the same issue, as is made explicit.

Bavli to M. Q. 1:7-8 I.1/8b-9a: four reasons for one rule, each bearing its own implications, then an objection is raised plus There is no problem from the perspective of him who has said,... And from the perspective of him who has said... And from the perspective of him who has said...

### 2. CONFLICTING READING OF SCRIPTURE YIELDING A COMMON RESULT: ARGUMENTS BASED ON EXEGESIS OF SCRIPTURE

Bavli to M. M.Q. 1:5A-B I.5: How does the cited verse yield this conclusion? If the verse yielded no such conclusion, the All-Merciful could as well have written...Why say...? That yields the conclusion that there is... vs. "The whole of the verse is redundant, for otherwise Scripture could have said... Why add, ... That yields the conclusion that...

The Bavli's contribution emphasizes the rational foundations of disputes, which conflict on reasonable grounds and represent negotiable differences. The

## Eight. Moed Qatan. Chapter One

emphasis is the construction of argument based on shared premises of the participants, so that each party has the possibility of claiming, "even on the basis of your position, I can prove mine right." The upshot is, argumentation appears meant not only to articulate bases of difference but also severely to restrict those bases to the realm of rationality and reason: disagreement confirms consensus on all things that matter. We may characterize this type of argumentation as arguments from shared reason or conflicts over different formulations of the law. Its companion type of argumentation flows from shared exegetical principles producing contradictory results.

Two results lay the foundations for further inquiry. First, we have found two types of argumentation and are ready to examine further texts. Second, so far as argument represents the medium for exposing the reason behind the rule, the Bavli takes the lead in laying out not only the law but its logic. In due course, however, we shall find ample evidence that the framers of the Bavli carried forward a rooted tradition of critical inquiry.[1]

---

[1] Nonetheless, I found the same odd result in my repertoire of dialectics of the Rabbinic canon, Mishnah-Tosefta-Yerushalmi-Bavli. First, dialectics is particular to Halakhic discourse. Second, the resort to the moving argument in the exposition of the logic of the law is rare; the Mishnah, Tosefta, and Yerushalmi cannot be characterized as dialectical in any but the most formal and superficial sense. Only the Bavli builds some major composites, and certainly its most successful ones, on dialectical arguments, and even there, it is only on rare occasion. See my *Talmudic Dialectics: Types and Forms.* Atlanta, 1995: Scholars Press for South Florida Studies in the History of Judaism. I. *Introduction. Tractate Berakhot and the Divisions of Appointed Times and Women,* and II. *The Divisions of Damages and Holy Things and Tractate Niddah.*

# 9

# Moed Qatan Chapter Two

## I. ARGUMENTS EXECUTED THROUGH APPEAL TO TRADITION AND REASON

### BAVLI TO MOED QATAN 2:4A I.1

A. They buy houses, slaves, and cattle, only for the needs of the festival or for the needs of a seller who has nothing to eat.

I.1 A. *Raba raised this question to R. Nahman:* "As to hiring for make-work jobs someone who has not got food — what is the law?"
B. *He said to him, "We have learned in the Mishnah,* **or for the needs of a seller who has nothing to eat.** *Now what does* who has nothing to eat *encompass? It is surely make-work for starving workers."*
C. *He said to him, "No, it serves to amplify the clause."*
D. Objected Abbayye, "**They do not write writs of indebtedness on the intermediate days of a festival. But if one does not trust him, or if he had nothing to eat, lo, this one should write [a writ of indebtedness]** [M. 3:4A-D]. *Now what does* if he had nothing to eat *encompass? It is surely make-work for starving workers."*
E. *That is decisive proof.*
F. *Objected R. Sheshet,* "**And sages say, 'Three sorts of craftsmen perform work on the eve of Passover up to noon, and these are they: tailors, barbers, and laundry-men.' R. Yosé b. R. Judah says, 'Also: shoemakers'** [M. Pes. 4:6D-F]. tailors, barbers, and laundry-men — for the same reason that an individual may do some sewing in the ordinary way during the intermediate days of the festival; hairdressers and fullers, for the same reason that persons coming home from abroad or coming out of prison may have a hair cut and wash their clothes during the intermediate days of the festival. *Now if you assume that it is permitted to hire for make-work jobs starving people, then all other work should have been permitted hear, since, if make-work jobs are*

*permitted where one is starving, anything else should also be permitted on the same principle."*

G. Objected R. Pappa, *"Then how about the following [equally plausible objection, leading to an absurd result]: building too should be permitted, for the following rule applies:* **As to a wall that is hanging over into public domain, they may tear it down and rebuild it in the usual way, because it is a public nuisance [T. 1:7A-B].***"*

H. Objected Rabina, "Then how about the following: a scribe should be permitted to do his work, since in any event, **And these do they write on the intermediate days of a festival: (1) writs of betrothal for women, (2) writs of divorce, (3) receipts [for payment of the marriage settlement], (4) testaments, (5) deeds of gift, (6) prosbols [assigning to the court writs of indebtedness, so that the writs will not be nullified by the advent of the Sabbatical Year], (7) deeds of valuation, (8) deeds of alimony, (9) writs of the rite of removing the shoe and of the exercise of the rite of refusal, (10) deeds of arbitration, (11) court decrees, and (12) official decrees [M. Moed Qatan 3:3].***"*

I. [The premises throughout invoke an analogy that is inappropriate, namely, the intermediate days of the festival and the conduct of ordinary people on the fourteenth of Nisan, prior to the advent of Passover; but that day is not the counterpart to a festival day at all.] *Rather, said R. Ashi, "How can you compare the rules governing the intermediate days of the festival week and the rules concerning the fourteenth of Nisan? Those governing the intermediate days of the festival week are so as to avoid heavy labor, but where there is the possibility of severe loss, rabbis have permitted work; rules governing the fourteenth of Nisan are based on the requirements of the festival of Passover, so that whatever is needed for the observance of the festival of Passover have our rabbis permitted, but anything that is not needed for the observance of the festival f Passover have our rabbis not permitted."*

The conflict concerns priorities: sanctification of the intermediate days of the festival as against providing for the poor. Nahman reads the Mishnah to yield the rule that one provides work for the poor. Abbayye cites evidence to refute that result. But the proof itself is challenged: a consistent rule, based on established facts, would not concur. A sequence of absurd results is adduced. But at the end, the argument turns on whether correct analogies have been introduced. This is a well-crafted, completely cogent composition, made up for the purpose of the extension of the law of the Mishnah. Here is a model of a composition that amplifies not the Mishnah-paragraph's wording or rule but its principle, allowing us to clarify the law that covers a variety of topics and to establish a more profound and decisive conception out of the details of the diverse topics: discover the valid analogy, and criticize a position on grounds of the appropriate or inappropriate character of said analogy. All parties are given plausible cases, and each step in the argument engages with the prior one; but in the end the decisive consideration registers.

*Nine. Moed Qatan. Chapter 2*

## II. Arguments Executed through Exegesis of Scripture

    A.    Mishnah: —
    B.    Tosefta: —
    C.    Yerushalmi
    D.    Bavli: —

## III. The Types of Argumentation

A fully-articulated argument occurs only once in the entire presentation of Moed Qatan Chapter Two, in all four documents. That is a surprising result.

    i.    Arguments Based on Tradition and Reason: B. to M. 2:4A I is our sole entry.
    ii.   Arguments Executed through Exegesis of Scripture: —

# PART FIVE

# A SECONDARY PROBE: TYPES OF ARGUMENTATION IN SELECT TRACTATES: QIDDUSHIN, ABODAH ZARAH

# 10

# Qiddushin

## I. Arguments Based on Tradition and Reason

    A.    Mishnah: —
    B.    Tosefta: —
    C.    Yerushalmi —
    D.    Bavli

### Bavli to Mishnah Qiddushin 1:1

X.1  A.  **And through the levir's death:**
    B.  *How do we know it?*
    C.  It derives from an argument a fortiori: If a married woman, who, if she commits adultery, is put to death through strangulation, is released by the death of the husband, a levirate widow, who is forbidden merely by a negative commandment [from marrying someone else] all the more so should be freed by the death of the levir!
    D.  But what distinguishes a married woman is that she goes forth with a writ of divorce. Will you say the same of this woman, who does not go forth with a writ of divorce?
    E.  But she, too, goes forth with the rite of removing the shoe [which is comparable to a writ of divorce].
    F.  Rather: What is special about the married woman is that the one who forbids her to other men also frees her [which is not the case with the levirate widow, since she is forbidden to others because of her childless deceased husband, but that the death of the levir frees her has yet to be proved].
    G.  *Said R. Ashi, "Lo, here too, he who forbids her also frees her: The levir forbids her, the levir frees her"* [since if there were no levir, her husband's death alone would have freed her, so he really is responsible (Freedman. *Qiddushin, ad loc.*)].

The thrust of argument, D, is to reject the analogy on which the argument a fortiori is based, C. The things deemed comparable in fact are to be differentiated, so the argument a fortiori does not serve. This is a familiar procedure. One precipitant of sustained argument, we see, is the issue of analogy and contrast. One party alleges the former, the contrary, the latter. Then what makes the engine of thought work is the analogical-contrastive principle, which fuels arguments and precipitates analysis.

### Bavli to Mishnah Qiddushin 1:2

VI.1 A. **The Hebrew slave girl has an advantage over him** [that is, over the Hebrew slave, M. 1:2A-B: A Hebrew slave is acquired through money and a writ. And he acquires himself through the passage of years, by the Jubilee year, and by deduction from the purchase price, redeeming himself at this outstanding value (Lev. 25:50-51)]. **For she acquires herself [in addition] through the appearance of tokens [of puberty].**

B. Said R. Simeon b. Laqish, "A Hebrew slave girl has acquired from the domain of her master possession of herself [as a free woman] upon the death of her father. That is the result of an argument a fortiori: If the appearance of puberty signs, which do not free her from her father's authority, free her from the authority of her master, then death, which does free her from her father's authority [the father's heirs have no claim on her], surely should free her from her master's authority [whose heirs should not inherit her]!"

C. *Objected R. Oshayya,* "**The Hebrew slave girl has an advantage over him. For she acquires herself [in addition] through the appearance of tokens [of puberty].** *But if what he has said were so, then the list should include reference to her father's death as well!"*

D. *The Tannaite authority has listed some items and left out others.*

E. *Well, then, what else has he left out, if he has left out this item?*

F. *He leaves out reference to her master's death.*

G. *Well, if that is all he has left out, then he has left out nothing; since that would pertain also to a male slave as well, it is omitted anyhow.*

H. *But why not include it?*

I. *The Tannaite framer of the passage has encompassed what is subject to a fixed limit [the six years, the proportionate repayment of the purchase price, the Jubilee], but what is not subject to a fixed limit he does not include in his Tannaite rule.*

J. *But lo, there is the matter of puberty signs, which are not subject to a fixed limit, but the Tannaite framer of the passage has covered them too.*

K. Said R. Safra, "They have no fixed limit above, but they are subject to a fixed limit **[16B]** below. *For it has been taught on Tannaite authority:* A boy aged nine who produced two puberty hairs — these are classified as a mere mole; from the age of nine years to twelve years and one day, they are classified as a mere mole. R. Yosé b. R. Judah says, 'They are classified as a mark of puberty.' From thirteen years and one day onward, all parties concur that they are classified as a mark of puberty."

Ten. Qiddushin  161

L. *Objected R. Sheshet,* "R. Simeon says, 'Four are given severance pay, three in the case of males, three in the case of females. And you cannot say there are four in the case of the male, because puberty signs are not effective in the case of a male, and you cannot say there is boring of the ear in the case of the female.' *Now if what R. Simeon b. Laqish has said were valid* ['A Hebrew slave girl has acquired from the domain of her master possession of herself as a free woman upon the death of her father'], *then the death of the father also should be included here. And should you say, the Tannaite authority has listed some items and left out others, lo, he has said matters explicitly in terms of four items! And if you should say, the Tannaite framer of the passage has encompassed what is subject to a fixed limit [the six years, the proportionate repayment of the purchase price, the Jubilee], but he has left off what is not subject to a fixed limit, lo, there is the matter of puberty signs, which are not subject to a fixed limit, and he has encompassed them in the Tannaite statement. And should you say, here as a matter of fact he, too, accords with R. Safra, well, then, there is the matter of the death of the master, which is not subject to a fixed definition as to time, and yet the Tannaite framer has included it. So what are the four items to which reference is made?"*

M. [1] Years, [2] Jubilee, [3] Jubilee for the one whose ear was bored, and [4] the Hebrew slave girl freed by puberty signs. *And that stands to reason, since the concluding clause goes on to say,* and you cannot say there are four in the case of the male, because puberty signs are not effective in the case of a male, and you cannot say there is boring of the ear in the case of the female. *But if it were the case [that the master's death is covered], then you would have four items for the woman. So that's decisive proof.*

N. *Objected R. Amram,* "And these are the ones that get severance pay: Slaves freed by the passage of six years of service, the Jubilee, the master's death, and the Hebrew slave girl freed by the advent of puberty signs. *And if the stated proposition were valid, the father's death also should be on the list. And should you say, the Tannaite authority has listed some items and left out others, lo, he has said,* and these are the ones [which is exclusionary, these — no others]. *And if you should say, the Tannaite framer of the passage has encompassed what is subject to a fixed limit [the six years, the proportionate repayment of the purchase price, the Jubilee], but he has left off what is not subject to a fixed limit, lo, there is the matter of puberty signs, which are not subject to a fixed limit, and he has encompassed them in the Tannaite statement. And should you say, here as a matter of fact he, too, accords with R. Safra, well, then, there is the matter of the death of the master. So isn't this a refutation of R. Simeon b. Laqish's position?"*

O. Sure is.
P. But lo, R. Simeon b. Laqish has set forth an argument a fortiori!
Q. It's a flawed argument a fortiori, along these lines: The distinguishing trait of puberty signs is that they mark a change in the body of the girl, but will you say the same of the death of the father, by which the body of the girl is left unaffected?

We now see that the argument a fortiori represents a translation, into the language of argumentation, of the analytical mode of category- and analogy-criticism. That is, once a problem is solved, for one party, by appeal to an analogy or a categorical judgment, the other party will challenge the accuracy of the categorical- or analogical comparison. That requires the making of a distinction by the second party, where the first party recognized none. Here the issue is, Does the Hebrew slave girl acquire possession of herself as a free woman upon the death of her father? The dispute between Simeon b. Laqish and Oshayya has to be shown to have a rational foundation. This is proposed as the formal one of the omission of an item, D, along with other items, E-F. That is challenged, G. But the challenge is reasonably countered, H-I. Then the theory of deliberate omission is further challenged, J. But a distinction is proposed to account for the inclusion of what can have been omitted, K. Sheshet, L, reverts to the primary issue of substance, turning away from the formal analysis that has preceded. But the established mode of inquiry moves forward.

### Bavli to Mishnah Qiddushin 4:3

A. **All those who are forbidden from entering into the congregation are permitted to marry one another.**
B. **R. Judah prohibits [their marrying one another].**
C. R. Eliezer says, "Those who are of certain status are permitted to intermarry with others who are of certain status.
D. "Those who are of certain status and those who are of doubtful status, those who are of doubtful status and those who are of certain status, those who are of doubtful status and those who are of doubtful status –
E. "[intermarriage among persons in such classifications] is prohibited."
F. And who are those who are of doubtful status?
G. The "silenced one," the foundling, and the Samaritan.

I.1 A. **All those who are forbidden from entering into the congregation:**
B. *What is the meaning of,* **all those who are forbidden from entering into the congregation***? Should I say this refers to Mamzers, Netins, silenced ones, and foundlings? Lo, the opening clause states explicitly:* **Converts, freed slaves, mamzers, Netins, "silenced ones," and foundlings are permitted to marry among one another***. And furthermore, with reference to the statement,* **R. Judah prohibits [their marrying one another]**, *to which clause does R. Judah's*

*Ten. Qiddushin* 163

*statement pertain? Should I say, it refers to the marriage of persons whose status is certain and persons whose status is subject to doubt? Now, since the concluding clause states,* **R. Eliezer says, "Those who are of certain status are permitted to intermarry with others who are of certain status. Those who are of certain status and those who are of doubtful status, those who are of doubtful status and those who are of certain status, those who are of doubtful status and those who are of doubtful status —** [intermarriage among persons in such classifications] **is prohibited,"** *it must follow that R. Judah does not take that position. And should you say* **R. Judah forbids** *pertains to the marriage of a proselyte and a mamzer girl, then does the language at hand state,* a proselyte with a mamzer girl? *What it states is,* **All those who are forbidden from entering into the congregation!**

C. Said R. Judah, **[74B]** *"This is the sense of the statement at hand:* **All those who are forbidden from entering into the congregation** of the priesthood — *and who might that be? It is a proselyte girl who converted at less than three years and a day old, thus not in accord with R. Simeon b. Yohai [as will be explained presently]* — **are permitted to marry one another**." [Then the statement, **R. Judah prohibits** their marrying one another refers to the marriage of a proselyte and a mamzer girl (Freedman).]

D. *Well, why not assign the rule to a girl three years and a day old, in accord also with R. Simeon b. Yohai?*

E. *If that were the case, the refutation would stand right along side, in the following argument: So the operative consideration is that it is a girl three years and a day old; lo, in the case of one less than that age, since she may enter the congregation of the priests, she is forbidden to intermarry with the others [mamzers and the like]. Then what about the one who is less than three years and a day old from the perspective of R. Simeon b. Yohai, who, though she may enter into the assembly of priests, nonetheless may intermarry with the others?* [Freedman: For since she may marry a mamzer, it follows that the assembly of proselytes does not fall into the category of an assembly, so the same would hold good if she is a proselyte prior to that age as well.]

I.2 A. *And is it an encompassing generalization that* **all those who are forbidden from entering into the congregation are permitted to marry one another**? What about a widow, a divorcée, a woman of impaired priestly genealogy, and a whore [Lev. 21:7], all of whom are prohibited from entering into the congregation of the priesthood, but who also are forbidden to marry with these others? *Furthermore,* then is one who is permitted to marry into the priesthood forbidden to marry with these? But what about a proselyte, who is permitted to marry a priest's daughter but also is permitted to marry a mamzer girl?

B. *Rather, said R. Nathan bar Hoshayya, "This is the sense of the statement:* Anyone whose daughter a priest is forbidden to marry — *and who might that be? it is a proselyte man who married a proselyte women, and that is in accord with the position of R. Eliezer b. Jacob* — is permitted to marry with one another.

C. *And is it an encompassing generalization that* anyone whose daughter a priest is forbidden to marry is permitted to marry with one another? *What about the case of* a priest of impaired genealogical status who married a daughter of Israelite status, in which case, a priest is forbidden to marry his daughter, but,

nonetheless, he may not intermarry with these others [the mamzer and the like]?
D. *No problem, the rule accords with R. Dosetai b. Judah* ["Israelite women constitute an immersion pool for the purpose of purification of priests who have been profaned"].
E. *What about the case of a priest of impaired genealogical status who married a priest girl of impaired genealogical status?* Here, though a priest may not marry his daughter, yet such a one may intermarry with those others! *And furthermore, the formulation implies, but one whose daughter is permitted to marry a priest is forbidden to intermarry with these* — then what about the case of a proselyte who married an Israelite woman, in which case a priest is permitted to marry his daughter, but he may intermarry with these others!
F. *Rather, said R. Nahman said Rabbah bar Abbuha, "Here at issue between them is the case of a mamzer born of a sister and a mamzer born of a married woman. The first Tannaite position is that even a mamzer born of his sister is classified as a mamzer. And R. Judah takes the view that a mamzer born of a married woman is a mamzer, but one born of a sister is not."* [Freedman: The rule does not refer to a proselyte at all, but to the question of whether these two mamzer children may intermarry. A sister is forbidden on pain of extirpation, adultery with a married woman is forbidden on pain of the death penalty. The first authority treats the offspring of both unions as a mamzer and holds those who are forbidden to enter the assembly as Mamzerim may nonetheless intermarry; Judah holds that only the latter, forbidden on pain of death, is a mamzer, but not the former, so they may not intermarry.]
G. *Well, if that's the case, then what does the framer of our Mishnah paragraph propose to tell us that is fresh and interesting, when we have already learned the same point in the Mishnah elsewhere:* **What is the definition of a "mamzer"?** "**[The offspring of] any [marriage of near of kin — the rubric, 'He shall not come into the congregation of the Lord' (Deut. 23:3),"** the words of R. Aqiba. Simeon of Teman says, "**[The offspring of] any [marriage] for which the participants are liable to extirpation by Heaven."** And the law follows his opinion. R. Joshua says, "**[The offspring of] any [marriage] for which the participants are liable to be put to death by a court"** [M. Yeb. 4:13]?
H. *Rather, said Raba, "Here at issue between them is the case of an Ammonite and Moabite proselyte, and this is the sense of the statement:* **All those who are forbidden from entering into the congregation** — *and who might that be? an Ammonite and a Moabite proselyte —* **are permitted to intermarry**."
I. *If so, what is the meaning of,* **R. Judah prohibits [their marrying one another]**?
J. *This is the sense of his statement,* "Even though **R. Judah prohibits** a proselyte to marry a mamzer girl, that is a proselyte who is eligible to enter into the assembly; but it does not apply to Ammonite and Moabite proselytes, who are not eligible to enter into the assembly."

The argument commences at C with Judah's thesis, which is then challenged at D. That is, why adopt premise A when we can choose premise B. This is dismissed at E. A new phase commences with I.2, once more with a thesis proposed at B and

*Ten. Qiddushin*

challenged at C. Now the basis of the challenge is articulate: what about exceptions to the generalization that is the premise of the thesis. The continuation of the argument proceeds through familiar patterns of argument, e.g., G's challenge based on the banality of the result of the proposed explanation.

## II. ARGUMENTS EXECUTED THROUGH EXEGESIS OF SCRIPTURE

    A.    MISHNAH: —
    B.    TOSEFTA: —
    C.    YERUSHALMI

### YERUSHALMI TO MISHNAH QIDDUSHIN 1:1

[A] [58b] **A woman is acquired [as a wife] in three ways, and acquires [freedom for] herself [as a free agent] in two ways.**
[B] **She is acquired through money, a writ, or sexual intercourse.**

[I.3 A] [Why is it necessary to adduce evidence via a verse of Scripture, if the logical argument of an argument a fortiori could produce the same result? We shall now see the answer:] Said R. Abin, "And Hezekiah taught: 'When a man takes a wife' (Deut. 24:1) tells us that a woman is acquired through a money payment.
[B] "Now, it is a matter of logical argument, if a Hebrew slave girl. who is not acquired through sexual relations, is acquired through a money payment [Ex. 21: 7: 'When a man sells his daughter'], this one, who may be acquired through sexual relations, is it not reasonable to suppose that she should be acquired through a money payment?
[C] "The childless brother-in-law's widow will prove [to the contrary], for she indeed is acquired through an act of sexual relations, but she is not acquired through a money payment. [So there is no anomaly in the case of B, hence no argument a fortiori.]
[D] "This one too should cause no surprise, that even though she is acquired through sexual relations, [on the analogy with the childless sister-in-law] she still is not acquired through a money payment.
[E] "Accordingly, Scripture is required to state, 'When a man takes a wife'— indicating that she is acquired through a money payment.
[F] "'And has sexual relations with her'— indicating that she is acquired through an act of sexual relations.
[G] "Now is it not logical to argue as follows: If the childless widow, who is not acquired through a money payment, is acquired through an act of sexual relations, this one, who is acquired through a money payment, is it not logical that she should also be acquired through an act of sexual relations?
[H] "The Hebrew slave girl proves to the contrary. For she is acquired through a money payment and is not acquired through an act of sexual relations.
[I] "This one too should cause no surprise, for even though she is acquired through a money payment, she is not to be acquired through an act of sexual relations.

[J] "Accordingly, Scripture is required to state, 'When a man takes a wife'—indicating that she is acquired through a money payment.

[K] "'And has sexual relations with her'— indicating that she is acquired through an act of sexual relations.

[L] "As to a writ: Now if a payment of money, which does not have the power to free the woman from her husband, has the power to bring her under the domain of her husband, a writ, which does have the power to take her out of his domain—is it not logical that it should also have the power to bring her into his domain?

[M] "No, if you have stated that rule in regard to a money payment, which has the power to remove what has been sanctified from consecrated status through redemption [substitution], will you say the same of a writ, which does not have the power to redeem what has been consecrated and so remove it from its consecrated status?

[N] "The argument a fortiori has been shattered, and, accordingly, you must return to Scripture.

[O] "So it was necessary for Scripture to state: 'When a man takes a wife and marries her, if then she finds no favor in his eyes because he has found some indecency in her, and he writes her a bill of divorce and puts it in her hand and sends her out of his house, and she departs out of his house, and if she goes and becomes another man's wife . . .' (Deut. 24:1, 2).

[P] "The 'becoming' [another man's wife] thus is joined to the sending forth. Just as the sending forth is through a writ, so the becoming another man's wife is through a writ."

The question, why ask Scripture to prove what we on the basis of our own reasoning through an argument a fortiori can demonstrate, finds a simple answer. The logical argument does not serve, because the category-formations of which it is comprised in fact do not match exactly. Hence the argument is based on the false premise of comparability, and the only route open is via Scripture.

D. BAVLI

BAVLI TO MISHNAH QIDDUSHIN 1:2

A. A Hebrew slave is acquired through money and a writ.

II.1 A. [A Hebrew slave is acquired through money] or a writ:
B. *How on the basis of Scripture do we know that fact?*
C. Said Ulla, "Said Scripture, 'If he take him another wife' (Ex. 21:10) [in addition to the Hebrew slave girl] — Scripture thus treats the Hebrew slave girl as another wife: Just as another wife would be acquired by a writ, so a Hebrew slave girl is acquired through a writ."
D. *Well, that proof would clearly pose no problem to him who says, "The writ of a Hebrew slave girl — the master writes it," but from the perspective of him who says, "The father writes it," what is to be said? For it has been stated:*

*Ten. Qiddushin* 167

- E. The writ of a Hebrew slave girl — who writes it?
- F. R. Huna said, "The master writes it."
- G. R. Hisda said, "The father writes it."
- H. *So the proposed derivation from Scripture poses no problems, but from the perspective of R. Hisda, what is to be said?*
- I. Said R. Aha bar Jacob, "Said Scripture, 'She shall not go forth as slave boys do' (Ex. 21:7) [if the master blinds them or knocks out their teeth] — but she may be purchased in the manner in which slave boys are purchased. *And what might that way be? A* writ."
- J. *Well, why not say:* But she may be purchased in the manner in which slave boys are purchased. *And what might that way be?* usucaption?
- K. Said Scripture, "And you shall make [gentile slaves] an inheritance for your children after you" (Lev. 25:46) — they are acquired by usucaption, and slaves of no other classification are acquired by usucaption.
- L. *Well, why not say:* They are acquired by a writ, and slaves of no other classification are acquired by a writ?
- M. But isn't it written, "She shall not go forth as slave boys do" (Ex. 21:7)?
- N. Well, then, how come you prefer the one reading rather than the other?
- O. *It stands to reason that a writ is encompassed as a medium of acquiring title,* since a writ serves to divorce an Israelite woman [Freedman: just as it is effective in one instance, so in another].
- P. *To the contrary, usucaption should have been encompassed as a medium of acquiring title,* since it serves to effect acquisition of the property of an heirless proselyte.
- Q. *But we don't find such a medium of acquisition relevant when it comes to matters of marital relationship. Or, if you prefer, I shall say that the language,* "if he takes another" *serves to make that very point.* [Freedman: "She shall not go out" teaches that she may be acquired by deed, as is implied by the analogy of "another."]
  - R. *Now how does R. Huna deal with the clause,* "She shall not go forth as slave boys do" (Ex. 21:7) [if the master blinds them or knocks out their teeth]?
  - S. *He requires that verse to indicate that* she does not go forth at the loss of the major limbs, as does a slave boy.
  - T. And R. Hisda?
  - U. *If so, Scripture should have said,* "She shall not go forth like slave boys." *Why say,* "She shall not go forth as slave boys do" (Ex. 21:7) [if the master blinds them or knocks out their teeth]? *That yields two points.*

The demonstration from Scripture must respond to the challenge of D, that is, to the premise of the demonstration. Then the parties to the challenge are required to participate, H. The successive challenges offer possibilities other than the principal one. The key point in the argument is at L, why not consider contrary propositions, why prefer one reading over the other? Then reason is invoked, O, and challenged, P.

### III. ARGUMENTS CONCERNING THE GOVERNING ANALOGY

    A. MISHNAH: —
    B. TOSEFTA: —
    C. YERUSHALMI: —
    D. BAVLI: —

### IV. THE TYPES OF ARGUMENTATION

Arguments based on tradition involve the mere assertion that one or another party has received from prior sages a statement accorded the status of decided law. In the end, then, the "argument" formalizes what is no more penetrating than a mere exchange of opinion. Arguments based on reason, by contrast, involve an assertion deemed self-evident and compelling. And that is, more often than not, the allegation that one category-formation is comparable to another, therefore follows the rule of the other. The contrary argument, then, requires the differentiation of the two category-formations and the identification of distinction where the other party has alleged equivalence. In the present tractate, B. to M. Qid. 1:1 involves an argument a fortiori, therefore an allegation of analogy and contrast (X is like Y, but if X, the lesser of the two species, is such, then Y, the greater, all the more so must be such). The same interest in differentiating what is allegedly to be comparable recurs at B. to M. Qid. 1:2; now the making of distinctions is primary. B to M. Qid. 4:3 works out a different line of argumentation in the realm of analogy and contrast, now challenging the proposed generalization, another way of showing difference where another party has proposed correspondence or likeness.

Argumentation in the context of scriptural proof for propositions takes two forms. First, we want to know why, with access to pure reason, we have nonetheless to resort to Scripture's proof. The answer, familiar from Sifra, is that reason on its own does not effect unflawed category-formation; classification without Scripture's intervention proves imperfect, e.g., Y. to M. Qid. 1:1.I.3.

# 11

# Abodah Zarah

## I. Arguments Based on Tradition and Reason

### A. Mishnah

#### Mishnah Abodah Zarah 2:5

A. Said R. Judah, "R. Ishmael asked R. Joshua as they were going along the road.
B. "He said to him, 'On what account did they prohibit cheese made by gentiles?'
C. "He said to him, 'Because they curdle it with rennet from carrion.'
D. "He said to him, 'And is not the rennet from a whole offering subject to a more stringent rule than rennet from carrion, and yet they have said, 'A priest who is not squeamish sucks it out raw?'
E. (But they did not concur with him and ruled, "It is not available for [the priests'] benefit, while it also is not subject to the laws of sacrilege."
F. "He went and said to him, 'Because they curdle it with rennet of calves sacrificed to idols.,
G. "He said to him, 'If so, then why have they not also extended the prohibition affecting it to the matter of deriving benefit from it?'
H. "He moved him on to another subject.
I. "He said to him, 'Ishmael, my brother, "How do you read the verse: For your [masculine] love is better than wine, or, Your [feminine] love is better than wine" (Song 1:2)?'
J. "He said to him, 'For your [feminine] love is better than wine.'
K. "He said to him, 'The matter is not so. For its neighbor teaches concerning it, "Your [masculine] ointments have a goodly fragrance" (Song 1:3).'"

The key point in the argument occurs at G, which challenges the given reason on the basis of inconsistency. The reason does not adequately explain the rule, leaving the hole that is identified.

### Mishnah Abodah Zarah 4:7

A. They asked sages in Rome, "If [God] is not in favor of idolatry, why does he not wipe it away?"
B. They said to them, "If people worshipped something of which the world had no need, he certainly would wipe it away.
C. "But lo, people worship the sun, moon, stars, and planets.
D. "Now do you think he is going to wipe out his world because of idiots?"
E. They said to them, "If so, let him destroy something of which the world has no need, and leave something which the world needs!"
F. They said to them, "Then we should strengthen the hands of those who worship these [which would not be destroyed], for then they would say, 'Now you know full well that they are gods, for lo, they were not wiped out!'"

God's not wiping out idolatry is explained, B-D, and the rather commonplace explanation is challenged, E; the challenge is disposed of at F. The argument then follows a simple course: reason, challenge, response to the challenge, at each point considerations of common sense and practicality entering in.

### B. Tosefta

### Tosefta Abodah Zarah 6:7

A. Philosophers asked sages in Rome, "If God's will is not for idolatry, why does he not wipe it away?"
B. They said to them, "If people worshipped something of which the world had no need, he certainly would wipe it away. But lo, people worship the sun, moon, and stars. Now do you think he is going to wipe out his world because of idiots? [M. A.Z. 4:7A-D].
C. "But let the world be in accord with its accustomed way, and the idiots who behave ruinously will ultimately come and give a full account of themselves.
D. "[If] one has stolen seeds for planting, are they not ultimately going to sprout?
E. "[If] one has had sexual relations with a married woman, will she not ultimately give birth?
F. "But let the world be in accord with its accustomed way, and the idiots who behave ruinously will ultimately come and give a full account of themselves."

The reprise amplifies and improves but presents no surprises.

*Eleven.* 171

    C.    YERUSHALMI: —
    D.    BAVLI

### BAVLI TO MISHNAH ABODAH ZARAH 4:7

A. They asked sages in Rome, "If [God] is not in favor of idolatry why does he not wipe it away?"

B. They said to them, "If people worshipped something of which the world had no need, he certainly would wipe it away.

C. "But lo, people worship the sun, moon, stars, and planets.

D. "Now do you think he is going to wipe out his world because of idiots?

E. They said to them, "If so, let him destroy something of which the world has no need, and leave something which the world needs!"

F. They said to them, "Then we should strengthen the hands of those who worship these [which would not be destroyed], for then they would say, 'Now you know full well that they are gods, for lo, they were not wiped out!'"

I.1  A. *Our rabbis have taught on Tannaite authority:*

B. Philosophers asked sages in Rome, "[If] [God] is not in favor of idolatry, why does he not wipe it away?"

C. They said to them, "[If] people worshipped something of which the world had no need, he certainly would wipe it away. But lo, people worship the sun, moon, and stars. Now do you think he is going to wipe out his world because of idiots? [M. 4:7A-D].

D. "But let the world be in accord with its accustomed way, and the idiots who behave ruinously will ultimately come and give a full account of themselves.

E. "Another matter: [If] one has stolen a seah of seeds for planting and gone and planted them in the ground, it is a matter of justice that they should not sprout. But let the world be in accord with its accustomed way, and the idiots who behave ruinously will ultimately come and give a full account of themselves.

F. "Another matter: [If] one has had sexual relations with a married woman, it is a matter of justice that she should not give birth. But let the world be in accord with its accustomed way, and the idiots who behave ruinously will ultimately come and give a full account of themselves" [T. A.Z. 6:7A-F].

G. *That is in line with what* R. Simeon b. Laqish said, "Said the Holy One, blessed be He, 'It is not sufficient for the wicked to make my coinage common, but they go on to give me the trouble of putting my seal on it'" [Cohen: The wicked make wrong use of the sexual instinct with which they have been endowed by God and trouble him to form the embryo which results from their immorality].

I.2  A. A philosopher asked Rabban Gamaliel, "It is written in your Torah, 'For the Lord your God is a devouring fire, a jealous God' (Dt. 4:24). How come he is more jealous against the worshippers of the idol than against the idol itself?"

|   | B. | He said to him, "I shall give you a parable. To what is the matter to be compared? To a mortal king who had a single son, and this son raised a dog for himself, which he called by his father's name, so that, whenever he took an oath, he exclaimed, 'By the life of this dog, my father!' When the king heard, with whom was he angry? Was he angry with the son, or what he angry with the dog? One has to say it was with the son that he was angry." |
|---|---|---|
|   | C. | [The philosopher] said to him, "Are you going to call the idol a dog? But there is some substance to it." |
|   | D. | He said to him, "What makes you say so?" |
|   | E. | He said to him, "One time a fire broke out in our town and the entire town burned up, but that temple was not burned up." |
|   | F. | He said to him, "I shall give you a parable. To what is the matter to be compared? To a mortal king against whom one of the provinces rebelled. When he makes war, with whom does he do it? With the living or with the dead? You must say it is with the living he makes war." |
|   | G. | He said to him, "So you're just calling it names — a dog, a corpse. In that case, then let him just destroy it out of the world." |
|   | **H.** | **He said to him, "If people worshipped something of which the world had no need, he certainly would wipe it away. But lo, people worship the sun, moon, stars, and planets,** brooks and valleys. **Now do you think he is going to wipe out his world because of idiots?** And so Scripture says, [55A] 'Am I utterly to consume all things from off the face of the ground, says the Lord, am I to consume man and beast, am I to consume the bird of the heaven and the fish of the sea, even the stumbling blocks of the wicked' (Zeph. 1:2). Now simply because the wicked stumble on account of these things, is he going to destroy them from the world? Don't they also worship the human being, 'so am I to cut off man from off the face of the ground'?" |
| I.3 | A. | General Agrippa asked Rabban Gamaliel, "It is written in your Torah, "For the Lord your God is a devouring fire, a jealous God' (Dt. 4:24). Is there jealousy, except on the part of a sage for another sage, on the part of a great athlete for another great athlete, on the part of a wealthy man for another wealthy man?" |
|   | B. | He said to him, "I shall give you a parable. To what is the matter to be compared? To a man who married a second wife. If she is more important than she, she will not be jealous of her. If she is less than she, she will be jealous of her." |
| I.4 | A. | *Zeno asked R. Aqiba, "In my heart and in your heart we both know that there is no substance whatsoever in idolatry. But lo, we see people go into a shrine crippled and come out cured. How come?"* |
|   | B. | He said to him, "I shall give you a parable. To what is the matter to be compared? To a reliable person who was in a town, and all the townsfolk would deposit their money into his care without witnesses. One man came and left a deposit in his charge with witnesses, but once he forgot and left his deposit without witnesses. The wife of the reliable man said to him, 'Come, let us deny it.' He said to her, 'Because this idiot acted improperly, shall we destroy our good name for reliability?' So it is with troubles. When they send them upon a person, they are made to take the oath, 'You shall come upon him only on such-and-such a day, and you shall depart from him only on such-and-such a day, and at such-and-such an hour, through the medium of so-and-so, with such-and-such |

*Eleven.* 173

a remedy.' When it is time for them to take their leave, it just happened that the man went to a temple of an idol. So the afflictions plea, 'It is right and proper that we not leave him and go our way, but because this fool acts as he does, are we going to break our oath?'"

C. *That is in line with what R. Yohanan said, "What is the meaning of the verse of Scripture:* 'And sore and faithful sicknesses' (Dt. 28:59) — 'sore' in their mission, 'faithful' to their oath."

I.5 A. *Raba b. R. Isaac said to R. Judah, "There is a temple to an idol in our locale. When there is need for rain, the idol appears in a dream and says to them, 'Kill someone for me and I shall bring rain.' So they kill someone for her, and she brings rain."*

B. *He said to him, "If I were dead, no one could tell you this statement which Rab said, 'What is the meaning of the verse of Scripture, "...which the Lord your God has divided to all the peoples under the whole heaven"* (Dt. 4:19)? [Since the letters of the word 'divided' may be read as 'smooth,' the verse means this:] this teaches that he made them smooth talkers, so as to banish them from the world."

C. *That is in line with what R. Simeon b. Laqish said, "What is the meaning of the verse of Scripture,* 'Surely he scorns the scorners, but he gives grace to the lowly' (Prov. 3:34)? If someone comes along to make himself unclean, they open the gate for him. If he comes along to purify himself, they also help him do so."

The Bavli's expanded repertoire of arguments amplifies but does not innovate. But there is an innovation, the introduction of an argument based on self-evidence, namely, the parable, which suffers no substantive refutation but must be confronted. The argument through a parable, I:2, is challenged at the analogy: the idol is no dog, but sometimes performs as asked. That too provokes a parable, with the same objection repeated: that is just name-calling. That ends, I.2, at a reprise of the basic argument: God is not going wantonly to destroy idols at the expense of the world. The parabolic mode of argument continues at I:3, I:4. We note that that mode of argument has not proved common in our sample.

## II. ARGUMENTS EXECUTED THROUGH EXEGESIS OF SCRIPTURE

### A. MISHNAH

#### MISHNAH ABODAH ZARAH 3:4

A. Peroqlos b. Pelosepos asked Rabban Gamaliel in Akko, when he was washing in Aphrodite's bathhouse, saying to him, "It is written in your Torah, And there shall cleave nothing of a devoted thing to your hand (Dt. 13:18). How is it that you're taking a bath in Aphrodite's bathhouse?"

B. He said to him, "They do not give answers in a bathhouse."

C. When he went out, he said to him, "I never came into her domain. She came into mine. They don't say, 'Let's make a bathhouse as an ornament for Aphrodite.' But they say, 'Let's make Aphrodite as an ornament for the bathhouse.'

D. "Another matter: Even if someone gave you a lot of money, you would never walk into your temple of idolatry naked or suffering a flux, nor would you piss in its presence.

E. "Yet this thing is standing there at the head of the gutter and everybody pisses right in front of her."

F. It is said only, ". . . their gods" (Dt. 12:3)-that which one treats as a god is prohibited, but that which one treats not as a god is permitted.

The challenge based on Scripture, A, is met not through exegesis of the cited verse but through the reason: the sage is not deriving benefit from Aphrodite's bath house at all.

## B. TOSEFTA

### TOSEFTA ABODAH ZARAH 3:19

K. R. Judah says, "As to an idol itself, one breaks it and crushes it to powder and scatters it to the wind or tosses it into the sea."

L. They said to him, "Also: it may be made into manure, as it is said, 'None of the devoted things shall cleave to your hand' (Deut. 13:17) [M. A.Z. 3:3D]."

M. Said to them R. Yosé, "Lo, it says, 'Then I took the sinful thing, the calf which you had made, and burned it with fire and crushed it, grinding it very small, until it was as fine as dust, and I threw the dust of it into the brook that descended out of the mountain' (Deut. 9:21)."

N. They said to him, "Is there proof from that Scripture? [But lo, it has also been said,] 'And he took the calf which they had made and burnt it with fire and ground it to powder and scattered it upon the water and made the people of Israel drink it' (Ex. 32:20).

O. "For he wanted to test them just in the way in which they test women accused of adultery."

P. Said to them R. Yosé, "Lo, Scripture says, 'And the Philistines left their idols there, and David and his men carried them away' (11 Sam. 5:21)."

Q. They said to him, "Now is there any proof from that verse? [And lo, it has also been said,] 'And they left their gods there, and David gave command, and they were burned' (I Chron. 14:12)."

R. Said to them R. Yosé, "Lo, Scripture says, 'Even Maacah, his mother, King Asa removed from being queen mother, because she had made an abominable image for Asherah' (2 Chron. 15:16).

S. "He removed it and took it out."

T. They said to him, "Is there any proof from that matter? 'And Asa cut down her image, crushed it, and burned it at the brook Kidron' (11 Chron 15: 16)."

*Eleven.*  175

U.  Said to them R. Yosé, "Lo, Scripture says, 'He removed the high places and broke the pillars and cut down the Asherah. And he broke in pieces the bronze serpent that Moses had made, for until those days the people of Israel had burned incense to it; it was called Nehushtan' (2 Kings 18:4) "

V.  They said to him, "Now was this an idol! Did not Moses our rabbi make it? This teaches that the Israelites followed it in error until Hezekiah came along and hid it away."

Judah's position on the disposition of the idol, K, is augmented at L: there is more than one proper way of doing the deed. At M Yosé then finds a text that specifies the procedure he has named. The exchange of verses continues to the end.

### C. YERUSHALMI

#### YERUSHALMI TO MISHNAH ABODAH ZARAH 1:1

[A]  [39a] **Before the festivals of gentiles for three days it is forbidden to do business with them...**

[I:1 A]  *R. Hama bar Uqbah derived scriptural support for all of those [statements about the interval of three days during which it is prohibited to do business with gentiles prior to a festival of theirs] from the following verse:* "[Come to Bethel and transgress; to Gilgal and multiply transgression;] bring your sacrifices every morning, your tithes on the third day" (Amos 4:4).

[B]  *Said to him R. Yosé, "If so, then even in the exilic communities [the rule should be the same].*

[C]  *"Yet it has been taught in a Tannaitic tradition:* **'Nahum the Mede says, "One day in the exilic communities [before their festival] it is prohibited [to do business with gentiles, and not the three days specified by M. A.Z. 1:1, which apply only to the Holy Land]"'** [T. A.Z. 1:1A]."

[D]  *Why so?*

[E]  *There* [in Babylonia] *they looked into the matter and found out that* [the pagans] *prepare their requirements* [for celebrating a festival] *in only a single day, so they forbade business dealings with them for a single day. But here* [in the Holy Land] *they looked into the matter and found out that they prepare their requirements* [for celebrating a festival] *in a full three days, so they forbade business dealings with them for a full three days.*

[F]  *How then does R. Yosé interpret the cited verse of Scripture,* "Bring your sacrifices every morning [etc.]"?

[G]  Concerning the reign of Jeroboam does Scripture speak.

[H]  Once Jeroboam took up the reign over Israel, he began to entice Israel [toward idolatry], saying to them, "Come and let us practice idolatrous worship. Idolatry is permissive."

[I]  *That is the meaning of the following verse of Scripture:* "[Because Syria with Ephraim and the son of Remaliah has devised evil against you, saying,] 'Let us go up against Judah and terrify it, and let us conquer it for ourselves and set up the son of Tabeel as king in the midst of it'" (Is. 7:5-6).

The Yerushalmi not only lays out the pertinent verses, A, but also constructs a response to the proof-text, F-I.

### YERUSHALMI TO MISHNAH ABODAH ZARAH 1:2

[A] These are the festivals of gentiles:
[B] [1] Calends, [2] Saturnalia, [3] Kratesis [the commemoration of the empire],
[C] and [4] the emperor's anniversary, [5] his birthday,
[D] "and [6] the day of his death," the words of R. Meir.
[E] And sages say, "In any case of death rites in which there is a burning, there is idolatry, and in which there is no burning, there is no idolatry."

[I:1 A] Rab said, "Their testimonies [spelling the word for festivals at M. 1:2A with an 'ayin]."
[B] And Samuel said, "Their calamity [with an 'alef]."
[C] He who claims that the word is spelled with an 'ayin [as "their testimonies,"] draws evidence from the following verse: "Let them bring their witnesses to justify them" (Is. 43:9).
[D] And he who claims that the word is spelled with an 'alef, as "their festivals," draws evidence from the following verse: "For the day of their calamity ('YDM) is at hand" (Deut. 32:35).

Both parties are able to find evidence for their preferred spellings.

D.  BAVLI: —

## III. ARGUMENTS CONCERNING THE GOVERNING ANALOGY

A.  MISHNAH: —
B.  TOSEFTA: —
C.  YERUSHALMI: —
D.  BAVLI: —

## IV. THE TYPES OF ARGUMENTATION

The arguments with idolatry, M. A.Z. 4:7 and their amplifications at T. A.Z. 6:7 and Bavli to M. A. Z. 4:7, invoke parables, rather than evidence of nature or Scripture, to make their points. The Halakhic argumentation rarely utilizes parables in such a manner. So too, the arguments executed through exegesis of Scripture in the present category-formation do not correspond to Halakhic counterparts, reason replacing exegesis in any meaningful sense.

# 12

# Dialectical versus Non-Dialectical Arguments

I. A SIMPLE TYPOLOGY OF ARGUMENTATION: DIALECTICAL VERSUS NON-DIALECTICAL ARGUMENTS

While the initial probe proved unsuccessful, being at once too complex and insufficiently differentiated (!), an already-completed study of Halakhic argumentation makes possible a simple comparison of Halakhic and Aggadic types of argumentation. I have already shown that all Halakhic argumentation may be classified as either dialectical or not dialectical.[1] With so broad and loose a typology, we are able to ask whether we find, in the Aggadic documents, types of argumentation that correspond to one of the two sorts characteristic of the Halakhic writings: dialectical or other. Here are clearly defined choices, as I shall explain, and all forms of argumentation in the Halakhic documents may be classified as either dialectical or non-dialectical.

Not only so, but once the taxonomy of "non-dialectical" pertains, the Aggadah will signal its own subdivisions and point us toward their Halakhic counterparts. So the result, while disappointing, is not hopeless. The question at hand comes down to a simple issue. To what extent do we find, in Aggadic documents, any sort of systematic argument at all that corresponds to any sort of systematic argument characteristic of the Halakhic ones?

---

[1] *Talmudic Dialectics: Types and Forms.* Atlanta, 1995: Scholars Press for South Florida Studies in the History of Judaism. I. *Introduction. Tractate Berakhot and the Divisions of Appointed Times and Women. And Talmudic Dialectics: Types and Forms.* Atlanta, 1995: Scholars Press for South Florida Studies in the History of Judaism. II. *The Divisions of Damages and Holy Things and Tractate Niddah.*

## II. DEFINING THE DIALECTICAL ARGUMENT. AND TWO INSTANCES OF A NON-DIALECTICAL ARGUMENT

Since the simplest possible taxonomy rests on the distinction between dialectical and non-dialectical argument, let us begin with the positive, the definition of the dialectical argument. That definition will serve to accommodate the negative, the non-dialectical as well. A preliminary and rather general definition of the mode of writing set forth as a dialectical argument is called for.[2] The Rabbinic dialectical argument, — the protracted, sometimes meandering, always moving flow of contentious thought, — raises a question and answers it, then raises a question about the answer, and, having raised another question, it then gives an answer to that question, and it continues onward through a theoretically unlimited number of exchanges, all in the same fashion. So it moves hither and yon; it is always continuous, start to finish, but it is never the same. A non-dialectical argument takes the form of an exchange — question and answer — but lacks the movement, continuity, and dynamic of thesis and antithesis and (ultimate) synthesis, characteristic of Rabbinic dialectics.

Dialectical argument is best defined as the trajectory of thought unfolding through challenge and response, initiative and reaction thereto. The dialectical, or moving, argument is important because, in the sustained conflict provoked by the testing of proposition in contention and response, the upshot of argument is to turn fact into truth. Two steps are involved, making a point, then challenging that point, and together these mark a stage in the unfolding of the argument. Making a point forms of data important propositions. The challenge involves exchanges of contradictory propositions and arguments in behalf of one or the other of them, objections and ripostes. The whole holds together, however protracted, by the continuous flow of argument, from point A to point B to point C, as secondary and tertiary issues are raised.

"Dialectical" then means, moving, and a dialectical argument is a systematic exposition, through give and take, moving from point to point; the argument is the thing, since the dialectical argument strays from its original, precipitating point and therefore does not ordinarily undertake the demonstration of a fixed proposition. Rather, it moves along, developing an idea through questions and answers, sometimes implicit, but commonly explicit. The dialectical character derives not from the mere rhetorical device of question and answer, but from the pursuit of an argument, in a single line, but in many and diverse directions: not the form but the substantive continuity defines the criterion. And the power of the dialectical argument flows from that continuity. We find the source of continuity in the author's capacity to show connections through the momentum of rigorous analysis, on the one side, and free-ranging curiosity, on the other.

---

[2] Only when we have examined the repertoire of cases will a clear and reliable definition emerge.

## Twelve. Dialectical vs. Non-Dialectical Arguments

Now to underscore the difference between dialectical and non-dialectical arguments. It lies in those second and third and fourth turnings. These differentiate a dialectical from a static argument, much as the bubbles tell the difference between still and sparkling wine. The always-sparkling dialectical argument is one principal means by which Rabbinic writing accomplishes its goal of showing the connections between this and that, ultimately demonstrating the unity of many "thises and thats." These efforts at describing the argument serve precisely as well as program notes to a piece of music: they tell us what we are going to hear; they cannot play the music. What "moves" therefore is the flow of argument and thought, and that is — by definition — from problem to problem. The movement is generated specifically by the raising of contrary questions and contradictory theses: "is not the opposite more reasonable?". What characterizes the dialectical argument in Rabbinic literature is its meandering, its moving hither and yon. It is not a direct or straight-line or a set-piece movement, e.g., the dialectical argument with which we are familiar in the modern West, thesis, antithesis, synthesis. It also does not correspond to any propositional or syllogistic argument, even though such arguments may take place in three or more steps, inclusive of counter-arguments.[3]

An important qualification is in order, and that concerns the exclusion from consideration of protracted presentations of data, in the form of questions and answers, that simply set forth a mass of well-crafted information, but no sustaining and continuous proposition. Such agglutinations of compositions and even composites prove informative; they collect information, much of it serving as on-

---

[3] The comparison of Talmudic dialectics to Platonic dialectics in the Dialogues has not taken place, so far as I know. I argue that the power of the Talmud lies in its translation into concrete and everyday matters of the two most powerful intellectual components of Western civilization from its roots to our own time, science and philosophy, specifically, [1] Aristotle's principles of knowledge and [2] Socrates' (Plato's) principles of rational inquiry and argument. The modes of scientific inquiry of the one and of reasoned analysis of the other are translated by the Talmud into everyday terms, so that the experience of the everyday is turned into the academy for reasoned explanation of how things are: a book that turns concrete facts of the home and street into propositions of scientific interest and problems of philosophical inquiry. The Talmud turns the world into a class room, people into disciples, and culture into a concrete exemplification of abstract and reliable truth. Specifically: the Talmud is made up of two components, a philosophical law code, the Mishnah, which, in concrete ways, inculcates the principles of rational classification that Aristotle stated in abstract form; and a commentary to the Mishnah, called the Gemara (or simply, the Talmud proper), which, through the utilization of applied reason and practical logic, forms a moving ("dialectical") and analytical argument about the working of those principles in concrete cases. The importance of the moving argument lies in its open-endedness, so that successive generations found themselves not merely invited, but empowered, to join in the argument and so assume the disciplines of rational argument that the Talmud exemplifies. In both aspects, therefore, the document serves as the medium of inductive instruction into the principles of science and philosophy that define the structure of the well-ordered society.

site footnotes. But they follow no analytical problem, and they aim at little more than the provision of information. Readers who follow the survey with the text in hand and wish to know why I have not referred to a given item may appeal to the present criterion: an analytical program or a merely illuminating collection of information. Both will exhibit connections from one item to the next, but the dialectical-analytical argument will always pursue an abstract and generalizing question, and the agglutinative composite will ordinarily turn out to be a set of footnotes. To be sure, reasonable people can disagree in specific problems of classification. But the general distinction will stand.

What of a non-dialectical argument? Let me give one example of discourse that moves forward through rhetorical questions and answers but does not demand classification as dialectical, in that the movement proves superficial, the basic argument static and narrowly propositional. In the following case we see how a rhetorical form of questions and answers conceals a perfectly standard exchange of information, nothing more:

I.6  A.  Said R. Huna, "He who enters the synagogue and finds the community saying the Prayer, if he can begin and complete the Prayer before the leader of the community in his repetition, reaches the blessing, 'We acknowledge...,' should say the Prayer, and if not, he should not say the Prayer."
B.  And R. Joshua b. Levi said, "If he can begin and complete the Prayer before the leader of the community in his repetition reaches the Sanctification, he should say the Prayer, and if not, he should not say the Prayer."
C.  *Concerning what principle do they differ?*
D.  *One master [A] takes the view that* an individual may say the Sanctification-prayer [by himself].
E.  *The other [B] takes the view that t*he individual may not say the Sanctification-prayer [by himself].
F.  So too [B] did R. Ada bar Ahbah say, "How do we know on the basis of Scripture that an individual [praying by himself] does not say the Sanctification-prayer? As it is said, 'And I shall be sanctified among the children of Israel' (Lev. 22:32). Every matter involving sanctification may be conducted among no fewer than ten men."
G.  *How does the besought proof derive from the cited verse?*
H.  *It accords with that which Rabbinai, brother of R. Hiyya bar Abba, taught on Tannaite authority,* "An analogy is drawn on the use of the word 'among.'
I.  "Here it is written, 'And I shall be sanctified among the children of Israel' (Lev. 22:32), and elsewhere it is written, 'Separate yourselves from among this congregation' (Num. 16:21). Just as, in the latter instance, 'among' involves ten men, so here ten are required."
J.  *Both authorities concur, in the end, that one does not interrupt [the Prayer. If a person has begun to recite the Prayer, when the congregation comes to recite the Sanctification, the person does not interrupt his prayer to recite the Sanctification with the congregation.]*

*Twelve. Dialectical vs. Non-Dialectical Arguments* 181

What we have is little more than a first-rate exposition of the point at issue in a dispute, followed by a secondary datum, which shows how a proposition emerges from a proof-text. Merely presenting a dispute in a fair and balanced way, utilizing the form of question and answer, does not lead us into the realm controlled by authentic dialectics. We cannot confuse the deft presentation of conflicting propositions, along with required information, with the rich intellectual movement, hither and yon, that dialectics involves.

This distinction, between the rhetoric of dialectics and the logic thereof, forms so central a point of differentiation in all that follows as to justify introducing a second example of what I class as other than an analytical-dialectical argument. It is a case in which the formal utilization of questions and answers masks a quite static argument, in which set-piece positions are intertwined, compared and contrasted, without a trace of movement from one point to some other:

### Serving Mishnah-tractate Erubin 6:3-4

VI.2 A. *Abbayye asked Rabbah,* "Five tenants lived in a single courtyard, and one of them forgot and did not participate in the fusion meal —when he renounces his rights of access, does he have to renounce it in favor of each and every tenant or does he not have to do so?"

B. He said to him, "He has to renounce his right in favor of each and every tenant."

C. *An objection was raised:* One party who did not participate in the fusion meal abrogates his right in favor of one party who did participate in the fusion meal; two persons who participated in the fusion meal assign their right to one who didn't, and two who didn't participate in the fusion meal abrogate their right to two who did participate in the fusion meal or to one who did not participate in the fusion meal. But one who participated in the fusion meal doesn't abrogate his right to one who didn't participate, and two who participated in the fusion meal do not abrogate their right in favor of two who didn't participate, and two who didn't participate in the fusion meal don't abrogate their right in favor of two who didn't participate in the fusion meal. *Now the Tannaite formulation in any event states at the outset,* one party who did not participate in the fusion meal abrogates his right in favor of one party who did participate in the fusion meal. *Now how are we to imagine the case? If there is no other with him, then with whom might he have joined in the fusion meal? So it must follow, there must have been another tenant alongside, and yet it is stated,* one party who did participate in the fusion meal! [Slotki: How could Rabbah maintain that renunciation must be made in favor of each and every tenant individually?]

D. And Rabbah?

E. *Here with what situation do we deal? It is a case in which there was a tenant with whom the fusion meal was made, but who died* [Slotki: by the time the third party presented his share; so there were only two tenants in the courtyard, and one may renounce in favor of the other].

F. *Well, then, what about what follows:* But one who participated in the fusion meal doesn't abrogate his right to one who didn't participate? *Now, if he had* been there but died, why shouldn't it be permitted [for the survivor to renounce his share (Slotki)]? *So it's obvious that the tenant with whom the meal was prepared was still around, and, since the final clause takes for granted that he was still around, the initial clause also deals with a case in which he was still around [and Rabbah's got a problem]!*

G. What makes you see things that way? The one clause deals with its case, the other deals with its situation. You may know that that is the case, for the concluding part of the opening formulation says, two who didn't participate in the fusion meal abrogate their right to two who did participate in the fusion meal. *So to two they may do so, but not to one.*

H. And Abbayye?

I. *He may say, what is the meaning of* "to two"? *It is,* "to one of the two."

J. *If so, why instead of* "two" *wasn't it said,* "To one who joined in the fictive fusion meal or to one who did not" [Slotki: since one tenant cannot join in a fictive meal with himself, it would then be obvious that the sense was, to one of two]?

K. *Well, that's a legitimate problem.*

L. ...one party who did not participate in the fusion meal abrogates his right in favor of one party who did participate in the fusion meal –

M. *in Abbayye's view,* this speaks of a case in which the other tenant [who joined in the fiction meal with the one mentioned] was still alive, *and so we are informed that* it is not necessary to renounce one's rights in favor of each and every tenant.

N. *In Rabbah's view, it is a case in which he was around but then died, and so we are informed that no precautionary decree is enacted to deal with the possibility that someone may yet be around [and yet the same procedure might be followed].*

O. ...two parsons who participated in the fusion meal assign their right to one who didn't –

P. *So that's pretty obvious.*

Q. What might you otherwise have imagined? That since he did not participate in the fusion meal, an extra-judicial penalty is to be imposed on him? So we are informed that that is not the case.

R. ...and two who didn't participate in the fusion meal abrogate their right to two who did participate in the fusion meal –

S. *In Rabbah's view, the Tannaite formulation of the concluding clause was meant to clarify the sense of the opening clause. To Abbayye, it was necessary to include the clause concerning two who didn't participate in the fusion meal. For it might have entered your mind that we should make a precautionary decree, to cover the possibility that they may come and renounce in their favor [which is forbidden[, but so we are informed that that is not the case.*

T. ...or to one who did not participate in the fusion meal –

U. *What do I need this item for?*

V. What might you otherwise have supposed? That the rule applies to a case in which some of the tenants participated in the fusion meal and some didn't, but in a case in which all of them didn't, we impose a penalty, so that the rule of the fusion meal should not be forgotten? So we are informed that that is not so.

## Twelve. Dialectical vs. Non-Dialectical Arguments

W. But one who participated in the fusion meal doesn't abrogate his right to one who didn't participate –

X. From Abbayye's perspective, the Tannaite formulation of the concluding clause serves to explain the sense of the opening one. From Rabbah's perspective, since the opening clause was set forth, the closing clause was put in to match it.

Y. ...and two who participated in the fusion meal do not abrogate their right in favor of two who didn't participate –

Z. *So for what do I need to be told this again?*

AA. *It was necessary to cover the case in which one of them renounced his share in favor of the other [of those who didn't share in the fusion meal]. What might you have supposed? That the latter should then have the right to use the courtyard? So we are informed that that is not the case, since at the time the former renounced his share, he had no right to use the courtyard.*

BB. ...and two who didn't participate in the fusion meal don't abrogate their right in favor of two who didn't participate in the fusion meal –

CC. *So for what do I need to be told this again?*

DD. *It was necessary to cover even the case in which they said to him, "Acquire our share on the stipulation that you transfer them."*

Here is a superb exercise in fair and equitable presentation of two positions; but it is not a dialectical argument, because the positions stand still and the argument leads no where; without motion, the dialectic or movement proves merely formal but in no way substantive, the basic point at issue being made manifest but not made to move. Time and again, a closer look at what appears to be a moving argument shows us that all we have is a rhetorical device to secure the proper and orderly balance between two contradictory positions. We shall return to this point once more, to underscore the contrast between rhetorical and logical dialectics.

The dialectical argument opens the possibility of reaching out from one thing to something else, not because people have lost sight of their starting point or their goal in the end, but because they want to encompass, in the analytical argument as it gets underway, as broad and comprehensive a range of cases and rules as they possibly can. The movement from point to point in reference to a single point that accurately describes the dialectical argument reaches upward toward a goal of proximate abstraction, leaving behind the specificities of not only cases but laws, carrying us upward to the law that governs many cases, the premises that undergird many rules, and still higher to the principles that infuse diverse premises; then the principles that generate other, unrelated premises, which, in turn, come to expression in other, still-less intersecting cases. The meandering course of argument comes to an end when we have shown how things cohere. Or, sometimes, the argument simply stops, leaving open possibilities for coming generations to take up.

## III. AN EXAMPLE OF A DIALECTICAL ARGUMENT

We have now completed our theoretical definitions, amply illustrated on the negative side. It is time to consider what I regard as an authentic instance of a dialectical argument: not formal but substantive in movement. The passage that we consider occurs at the Babylonian Talmud Baba Mesia 5B-6A, which is to say, Talmud to Mishnah Baba Mesia. 1:1-2. Our interest is in the twists and turns of the argument and what is at stake in the formation of a continuous and unfolding composition:

### BAVLI TO M. B.M. 1:1-2 IV.1.5B6A

[5B] IV.1. A. **This one takes an oath that he possesses no less a share of it than half, [and that one takes an oath that he possesses no less a share of it than half, and they divide it up]:**

The rule of the Mishnah, which is cited at the head of the sustained discussion, concerns the case of two persons who find a garment. We settle their conflicting claim by requiring each to take an oath that he or she owns title to no less than half of the garment, and then we split the garment between them.

Our first question is one of text-criticism: analysis of the Mishnah-paragraph's word choice. We say that the oath concerns the portion that the claimant alleges he possesses. But the oath really affects the portion that he does not have in hand at all:

    B.  *Is it concerning the portion that he claims he possesses that he takes the oath, or concerning the portion that he does not claim to possess?* [Daiches: "The implication is that the terms of the oath are ambiguous. By swearing that his share in it is not "less than half," the claimant might mean that it is not even a third or a fourth (which is 'less than half'), and the negative way of putting it would justify such an interpretation. He could therefore take this oath even if he knew that he had no share in the garment at all, while he would be swearing falsely if he really had a share in the garment that is less than half, however small that share might be].

    C.  *Said R. Huna, "It is that he says,* 'By an oath! I possess in it a portion, and I possess in it a portion that is no more than half a share of it.'" [The claimant swears that his share is at least half (S. Daiches, *Baba Mesia*, London, 1948: Soncino. *Ad Loc.* )].

Having asked and answered the question, we now find ourselves in an extension of the argument; the principal trait of the dialectical argument is now before us: [1] but [2] maybe the contrary is the case, so [3] what about — that is, the setting aside of a proposition in favor of its opposite. Here we come to the definitive trait of the dialectic argument: its insistence on challenging every proposal

## Twelve. Dialectical vs. Non-Dialectical Arguments     185

with the claim, "maybe it's the opposite?" This pestering question forces us back upon our sense of self-evidence; it makes us consider the contrary of each position we propose to set forth. It makes thought happen. True, the Talmud's voice's "but" — the whole of the dialectic in one word! — presents a formidable nuisance. But so does all criticism, and only the mature mind will welcome criticism. Dialectics is not for children, politicians, propagandists, or egoists. Genuine curiosity about the truth shown by rigorous logic forms the counterpart to musical virtuosity. So the objection proceeds:

> C. *Then let him say, "By an oath! The whole of it is mine!"*

Why claim half when the alleged finder may as well demand the whole cloak?

> D. *But are we going to give him the whole of it?* [Obviously not, there is another claimant, also taking an oath.]

The question contradicts the facts of the case: two parties claim the cloak, so the outcome can never be that one will get the whole thing.

> E. *Then let him say, "By an oath! Half of it is mine!"*

Then — by the same reasoning — why claim "no less than half," rather than simply, half.

> F. *That would damage his own claim* [which was that he owned the whole of the cloak, not only half of it].

The claimant does claim the whole cloak, so the proposed language does not serve to replicate his actual claim. That accounts for the language that is specified.

> G. *But here too is it not the fact that, in the oath that he is taking, he impairs his own claim?* [After all, he here makes explicit the fact that he owns at least half of it. What happened to the other half?]

The solution merely compounds the problem.

> H. *[Not at all.] For he has said,* "The whole of it is mine!" [And, he further proceeds,] "And as to your contrary view, By an oath, I do have a share in it, and that share is no less than half!"

We solve the problem by positing a different solution from the one we suggested at the outset. Why not start where we have concluded? Because if we had done so, we should have ignored a variety of intervening considerations and so should have expounded less than the entire range of possibilities. The power of the dialectical argument now is clear: it forces us to address not the problem and the solution alone, but the problem and the various ways by which a solution may be reached; then, when we do come to a final solution to the question at hand, we have reviewed all of the possibilities. We have seen how everything flows together, nothing is left unattended.

The dialectical argument in the Talmud and in other Rabbinic writings therefore undertakes a different task from the philosophical counterpart. What we have here is not a set-piece of two positions, with an analysis of each, such as the staid philosophical dialogue exposes with such elegance; it is, rather, an analytical argument, explaining why this, not that, then why not that but rather this; and onward to the other thing and the thing beyond that — a linear argument in constant motion. When we speak of a moving argument, this is what we mean: what is not static and merely expository, but what is dynamic and always contentious. It is not an endless argument, an argument for the sake of arguing, or evidence that important to the Talmud and other writings that use the dialectics as a principal mode of dynamic argument is process but not position. To the contrary, the passage is resolved with a decisive conclusion, not permitted to run on.

But the dialectical composition proceeds — continuous and coherent from point to point, even as it zigs and zags. We proceed to the second cogent proposition in the analysis of the cited Mishnah-passage, which asks a fresh question: why an oath at all?

2.     A.     [It is envisioned that each party is holding on to a corner of the cloak, so the question is raised:] Now, since this one is possessed of the cloak and standing right there, and that one is possessed of the cloak and is standing right there, why in the world do I require this oath?

Until now we have assumed as fact the premise of the Mishnah's rule, which is that an oath is there to be taken. But why assume so? Surely each party now has what he is going to get. So what defines the point and effect of the oath?

    B.     Said R. Yohanan, "This oath [to which our Mishnah-passage refers] happens to be an ordinance imposed only by rabbis,
    C.     "so that people should not go around grabbing the cloaks of other people and saying, 'It's mine!'" [But, as a matter of fact, the oath that is imposed in our Mishnah-passage is not legitimate by the law of the Torah. It is an act taken by sages to maintain the social order.]

We do not administer oaths to liars; we do not impose an oath in a case in which we may end up one of the claimants would take an oath for something he knew to be untrue, since one party really does own the cloak, the other really has grabbed it. The proposition solves the problem — but hardly is going to settle the

## Twelve. Dialectical vs. Non-Dialectical Arguments

question. On the contrary, Yohanan raises more problems than he solves. So we ask how we can agree to an oath in this case at all?

> D. *But why then not advance the following argument: since such a one is suspect as to fraud in a property claim, he also should be suspect as to fraud in oath-taking?*

Yohanan places himself into the position of believing in respect to the oath what we will not believe in respect to the claim on the cloak, for, after all, one of the parties before us must be lying! Why sustain such a contradiction: gullible and suspicious at one and the same time?

> E. *In point of fact, we do not advance the argument: since such a one is suspect as to fraud in a property claim, he also should be suspect as to fraud in oath-taking, for if you do not concede that fact, then how is it possible that the All-Merciful has ruled, "One who has conceded part of a claim against himself must take an oath as to the remainder of what is subject to claim"?*

If someone claims that another party holds property belonging to him or her, and the one to whom the bailment has been handed over for safe-keeping, called the bailee, concedes part of the claim, the bailee must then take an oath in respect to the rest of the claimed property, that is, the part that the bailee maintains does not belong to the claimant at all. So the law itself — the Torah, in fact — has sustained the same contradiction. That fine solution, of course, is going to be challenged:

> F. *Why not simply maintain, since such a one is suspect as to fraud in a property claim, he also should be suspect as to fraud in oath-taking?*
> G. *In that other case, [the reason for the denial of part of the claim and the admission of part is not the intent to commit fraud, but rather,] the defendant is just trying to put off the claim for a spell.*

We could stop at this point without losing a single important point of interest; everything is before us. One of the striking traits of the large-scale dialectical composition is its composite-character. Starting at the beginning, without any loss of meaning or sense, we may well stop at the end of any given paragraph of thought. But the dialectics insists on moving forward, exploring, pursuing, insisting; and were we to remove a paragraph in the middle of a dialectical composite, then all that follows would become incomprehensible. That is a mark of the dialectical argument: sustained, continuous, and coherent — yet perpetually in control and capable of resolving matters at any single point.

Now, having fully exposed the topic, its problem, and its principles, we take a tangent indicated by the character of the principle before us: when a person will or will not lie or take a false oath. We have a theory on the matter; what we now do is expound the theory, with special reference to the formulation of that theory in explicit terms by a named authority:

> H. This concurs with the position of Rabbah. [For Rabbah has said, "On what account has the Torah imposed the requirement of an oath on one who confesses to only part of a claim against him? It is by reason of the presumption that a person will not insolently deny the truth about the whole of a loan in the very presence of the creditor and so entirely deny the debt. He will admit to part of the debt and deny part of it. Hence we invoke an oath in a case in which one does so, to coax out the truth of the matter."]
> 
> I. For you may know, [in support of the foregoing], that R. Idi bar Abin said R. Hisda [said]: "He who [falsely] denies owing money on a loan nonetheless is suitable to give testimony, but he who denies that he holds a bailment for another party cannot give testimony."

The proposition is now fully exposed. A named authority is introduced, who will concur in the proposed theoretical distinction. He sets forth an extra-logical consideration, which of course the law always will welcome: the rational goal of finding the truth overrides the technicalities of the law governing the oath.

Predictably, we cannot allow matters to stand without challenge, and the challenge comes at a fundamental level, with the predictable give-and-take to follow:

> J. But what about that which R. Ammi bar. Hama repeated on Tannaite authority: "[If they are to be subjected to an oath,] four sorts of bailees have to have denied part of the bailment and conceded part of the bailment, namely, the unpaid bailee, the borrower, the paid bailee, and the one who rents."
> 
> K. *Why not simply maintain, since such a one is suspect as to fraud in a property claim, he also should be suspect as to fraud in oath-taking?*
> 
> L. *In that case as well, [the reason for the denial of part of the claim and the admission of part is not the intent to commit fraud, but rather,] the defendant is just trying to put off the claim for a spell.*
> 
> M. He reasons as follows: "I'm going to find the thief and arrest him." Or: "I'll find [the beast] in the field and return it to the owner."

Once more, "if that is the case" provokes yet another analysis; we introduce a different reading of the basic case before us, another reason that we should not impose an oath:

> N. *If that is the case, then why should one who denies holding a bailment ever be unsuitable to give testimony? Why don't we just maintain that the defendant is just trying to put off the claim for a spell. He reasons as follows: "I'm going to look for the thing and find it."*
> 
> O. *When in point of fact we do rule,* He who denies holding a bailment is unfit to give testimony, *it is in a case in which witnesses come and give testimony against him that at that very moment, the bailment is located in the bailee's*

Twelve. Dialectical vs. Non-Dialectical Arguments

domain, and he fully is informed of that fact, or, alternatively, he has the object in his possession at that very moment.

The solution to the problem at hand also provides the starting point for yet another step in the unfolding exposition. Huna has given us a different resolution of matters. That accounts for No. 3, and No. 4 is also predictable:

3. A. *But as to that which R. Huna has said* [when we have a bailee who offers to pay compensation for a lost bailment rather than swear it has been lost, since he wishes to appropriate the article by paying for it, (Daiches)], "They impose upon him the oath that the bailment is not in his possession at all,"
   B. *why not in that case invoke the principle, since such a one is suspect as to fraud in a property claim, he also should be suspect as to fraud in oath-taking?*
   C. In that case also, he may rule in his own behalf, I'll give him the money.
4. A. Said R. Aha of Difti to Rabina, "But then the man clearly transgresses the negative commandment: 'You shall not covet.'"
   B. *"You shall not covet" is generally understood by people to pertain to something for which one is not ready to pay.*

Yet another authority's position now is invoked, and it draws us back to our starting point: the issue of why we think an oath is suitable in a case in which we ought to assume lying is going on; so we are returned to our starting point, but via a circuitous route:

5. A. [6A] *But as to that which R. Nahman said,* "They impose upon him [who denies the whole of a claim] an oath of inducement," *why not in that case invoke the principle, since such a one is suspect as to fraud in a property claim, he also should be suspect as to fraud in oath-taking?*
   B. *And furthermore, there is that which R. Hiyya taught on Tannaite authority:* "Both parties [employee, supposed to have been paid out of an account set up by the employer at a local store, and store-keeper] take an oath and collect what each claims from the employer," *why not in that case invoke the principle, since such a one is suspect as to fraud in a property claim, he also should be suspect as to fraud in oath-taking?*
   C. *And furthermore, there is that which R. Sheshet said,* "We impose upon an unpaid bailee [who claims that the animal has been lost] three distinct oaths: first, an oath that I have not deliberately caused the loss, that I did not put a hand on it, and that it is not in my domain at all," *why not in that case invoke the principle, since such a one is suspect as to fraud in a property claim, he also should be suspect as to fraud in oath-taking?*

We now settle the matter:

   D. *It must follow that we do not invoke the principle at all, since such a one is suspect as to fraud in a property claim, he also should be suspect as to fraud in oath-taking?*

What is interesting is why walk so far to end up where we started: do we invoke said principle? No, we do not. What we have accomplished on our wanderings is a survey of opinion on a theme, to be sure, but opinion that intersects at our particular problem as well. The moving argument serves to carry us hither and yon; its power is to demonstrate that all considerations are raised, all challenges met, all possibilities explored. This is not merely a set-piece argument, where we have proposition, evidence, analysis, conclusion; it is a different sort of thinking altogether, purposive and coherent, but also comprehensive and compelling for its admission of possibilities and attention to alternatives. What we shall see, time and again, is that the dialectical argument is the Talmud's medium of generalization from case to principle and extension from principle to new cases.

### IV. A CONTRASTING EXAMPLE OF AN ARGUMENT OF AN OTHER-THAN-DIALECTICAL CHARACTER

The survey that follows excludes merely-rhetorical dialectics, that is, arguments framed in terms of sequences of questions and answers, since, in my judgment, such compositions and composites set forth exchanges of information and principle, but do not establish that wide-ranging analytical inquiry that encompasses within an extending frontier broad areas of law. Another rhetorical argument that serves only to set forth information in a balanced and proportionate manner takes an important role in the Talmud but in no way constitutes that logical marvel of dialectics that the Talmud occasionally creates. Readers who follow the Talmud along with my survey will note that I have not included numerous examples of exquisite exposure of balanced opposites. Two or more positions will be set forth, amplified, analyzed, without the intrusion of that logic of dialectics that requires us to move beyond the limits of the case. Here is a single example, and an especially lucid and appealing one, of how the Talmud's sense of equity and classicism comes to expression in the orderly representation of conflicting views:

I.1    A.    **[Mishnah-tractate Erubin 4:7A: He who was coming along the way and darkness overtook him, and who knew about a certain tree or a fence and said, "My place of residence for the Sabbath will be under it," has said nothing at all:]** *What is the meaning of* **he has said nothing at all***?*

       B.    Said Rab, "**He has said nothing at all** in any way, shape, or form, *so that he may not even continue to the space under the tree."* [Slotki: He must not move from his position until after the Sabbath, since he has acquired no place for his Sabbath rest, from which he could be entitled to walk within a permitted Sabbath limit; his right to the place on which he stood when the Sabbath came into effect has been expressly renounced by his choosing another one, and the area under the tree couldn't be acquired by him, since he had not specified which particular four cubits of that space he chose.]

       C.    And Samuel said, "**He has said nothing at all** in respect to going on to his home. *But he may go to the space under the tree."*

## Twelve. Dialectical vs. Non-Dialectical Arguments

D. The space under the tree is treated as in the case of an ass driver and a camel driver [so the man can't move in any direction for very far]. If he wanted to measure from the north side of the tree, they tell him to begin measuring from the south side. [Slotki: In appointing the tree as his Sabbath base, he didn't specify which particular four cubits of space under the tree he wanted to acquire, so any four cubits of space within the circumference of the tree and the branches may be assumed to be the appointed spot. In measuring the distances, therefore, a course must be adopted that under all circumstances could not possibly lead to an infringement of any of the restrictions involved. If the diameter of the circumference of the tree and its branches measured twenty cubits, and the distance from the northern point to the man's house was exactly two thousand cubits, the measuring must not begin from that point, but from the southern point of the diameter, which is two thousand and twenty cubits distant from the house. And since it is forbidden to proceed beyond two thousand cubits, the man's Sabbath limit would terminate at a point twenty cubits away from his house, which, in consequence, he would not be able to enter during the Sabbath.] So, too, if he came to measure from the south side of the tree, they tell him to measure from the north side.

E. [50A] *Said Rabbah, "What is the operative consideration behind the ruling of Rab? Because the man didn't specify the exact spot."*

F. *There are those who say: Said Rabbah, "What is the operative consideration behind the ruling of Rab? Because he takes the view, in any case in which if a statement would not be valid if one statement followed another, then even if the statements are made simultaneously, they are also null."* [Freedman, *Nedarim* 69B: Whatever is not valid consecutively is not valid even simultaneously.] [Slotki: The man's appointment of the entire area under the tree, including both the northern and southern sides, is therefore null; an area of four cubits on the northern side of the tree cannot be acquired after such an area had been acquired on the southern side or vice versa.]

G. *What's the difference between these two explanations?*

H. *At issue between the two explanations would be a case in which someone said, "Let me acquire an area of four cubits out of eight." One who has said that the operative consideration is that the man didn't specify the exact spot will hold that here he didn't specify the spot. And one who said that the operative consideration is, In any case in which if a statement would not be valid if one statement followed another, then even if the statements are made simultaneously, they are also null, lo, such a statement is valid if an area of four cubits has been specified, for here the man said he wanted to acquire no more than four cubits.*

I.2 A. *Reverting to the body of the foregoing:* Said Rabbah, "In any case in which if a statement would not be valid if one statement followed another, then even if the statements are made simultaneously, they are also null"–

B. *Objected Abbayye to Rabbah,* "**He who gave too much tithe —while the produce is properly tithed, the tithe is ruined [since part of what is included within the tithe is in fact not tithe at all] [T. Dem. 8:13A-B].** *But why should this be the case? Why not say, 'What cannot be done consecutively also cannot be done simultaneously'?"*

C. *He said to him, "That case is exceptional, because, as to tithes, it is possible in the case of half-grain to do it, for if one said, 'Let half of each grain be sanctified,' it is indeed sanctified; but as to tithes of cattle, it is impossible to do it by halves, and it is also impossible to do it consecutively; and yet Rabbah has said, 'If two animals came out of the corral simultaneously as tenth, and he called them tenth, the tenth and the eleventh are treated as a group together [the tenth is actually tithe, the eleventh is a peace-offering].'" [If he had declared them so in sequence, the second would be invalid; why is the simultaneous declaration valid? (Freedman)].*

D. *The tithing of cattle is exceptional, since it is valid even when done in error, for we have learned in the Mishnah:* **[If] he called the ninth, tenth, and the tenth, ninth, and the eleventh, tenth, all three are sanctified [M. Bekh. 9:8D].**

E. *Lo, what about the matter of the thanksgiving-offering, which cannot be designated in error nor consecutively [that is, the thanksgiving-offering was accompanied by forty loaves that were sanctified; if the animal was sacrificed to sanctify certain loaves, which weren't the intended ones, they are not sanctified; if after forty loaves are sanctified, another forty are declared holy, the declaration is null (Freedman)], and yet it has been stated:* A thank-offering that one slaughtered in connection with eighty loaves of bread –

F. Hezekiah said, "Forty of the loaves among the eighty have been sanctified."

G. R. Yohanan said, "Forty of the loaves among the eighty have not been sanctified."

H. *Hasn't it been stated in that connection: Said Zira, "All concur that if the officiating priest said, 'Let forty out of the eighty be sanctified,' they are sanctified. 'The forty shall not be sanctified unless all eighty are sanctified,' they are not sanctified. Where they differ is only when*

Twelve. Dialectical vs. Non-Dialectical Arguments 193

the matter has not been made explicit. One authority takes the view that the unstated intention of the donor in presenting eighty loaves was to make sure that at least forty would be found suitable, **[50B]** and the other authority maintains that the intention was merely to provide a very large offering [so all eighty have to be valid]"?

I.3 A. [With reference to the statement, said Rab, "**He has said nothing at all** in any way, shape, or form, *so that he may not even continue to the space under the tree,*"] said Abbayye, "That has been taught only with regard to a tree with a diameter underneath of no less than twelve cubits [Slotki: the length comprising no less than three sections of four cubits each, so it is impossible to ascertain whether it was the middle section or one of the outer ones that the man wanted to acquire as his Sabbath base]. But in the case of a tree with a diameter underneath of less than twelve cubits, at least part of the man's house is well marked out." [Slotki: If the diameter was only eleven cubits, each four cubits at either of the extremities must inevitably overlap half a cubit with the middle four cubits; if the man chose the middle section, all of his Sabbath base is obviously well defined; but even if he intended one of the outer sections to be his Sabbath base, each of them is at least partially defined in that part where it overlaps with the middle sections; his base may therefore be regarded as located in full or in part in that section.]

B. *Objected R. Huna b. R. Joshua, "But how do you know that he ever intended to utilize the middle four cubits? Maybe he intended to utilize either the four cubits on one side or the four on the other!"*

C. Rather, said R. Huna b. R. Joshua, "That has been taught only with regard to a tree with a diameter underneath of no less than eight cubits [where we don't know what section he intended], but if it has seven cubits underneath, then in such a situation at least part of the man's house is well marked out."

I.4 A. [With regard to the statements above, said Rab, "**He has said nothing at all** in any way, shape, or form, *so that he may not even continue to the space under the tree.*" And Samuel said, "**He has said nothing at all** in respect to going on to his home. *But he may go to the space under the tree,*"] *it has been taught on Tannaite authority in accord with the position of Rab, and it has been taught on Tannaite authority in accord with the position of Samuel.*

B. *It has been taught on Tannaite authority in accord with the position of Rab:* He who was going along the way and it got dark and he knew a certain tree or fence and said, "My place of Sabbath rest will be under it," has said nothing at all. But if he said, "My place of Sabbath rest will be in such and such a place," he may continue the trip till he gets to that place. Once he has gotten to that place, he may walk throughout the place and outside of it for two thousand cubits. Under what circumstances? If it is a place that is well defined, for instance, a mount ten handbreadths high and from four cubits to

*194*    *Analysis and Argumentation in Rabbinic Judaism*

two bet seahs in area, or a valley ten handbreadths deep and from four cubits to two bet seahs in area; but if it was a place that was not well defined, he is not allowed to move for more than four cubits. If there were two people traveling together, and one of them knows of a well-delineated spot and the other doesn't, the latter assigns to the former his right to choose a place for Sabbath rest, and the other says, "My place of Sabbath rest will be in such and such a place." Under what circumstances? Where the man indicated the four cubits he selected by a clearly defined landscape marker. But if he did not define the four cubits by a clearly defined landscape marker, he may not move from his place.

C. *May we then say that this is a refutation of the position of Samuel?*

D. *Samuel may say to you, "Here with what case do we deal? It would be one in which from the place where the man stood to the root of a tree were two thousand four cubits, so that if you set him up on the far side of the tree, he would be standing outside of his permitted limit; so, if he indicated that the spot was four cubits on the hither side of the tree, he may go there, but otherwise, not."*

E. *And it has been taught on Tannaite authority in accord with the position of Samuel:* If someone erred and made fusion meals in two opposite directions in the belief that it is permitted to set out fusion meals in two opposite directions, or if he said to his servants, "Go and set out a fusion meal for me," and one of them set out a fusion meal to the north and the other to the south, he may go northward as far as the limit of the southern fusion meal, and southward up to the limit of the northern fusion meal. But if they measured each limit exactly, he may not stir from the place.

F. *May we then say that this is a refutation of the position of Rab?*

G. *Well, not exactly: Rab has the standing of a Tannaite authority and so has every right to differ from this Tannaite formulation.*

The point is now self-evident. This argument stands still, a static presentation of beautifully articulated and amplified exchanges of principles. The argument utilizes the rhetoric of question and answer — but does not move. In Hegelian terms, we have a thesis, an antithesis, but no synthesis, hence, no dialectics of logic, merely of rhetoric. The balance between B and its articulation against C, then the introduction in Rabbah's name, of the consideration underlying Rab's position, simply deepens the presentation, but does not expand it in any way. The same static trait characterizes G-H. I:2 forms nothing more than a footnote. That is shown by I:3, which simply reverts to our starting point; I:4 follows suit. And the

*Twelve. Dialectical vs. Non-Dialectical Arguments* 195

appendix at I:4B draws us back to the contrary position of Samuel. So, as I said, what we have is balanced, orderly, fair — but in the end merely an exercise in paraphrase, recapitulation, and amplification. And these valued modes of clarification of conflicting principles stand still and find no resolution, such as dialectics effects. Within this classification of rhetorical dialectics falls the bulk of the cases that are not reproduced here and that play no role in my account of matters.

The Talmud presents a vast quantity of exquisitely balanced expositions of various positions, that is, essentially syllogistic arguments, in which two contrary propositions are argued. These exhibit a pure classicism, according to each party to a proposition a balanced and proportionate share of the whole, with both sides given equal opportunity to answer one another. The result is the construction, in words, of a discourse that compares in balance and order and exact proportion to the Parthenon. Here is yet another instance of that perfection of presentation that may readily be confused with a dialectical argument, but that is not, in fact, dialectical at all:

**I.1**  A.  *It has been stated:*
B.  He who enters into the rite of removing the shoe with a pregnant woman who then miscarried —
C.  R. Yohanan said, "She does not perform the rite of removing the shoe [with the brothers]."
D.  And R. Simeon b. Laqish said, "She does perform the rite of removing the shoe [with the brothers]."
E.  R. Yohanan said, "She does not perform the rite of removing the shoe [with the brothers]:" the rite of removing the shoe performed by a pregnant woman who has miscarried is classified as a valid rite of removing the shoe, and the act of sexual relations of a pregnant woman is classified as a valid act of sexual relations.
F.  And R. Simeon b. Laqish said, "She does perform the rite of removing the shoe [with the brothers]:" the rite of removing the shoe performed by a pregnant woman who has miscarried is not classified as a valid rite of removing the shoe, and the act of sexual relations of a pregnant woman is not classified as a valid act of sexual relations.
G.  *What is at stake in this dispute?*
H.  *If you wish, I shall say that at issue is the interpretation of a verse of Scripture, and if you wish, I shall say that at issue is a matter of reasoning.*
I.  *If you wish, I shall say that at issue is the interpretation of a verse of Scripture:* "R. Yohanan takes the view that the language, "And have no child" *is what Scripture has said, and lo, this one has no child. And R. Simeon b. Laqish maintains that the language,* "And have no child" *implies,* "look into the matter" *[and find out whether there has been any kind of offspring; here the miscarriage then qualifies].*

J. *and if you wish, I shall say that at issue is a matter of reasoning. R. Yohanan takes the view that, if Elijah should come and say that the woman is going to miscarry, would she not in any event have been subject to the rite of removing the shoe or levirate marriage? [She most certainly would.] So here too, it is a fact that is subject to retrospective clarification. And R. Simeon b. Laqish maintains that we do not invoke the principle that a fact is subject to retrospective clarification [but we settle matters as they are at the moment of decision].*

K. *R. Yohanan objected to R. Simeon b. Laqish, "* **[If] the offspring is not timely, he is prohibited from marrying her relatives, and she is prohibited from marrying his relatives, and he has invalidated her from marrying into the priesthood.** *Now from my perspective, in holding that* the rite of removing the shoe performed by a pregnant woman who has miscarried is classified as a valid rite of removing the shoe, and the act of sexual relations of a pregnant woman is classified as a valid act of sexual relations, *that explains why he renders her unfit. But from your perspective, in holding that,* the rite of removing the shoe performed by a pregnant woman who has miscarried is not classified as a valid rite of removing the shoe, and the act of sexual relations of a pregnant woman is not classified as a valid act of sexual relations, *why in the world can he have* **invalidated her from marrying into the priesthood?***"*

L. *He said to him, "It is based on rabbinical authority and represents merely a stricter ruling than the law would require"* [Slotki: one not knowing the circumstances of this particular case would erroneously assume that any other woman who has performed the rite of removing the shoe likewise may be married to a priest].

M. *There are those who represent matters as follows: R. Simeon b. Laqish objected to R. Yohanan, "* **[If] the offspring is not timely, he is prohibited from marrying her relatives, and she is prohibited from marrying his relatives, and he has invalidated her from marrying into the priesthood.** *Now from my perspective, in holding that* the rite of removing the shoe performed by a pregnant woman who has miscarried is not classified as a valid rite of removing the shoe, *that explains why he renders her unfit — that is, as a strict interpretation of the law. But it is not taught as the Tannaite rule,* she does not have to undergo the rite of removing the shoe with the brothers. *But from your perspective, the rule should be stated:* she does not have to undergo the rite of removing the shoe with the brothers."

N. *He said to him, "True enough. But since the Tannaite formulation in the first clause is,* **and he has not invalidated her from marrying into the priesthood,** *it is stated in the second clause,* **and he has invalidated her from marrying into the priesthood."**

Twelve. Dialectical vs. Non-Dialectical Arguments    197

O.   R. Yohanan objected to R. Simeon b. Laqish, " **[If] the offspring is not timely, he may confirm [the marriage]:** *now from my perspective, in holding that* the rite of removing the shoe performed by a pregnant woman who has miscarried is classified as a valid rite of removing the shoe, and the act of sexual relations of a pregnant woman is classified as a valid act of sexual relations, *that explains why* **he may confirm [the marriage].** *But from your perspective, in holding that,* the rite of removing the shoe performed by a pregnant woman who has miscarried is not classified as a valid rite of removing the shoe, and the act of sexual relations of a pregnant woman is not classified as a valid act of sexual relations, *why in the world [can he* **confirm the marriage]***? Rather, the rule should state,* he must go and have sexual relations with her again, and only then may he confirm the marriage!'"

P.   "But what is the meaning of, **he may confirm [the marriage]***? It is,* he must go and have sexual relations with her again, and only then may he confirm the marriage. That is, it is not sufficient [without doing so]."

Q.   There are those who represent matters as follows: R. Simeon b. Laqish objected to R. Yohanan, " **[If] the offspring is not timely, he may confirm [the marriage]:** *now from my perspective, in holding that* the rite of removing the shoe performed by a pregnant woman who has miscarried is not classified as a valid rite of removing the shoe, and the act of sexual relations of a pregnant woman is not classified as a valid act of sexual relations, *that explains why* **he may confirm [the marriage]** — *meaning:* he must go and have sexual relations with her again, and only then may he confirm the marriage. That is, it is not sufficient [without doing so]. *But from your perspective, the rule should be,* if he wants, he may divorce her, but if he wants, he may confirm the marriage with her."

R.   *He said to him,* "True enough. *But since in the prior clause it says,* **he must put her away,** *in the following clause it says,* **he may confirm [the marriage]***.*"

S.   *An objection was raised:* He who marries his deceased childless brother's widow and she turns out to be pregnant, lo, her co-wife should not remarry, lest the offspring turn out to be viable. *To the contrary, what it should say is this: if the offspring is viable, her co-wife is exempt [and free to marry, so none of the widows of the deceased is subject to the levirate connection is any form]. So rather read:* it is possible that the offspring will not be viable. *Now, if it should enter your mind that* the act of sexual relations of a pregnant woman is classified as a valid act of sexual relations, *why is the rule that* her co-wife should not remarry, lest the offspring turn out to be viable? *Let her be freed of the levirate connection through the act of sexual relations of her fellow!"*

T. Said Abbayye, *"As to the sexual relations, both parties concur that she does not exempt her co-wife. What separates them is only the question of the rite of removing the shoe. R. Yohanan maintains that that* the rite of removing the shoe performed by a pregnant woman who has miscarried is classified as a valid rite of removing the shoe but the act of sexual relations of a pregnant woman is not classified as a valid act of sexual relations, *and R. Simeon b. Laqish holds the view that that* the act of sexual relations of a pregnant woman is not classified as an act of sexual relations, and the rite of removing the shoe performed by a pregnant woman who has miscarried is not classified as a valid rite of removing the shoe."

U. Said to him Raba, *"Well, how do you want it?* If the act of sexual relations of a pregnant woman is classified as an act of sexual relations, then the rite of removing the shoe performed by a pregnant woman should be regarded as valid, and if the act of sexual relations of a pregnant woman is not classified as an act of sexual relations, then the rite of removing the shoe performed by a pregnant woman should not be regarded as valid. *For we have it as an established rule* **[36A]** that anyone who is subject to marriage with the levir is subject to the rite of removing the shoe, and anyone who is not subject to marriage with the levir is not subject to the rite of removing the shoe."

V. *Rather, said Raba, "This is the sense of the matter:* 'He who marries his deceased childless brother's widow and she turns out to be pregnant, lo, her co-wife should not remarry, lest the offspring turn out to be viable, and sexual relations with a pregnant woman are not classified as sexual relations, and the rite of removing the shoe done with a pregnant woman is not classified as a valid rite of removing the shoe, and the offspring does not exempt the co-wives from the levirate connection until it is actually born.'"

  W. *It has been taught on Tannaite authority in accord with the position of Raba:* He who marries his deceased childless brother's widow and she turns out to be pregnant, lo, her co-wife should not remarry, lest the offspring turn out to be viable, and sexual relations with a pregnant woman or the rite of removing the shoe does not exempt the co-wives from the levirate connection, but only the offspring exempts the co-wives, and the offspring does not exempt the co-wives from the levirate connection until it is actually born.

X. *The operative consideration therefore in exempting the co-wives from the levirate connection is,* lest the offspring turn out to be viable. *But then, if the offspring is not viable, the co-wife is exempt*

## Twelve. Dialectical vs. Non-Dialectical Arguments

[Slotki: on the strength of the sexual relations that took place prior to the miscarriage of the child, no repeated sexual relations being necessary]. *May we then say that this refutes the position of R. Simeon b. Laqish?*

Y. *R. Simeon b. Laqish will say to you, "This is the sense of the statement:* He who marries his deceased childless brother's widow and she turns out to be pregnant, lo, her co-wife should not remarry, lest the offspring not turn out to be viable, and sexual relations with a pregnant woman are not classified as valid sexual relations, and the rite of removing the shoe performed with her is not classified as a valid rite of removing the shoe. And if you should say, 'well, follow the rule governing the majority of women, and the majority of women produce perfectly healthy offspring,' still it is the fact that an offspring exempts the co-wives from the levirate connection only when it is actually born."

Z. *Said R. Eleazar, "Well, how is it possible that there should be such a ruling as that which R. Simeon b. Laqish has laid down, and yet we have not learned it as a Tannaite formulation in our Mishnah?" He went forth and took a close look, and found the following, which we have learned in the Mishnah:* **A woman whose husband and co-wife went overseas and they came and said to her, "Your husband has died," should not remarry [without the rite of removing the shoe or enter into levirate marriage, until she ascertains whether her co-wife is pregnant [M. 16:1A-B].** *Now it is easy to understand why she should not enter into levirate marriage, lest the offspring be viable, so the levir would violate the Torah's prohibition against marrying a brother's wife. But why should she not perform the rite of removing the shoe? Now there is no problem in understanding why she should not perform the rite of removing the shoe within the nine months after the husband's death, and not contract a marriage in that same period, on account of doubt [as to whether the offspring is viable; if it is, the rite and the levirate marriage would be invalid; the exemption is brought into force by the actual birth]. But why should she not* perform the rite of removing the shoe within the nine months of the husband's death and enter into marriage after nine months?" [Slotki: this should be permitted by Yohanan in any event: if the rival had been pregnant and miscarried or had not been pregnant at all, the rite of removing the shoe was valid; if a viable child had been born, the exemption took effect at his birth, and the subsequent marriage would be lawful; since the rule forbids the rite of removal and marriage even after nine months unless definite information about the rival has been received, it must be assumed to represent the view of Simeon b. Laqish, who deems the rite of removal invalid wherever the child is not viable and the ceremony took place during pregnancy.]

AA. *But even in accord with your position* [the rite of removal is forbidden because the co-wife may have been pregnant when the rite took place (Slotki)], *let her perform the rite of removal and then marry after nine months* [when there will be no doubt on the pregnancy; why wait to find out whether the co-wife has been pregnant at all]? *So this passage must be excluded from consideration, for Abbayye and Bar Abba and R. Hinena bar Abbayye all maintained,* "It is possible that the offspring of the co-wife might be viable, and you would then make it necessary to proclaim concerning her with regard to the priesthood [that the rite of removal was unnecessary and therefore null, so she remains eligible to the priesthood]."

BB. *So make it necessary to issue such a proclamation!*

CC. *There may be someone who witnessed the rite of removing the shoe but did not hear about the proclamation and so would imagine that a woman who has performed the rite of removing the shoe may marry a priest [which is not the case].*

DD. *Said to him Abbayye,* "*Now has it been said,* 'She should not carry out the rite of removing the shoe nor enter into levirate marriage'? *What is stated is,* 'She shall not be married nor enter into levirate marriage' *that is, without the rite of removing the shoe. But if the rite of removing the shoe was carried out [even within the nine months of the death of the husband], she would be permitted to marry at the end of the period*" [Slotki: and the passage affords no support to Simeon b. Laqish].

EE. *It has been taught on Tannaite authority in accord with the position of R. Simeon b. Laqish:* He who carries out the rite of removing the shoe with a pregnant woman, who subsequently miscarried — she has to enter into the rite of removing the shoe with one of the other brothers.

2. A. *Said Raba,* "*The decided law accords with the position of R. Simeon b. Laqish in three matters. The first is the one that we have just now been discussing.*

   B. "*The second is in accord with that which we have learned in the Mishnah:* **He who divides his estate among his sons by a verbal [donation], [and] gave a larger portion to one and a smaller portion to another, or treated the firstborn as equivalent to all the others — his statement is valid. But if he had said, "By reason of an inheritance [the afore-stated arrangements are made]," he has said nothing** whatsoever. [If] he had written, whether at the beginning, middle, or end, [that these things are handed over] as a gift, his statement is valid [M. B.B.8:5E-J]. [36B] And said R. Simeon b. Laqish, 'Title is not transferred unless he said, "Let Mr. X and Mr. Y will inherit such-and-such a field, which I have assigned to them as a gift, so that they may inherit them."'

C. *"And the third is in line with that which we have learned in the Mishnah:* **He who writes over his property to his son [to take effect] after his death — the father cannot sell the property, because it is written over to the son, and the son cannot sell the property, because it is [yet] in the domain of the father. [If] the father sold [it], the property is sold until he dies. If the son sold the property, the purchaser has no right whatever in the property until the father dies. The father harvests the crops and gives the usufruct to anyone whom he wants. And whatever he left already harvested-lo, it belongs to his heirs [M. B.B. 8:7].** *And it has been stated:* if the son sold the property in the lifetime of the father and died in the lifetime of the father — R. Yohanan said, "The purchaser has not acquired the property." R. Simeon b. Laqish said, "The purchaser has acquired the property." R. Yohanan said, "The purchaser has not acquired the property," *for the right to the usufruct [such as the step father in our case had] is tantamount in law to the right to the substance of the estate, [so that when the son sold the estate during the lifetime of the father, he sold something that he did not own.]* [R. Simeon b. Laqish said, "The purchaser has acquired the property," for *the right to the usufruct [such as the step father in our case had] is not tantamount in law to the right to the substance of the estate, so that when the son sold the estate during the lifetime of the father, he sold something that he did own."*

The first initiative takes place at 1.E-F, the second at Gff. In the former, each party gets to amplify his position, in the latter, the anonymous voice articulates the principle at issue, and each of the choices is then worked out in detail and in balance. Then each party is given the opportunity to object to the position of the other, with an appropriate rejoinder. Even when we have new versions of the several statements, these exhibit that same proportion and balance. When T-U then introduce a new perspective, the two positions once more are carefully balanced. And so throughout. All of this captures our admiration, but none of it falls into the category of an argument that moves out of its original framework, and, viewed whole, the composition falls into the category of a syllogism, brilliantly executed.

### v. The Importance of the Dialectical Argument in the Halakhic Literature

What then is at stake in the dialectical argument? I see three complementary results. All of them, in my view, prove commensurate to the effort required to follow these protracted, sometimes tedious disquisitions.

First, we test every allegation by a counter-proposition, so serving the cause of truth through challenge and constant checking for flaws in an argument.

Second, we survey the entire range of possibilities, which leaves no doubts about the cogency of our conclusion. And that means, we move out of our original case, guided by its generative principle to new cases altogether.

Third, quite to the point, by the give and take of argument, we ourselves are enabled to go through the thought processes set forth in the subtle markings that yield our reconstruction of the argument. We not only review what people say, but how they think: the processes of reasoning that have yielded a given conclusion. Sages and disciples become party to the modes of thought; in the dialectical argument, they are required to replicate the thought-processes themselves.

Let me give a single example of the power of the dialectical argument to expose the steps in thinking that lead from one end to another: principle to ruling, or ruling to principle. In the present instance, the only one we require to see a perfectly routine and obvious procedure, we mean to prove the point that if people are permitted to obstruct the public way, if damage was done by them, they are liable to pay compensation. First, we are going to prove that general point on the basis of a single case. Then we shall proceed to show how a variety of authorities, dealing with diverse cases, sustain the same principle.

### TALMUD Baba Mesia 10:5/O-X

O. He who brings out his manure to the public domain —
P. while one party pitches it out, the other party must be bringing it in to manure his field.
Q They do not soak clay in the public domain,
R. and they do not make bricks.
S. And they knead clay in the public way,
T. but not bricks.
U. He who builds in the public way —

Twelve. Dialectical vs. Non-Dialectical Arguments          203

    V.       while one party brings stones, the builder must make use of them in the public way.

    W.      And if one has inflicted injury, he must pay for the damages he has caused.

    X.       Rabban Simeon b. Gamaliel says, "Also: He may prepare for doing his work [on site in the public way] for thirty days [before the actual work of building]."

We begin with the comparison of the rule before us with another Tannaite position on the same issue, asking whether an unattributed, therefore authoritative, rule stands for or opposes the position of a given authority; we should hope to prove that the named authority concurs. So one fundamental initiative in showing how many cases express a single principle — the concrete demonstration of the unity of the law — is to find out whether diverse, important authorities concur on the principle, each ruling in a distinctive case; or whether a single authority is consistent in ruling in accord with the principle at hand, as in what follows:

I.1    A.    *May we say that our Mishnah-paragraph does not accord with the view of R. Judah? For it has been taught on Tannaite authority:*

        B.    **R. Judah says, "At the time of fertilizing the fields, a man may take out his manure and pile it up at the door of his house in the public way so that it will be pulverized by the feet of man and beast, for a period of thirty days. For it was on that very stipulation that Joshua caused the Israelites to inherit the land"** [T. B.M. 11:8E-H].

        C.    You may even maintain that he concurs with the Mishnah's rule [that **while one party pitches it out, the other party must be bringing it in to manure his field**]. R. Judah concedes that if one has caused damage, he is liable to pay compensation.

In line with the position just now proposed, then Judah will turn out to rule every which way on the same matter. And that is not an acceptable upshot.

        D.    *But has it not been taught in the Mishnah:* **If the store-keeper had left his lamp outside the store-keeper is liable [if the flame caused a fire]. R. Judah said, "In the case of a lamp for Hanukkah, he is exempt"** [M. B. Q. 6:6E-F], because he has acted under authority. *Now surely that must mean,* under the authority of the court [and that shows that one is not responsible for damage caused by his property in the public domain if it was there under the authority of the court]!

The dialectic now intervenes. We have made a proposal. Isn't it a good one? Of course not, were we to give up so quickly, we should gain nothing:

        E.    *No, what it means is, on the authority of carrying out one's religious obligations.*

By now, the reader is able to predict the next step: "but isn't the contrary more reasonable?" Here is how we raise the objection.

F. But has it not been taught on Tannaite authority:
G. in the case of all those concerning whom they have said, "They are permitted to obstruct the public way," if there was damage done, one is liable to pay compensation. But R. Judah declares one exempt from having to pay compensation.
H. So it is better to take the view that our Mishnah-paragraph does not concur with the position of R. Judah.

The point of interest has been introduced: whether those permitted to obstruct the public way must pay compensation for damages they may cause in so doing. Here is where we find a variety of cases that yield a single principle:

2. A. Said Abbayye, "R. Judah, Rabban Simeon b. Gamaliel, and R. Simeon all take the position that i n the case of all those concerning whom they have said, 'They are permitted to obstruct the public way,' if there was damage done, one is liable to pay compensation.
B. "As to R. Judah, the matter is just as we have now stated it.

Simeon b. Gamaliel and Simeon now draw us to unrelated cases:

C. "As to Rabban Simeon b. Gamaliel, we have learned in the Mishnah: **Rabban Simeon b. Gamaliel says, 'Also: He may prepare for doing his work [on site in the public way] for thirty days [before the actual work of building].'**
D. "As to R. Simeon, we have learned in the Mishnah: **A person should not set up an oven in a room unless there is a space of four cubits above it. If he was setting it up in the upper story, there has to be a layer of plaster under it three handbreadths thick, and in the case of a stove, a handbreadth thick. And if it did damage, the owner of the oven has to pay for the damage. R. Simeon says, 'All of these measures have been stated only so that if the object did damage, the owner is exempt from paying compensation if the stated measures have been observed' [M. B.B. 2:2A-F].**"

We see then that the demonstration of the unity of the law and the issue of who stands, or does not stand, behind a given rule, go together. When we ask about who does or does not stand behind a rule, we ask about the principle of a case, which leads us downward to a premise, and we forthwith point to how that same premise underlies a different principle yielding a case — so how can X hold the view he does, if that is his premise, since at a different case he makes a point with a principle that rests on a contradictory premise. The Mishnah and the Talmud are comparable to the moraine left by the last ice age, fields studded with boulders. For the Talmud, reference is made to those many disputes that litter the pages and impede progress. That explains why much of the Talmud is taken up with not only sorting out disputes, but also showing their rationality, meaning, reasonable people have perfectly valid reasons for disagreeing about a given point, since both parties share the same premises but apply them differently; or they really do not differ at

*Twelve. Dialectical vs. Non-Dialectical Arguments* 205

all, since one party deals with one set of circumstances, the other with a different set of circumstances.

### VI. THE LAW BEHIND THE LAWS

The dialectical argument proves the ideal medium for the assertion, through sustained demonstration alone, of the union of laws in law. Specifically, if all we know is laws, then we want to find out what makes them cohere. We ask, what is at stake in them? Accordingly, the true issues of the law emerge from the detailed rulings of the laws. Generalization takes a variety of forms, some yielding a broader framework into which to locate a case, others a proposition of consequence. Let me give an obvious and familiar instance of what is to be done. Here is an example of a case that yields a principle:

### TALMUD BABA MESIA TO 9:11

A. **(1) A day worker collects his wage any time of the night.**
B. **(2) And a night worker collects his wage any time of the day.**
C. **(3) A worker by the hour collects his wage any time of the night or day.**

I.1 A. *Our rabbis have taught on Tannaite authority:*
    B. How on the basis of Scripture do we know, **A day worker collects his wage any time of the night**?
    C. "[You shall not oppress your neighbor or rob him.] The wages of a hired servant shall not remain with you all night until the morning" (Lev. 19:13).
    D. And how on the basis of Scripture do we know, **and a night worker collects his wage any time of the day**?
    E. "[You shall not oppress a hired servant who is poor and needy]...you shall give him hire his hire on the day on which he earns it, before the sun goes down" (Dt. 23:14-15).
    F. *Might I say that the reverse is the case [the night worker must be paid during the night that he does the work, in line with Lev. 19:13, and the day worker by day, in line with Dt. 23:15]?*
    G. Wages are to be paid only at the end of the work [so the fee is not payable until the work has been done].

What do we learn from this passage? Specifically, two points.
[1] Scripture yields the rule at hand;
[2] Scripture also imposes limits on the formation of the law; but one generalization, that the law of the Mishnah derives from the source of Scripture.

And, if we take a small step beyond, of course, we learn that the two parts of the Torah are one. The hermeneutics instructs us to ask, how on the basis of Scripture do we know...? Its premise then is that Scripture forms the basis for rules not expressed with verses of the written Torah. The theological principle conveyed in the hermeneutics expressed in the case is that the Torah is one and encompasses both the oral and the written parts; the oral part derives its truths from the written part.

Now if I had to identify the single most important theological point that the Talmud and other writings that use dialectics sets forth, it is that the laws yield law, the truth exhibits integrity, all of the parts — the details, principles, and premises — holding together in a coherent manner. To understand how generalizations are attained, however, we cannot deal only with generalizations. So we turn to a specific problem of category-formation, namely, in the transfer of property, whether or not we distinguish between a sale and a gift. That is, in both instances property is transferred. But the conditions of transfer clearly differ; in the one case there is a quid pro quo, in the other, not. Now does that distinction make a difference? The answer to that question will have implications for a variety of concrete cases, e.g., transfers of property in a dowry, divisions of inheritances and estates, the required documents and procedures for effecting transfer of title, and the like. If, then, we know the correct category-formation — the same or not the same category — we form a generalization that will draw together numerous otherwise unrelated cases and (more to the point) rules.

One way to accomplish the goal is to identify the issue behind a dispute, which leads us from the dispute to the principle that is established and confirmed by a dispute on details, e.g., whether or not the principle applies, and, if it does, how it does. In this way we affirm the unity of the law by establishing that all parties to a dispute really agree on the same point; then the dispute itself underlines the law's coherence:

### BAVLI TO M. BABA BATRA 1:3

- A. He whose [land] surrounds that of his fellow on three sides,
- B. and who made a fence on the first, second, and third sides —
- C. they do not require [the other party to share in the expense of building the walls].
- D. R. Yosé says, "If he built a fence on the fourth side, they assign to him [his share in the case of] all [three other fences]."

In the following dispute, we ask what is subject to dispute between the two named authorities, B-C.

2. A. *It has been stated:*
   B. R. Huna said, "All is proportional to the actual cost of building the fence [Simon: which will vary according to the materials used by the one who builds the fence]."
   C. Hiyya bar Rab said, "All is proportionate to the cost of a cheap fence made of sticks [since that is all that is absolutely necessary]."

Twelve. Dialectical vs. Non-Dialectical Arguments 207

To find the issue, we revert to our Mishnah-rule. The opinions therein guide the disputing parties. Each then has to account for what is subject to dispute in the Mishnah-paragraph. Then the point is, the Mishnah's dispute is not only rational, but it also rests upon a shared premise, affirmed by all parties. That is the power of D.

D. *We have learned in the Mishnah:* **He whose [land] surrounds that of his fellow on three sides, and who made a fence on the first, second, and third sides — they do not require [the other party to share in the expense of building the walls].** Lo, if he fences the fourth side too, he must contribute to the cost of the entire fence. *But then note what follows:* **R. Yosé says, "If he built a fence on the fourth side, they assign to him [his share in the case of] all [three other fences]."** *Now there is no problem from the perspective of R. Huna, who has said,* "All is proportional to the actual cost of building the fence [Simon: which will vary according to the materials used by the one who builds the fence]." *Then we can identify what is at issue between the first authority and R. Yosé. Specifically, the initial authority takes the view that we proportion the costs to what they would be if a cheap fence of sticks was built, but not to what the fence-builder actually spent, and R. Yosé maintains that under all circumstances, the division is proportional to actual costs. But from the perspective of Hiyya bar Rab, who has said,* "All is proportionate to the cost of a cheap fence made of sticks [since that is all that is absolutely necessary]," *what can be the difference between the ruling of the initial Tannaite authority and that of R. Yosé? If, after all, he does not pay him even the cost of building a cheap fence, what in the world is he supposed to pay off as his share?*

We now revert to the dialectics, but a different kind. Here we raise a variety of possibilities, not as challenges and responses in a sequence, but as freestanding choices; the same goal is at hand, the opportunity to examine every possibility. But the result is different: not a final solution but four suitable ones, yielding the notion that a single principle governs a variety of cases. That explains why we now have a set of four answers, all of them converging on the same principle:

E. *If you want, I shall say that what is at issue between them is the fee to be paid for a watchman. The initial authority holds that he pays the cost of a watchman, not the charge of building a cheap fence, and R. Yosé says that he has to pay the cost of building a cheap fence.*

F. *But if you prefer, I may say that at issue between them is the first, second, and third sides, in which instance the initial Tannaite authority has the other pay only the cost of fencing the fourth side, not the first three, and R. Yosé maintains he has to pay his share of the cost of fencing the first three sides too.*

G. *And if you prefer, I shall maintain that at issue between them is whether the fence has to be built by the owner of the surrounding fields or the owner of the enclosed field if the latter pays the cost of the whole. The initial Tannaite authority says that the consideration that leads the owner of the enclosed field* to have to contribute at all is that he went ahead and built the fourth fence, so he has to pay his share of the cost of the whole; but if the owner of the surrounding fields is the one who went ahead and did it, the other has to pay only the share of the fourth fence. For his part, R. Yosé takes the position that there is no distinction between who took the initiative in building the fourth fence, whether the owner of the enclosed field or the owner of the surrounding field. In either case the former has to pay the latter his share of the whole.

H. There are those who say, in respect to this last statement, that at issue between them is whether the fourth fence has to be built by the owner of the enclosed field or the surrounding fields so that the former has to contribute his share. The initial Tannaite authority holds that, even if the owner of the surrounding fields makes the fourth fence, the other has to contribute to the cost, and R. Yosé maintains that if the owner of the enclosed field takes it on himself to build the fourth fence, he has to pay his share of the cost of the whole, because through his action he has shown that he wants the fence, but if the owner of the surrounding fields builds the fourth side, the other pays not a penny [since he can say he never wanted a fence to begin with].

The premise of E is that the owner of the land on the inside has a choice as to the means of guarding his field; but he of course bears responsibility for the matter. F agrees that he bears responsibility for his side, but adds that he also is responsible for the sides from which he enjoys benefit. And of course G concurs that the owner of the inner field is responsible to protect his own property. H takes the same view. What we have accomplished is, first, to lay a foundation in rationality for the dispute of the Mishnah-paragraph, and, further, demonstrate that all parties to the dispute affirm the responsibility to pay one's share of that from which one benefits. Justice means, no free lunch.

### VII. THE UNITY OF THE LAW

In what follows, the unity of the law extends from agreements behind disputes to a more fundamental matter: identifying the single principle behind many, diverse cases. What do diverse cases have in common? Along these same lines, that same hermeneutics wants us to show how diverse authorities concur on the same principle, dealing with diverse cases; how where there is a dispute, the dispute represents schism vs. consensus, with the weight of argument and evidence favoring consensus; where we have a choice between interpreting an opinion as schismatic and as coherent with established rule, we try to show it is not schismatic; and so on and so forth. All of these commonplace activities pursue a single goal, which is to limit the range of schism and expand the range of consensus, both in political, personal terms of authority, and, more to the point, in the framework of case and principle. If I had to identify a single hermeneutical principle — that is, defining melody — that governs throughout, it is, the quest for harmony, consensus, unity, and above all,

*Twelve. Dialectical vs. Non-Dialectical Arguments*

the rationality of dispute: reasonable disagreement about the pertinence or relevance of established, universally-affirmed principles.

Here is a fine instance of the working of the hermeneutics that tells us to read the texts as a single coherent statement, episodic and unrelated cases as statements of a single principle. The principle is: it is forbidden for someone to derive uncompensated benefit from somebody else's property. That self-evidently valid principle of equity — "thou shalt not steal" writ small — then emerges from a variety of cases; the cases are read as illustrative. The upshot of demonstrating that fact is to prove a much-desired goal. The law of the Torah — here, the written Torah, one of the ten commandments no less! — contains within itself the laws of everyday life. So one thing yields many things; the law is coherence in God's mind, and retains that coherent as it expands to encompass the here and the now of the social order. The details as always are picayune, the logic practical, the reasoning concrete and applied; but the stakes prove cosmic in a very exact sense of the word. The problem involves a two-story house, owned by the resident of the lower story. The house has fallen down. The tenant, upstairs, has no where to live. The landlord, downstairs, does not rebuild the house. The tenant has the right to rebuild the downstairs part of the house and to live there as long as the landlord does not complete the rebuilding of the house and also refund to the tenant the cost of rebuilding the part that the tenant has reconstructed for himself. Judah rejects this ruling, and, in doing so, invokes a general principle, by no means limited to the case at hand. Then the Bavli will wish to show how this governing principle pertains elsewhere.

### Mishnah-tractate Baba Mesia 10:3
### and Bavli to M. Baba Mesia 10:3 I.1/117A-B

A. A house and an upper story belonging to two people which fell down —
B. [if] the resident of the upper story told the householder [of the lower story] to rebuild,
C. but he does not want to rebuild,
D. lo, the resident of the upper story rebuilds the lower story and lives there,
E. until the other party compensates him for what he has spent.
F. R. Judah says, "Also: [if so,] this one is [then] living in his fellow's [housing]. [So in the end] he will have to pay him rent.
G. "But the resident of the upper story builds both the house and the upper room,
H. "and he puts a roof on the upper story,
I. "and he lives in the lower story,
J. "until the other party compensates him for what he has spent."

At issue is a principle, which settles the case at hand. It is whether or not one may gratuitously derive benefit from someone else's property. We shall now show that Judah repeatedly takes that position in a variety of diverse cases:

I.1 A. [117B] Said R. Yohanan, "In three passages R. Judah has repeated for us the rule that it is forbidden for someone to derive benefit from somebody's else's property. *The first is in the Mishnah passage at hand. The next is in that which we have learned in the Mishnah.*"

The case that is now introduced involves an error in dyeing wool. The premise of the rulings is that dyeing always enhances the value of the wool, whether it is dyed of one color or some other. On that basis, the following is quite clear:

B. He who gave wool to a dyer to dye it red, and he dyed it black, or to dye it black, and he dyed it red —
C. R. Meir says, "The dyer pays him back the value of his wool."
D. And R. Judah says, "If the increase in value is greater than the outlay for the process of dyeing, the owner pays him back for the outlay for the process of dyeing. And if the outlay for the process of dyeing is greater than the increase in the value of the wool, the owner pays him [the dyer] only the increase in the value of the wool" [M. B.Q. 9:4G-K].
E. *And what is the third? It is as we have learned in the Mishnah:*
F. He who paid part of a debt that he owed and deposited the bond that has been written as evidence covering the remaining sum with a third party, and said to him, "If I have not given you what I still owe the lender between now and such-and-such a date, give the creditor his bond of indebtedness," if the time came and he has not paid,
G. R. Yosé says, "He should hand it over."
H. And R. Judah says, "He should not hand it over" [M. B.B. 10:5A-E]
I. *Why [does it follow that Judah holds that it is forbidden for someone to derive benefit from somebody's else's property]? Perhaps when R. Judah takes the position that he does here, it is only because there is blackening of the walls.*
J. [Freedman: the new house loses its newness because the tenant is living there, so the house owner is sustaining a loss, and that is why the tenant has to pay rent];
K. as to the case of the dyer who was supposed to dye the wool red but dyed it black, *the reason is that he has violated his instructions, and we have learned in the Mishnah:*
L. **Whoever changes [the original terms of the agreement] — his hand is on the bottom [M. B.M. 6:2E-F].** [That is to say, the decision must favor the other party, the claim of the one who has changed the original terms being subordinated.]
M. *And as to the third case,* **the one who has paid part of his debt,** *here we deal with an enticement, and we infer from this case that R. Judah takes the position that in the case of a come-on, there is no transfer of title.*

Yohanan's observation serves the purpose of showing how several unrelated cases of the Mishnah really make the same point: you shall not steal. The voice of the Talmud — that is to say, the dialectics itself — then contributes an objection

*Twelve. Dialectical vs. Non-Dialectical Arguments*

and its resolution, making Yohanan's statement plausible and compelling, not merely an observation that may or may not be so.

An ideal way of demonstrating the unity of the law is to expose the abstract premise of a concrete rule, and that without regard to the number of discrete cases that establish the same rule. Here is a case in which the theological principle, a stipulation made not be made contrary to what is written in the Torah, is shown to form the premise of a concrete case; then the case once more merely illustrates the principle of the Torah, which delivers its messages in just this way, through exemplary cases. 2.A commences with a common attributive formula, said x...said y.... This bears the meaning, said x in the name of y (and on his authority). Judah is then the tradent of the opinion or ruling, and Samuel the original source. Such an attributive formula may encompass three or more names and is common in both Talmuds.

### BAVLI TO M. MAKKOT 1:1L-N, 1:2, 1:3/I.2

2.  A. And said R. Judah said Samuel, "He who says to his fellow, '...on the stipulation that the advent of the Seventh Year will not abrogate the debts' — the Seventh Year nonetheless abrogates those debts."

    B. *May one then propose that Samuel takes the view that* that stipulation represents an agreement made contrary to what is written in the Torah, and, as we know, any stipulation contrary to what is written in the Torah is a null stipulation? *But lo, it has been stated:*

    C. He who says to his fellow, "[I make this sale to you] on the stipulation that you may not lay claim of fraud [by reason of variation from true value] against me"—

    D. Rab said, "He nonetheless may lay claim of fraud [by reason of variation from true value] against him."

    E. Samuel said, "He may not lay claim of fraud [by reason of variation from true value] against him."

    F. *Lo, it has been stated in that connection:* said R. Anan, "*The matter has been explained to me such that Samuel said,* 'He who says to his fellow, "[I make this sale to you] on the stipulation that you may not lay claim of fraud [by reason of variation from true value] against me" — he has no claim of fraud against him. [If he said,] "...on the stipulation that in the transaction itself, there is no aspect of fraud," lo, he has a claim of fraud against him.'"

    G. Here too, the same distinction pertains. If the stipulation was, "on condition that you do not abrogate the debt to me in the Sabbatical Year," then the Sabbatical Year does not abrogate the debt. But if the language was, "on condition that the Sabbatical Year itself does not abrogate the debt, the Sabbatical Year does abrogate the debt."

What is at stake in this issue is of course not only jurisprudential principles but theological truth, concerning the power of language. In the Torah, language is enchanted; it serves, after all, for the principal medium of the divine self-manifestation: in words, sentences, paragraphs, a book: the Torah. So what one says forms the foundation of effective reality: it makes things happen, not only records what has happened.

But what happens if one makes a statement that ordinarily would prove effective, but the contents of the statement contradict the law of the Torah? Then such a stipulation is null. Why? Because the Torah is what makes language work, and if the Torah is contradicted, then the language is no more effective — changing the world to which it refers, the rules or conditions or order of existence — than it would be if the rules of grammar were violated. Just as, in such a case, the sentence would be gibberish and not convey meaning, so in the case at hand, the sentence is senseless and null.

### VIII. DIALECTICS AND THE INTELLECTUAL DYNAMICS OF THE HALAKHIC LITERATURE

The main consequence for the Halakhah of formation through dialectical arguments is simply stated. It is the power of that mode of the representation of thought to show us — as no other mode of writing can show — not only the result but the workings of the logical mind. By following dialectical arguments, we ourselves enter into those same thought processes, and our minds then are formed in the model of rigorous and sustained, systematic argument. The reason is simply stated. When we follow a proposal and its refutation, the consequence thereof, and the result of that, we ourselves form partners to the logical tensions and their resolutions; we are given an opening into the discourse that lies before us. As soon as matters turn not upon tradition, to which we may or may not have access, but reason, specifically, challenge and response, proposal and counter-proposal, "maybe matters are just the opposite?" we find an open door before us.

For these are not matters of fact but of reasoned judgment, and the answer, "well, that's my opinion," in its "traditional form," namely, "that is what Rabbi X has said, so that must be so," finds no hearing. Moving from facts to reasoning, propositions to the process of counter-argument, the challenge resting on the mind's own movement, its power of manipulating facts one way rather than some other and of identifying the governing logic of a fact — that process invites the reader's or the listener's participation. The author of a dialectical composite presents a problem with its internal tensions in logic and offers a solution to the problem and a resolution of the logical conflicts.

What is at stake in the capacity of the framer of a composite, or even the author of a composition, to move this way and that, always in a continuous path, but often in a crooked one? The dialectical argument opens the possibility of reaching out from one thing to something else, and the path's wandering is part of the reason. It is not because people have lost sight of their starting point or their goal in the end, but because they want to encompass, in the analytical argument as it gets underway, as broad and comprehensive a range of cases and rules as they can. The movement from point to point in reference to a single point that accurately describes the dialectical argument reaches a goal of abstraction. At the point at which we leave behind the specificities of not only cases but laws, sages carry the argument upward to the law that governs many cases, the premises that undergird many rules, and still higher to the principles that infuse diverse premises; then the principles that generate other, unrelated premises, which, in turn, come to expression in other, still-less intersecting cases. The meandering course of argument comes to an end when we have shown how things cohere that we did not even imagine were contiguous at all.

The dialectical argument forms the means to an end. The distinctive character of the Talmuds' and other documents' particular kind of dialectical argument is dictated by the purpose for which dialectics is invoked. Specifically, the goal of all argument is to show in discrete detail the ultimate unity of the law. The hermeneutics of dialectics aims at making manifest how to read the laws in such a way as to discern that many things really say one thing. The variations on the theme then take the form of detailed expositions of this and that. Then our task is to move backward from result to the reasoning process that has yielded said result: through regression from stage to stage to identify within the case not only the principles of law that produce that result, but the processes of reasoning that link the principles to the case at hand. And, when we accomplish our infinite regression, we move from the workings of literature to its religious character and theological goal: it is to know God in heaven, represented, on earth, by the unity of the law, the integrity of the Torah.

These definitions in hand, we have a typology of argument that encompasses all data. We are now ready to ask, does the Aggadic literature correspond in its types of argumentation — dialectic/non-dialectic? Indeed, with a clear definition in hand of what we mean by "argumentation" in the broadest possible framework, we are ready to ask whether we find in the Aggadic documents any argumentation at all. The answer is, we certainly do, and, within the category, non-dialectical argumentation, we shall find meeting points between Halakhic and Aggadic discourse.

PART SIX

TYPES OF ARGUMENT,
AUTHENTIC AND INAUTHENTIC,
IN MIDRASH-COMPILATIONS

# 13

# Genesis Rabbah

### i. Dialectical Arguments

Genesis Rabbah contains no dialectical arguments.

### ii. Non-Dialectical Arguments

The document contains a few instances in which a dispute is articulated by the provision of reasons for the contradictory positions.

**I.III.**
1. A. R. Tanhum commenced discourse, "For you are great and do wonderful things, you alone are God "(Ps. 86:10).
   B. Said R. Tanhum b. R. Hiyya, "As to a skin, if it has a hole as small as the eye of a needle, all of the air will escape for from it.
   C. "But as to a human being, a person is made with many apertures and holes, but the spirit does not go forth through them.
   D. "Who has done it in such a way? 'You alone are God' (Ps. 86:10)."
2. A. When were the angels created?
   B. R. Yohanan said, "On the second day of creation [Monday] were they created.
   C. "That is in line with this verse of Scripture: 'Who lays the beams of your upper chambers in the waters' (Ps. 104:3), after which it is written, 'Who makes the spirits of your angels' (Ps. 104:4). [The waters were divided into upper and lower parts, and on that same day the angels were created.]"
   D. R. Hanina said, "They were created on the fifth day of creation [Thursday]. For it is written, 'Let fowl fly above the earth' (Gen. 1:20), and it is written, 'And with two did the angel fly' (Is. 6:21)."

What is noteworthy is that the inclusion of a secondary exercise of exchange of viewpoints and argument takes a subordinate position in the exposition of the composite. The primary, documentary interest is exhausted at No. 1. The creation of the angels is not essential to No. 1, but, tacked on, the composition fills in a gap left by the opening composition; once the creation of Man enters in, the natural next question is the location of the creation of angels. But the dispute between Yohanan and Hanina, between the second and the fifth days, yields no more of an argument than an exchange of proof texts. We can hardly regard the presentation of conflicting verses as a systematic argument, and I shall only rarely cite such an item. But it is important to take into account in our larger picture of argumentation in the Aggadic documents. What it shows is willingness to settle for a scriptural support for a factual claim, not an appeal to logic or reason or analysis.

## I:XV.

1. A. ["...the heaven and the earth" (Gen. 1:1):] The House of Shammai say, "The heaven was created first."
   B. The House of Hillel say, "The earth was created first."
   C. In the view of the House of Shammai the matter may be compared to the case of a king who first made a throne for himself and afterward the footstool for the throne, as it is said, "The heaven is my throne, and the earth the dust of my feet" (Is. 66:1).
   D. In the view of the House of Hillel the matter is to be compared to the case of a king who built a first palace for himself. Only after he had built the bottom floor did he build the upper floor, for so it is written, "On the day on which the Lord God made earth and [only then] heaven" (Gen. 2:4).
   E. Said R. Judah bar Ilai, "The following verse of Scripture supports the view of the House of Hillel: 'Of old you laid out the foundations of the earth...,' and afterward, '...and the heavens are the work of your hands' (Ps. 102:25).
      F. Said R. Hanin, "On the basis of the verse of Scripture that supports the position of the House of Shammai the House of Hillel find evidence to reject that same view: 'The earth was...' (Gen. 1:2), meaning that it had already come into being."
      G. R. Yohanan [said] in the name of sages, "As to the act of creation, heaven came first. As to the process of finishing off creation, the earth came first."
      H. Said. R. Tanhuma, "I shall supply a verse of Scripture to support that statement. As to creation, the heaven came first: 'In the beginning God created [the heaven, then the earth]' (Gen. 1:1). But as to the process of finishing off creation, the earth came first: 'On the day on which the Lord God made heaven and earth' (Gen. 2:4)."
         I. Said R. Simeon, "I should be surprised if the fathers of the world disputed concerning this matter. For both of them were created only as are the pot and its lid [which is to say, in a single act]. In this regard I recite the following verse of Scripture: '[My hand established the earth, and my right hand spread out the heaven.] When I call them, they stand up together' (Is. 48:13)."

*Thirteen. Genesis Rabbah* 219

      J.    Said R. Eleazar b. R. Simeon, "According to this opinion of my father, why is it that sometimes heaven comes before earth, sometimes earth comes before heaven. But what it teaches is that the two of them are equal [having been created at the same instant]."

I:XIV.1ff., and I:XV form a miscellany that is takes shape around its own theme and is introduced because of its general relevance to the theme, heaven and earth, of the verse at hand. Here again, there is no pretense that we engage in exegesis. Neither composite pretends to follow the dominant program or formal structure of the document. I.XV supplies a systematic *Auseinandersetzung* between the two Houses, in which the contradictory opinions are sustained by balanced arguments. The arguments are comprised by parables, C, D, then verses of Scripture, E, F. The secondary expansion is of no interest in this context. The main point is, it is possible to conduct a dispute through the provision of contradictory arguments that consist of a trade-off of relevant verses of Scripture, on the one side, and of parables, on the other. The utilization of a parable as an argument for a theological position corresponds to the utilization of a precedent (ma'aseh) in behalf of a Halakhic one.

## II:V.

**1.**    A.    R. Abbahu and R. Hiyya the Elder:
        B.    R. Abbahu said, "At the beginning of the act of creating the world, the Holy One, blessed be he, foresaw the deeds of the righteous and of the wicked.
        C.    "'And the earth was unformed' refers to the deeds of the wicked.
        D.    "'And God said, "Let there be light"' refers to the deeds of the righteous.
        E.    "But I do not know which of the two God prefers, the deeds of this sort or the deeds of that.
        F.    "On the basis of what is written, namely, 'And God looked upon the light, seeing that it was good,' one has to conclude that God prefers the deeds of the righteous to the deeds of the wicked."
**2.**    A.    Said R. Hiyya the Elder, "At the beginning of the creation of the world the Holy One, blessed be he, foresaw that the Temple would be built, destroyed, and rebuilt.
        B.    "'In the beginning God created' [refers to the Temple] when it was built, in line with the following verse: 'That I may plant the heavens and lay the foundations of the earth and say to Zion, You are my people' (Is. 51:16).
        C.    "'And the earth was unformed' — lo, this refers to the destruction, in line with this verse: 'I saw the earth, and lo, it was unformed' (Jer. 4:23).
        D.    "'And God said, "Let there be light"' — lo, it was built and well constructed in the age to come.
        E.    "That is in line with this verse: 'Arise, shine, for your light has come, and the glory of the Lord is risen upon you' (Is. 60:1)."

The cited positions, 1.B vs. 2.A, are of interest because they do not conflict, but also do not cohere. We cannot regard the two propositions as mutually exclusive but may see them as complementary. The proof-texts are expounded, not just cited. But how this would serve to illustrate a type of argumentation, as distinct from a mode of exposition, I cannot say.

## XII:IV.
1.   A.   R. Judah and R. Nehemiah:
      B.   R. Judah says, "'And the heaven and earth were finished...' (Gen. 2:2) in their proper time, 'and all their host,' in their own time [each reaching completion separately]."
      C.   Said to him R. Nehemiah, "And lo, it is written, 'These are the generations of heaven and earth, when they were created' (Gen. 2:4). The meaning is, 'Just as they were when they were first created, on the day on which they were created, they brought forth all that was going to come forth from them [their generations]. [So creation took place simultaneously for all things that were created.]"
      D.   Said to him R. Judah, "And lo, it is written, 'And there was evening, and there was morning, 'one day,' 'a second day,' 'a third day,' a fourth day,' 'a fifth day,' a sixth day.' [That would surely indicate that creation was progressive and did not take place all at one moment]."
      E.   Said to him R. Nehemiah, "It was like the case of the harvesting of figs. Each one made its appearance when it was ready. [But all of them had been created, *in nuce* , at once.]"
      F.   R. Berekhiah: "In respect to this view of R. Nehemiah there is the following verse: 'And the earth produced...' (Gen. 1:12), meaning, [it produced] something that was ready at hand [and had only to be brought forth]."

The two positions are not articulated formally. Judah takes the view that the heaven and the earth and their host were individually completed in sequence, and Nehemiah, objecting to that position, cites a verse yielding a contrary result. The dispute then unfolds through an exchange of proof-texts, and the introduction of a metaphor, E.

## XIV:V.
1.   A.   "And the Lord God formed" (Gen. 2:7): The word is written with two Y's, representing two acts of creation,
      B.   creation in this world and creation in the world to come.
2.   A.   The House of Shammai and the House of Hillel:
      B.   The House of Shammai say, "The act of creation of man in this world is not the same as the act of creation of man in the world to come. In this world the act of creation begins with the skin and the flesh and is completed with the sinews and bones. But in the world to come the act of creation begins with the sinews and bones and is completed with the skin and flesh. For so does Scripture say with reference to the dead to whom Ezekiel preached: 'And I beheld and lo, there were sinews upon them and flesh came up and skin covered them above [in that order]' (Ez. 37:8)."
            C.   Said R. Jonathan, "One may not derive the facts from the case of the dead of whom Ezekiel spoke. For to what may the dead to whom

*Thirteen. Genesis Rabbah* 221

          Ezekiel spoke be compared? To one who entered the bath house [who leaves his clothes in a pile]. What he takes off first he puts on last."
- D. The House of Hillel say, "Just as the act of creation of man is done in this world, so is the act of creation of man done in the world to come. In this world the act begins with the skin and the flesh and is completed with the sinews and bones. So too in the age to come the act begins with the skin and the flesh and ends with the sinews and the bones. For so does Job say, 'Will you [in the age to come] not pour me out as milk and curdle me like cheese? You will clothe me with skin and flesh and knit me together with bones and sinews' (Job 10:10-11).
- E. "'You poured me out and curdled me' is not what is says, but rather, 'you *will* pour me out and *will* curdle me.' 'You have clothed me with skin and flesh' is not what it says, but rather, 'You *will* cloth me. 'And with bones and sinews you have knit me together' is not what it says but rather, 'You *will* knit me together.'
- F. "The matter may be compared to a bowl that is filled with milk. Until one puts rennet into the milk, the milk is flowing. Once one puts rennet into the milk, the milk congeals and becomes firm. That is in line with what Job said, 'Will you not pour me out as milk...skin and flesh...you have granted me life and favor' (Job 10:12)."

The theme introduced by the base verse, No. 1, accounts for the inclusion of No. 2, a well-articulated, balanced dispute. The two positions are balanced in their exposition, B, D, with the same type of argumentation, involving the provision of a reason ("for so does Scripture say") accorded to both parties. The Hillelite exposition undergoes secondary development, complete with a parable, which the Shammaite view is not accorded. But the character of the argumentation is consistent: a reason deriving from Scripture or from a parable.

## LXXIII:V.
2.
- A. "God has taken away my reproach:" in the incident of the concubine of Gibeah.
- B. "Cursed is he who gives a wife to Benjamin" (Judges 21:18).
- C. 'God has taken away my reproach:"
- D. In the days of Jeroboam: "Neither did Jeroboam recover strength again in the days of Abijah, and the Lord smote him and he died" (2 Chr. 13:20).
- E. Said R. Samuel bar Nahman, "Do you think that Jeroboam was smitten? But in fact Abijah was smitten."
- F. Why was Abijah smitten?
- G. Said R. Abba b. Kahana, "Because he removed the identifying marks of the faces of the Israelites, as it is written, 'The show of their countenance does witness for them' (Is. 3:9)."
- H. Said R. Assi, "Because he set up guards over them for three days until the features of their faces were disfigured.
  - I. "For so we have learned in the Mishnah: **People give testimony to the identity of a corpse only through the**

features of the face together with the nose, and that is the case even if there are other marks of identification on the body and the garments; and one may give testimony only within three days of death [beyond which point the face is disfigured] [M. Yeb. 16:3].

J. "And it says, 'The widows are increased to me above the sands of the seas' (Jer. 15:8)."

K. R. Yohanan said, "It was because he treated with contempt Ahijah the Shilonite: 'And there were gathered to him vain men, base fellows' (2 Chr. 13:7). So he treated Ahijah as worthless."

L. R. Simeon b. Laqish said, "It was because he humiliated them in public: 'And you are a great multitude and there are with you the golden calves' (2 Chr. 13:7)."

M. Rabbis said, "It was because an idol came into his possession and he did not nullify it: 'And Abijah pursued after Jeroboam and took cities from him, Bethel and the towns thereof, and Jeshanah and the towns thereof' (2 Chr. 13:19), and further: 'And he set the one [golden calf] in Bethel and the other in Dan' (1 Kgs. 12:29).

N. "Now is it not an argument *a fortiori* : If, in the account of Scripture, because a king insulted a king like himself and therefore was smitten, if an ordinary person insults an ordinary person, how much the more so!"

The dispute, 2.G, H, K, L, M, involves arguments deriving from Scripture. What is important from our perspective occurs at N, an explicit invocation of an argument a fortiori. As we have seen in the earlier chapters, in Halakhic contexts the argument a fortiori invokes considerations of analogy and contrast, resting on givens of classification. Here, by contrast, the argument rests on no such foundation. But it also has no bearing on the dispute before us.

### LXXXIII:V.

1. A. Wheat, straw, and stubble had a fight.
   B. Wheat said, "It was on my account that the field was sown."
   C. Stubble said, "It was on my account that the field was sown."
   D. Wheat said, "The day will come and you will see."
   E. When the harvest time came, the householder began to take the stubble and burn it, and the straw and spread it, but the wheat he made into heaps.
   F. Everyone began to kiss the wheat. [I assume this is a reference to the messianic passage, "Kiss the son" which is also to be translated, "Kiss the wheat" (Ps. 2:12).]
   G. So too Israel and the nations of the world have a fight.
   H. These say, "It was on our account that the world was created," and those say, "It was on our account that the world was created."
   I. Israel says, "The day will come and you will see."

Thirteen. Genesis Rabbah 223

    J.    In the age to come: "You shall fan them and the wind will carry them away" (Is. 41:16).
    K.    As to Israel: "And you shall rejoice in the Lord, you shall glory in the Holy One of Israel" (Is. 41:16).

The sole point of interest for us comes with the appeal of each party to future evidence: time will tell and prove us right.

## XCII:VII.

1.    A.    "When they had gone but a short distance from the city, Joseph said to his steward, 'Up, follow after the man, and when you overtake them, say to them, 'Why have you returned evil for good? Why have you stolen my silver cup? Is it not from this that my lord drinks, and by this that he divines? You have done wrong in so doing. When he overtook them, he spoke to them these words. They said to him, 'Why does my lord speak such words as these? Far be it from your servants that they should do such a thing. Behold, the money which we found in the mouth of our sacks we brought back to you from the land of Canaan; how then should we steal silver or gold from your lord's house?'" (Gen. 44:4-8):

    B.    Said R. Ishmael, "This is one of the ten examples of the argument *a fortiori* that are stated in the Torah.

    C.    "'Behold, the money which we found in the mouth of our sacks we brought back to you from the land of Canaan.' Now the argument *a fortiori* : '...how then should we steal silver or gold from your lord's house?'

    D.    "'Behold the children of Israel have not hearkened to me.' Now the argument *a fortiori* : 'How then shall Pharaoh hear me' (Ex. 6:12).

    E.    "'Behold, while I am yet alive with you this day, you have been rebellious against the Lord.' Now the argument *a fortiori* : 'And how much more after my death' (Deut. 31:27).

    F.    "'And the Lord said to Moses, If her father had but spit in her face...' Now the argument *a fortiori* : '...surely she should hide in shame for seven days' (Num. 12:14).

    G.    "'If you have run with the footmen and they have wearied you...' Now the argument *a fortiori* : 'how can you contend with the horses' (Jer. 12:5).

    H.    "'Behold, we are afraid here in Judah...' Now the argument *a fortiori:* How much more if we go to Keilah' (1 Sam. 23:3).

    I.    "'And if in a land of peace where you are secure you are overcome...' Now the argument *a fortiori* : 'how will you do in the thickets of the Jordan' (Jer. 12:5).

    J.    "'Behold, the righteous shall be requited in the earth...' Now the argument *a fortiori* : 'How much more the wicked and the sinner' (Prov. 11:31).

    K.    "'And the king said to Esther the queen, The Jews have slain and destroyed five hundred men in Shushan the castle...' Now the argument *a fortiori* : 'What then have they done in the rest of the king's provinces' (Est. 9:12).

    L.    "'Behold, when it was whole, it was meet for no work...' Now the argument *a fortiori* : 'How much less, when the fire has devoured it and it is singed' (Ez. 15:5)."

What is important is the articulated view that one type of argumentation such as the sages routinely utilize in the Halakhic documents derive from Scripture. But in the present cases, the issues of classification, comparison and contrast, do not figure. There is no contrary position, and the argument is deemed unanswerable. That is rarely the upshot in Halakhic discourse.

## C:VII.

1. A. "When they came to the threshing floor of Atad, which is beyond the Jordan, they lamented there with a very great and sorrowful lamentation, and he made a mourning for his father seven days" (Gen. 50:10):
   B. How on the basis of Scripture do we know that mourning lasts for seven days?
   C. R. Aha derives proof from the following: "...and he made a mourning for his father seven days" (Gen. 50:10).
   D. But does proof derive from a matter pertaining to the age prior to the giving of the Torah?
   E. R. Simeon b. Laqish in the name of Bar Qappara derives proof from the following: "And you shall not go out from the door of the tent of meeting for seven days' (Lev. 8:13). Just as you are anointed with anointing oil for seven days, so you will observe for your brothers seven days [of mourning]."
   F. R. Hoshaiah derives proof from the following: "'And at the door of the tent of meeting you shall dwell day and night for seven days and keep the observance of the Lord' (Lev. 8:35). Just as the Holy One, blessed be he, kept an observance for his world for seven days, so you must observe seven days of mourning for your brothers."
   G. For R. Joshua b. Levi said, "For seven days the Holy One, blessed be he, went into mourning for his world [before he brought the flood, as it is said, 'And it grieved him in his heart' (Gen. 6:5), and further it says, 'For the king grieved for his son' (2 Sam. 19:3)]."
   H. R. Yohanan derives proof from the following: "'Let her not, I pray you, be as one dead,' but rather: 'let her be shut up seven days' (Num. 12:12, 14). Just as the days of shutting up last for a week, so the mourning lasts for seven days."
   I. One of the masters told this statement of R. Yohanan to R. Simeon b. Laqish, who did not accept it. Why did he not accept it? He said, "[Freedman:] There the rule treats the case as a matter of shutting up, while here it is treated as a matter of decided and definite illness."
   J. R. Abbahu in the name of R. Yohanan came and said, "'Let her not, I pray you, be as one dead,' (Num. 12:12, 14). Just as the days of mourning for the deceased last for a week, so the period of probationary waiting lasts for seven days."
   K. Said R. Jeremiah and R. Hiyya bar Abba in the name of R. Simeon b. Laqish, "'And I will turn your feasts into mourning' (Amos 8:10).
   L. "Just as the days of the Festival [of Tabernacles] are seven, so the period of mourning should be seven days."

*Thirteen. Genesis Rabbah* 225

Q. [Reverting to the question with which we began:] R. Berekhiah and R. Jonah in the name of R. Simeon b. Laqish in the name of R. Judah the Patriarch: "It is written, 'So the days of weeping in the mourning for Moses were ended' (Deut. 34:8).

R. "'Days' stands for two, 'weeping' stands for seven, and 'mourning' stands for thirty."

S. There are those who reverse matters: "Days" stands for seven, "weeping" stands for two, and "mourning" stands for thirty.

T. Now we understand the references to seven and to thirty days [respectively, since these are known periods involved in the mourning procedure]. But what is the point of a reference to two days?

U. It deals with the case of a poor person, who cannot afford to take off time from work. If such a person is very poor, he does not do any work on the first and second days of the bereavement, on the third he works in private. But a curse be on the heads of his neighbors, who made it necessary [by their neglect] for him to conduct himself in that way.

V. Bar Qappara said, "Even on the third day he should not do anything at all, because that is the time when the grief is at its strongest."

W. Bar Qappara taught, "The entire depth of grief comes only on the third day."

X. Up to the third day the soul keeps returning to the body, thinking that it will go back in. When it sees that the features of the face have crumbled, it goes its way and leaves the body. That is in line with this verse: "But his flesh grieves for him, and his soul mourns over him" (Job 14:22).

Y. In the age to come the mouth and the belly will have a quarrel with one another. The mouth will say to the belly, "Whatever I stole and grabbed I gave you." After three days the body bursts and says to the mouth, "Here is what is everything you stole and grabbed."

Z. "And the pitcher is broken at the fountain" (Qoh. 12:6).

The dispute concerns the proof for a shared proposition, a fact of law. Each principal player then explains the probative value of his chosen proof-text, treating it as the foundation for a comparison between the subject of his proof-text and Israel in general, e.g., if God does it this way, so must you. So the weight of argumentation rests on the validity of the proposed metaphor or parable (as the case may be). Then a secondary argument, I, explains grounds for rejecting the proposed proof, namely, distinguishing between one case and the other, or, more simply, rejecting the simile or parable.

### III. TYPES OF ARGUMENTATION IN GENESIS RABBAH

What is noteworthy is the recognition that one important type of argumentation, the argument *a fortiori,* finds ample instantiation in Scripture. It is the only type of argumentation that is identified articulately and given its scriptural foundation.

Through the exchange of proof-texts Genesis Rabbah presents arguments in behalf of conflicting propositions. These are only rarely expounded in any secondary interchange; it is taken for granted that each party has sufficient reason to sustain his position. But occasionally, the reasoning behind the argument will be made explicit. Arguments may take the form of an exchange of parables, each party's parable sustaining his basic position. I cannot overstress that parables, in the context of Aggadic argumentation, form the counterpart, for Halakhic argumentation, of analogical arguments: that is like this, therefore that follows the rule or yields the principle characteristic of this. Where we find disputes joined to arguments, they are rarely primary to the documentary program.

The entire corpus of data hardly compares with the extensive, complex, and dense repertoire of argumentation characteristic of the Halakhic documents. What makes Genesis Rabbah Aggadic — its systematic exposition, in terms of generalizations of Scripture's narratives of particular persons and unique events — also places the document into that larger classification of Rabbinic writing, the effort at critical generalization, that forms of the Halakhah and the Aggadah a single, coherent intellectual structure. The topics differ, the genres of writing are readily differentiated from one another. But a single fundamental mode of thought — the effort to transform cases into rules, rules into principles, bodies of data into systematic statements — and, consequently, one cogent body of argumentation come to realization throughout.

# 14

# Leviticus Rabbah

i. Dialectical Arguments

The document presents nothing comparable to a dialectical argument. More to the point, Leviticus Rabbah contains no instances of systematic, sustained argumentation that is primary to the document. The fine cases that we do identify are primary to the Talmud (the Yerushalmi in the case at hand) and intruded here, as formal traits indicate in all instances.

ii. Non-Dialectical Arguments

An argument requires the premise that both parties to conflict on a common proposition cannot be right. Then an exchange of evidence and reason will take place to make the case for each party to the dispute, and that exchange constitutes the argument; the rules governing the exchange define the protocol of argumentation. They dictate what kind of considerations prevail. Now, in Leviticus Rabbah and comparable compilations of Midrash-exegeses and propositions, we find tolerance for diverse readings of a single verse of Scripture. These are composites made up of compositions concerning the exposition of a given verse, the composites beyond joined by the signal, "another matter." In no case does an "another-matter"-composite encompass an argument not only in behalf of one reading but also in opposition to an alternative reading of the verse held in common. The "another-matter" constructions form a kind of sustained exchange of views, but there is no hint that at issue is who is right and who is wrong, that is, an argument in behalf of an exclusive proposition. Each "another-matter" composite represents a possibility among possibilities. It is not necessary to reproduce more than a single composite to make that point clear.

## VI:I
1. A. "If any one sins, in that he hears a public adjuration to testify, (and, though he is a witness, whether he has seen or come to know the matter, yet does not speak, he shall bear his iniquity)" (Lev. 5:1).
   B. "Be not a witness (against your neighbor) without cause" (Prov. 24:28).
   C. This refers to Israel: "You are my witnesses, says the Lord, and I am God" (Is. 43:12).
   D. "... against your neighbor..." (Prov. 24:28).
   E. This refers to the Holy One, blessed be he: "Your friend and your father's friend do not forsake" (Prov. 27:10).
   F. "(Be not a witness against your neighbor without cause,) and do not deceive with your lips" (Prov. 24:28).
   G. After you inveigled me at Sinai and said to me, "Whatever the Lord has spoken, we shall do and we shall hear" (Ex. 24:7), forty days later you said to the calf, "This is your God, O Israel" (Ex. 32:4).

## VI.IV
1. A. R. Yosé b. R. Hanina interpreted the passages at hand to speak of the accused wife:
   B. "'If any one sins' (Lev. 5:1) — this is a woman who had sinned against her husband. This one supports and feeds her, and she goes and misbehaves with a perfect stranger.
   C. "'In that he hears a public adjuration to testify' (Lev. 5:1). 'Then let the priest make the woman take the oath of adjuration' (Num. 5:21).
   D. "'Though he is a witness' (Lev. 5:1). 'And there is no witness' (Num. 5:13).
   E. "'Whether he has seen' (Lev. 5:1). 'And she is undetected though she has defiled herself' (Num. 5:13).
   F. "'... or known' (Lev. 5:1). 'And it is hidden from the eyes of her husband' (Num. 5:13).
   G. "'And it is hidden from the eyes of her husband' (Num. 5:13) — and not from the eyes of her levirate husband (who cannot impose the rite upon her).
   H. "'Yet does not speak, he shall bear his iniquity' (Lev. 5:1). If she does not confess to the priest: 'And her belly will swell and her thigh will fall away'" (Num. 5:27).

## VI:V
1. A. R. Phineas interpreted the verses (Lev. 5:1) to speak of Israel at Mount Sinai:
   B. "'If any soul sins' (Lev. 5:1). 'And I saw, and lo, you had sinned against the Lord your God' (Deut. 9:16).
   C. "'And heard the sound of a public adjuration' (Deut. 5:1). 'His sound did we hear from the midst of the fire'" (Deut. 5:21).
2. A. Said R. Yohanan, "They made a mutual agreement between them,
   B. "that (God) would not reject them, and that they would not reject him."

I give the base-exposition of the base-verse and the intersecting verse, VI:I, and then the exchange of views of Yosé b. R. Hanina and Phineas on the matter. As we see, each invokes his own reference-point for the verse, "If anyone sins....:"

*Fourteen. Leviticus Rabbah* 229

bearing witness and failing to give testimony. Yosé invokes the accused wife, Phineas, Israel at Sinai. Now the two expositions stand quite independent of one another, but, juxtaposed, invite us to suppose a dispute is at hand. But the "another-matter"-composites not only do not sustain disputes, but they mean to show the opposite. The intent is to demonstrate through the diverse readings a common point. In the present case the demonstration is self-evident: Israel at Sinai was like the wife accused of adultery, for in the background, by reason of VI.IV, is the golden calf. Then VI:V.1 is truncated, not corresponding in execution, point by point, to the details of VI:IV. For our purpose the point is clear: an "another-matter"-composite does not present us with a glimpse at modes of argumentation in play in the Rabbinic mind.

## XI:V

1. A. "With the merciful you show yourself merciful, with the innocent you show yourself innocent, with the pure you show yourself pure, with the crooked you show yourself perverse. (For you deliver a humble people, but the haughty eyes you bring down)" (Ps. 18:26-27).
   B. R. Judah and R. Nehemiah:
   C. R. Judah interpreted the verse to speak of Abraham, our father.
   D. "When Abraham came in a spirit of mercy (to travelers), the Holy One, blessed be he, dealt with him in a merciful way; when he acted in an innocent way, the Holy One, blessed be he, dealt with him in an innocent way; and when he dealt with him in a crooked way, the Holy One, blessed be he, dealt with him in a crooked way, and when he sought a frank statement of his affairs, the Holy One, blessed be he, made a frank statement about his affairs.
   E. "When did he come in a spirit of mercy?
   F. "When he said, 'My Lord, do not go away, I pray you, from your servant, (and he stood by them under the tree while they ate)' (Gen. 18:3).
      G. "What is written there? 'And Abraham was still standing before the Lord'" (Gen. 18:22).
      H. Said R. Simon, "It is an improvement made by scribes. In fact, it was the Presence of God that was waiting for him."
   I. (Judah continues:) "When did he come in a blameless spirit?
   J. "When he said to him, 'Perhaps there will lack five of the fifty righteous men. (Will you destroy the entire city for the lack of the five?)' (Gen. 18:28).
   K. "What is written there?
   L. "'I shall not destroy the city if I find there forty-five righteous men' (Gen. 18:28).
   M. "When did he deal with him in a crooked way?
   N. "When he said to him. 'And I go childless' (Gen. 15:2) (without directly saying what he wanted).
   O. "What is written there?
   P. "(In an equally roundabout way, God replied): 'This man will not inherit your estate' (Gen. 15:4).
   Q. "When did he seek a frank statement of his affairs?

R. "When he said to him, 'How shall I know that I shall inherit it?' (Gen. 15:8).
S. "What is written there? 'You should know for certain that your seed will be a stranger' (Gen. 15:13)."
T. R. Nehemiah interpreted the passage to speak of Moses.
U. "When he came in a spirit of mercy the Holy One, blessed be he, dealt with him in a merciful way; when he acted in an innocent way, the Holy One, blessed be he, dealt with him in an innocent way; when he dealt with him in a crooked way, the Holy One, blessed be he, dealt with him in a crooked way, and when he sought a frank statement of his affairs, the Holy One, blessed be he, made a frank statement about his affairs.
V. "When did he come in a spirit of mercy?
W. "When he said to him, 'Why is the bush not burned up?' (Ex. 3:3).
X. "He said to him (In Aramaic:) 'Because my glory is present in it.'
Y. "When did he act in an innocent way?
Z. "When he said to him, 'Show me, I pray you, your glory' (Ex. 33:18).
AA. "What is written there? 'I shall cause all my goodness to pass before you' (Ex. 33:19).
BB. "When did he deal in with him in a crooked way? When he said to him, 'And when they say to me, what is his name? what should I answer them?' (Ex. 3:13).
CC. "What did he say to him? 'This is my name' for the time being, 'I am what I am' (Ex. 3:14).
DD. "And when did he seek a frank statement of his affairs? When he said to him, 'And now, go, and I shall send you to Pharaoh, so that you may bring forth my people, the children of Israel, out of Egypt' (Ex. 3:10).
EE. "He said to him, 'Send, I pray you, whomever you will send'" (Ex. 4:13).

Does the cited verse refer to Abraham or to Moses? Each party attends to the same details as are worked out by the other: a case of mercy, innocence ("blameless spirit"), dealing in a crooked way (not saying just what he had in mind), and, finally, making a frank statement. In a true argument, however, at the point at which the exposition of the two positions is complete, one party should take up evidence adduced by the other and controvert it, or an argument and counter it. But that is not what takes place in compositions such as the one before us, which therefore do not qualify as evidences for types of argumentation of Rabbinic Judaism.

We shall now see an authentic exercise of argumentation, with objections and answers, thrusts and parries, evidence and pertinent argument, the whole in a sustained and continuous exposition. What is self-evident is, the pericope is primary to the Yerushalmi, where it occurs, and violates the formal structure otherwise paramount in Leviticus Rabbah: parachuted down from another document altogether.

## IX:VI

1. A. (Y. Megillah 1:11.IV:) R. Eleazar and R. Yosé b. Haninah:
   B. R. Eleazar said, "Peace offerings did the children of Noah offer up."
   C. R. Yosé b. Haninah said, "Burnt offerings did the children of Noah offer up."

## Fourteen. Leviticus Rabbah

D. R. Eleazar objected to R. Yosé b. Haninah, "(And has it not been written,) 'And Abel brought of the firstlings of his flock and of their fat portions. (And the Lord had regard for Abel and his offering)' (Gen. 4:4)? (This indicates that the animals were offered as peace offerings, of) which the fat portions are offered, (not the whole beast)."

E. How does R. Yosé b. Haninah (interpret) this (verse)? He offered up their fat parts (along with the whole beast).

F. R. Eleazar objected to R. Yosé b. Haninah, "(And lo, it is written,) 'And he sent young men of the people of Israel, (who offered burnt offerings and sacrificed peace offerings of oxen to the Lord)' (Ex. 24:5). (This verse explicitly refers to peace offerings.)"

G. How does R. Yosé b. Haninah interpret this verse? He reads it in accord with the view of him who said that they were whole in their body (reading the word for peace offerings as "whole"), meaning that they were not flayed or chopped up.

H. R. Eleazar objected to R. Yosé b. Haninah, "(And lo, it is written), 'And Jethro, Moses' father-in-law, offered a burnt offering and sacrifices to God, (and Aaron came with all the elders of Israel to eat bread with Moses' father-in-law before God)' (Ex. 18:12). (This indicates that there were peace offerings as well as burnt offerings.)"

I. How does R. Yosé b. Haninah deal with this? He concurs with him who says that it was only after the giving of the Torah that Jethro converted.

J. R. Huna said, "Judah b. Rabbi and R. Yannai differed. One said, 'It was after the giving of the Torah that Jethro converted.' The other said, 'It was before the giving of the Torah that Jethro converted.'"

K. He who maintains that it was prior to the giving of the Torah that Jethro converted concurs with him who says that the children of Noah offered peace offerings.

L. He who says that it was after the giving of the Torah that Jethro converted concurs with him who said that the children of Noah offered burnt offerings.

    M. The following supports the position of R. Yosé b. Haninah: "Awake, O north wind, and come, O south wind! (Blow upon my garden, let its fragrance be wafted abroad. Let my beloved come to his garden, and eat its choicest fruits)" (Song 4:16).

    N. "Awake, O north wind" refers to the burnt offering, which is slaughtered at the north side of the altar.

    O. And why does Scripture call it (the burnt offering) uri (awake)? It means that this is something that was sleeping (prior to the coming of Israel) and was then awakened (at the building of the Israelite cult).

    P. "And come, O south wind" refers to peace offerings, which are slaughtered at the south side of the altar. Why call it (the peace offering)? It speaks of something "come south wind"? (This then refutes Yosé's view after all.)

    Q. Also this verse of Scripture supports the view of R. Yosé b. Haninah: "This is the law of the burnt offering, this is (that same) burnt offering" (Lev. 6:9) that the children of Noah had been offering. Now when (Scripture) came to peace offerings, it said, 'And this is the law of the sacrifice of peace offerings (which they will offer to the Lord)'" (Lev. 7:11).

232                           *Analysis and Argumentation in Rabbinic Judaism*

R. "Which they offered" is not written here, but rather, "which they will offer." The meaning then is, "from now on." (That supports Yosé's view that in olden times peace offerings were not offered.)

S. How does R. Eleazar deal with the verse that supports the position of R. Yosé b. R. Haninah, that is, "Awake, O north wind, (and come, O south wind)"?

T. ("Awake, O north wind"): When the exiles who are located in the north will awake, they will come and make camp in the south.

U. "Lo, I shall bring them from the north country" (Jer. 31:8).

V. When Gog, who is located in the north, will awake, he will come and fall in the south.

W. That accords with the following verse of Scripture: "I will turn you about and lead you on and will bring you up from the uttermost parts of the north" (Ez. 39:2).

X. When the anointed king (or: king messiah), who is now located in the north, will awake, he will come and rebuild the house of the sanctuary, which is located in the south.

Y. That accords with the following verse of Scripture: "I have roused up one from the north and he has come" (Is. 41:25).

Z. R. Yosé in the name of R. Benjamin b. R. Levi: "Now in this world, when the north wind blows, the south wind does not blow, and when the south wind blows, the north wind does not blow. But in the world to come, the Holy One, blessed be he, will say, 'I shall bring an <u>argestes</u> wind into the world, which blows from two directions at once.'

AA. "That is in line with the following verse of Scripture: 'I will say to the north, "Give up," and to the south, "Keep not back"'" (Is. 43:6)

BB. R. Yohanan said, "The Torah teaches you proper conduct. For a bridegroom does not enter into the marriage canopy until the bride gives him permission to come in. That is in line with the following verse of Scripture: 'Let my beloved come into my garden and enjoy its precious fruits' (Song 4:16), and afterward, 'I have come into my garden, my sister, my bride'" (Song 4:17).

The realization of one kind of argumentation — exchange of opinion, then proof-texts and their refutation, each party given an opportunity not only to refute the proofs of the other but also to present his own contrary evidence. The exact balance maintained throughout concludes at L. Then come supports for one position, not balanced by those for the other. The formal balance gives way. From our perspective what matters is the egregious standing of the composite: it breaks the formal rules of the document that contains it.

## XXXII:I

1. A. "On every side the wicked walk (as the reviled is exalted among the sons of men" (Ps. 12:8).

   B. R. Judah and R. Nehemiah.

## Fourteen. Leviticus Rabbah

C. R. Judah said, "(The meaning of the cited verse is) 'round about the wicked, the righteous walk.' How so? When the righteous go forth from the Garden of Eden and see that the wicked are judged in Gehenna, their souls rejoice.

D. "That is in line with the following verse of Scripture: 'They shall go forth and look upon the carcasses of the men (who have rebelled against me)' (Is. 66:24).

E. "At that moment they praise and give glory to the Holy One, blessed be he, for the suffering that he brought on them in this world (so that they enjoy the world to come).

F. "That is in line with the following verse of Scripture: 'In that day you will say, "I shall give thanks to you, O Lord, for though you were angry with me (in this world), (your anger is turned and you comfort me)"' (Is. 12:1).

G. "'Your anger is turned' against the nations of the world.

H. "'And you comfort me' through their (suffering).

I. "When? 'When the reviled (Israel) is exalted (KRWM)' (Ps. 12:8).

J. "When the Holy One, blessed be he, exalts the vineyard (KRM) that is despised in his world. And the vineyard of the Holy One, blessed be he, can only be Israel, as it is said, 'For the vineyard of the Lord of hosts is the house of Israel'" (Is. 5:7).

K. Said to him R. Nehemiah, "My noble lord, how long are you going to twist verses of Scripture against us?

L. "But the meaning of the cited verse is that it is around the righteous that the wicked walk, as it is written, 'On every side the wicked walk' (Ps. 12:8).

M. "How so? When the wicked come up out of Gehenna and see how the righteous dwell happily in the Garden of Eden, their soul shrivels inside them.

N. "That is in line with the following verse of Scripture: 'The wicked shall see and be vexed' (Ps. 112:10).

O. "When? 'When the reviled is exalted' (Ps. 12:8). When the Holy One, blessed be he, exalts in his world those religious duties that are despised (by the gentiles).

P. "'Why are you going out to be stoned (to death)?' 'Because I circumcised my son.'

Q. "'Why are you going forth to be burned (to death)?' 'Because I kept the Sabbath day.'

R. "'Why are you going forth to be put to death?' 'Because I ate unleavened bread (on Passover).'

S. "'Why are you going to be flogged with the strap?' 'Because I built a tabernacle (for the Festival), because I took up the palm branch (on the Festival),' 'because I put on phylacteries,' 'because I inserted blue thread (into the fringes of my garment),' 'because I kept the will of my father who is in heaven.'

T. "That is in line with the following verse of Scripture: 'And he said to me, "What are these wounds (that are on your hands?)" Then he shall answer, "Those with which I was wounded in the house of those who caused me to be loved"' (Zech. 13:6).

U. "'These wounds have caused me to be loved by our father who is in heaven.' When? 'When the reviled is exalted.'"

Judah reads the cited verse in one way, Nehemiah in the opposite way; Judah explains the sense of his reading, C, Nehemiah gives his reading and explains it in perfect balance at L-M. I cannot point to the passage at which Judah responds to Nehemiah's reading, or Nehemiah's to Judah's, in the manner in which the parties to the dispute on the character of the sacrifices of Noah join issue head-on. The secondary exposition in both cases simply amplifies matters; there is no Auseinandersetzung beyond the explicit language of K; without K, the two positions are closely balanced, point by point. P-U are tacked on and add nothing to the dispute. We cannot regard the composite as an exemplification of rules of argumentation, other than the obvious one that in a valid dispute, each party is given its opportunity to state its position and evidence.

## XXXVI:I

1.   A.   "Of old you laid out the foundation of the earth, and the heavens are the work of your hands" (Ps. 102:25).

### TOPICAL COMPOSITE ON PRECEDENCE

B.   The House of Shammai and the House of Hillel:
C.   The House of Shammai say, "The heaven was created first, and then the earth."
D.   The House of Hillel say, "The earth was created first, then the heaven."
E.   This party brings a proof text for its opinion, and that party brings a proof text for its view.
F.   In the view of the House of Shammai, who maintain that the heaven was created first and then the earth, we may make a comparison. To what is the matter comparable?
G.   To the case of a king who made a throne. Only after he made the throne did he make its footstool. Thus: "So says the Lord, 'The heaven is my throne, and the earth the dust at my feet'" (Is. 66:1).
H.   In the view of the House of Hillel, who maintain that the earth was created first and then the heaven, we may make a comparison. (To what is the matter comparable?)
I.   To the case of a king who built himself a palace. Only after he builds the lower floors does he build the upper floors.
J.   So it is written, "My hand laid the foundation of the earth, and my right hand (then) spread out the heaven" (Is. 48:13).
    K.   Said R. Haninah, "Also the following verse of Scripture supports the position of the House of Hillel: 'Of old you laid out the foundations of the earth,' and afterward: 'and the heavens are the work of your hands'" (Ps. 102:25).
    L.   Said R. Judah, "From the very passage of Scripture which is adduced in support of the position of the House of Shammai, the House of Hillel find proof to dismiss that same position.
    M.   "In the view of the House of Shammai, who maintain that the heaven was created first and then the earth, (the following proof text confirms

*Fourteen. Leviticus Rabbah* 235

their position:) 'In the beginning God created the heaven and the earth' (Gen. 1:1).

N. "In the view of the House of Hillel, who say that the earth was created first, then the heaven: 'And the earth was unformed and void' (Gen. 1:2), indicating that the earth already was in being."

The argument consists of (1) a proof text and (2) a parable, and the parables do meet head-on: the king who made a throne versus the king who built a palace, each parable then yielding the desired implications for the respective parties. Here, then, we find something akin to a sustained, systematic argument, formulated within the data of Midrash-Aggadah to be sure: exegesis of Scripture, re-presentation of a case or rule through a narrative bearing self-evident meaning (parable). The composition (including the tack-on glosses, K-N) is intruded into its context in Leviticus Rabbah, as the indentation here and as the outline in *Components of the Rabbinic Tradition ad loc.* Indicate.

### III. TYPES OF ARGUMENTATION IN LEVITICUS RABBAH

In Leviticus Rabbah I cannot point to a single case primary to Leviticus Rabbah in which a dispute is amplified by an exercise of argumentation in behalf of one position and against the contrary. The "another-matter"-composites embody the basic attitude of the document, which is to accommodate diverse readings of the same matter, each yielding its own proposition, all propositions deemed coherent with one another. The exchange of Judah and Nehemiah, XI:V, simply juxtaposes two matched positions on the meaning of the same verses; balancing opinions yields no argument as to which party prevails, on the contrary, the composition could as well bear the heading, "another matter" before Nehemiah's statement. What differentiates "another-matter"-composites from authentic arguments is the secondary effort to refute the proof adduced by one party against the other. Not merely juxtaposing contradictory evidence and propositions but seeing to the engagement of each side with the position of the other, the articulate refutation by one party of the evidence presented by the other — these are the marks of authentic argumentation. By that criterion, Leviticus Rabbah in the compositions and composites that are primary to the document and that comply with its formal requirements contains nothing that pertains.

# 15

# Sifré to Numbers

Sifré to Numbers, like its companions, Sifra (Leviticus) and Sifré to Deuteronomy, takes up both Halakhic and Aggadic problems in its exegetical work on its base-document. We should not find surprising, therefore, that the document encompasses argumentation suitable for Halakhic, not only Aggadic, problems. To be sure, in Sifré to Numbers I find no exercises in moving arguments. The arguments that are traced are protracted and systematic, but that is not the same thing. But the document unites Halakhic and Aggadic materials within its program and — by its very nature and calling — well demonstrates the unity of Rabbinic modes of thought in this regard, which is what we set out to investigate.

### I. DIALECTICAL ARGUMENTS

The sustained and beautifully articulated argument concerning the priority of scriptural definitions of governing analogies over those the definitions provided by indicative traits of things, which we shall examine at some length in a moment, presents a protracted discussion. But the extensive articulation of matters does not qualify as a dialectical argument, only as a balanced and fully-realized one.

### II. NON-DIALECTICAL ARGUMENTS

One type of argument captures our attention, the polemic worked out by showing that intrinsic traits of things do not, in fact, suffice to establish analogies for hierarchical classification. Sifré to Numbers, like its companions, Sifra and (to a lesser extent) Sifré to Deuteronomy, contains a variety of well-articulated arguments, all of them explicit as to the logic that governs. Certainly the most characteristic is the demonstration that logic — the logic of hierarchical classification — on its own cannot suffice to yield the Halakhah, but that Scripture is required to make matters explicit. To advance that fundamental polemic, a very particular kind of argument is required, one that differentiates categories of data that are assumed to be uniform. Hierarchical classification depends upon the premise that categories, or classifications, of data are uniformly indicated, derive from common indicative characteristics. Then to show that analogical-contrastive reasoning does not serve, the holder of the contrary view must call into question the definitive power of indicative characteristics. He must find distinctions where the protagonist of the method sees uniformity. This may be done, for example, by showing that species of a common genus do not conform to the same rule and so are to be differentiated from one another — a very routine challenge to the method of deriving the law for an unknown case by appeal to a known case deemed to be similar.

I have placed these polemics and the reason governing them into perspective in *Uniting the Dual Torah: Sifra and the Problem of the Mishnah.* Cambridge and New York, 1989: Cambridge University Press. The Mishnah derives its rules through a process of classification of data by appeal to its indicative traits, then the hierarchization of the consequent classifications. Sifra, Sifré to Numbers, and Sifré to Deuteronomy persistently criticize those results and insist upon the indeterminacy of indicative traits in a process of classification and, therefore, demonstrate the priority of Scripture in the classification of data. When it comes to the classification, comparison and contrast, of data, only Scripture produces reliable results.

One typical way of introducing the critique of logic in behalf of Scripture is to propose that, without Scripture's articulation of a rule, we could on the basis of logic have discovered the same rule. That is ordinarily through an argument a fortiori, as I shall point out when we have examined our first case.

## I:IV
1. A. "[The Lord said to Moses, 'Command the people of Israel that] they put out of the camp [every leper and every one having a discharge, and every one that is unclean through contact with the dead']" (Num. 5:1-2).
   B. Is it from the [innermost] camp, of the Presence of God, or should I infer that it is only from the camp of the Levites?
   C. Scripture states, "...they put out them of the camp." [The sense is that they are to be put outside of the camp of the Presence.]
   D. Now even if Scripture had not made the matter explicit, I could have proposed the same proposition on the basis of reasoning [that they should be put outside of the camp of the Presence]:
   E. If unclean people are driven out of the camp that contains the ark, which is of lesser sanctity, all the more so should they be driven out of the camp of the Presence of God, which is of greater sanctuary.
   F. But if you had proposed reasoning on that basis, you would have found yourself in the position of imposing a penalty merely on the basis of reason [and not on the basis of an explicit statement of Scripture, and one does not impose a penalty merely on the basis of reason].
   G. Then is why it is stated: "...they put out of the camp."

*Fifteen. Sifré to Numbers* 239

    H.    Making that matter explicit in Scripture serves to teach you that penalties are not to be imposed merely on the basis of logic [but require explicit specification in Scripture]. [That is, Scripture made a point that reason could have reached, but Scripture made the matter explicit so as to articulate a penalty applicable for violating the rule.]
      I.    [Rejecting that principle,] Rabbi says, "It is not necessary for Scripture to make the matter explicit, since it is a matter of an argument *a fortiori*:
      J.    "If the unclean people are driven out of the camp that contains the ark, which is of lesser sanctity, all the more so should they be driven out of the camp of the Presence of God, which is of greater sanctity.
      K.    "Then is why it is stated: '...they put out of the camp every leper and every one having a discharge, and every one that is unclean through contact with the dead'?
      L.    "[By specifying that all three are put out of the camp,] Scripture thereby served to assign to them levels or gradations [of uncleanness, with diverse rules affecting those levels, as will now be spelled out. Since we know that that rule applies to the ostracism of the leper, the specification that the others also are to be put out of the camp indicates that a singular rule applies to each of the category. If one rule applied in common, then the specification with respect to the leper alone would have sufficed to indicate the rule for all others.]"

The nub of the argument is at D, even if Scripture had not made the matter explicit, logic yields the same result. It is based on an argument a fortiori, If the lesser class is subject to the rule, the greater class should also be. That argument, on its own, stands, but produces an anomaly. One may not impose a penalty merely by a process of reasoning; Scripture must make the matter explicit. The fundamental type of argumentation, therefore, the argument a fortiori, is allowed to stand. We shall presently examine how that type of argument is subjected to criticism.

### VIII:IV
1.    A.    "...a tenth of an ephah of barley meal...:"
      B.    Why is this matter made explicit?
      C.    Because one might have argued to the contrary:
      D.    Since the meal-offering brought by a sinner [accompanying a sin-offering] has to be brought on account of a sin, and this one too is brought on account of sin, if I draw an analogy to the meal-offering of a sinner, which is brought only as fine flour, so this one also should bring only meal of fine flour.
      E.    Accordingly, Scripture makes explicit the contrary fact, that this meal-offering derives from barley-meal [and not fine flour].

### VIII:V
1.    A.    "...barley....:"
      B.    Why is this matter made explicit?
      C.    Because one might have argued to the contrary:
      D.    Since the meal-offering brought by a sinner [accompanying a sin-offering] comes on account of a sin, and this one is brought on account of sin, if I draw an

analogy to the meal-offering of a sinner, which is brought only as wheat, so this one also should bring only a meal-offering of wheat.

E. Accordingly, Scripture makes explicit the contrary fact, that this meal-offering derives from barley [and not wheat].

The critique of arguing from analogy is explicit: analogy yields false results. Once we establish a common category by reason of indicative traits ("brought on account of sin") we impose upon the unknown rule governing the known. But, in the case of VIII:IV, that is contrary to fact, and so too in VIII:V. The upshot is a critique of the argumentation of analogy and contrast. But this is a simple example. A comparable critique follows.

## XXII:II

1. A. "...When either a man or a woman makes a special vow, the vow of a Nazirite, to separate himself to the Lord" (Num. 6:1-4).
   B. The present specification serves to impose the same rule on women as on men.
   C. For one might on the basis of logic have reached the contrary conclusion:
   D. if in a case in which the law has treated minors as equivalent to adults [namely, minor priests are forbidden to contract corpse uncleanness as much as are adult priests], it has not treated women as equivalent to men, [since women-priests are not prohibited from contracting corpse uncleanness], in the present case, in which the law has not treated minors as equivalent to adults, is it not logical that we should *not* impose the same rule on women as on men?
   E. Accordingly, Scripture states, "When either a man or a woman makes a special vow, the vow of a Nazirite," so serving to impose the same rule on women as on men.

## XXII:III

1. A. "When either a man or a woman makes a special vow, the vow of a Nazirite, to separate himself to the Lord:"
   B. The phrase at hand further serves to exclude minors [from the Nazirite vow].
   C. For logic might have led us to the contrary conclusion: if in a case in which the law has not treated women as equivalent to men, the law has treated minors as equivalent to adults, in the present case, in which the law has treated women as equivalent to men, is it not logical that minors should be treated as adults?
   D. Accordingly, Scripture states, "When either a man or a woman makes a special vow, "to exclude minors from the rule.
2. A. If so, why is it further stated, "...makes a special vow"?
   B. That phrase further serves to encompass only those who know the meaning of making a special vow,
      C. and on that basis the rule is given: **A boy twelve years and one day old is subject to having vows that he may take investigated [as to their validity. If he understood what he was doing, the vows are valid, and if not, they are not valid]** [M. Nid. 5:6].

*Fifteen. Sifré to Numbers* 241

Once more, Scripture is required, because logic produces a false result. Women are treated differently from men in one case, so logic suggests, that should be so in all cases. But that is not correct.

## XXIII:I
1.  A. "'...he shall separate himself from wine and strong drink; he shall drink no vinegar made from wine or strong drink, [and he shall not drink any juice of grapes or eat grapes, fresh or dried. All the days of his separation he shall eat nothing that is produced by the grapevine, not even the seeds or the skins]'" (Num. 6:1-4).
    B. [The reference to strong drink] serves to treat wine drunk as a matter of religious duty as equivalent to wine drunk for mere pleasure.
    C. For one might have argued as follows: just as one who has suffered a bereavement but not yet buried his dead is forbidden to drink wine, and a Nazirite is forbidden to drink wine, if I draw an analogy from the case of the bereaved, in which case the law has not treated wine drunk as a matter of religious duty as equivalent to wine drunk as a matter of mere pleasure [for the bereaved may drink the former but not the latter], so in the case of the Nazirite we should not treat wine drunk as a matter of religious duty as equivalent to wine drunk as a matter of mere pleasure.
    D. And the view contrary to this one would be on the basis of an argument *a fortiori:*
    E. now if in the case of one who has not yet buried his deceased, in which instance the law has placed in the same classification a religiously required meal and the drinking of wine as a religious duty, the law still has not placed in the same classification wine drunk as a religious duty and wine drunk as mere pleasure,
    F. a Nazirite, in which case the law has *not* placed in the same classification the eating of a meal as a religious duty and the drinking of wine as a religious duty [since the latter is forbidden under all circumstances, even as a religious duty], is it not a matter of logic that the drinking of wine as a religious duty should not fall into the same classification as the drinking of wine as a matter of sheer enjoyment? [Hence on this basis we should not treat wine drunk as a matter of religious duty as equivalent to wine drunk as a matter of mere pleasure.]
    G. But lo, the one who carries out an act of cultic service to an idol will prove the contrary. For in that matter the law has not placed in the same classification the eating of a meal as a religious duty and the drinking of wine as a religious duty, but the law has treated in his case the drinking of wine as a religious duty and the drinking of wine as a matter of sheer pleasure. [One who drinks wine used for a libation is guilty, no matter the purpose of drinking the wine.] So that case will prove in the case of the Nazir, that even though the law has not treated the eating of a meal as a religious duty as belonging to the same classification as the drinking of wine as a religious duty, nonetheless the drinking of wine as a religious duty should be treated as equivalent to the drinking of wine as a matter of sheer pleasure.
    H. Now lo, there is this argument *a fortiori* : now if in the case of one who performs an act of service to an idol, in which the law has not treated the refuse of food

as equivalent to food, eating is equivalent to drinking and eating grapes is equivalent to drinking wine, and, in such a case wine drunk as a matter of religious duty is equivalent to wine drunk as a matter of sheer pleasure, in the case of a Nazirite, in which instance the refuse of food is treated as equivalent to food [since the Nazirite cannot eat grape pits as much as he cannot eat the grapes themselves], and eating is treated as equivalent to drinking, and eating grapes is treated as equivalent to drinking wine, is it not a matter of logic that we should treat the drinking of wine as a matter of religious duty to be equivalent to drinking wine as a matter of sheer pleasure?

I. No, at not at all. If you have made that rule in connection with the one who performs an act of service to an idol, such a one is subject to the death penalty, and it is for that reason that the law has treated the drinking of wine as a matter of religious duty as equivalent to the drinking of wine for sheer pleasure. But will you make the same rule in connection with the Nazirite, in which case violation of the law is not penalized by death? Since the death penalty does not apply, therefore wine drunk as a matter of religious duty is not to be treated as equivalent to wine drunk for sheer pleasure.

J. [We are left with a mass of contradictory propositions, all of them yielded by reason unguided by Scripture.] Accordingly, Scripture states, "...he shall separate himself from wine and strong drink; he shall drink no vinegar made from wine or strong drink, and he shall not drink any juice of grapes or eat grapes, fresh or dried. All the days of his separation he shall eat nothing that is produced by the grapevine, not even the seeds or the skins]'" (Num. 6:1-4).

K. [The reference to strong drink] serves to treat wine drunk as a matter of religious duty as equivalent to wine drunk for mere pleasure.

Now the critique of logic proves more complex. Scripture is necessary not only because logic yields a false result, but also because logic proves indeterminate. If I depend on analogies, C, then I produce an anomaly. But, D, can we not show the opposite through an argument a fortiori? If the law does not classify both types of wine as equivalent in the weightier case, will the law not do the same in the lesser case? G then introduces the critical turn. It is to differentiate what we thought were comparable cases. Here is a cased in which the law has not treated two categories within the same classification (rule), and yet it has treated as equivalent the two matters we wish to differentiate. That yields an argument a fortiori with diametrically-opposed results from the one that we originally constructed, H. A further distinction then is introduced, to differentiate what we treated as comparable, I, and that leads to the recognition of anomaly, J. Scripture is then required to settle matters. What we have seen, therefore, is two different modes of argumentation on the matter of the efficacy of reason/logic/argument in generating the Halakhah. The first two simply shows how logic on its own (the argument a fortiori) produces results contrary to fact. The second is more complex, and it shows that logic produces contradictory outcomes. This is done by introducing anomalies and distinctions that upset the classification-system upon which the proposed demonstration of the Halakhah on the basis of logic is supposed to rest.

*Fifteen. Sifré to Numbers*

Another example of the critique of the logic of hierarchical classification based on the uncertainty of comparison and contrast, equally complex, shows how the same type of argumentation applies to other materials altogether.

## VI:III
1. A. "'...every man's holy thing shall be his; whatever any man gives to the priest shall be his' (Num. 5:10).
   B. "Why does Scripture make this statement?
   C. "Because, with reference to the fruit of an orchard in the fourth year after its planting, it is said, 'And in the fourth year all their fruit shall be holy, an offering of praise to the Lord' (Lev. 19:24), [I do not know whether the sense is that] it is holy for the farmer or holy for the priesthood. Accordingly, Scripture says, '...every man's holy thing shall be his; whatever any man gives to the priest shall be his,' Scripture thereby speaks of produce of an orchard in the fourth year after its planting, indicating that it should belong to the farmer," the words of R. Meir.
   D. R. Ishmael says, "It is holy to the farmer.
   E. "You maintain that it is holy for the farmer.. Or is it holy for the priesthood? Lo, this is how you may logically [rather than by reference to the exegesis, B-C, based on Scripture] deal with the problem:
   F. "Produce in the status of second tithe is called holy, and the fruit of an orchard in the fourth year after its planting is called holy. If I draw the analogy to produce in the status of second tithe, which belongs only to the farmer, then likewise produce of an orchard in the fourth year after its planting should belong only to the farmer."
   G. No, produce separated as heave-offering [for priestly use] proves to the contrary, for it too is called Holy, but it belongs only to the priest. And that furthermore demonstrates for produce of an orchard in the fourth year after its planting that even though it is called holy, it should belong only to the priesthood.
   H. "You may then offer [the following argument to the contrary, [showing the correct analogy is to be drawn not to heave-offering but to produce in the status of second tithe, as follows:] the correct separation of produce in the status of second tithe involves bringing the produce to the holy place [of Jerusalem, where it is to be eaten], and, along these same lines, produce of an orchard in the fourth year after its planning likewise involves bringing that produce to the holy place. If, therefore, I draw the rule for produce in the status of second tithe, maintaining that it belongs to the owner, so produce of an orchard in the fourth year after its planting likewise should belong only to the owner."
   I. [No, that argument can be disproved from another variety of produce entirely:] lo, produce designated as first fruits will prove to the contrary, for such produce likewise has to be brought to the holy place, but it belongs only to the priest. So produce in that classification will prove for produce of an orchard in the fourth year after its planting, showing that even though it has to be brought to the holy place, it also should belong only to the priests. [So the labor of classification continues.]
   J. "You may compose [the following argument to reply to the foregoing:] The [result of the] separation of produce in the status of second tithe falls into the

classification of holy and has to be brought to the holy place, but further is subject to redemption [in that one can redeem the actual fruit and replace it with ready cash, and one may then bring that cash to Jerusalem and buy for it produce to be eaten in Jerusalem under the rules governing second tithe]. Produce of an orchard in the fourth year after its planting likewise is called holy, has to be brought to the holy place, and is subject to the rules of redemption. But let the matter of heave offering not come into the picture, for even though it is called holy, it does not have to be brought to the holy place [but is eaten wherever it is located], and let the matter of first fruit likewise not enter the picture, for even though it is produce that has to be brought to the holy place, it is not called holy."

K. Lo, there is the case of the firstling, which *is* called holy, and which has to be brought to the holy place, but which belongs only to the priesthood. [So we can now provide an appropriate analogy.] And that case will prove [the rule for other sorts of produce subject to the same traits, specifically] produce of an orchard in the fourth year after its planting, for, even though it is called holy, and even though it has to be brought to the holy place, it should belong only to the priesthood.

L. "You may invoke the consideration of separating [the produce into one of its several classifications]. Let me call to account three distinct considerations in a single exercise:

M. "[1] Food in the status of second tithe is called holy, requires delivery to the holy place, and is subject to the rules of redemption.

N. "[2] Produce of an orchard in the fourth year after its planting is called holy, requires delivery to the holy place, and is subject to the rules of redemption.

O. "[1] But let not food that has been designated as heave-offering enter into consideration. For even though it is called holy, it does not require delivery to the holy place.

P. "And [2] let not first fruits enter into consideration. For even though it requires delivery to the holy place, it is not called holy.

Q. "Nor should [3] the firstling enter into consideration. For even though it is called holy and requires delivery to the holy place, it is not subject to the rules of redemption.

R. "Let me then draw the appropriate analogy from the correct source, and let me then compose a logical argument on the basis of the correct traits of definition.

S. "I shall draw an analogy on the basis of three shared traits from one matter to another, but I shall not drawn an analogy from something which exhibits three traits to something which does not share these same traits, but only one or two of them.

T. "If then I draw an analogy to produce in the status of second tithe, which belongs only to the owner, so too in the case of produce of an orchard in the fourth year after its planting, it should belong only to the owner."

2. A. R. Joshua says, "What is called holy belongs to the owner.

B. "You maintain that what is called holy belongs to the owner. But perhaps it belongs only to the priesthood?

C. "Scripture states, 'But in the fifth year you may eat of their fruit that they may yield more richly for you' (Lev. 19:25). To whom does the increase go? To him

*Fifteen. Sifré to Numbers*

to whom the produce already has been assigned [that is to say, the farmer, not the priesthood]."

The ambiguity of Scripture's wording yields to the problem of B-C and the dispute that flows therefrom. Ishmael, E, shows how logically, rather than exegetically, one may settle the dispute, showing that the produce is holy to the farmer, not the priest. This is done by establishing analogies or points of comparability: produce in the status of second tithe and produce of the orchard in the fourth year, both being called holy. The former belongs to the farmer, so the latter should as well, F. But, G, we can find a component of the same category — things called holy — that belongs to the priest, namely, heave-offering. Then that which is subject to debate should likewise go to the priest. Then the way forward is clear: distinguish among the categories that we have deemed comparable, eliminating the category that produces the unwanted result. Heave-offering is not the generative metaphor, H, but second tithe is. Then we meet the conditions set up at H, and in I we sustain our original objection, and so at J, K, L. Then, M-Q takes up the categories that have been entered into comparison and contrast and differentiates among them, showing those that belong together, M-N, and those that do not fit, O-P=Q. That produces the logical argument at the end: draw the appropriate analogy from the correct source and build, thereon, the logical argument. This is then summarized at S, T. No. 2 presents a simpler formulation of the same issue. I simply cannot improve on the clarity and power of logic that characterize this complex type of argumentation, which is articulate and compelling.

## XXVI:II

1.  A. "...he shall not go near a dead body:"
    B. May I infer that the corpses of beasts fall under consideration?
    C. Scripture says, "Neither for his father nor for his mother, [nor for brother or sister, if they die, shall he make himself unclean; because his separation to God]."
    D. Concerning what topic does Scripture speak? It concerns only human corpses.
    E. R. Ishmael says, "Such a proof is hardly necessary. For Scripture states, 'He shall not go near a corpse,' and the language at hand, speaking of a euphemism for sexual relations, can only speak of human beings. Why then does Scripture then make explicit the further matter: 'Neither for his father nor for his mother, nor for brother or sister, if they die, shall he make himself unclean'? The sense is, for such as these he may not contract corpse uncleanness, but he must contract corpse uncleanness on account of a neglected corpse [which under all circumstances he must bury, there being no alternative for the task]."
2.  A. [Building on the foregoing:] Now even if Scripture had not made that point [that for such as these he may not contract corpse uncleanness, but he must contract corpse uncleanness on account of a neglected corpse], I could have proved it on the basis of logic.
    B. Now the high priest is subject to the prohibition against contracting corpse uncleanness even for relatives, and the Nazirite is subject to that same

prohibition. If then I know as fact that the high priest nonetheless must contract corpse uncleanness on account of a neglected corpse, then so too should the Nazirite contract corpse uncleanness on account of a neglected corpse.

C. There is, moreover an argument *a fortiori* :

D. Now if a high priest, the sanctification of whom is permanent contracts corpse uncleanness on account of a neglected corpse, the Nazirite, whose sanctification is only temporary, surely should contract corpse uncleanness on account of a neglected corpse.

E. No, [there is a difference between the two cases,] for if you invoke that rule in the case of a high priest, who does not have to bring an offering on account of contracting uncleanness, and therefore contracts corpse uncleanness in the case of a neglected corpse, will you say the same of the Nazirite, who does have to bring an offering if he contracts uncleanness, and, therefore, he, but not the other, should not contract corpse uncleanness?

F. Accordingly, Scripture is needed to make the point:

G. "Neither for his father nor for his mother, nor for brother or sister, if they die, shall he make himself unclean."

H. For such as these he may not contract corpse uncleanness, but he must contract corpse uncleanness on account of a neglected corpse [which under all circumstances he must bury, there being no alternative for the task].

3. A.. May one argue a different view, namely:

B. "Neither for his father nor for his mother, nor for brother or sister, if they die, shall he make himself unclean:" — thus for his father and his mother he may not contract corpse uncleanness, but he *may* contract corpse uncleanness on account of any other corpses.

C. To prove the contrary you may construct an argument *a fortiori* as follows:

D. If an ordinary priest, who may contract corpse uncleanness to bury his relatives, may not contract corpse uncleanness on account of any other corpses, a Nazirite, who may not contract corpse uncleanness to bury his relatives, surely should not contract corpse uncleanness to bury anyone else.

E. Lo, what then is the sense of the verse, "Neither for his father nor for his mother, nor for brother or sister, if they die, shall he make himself unclean."?

F. For such as these he may not contract corpse uncleanness, but he must contract corpse uncleanness on account of a neglected corpse.

4. A.. Lo, even if the matter had not been made explicit, I still could have reached that conclusion on the basis of logic, as follows:

B. A general principle is stated with reference to a high priest, and the equivalent encompassing principle covers the Nazirite. Just as in the case of the high priest, the principle is that he may not contract corpse uncleanness on account of the need to bury relatives, so in the case of the Nazirite, he may not contract corpse uncleanness to bury relatives.

C. But why argue from the analogy of the high priest? I shall draw an analogy to an ordinary priest. Specifically: an encompassing principle applies to an ordinary priest, and the same applies to a Nazirite Just as in the former case, lo, the ordinary priest does contract corpse uncleanness to bury relatives, so in the case of the Nazirite, lo, he should contract corpse uncleanness to bury relatives.

*Fifteen. Sifré to Numbers*  247

    D. You draw the analogy from the case of the high priest, and I draw the analogy from the priest of the ordinary priest.
    E. Accordingly, Scripture is required to make the matter clear:
    F. "Neither for his father nor for his mother, nor for brother or sister, if they die, shall he make himself unclean:"
    G. He may not contract uncleanness on their account if they should day.

5. A. R. Aqiba says, "Such a proof is not required. For lo, Scripture states, 'Neither for his father nor for his mother, nor for brother or sister, if they die, shall he make himself unclean:'
    B. "if he was a high priest, as to his mother and father he may not contract corpse uncleanness, but he may contract corpse uncleanness in order to bury a neglected corpse.
    C. "If he was a Nazirite, as to his mother and father he may not contract corpse uncleanness, but he may contract corpse uncleanness in order to bury a neglected corpse.
    D. "If he was going to slaughter the lamb for his Passover offering, then, on account of the necessity of burying his brother he may not contract corpse uncleanness, but he may contract corpse uncleanness in order to bury a neglected corpse.
    E. "If he was an ordinary priest, he may contract corpse uncleanness in order to bury a neglected corpse.
    F. "But as to his son and daughter no statement is made, for even minors may become Nazirites."

Scripture yields the proposition that the Nazirite may not approach a human corpse but is not restricted from animal corpses, A-D. Ishmael interprets matters somewhat differently. The upshot is, the Nazirite may not contract corpse uncleanness for his near-relatives but he must do so for a neglected corpse, burial of which overrides all other prohibitions. Then, No. 2, the issue is raised, could logic not have produced the same outcome? 2.B begins with the argument by analogy: if the high priest, to whom contracting corpse uncleanness for near-relations is forbidden, is obligated to bury a neglected corpse, the Nazirite, in the same classification, also is so obligated. An argument a fortiori, C-D, is further included. But, the critique proceeds, the argument a fortiori fails, because there is a difference between the classifications that we have treated as analogous, the high priest and the Nazirite. So only Scripture serves. No. 3 then moves from Scripture to logic. Scripture yields the proposition that the prohibition against contracting corpse uncleanness pertains only to the near relatives but not to others (that is, a counter-intuitive proposition). An argument a fortiori is proposed against, C-D. That corrects the (mis-)reading of Scripture, E-F, producing the original result. Then, No. 4, we proceed along the same lines: without Scripture, logic would have served. Here we have the comparison of the high priest and the Nazirite. But that comparison is not compelling, since we can easily have drawn an analogy between the Nazirite and the ordinary priest, which produces a contrary result. Scripture, then, is required to clarify matters, analogies yielding indeterminate results. At No. 5, Aqiba goes over the same materials, A-F.

The critique of logic from the perspective of Scripture, the insistence that arguments from analogy depend upon uncertain classification-schemes — these yield a much more complex argument than is suggested in the foregoing cases. Let us turn, for the final instance of the critique of analogical logic, to a systematic exposition in which Scripture's exegetical logic and reason's analogical logic function side-by-side in a fully-articulated composition.

### XXXI:IV

1. 
   A. "[And he shall consecrate his head that same day,] and separate himself to the Lord for the days of his separation [and bring a male lamb a year old for a guilt offering; but the former time shall be void, because his separation was defiled]" (Num. 6:12):
   B. The purpose of that statement is to treat the days following the completion of the Nazirite vow as equivalent to the days within the spell of the vow, until the bringing of the required offering.
   C. Or perhaps he should be liable only until he completes the Nazirite vow [but not in the days between the conclusion of the vow and the bringing of the offering].
   D. For one may construct the following argument *a fortiori*:
   E. Since he is forbidden to drink wine and also forbidden to contract corpse uncleanness, if I draw an analogy to wine, in which case the days following the completion of the Nazirite vow as equivalent to the days within the spell of the vow, until the bringing of the required offering, so too as to the prohibition of corpse contamination, we should treat the days following the completion of the Nazirite vow as equivalent to the days within the spell of the vow, until the bringing of the required offering.
   F. And furthermore, one can construct an argument *a fortiori*:
   G. Now if wine, drinking which does not cause him to lose the credit for the days already observed, is such that the days following the completion of the Nazirite vow are equivalent to the days within the spell of the vow, until the bringing of the required offering, the matter of corpse uncleanness, which does cause the Nazirite to lose the credit for all the days he has observed, surely should be such that we treat the days following the completion of the Nazirite vow as equivalent to the days within the spell of the vow, until the bringing of the required offering.
   H. No, if you have stated that rule with regard to wine, which is at no point subject to remission from the prohibition affecting it, we may say that that is the reason that we treat the days following the completion of the Nazirite vow as equivalent to the days within the spell of the vow, until the bringing of the required offering.
   I. But will you say the same of corpse uncleanness, which is subject to a remission from the prohibition affecting it [e.g., in the case of the neglected corpse], and therefore in that case we should not treat the days following the completion of the Nazirite vow as equivalent to the days within the spell of the vow, until the bringing of the required offering.
   J. The matter of the cutting of the hair then will prove the point. For it is subject to a remission from the prohibition affecting it, and yet in that case we treat the

## Fifteen. Sifré to Numbers

days following the completion of the Nazirite vow as equivalent to the days within the spell of the vow, until the bringing of the required offering.

K. That will prove the matter as to contracting corpse uncleanness, for even though it is subject to a remission from the prohibition affecting it, we should in that regard treat the days following the completion of the Nazirite vow as equivalent to the days within the spell of the vow, until the bringing of the required offering.

L. And there is, moreover, an argument *a fortiori*: Now if the cutting of the hair, the violation of which will not cause the loss of all the days already observed, nonetheless is a rule in which we treat the days following the completion of the Nazirite vow as equivalent to the days within the spell of the vow, until the bringing of the required offering, the matter of corpse-uncleanness, which will cause the loss of the days already observed, should surely be a prohibition in connection with which we treat the days following the completion of the Nazirite vow as equivalent to the days within the spell of the vow, until the bringing of the required offering.

M. No, if you have stated that argument with regard to the cutting of the hair, in which matter the one who *gives* the haircut is in the same category [as to penalty] as the one who *gets* his hair cut, and therefore we treat the days following the completion of the Nazirite vow as equivalent to the days within the spell of the vow, until the bringing of the required offering, will you say the same in the matter of corpse uncleanness, in which instance the one who imparts uncleanness is not subjected to the same penalty as will come upon the Nazirite who is made unclean, and, in that case, we should therefore not treat the days following the completion of the Nazirite vow as equivalent to the days within the spell of the vow, until the bringing of the required offering.

N. But wine will prove the point, for the one who *provides* the wine is not treated as equivalent to the one who *drinks* it, but, nonetheless, we treat the days following the completion of the Nazirite vow as equivalent to the days within the spell of the vow, until the bringing of the required offering.

O. And that fact proves the case with regard to corpse-uncleanness, for even though in that case, while we do not subject the one who imparts uncleanness to the same sanctions as affect the one who is subject to uncleanness through corpse contamination, nonetheless we should treat the days following the completion of the Nazirite vow as equivalent to the days within the spell of the vow, until the bringing of the required offering.

P. And there is moreover an argument *a fortiori*:

Q. Now if wine, drinking of which does not cause the loss of the days already observed, is subject rule that we treat the days following the completion of the Nazirite vow as equivalent to the days within the spell of the vow, until the bringing of the required offering, corpse uncleanness, which will cause the loss of the days already observed, should surely be subject to the rule that we treat the days following the completion of the Nazirite vow as equivalent to the days within the spell of the vow, until the bringing of the required offering.

R. No, if you have stated the rule in connection with wine, which is never subject to a remission from the prohibition affecting it, and therefore we treat the days following the completion of the Nazirite vow as equivalent to the days within the spell of the vow, until the bringing of the required offering, will you say the

|     | same of corpse uncleanness, which is subject to remission from the prohibition affecting it [in the case of the neglected corpse]. Therefore we should not treat the days following the completion of the Nazirite vow as equivalent to the days within the spell of the vow, until the bringing of the required offering. |
| --- | --- |
| S.  | Now since logic leads us round in circles, we revert to Scripture, which says, "....and after that the *Nazirite* may drink wine" (Num. 6:20). |
| T.  | Now does he drink wine when he is a *Nazirite*? |
| U.  | Is it the case that a Nazirite drinks wine? [Obviously not, and he is not a Nazirite after the completion of the rites of purification.] The word therefore bears no meaning in context and provides the occasion for the construction of an analogy bringing into relationship two distinct passages. |
| V.  | Here the word "Nazirite" appears, and elsewhere the word likewise appears. Just as in the one case, the rule is that the days following the completion of the vow are subject to the prohibitions that apply during the spell of the vow, until the bringing of the sacrifices, so too the reference to Nazirite stated here means the same, namely, that the days following the completion of the vow are subject to the prohibitions that apply during the spell of the vow, until the bringing of the sacrifices. |

The point of law is raised at A-B+C. What is the status of the days from the end of the observation of the vow to the moment on which the required offerings are presented? Is the Nazirite still obligated in that interim, or has he completed his obligation? An analogy is proposed, based on the prohibition of wine. Just as the prohibition of wine applies to the days following the completion of the vow until the presentation of the required offering, so the prohibition against contracting corpse-uncleanness should apply. And an argument a fortiori further supports the same proposition., thus E-G. The way to demolish this argument is clear: show that the analogy to wine does not govern the matter of contracting corpse uncleanness; the latter is subject to remission, the former not, so H-I. J-K then matches the anomaly: cutting the hair is subject to remission but also marks those interim days as prohibited; and an argument fortiori sustains the same proposition. At M we differentiate the prohibition of cutting the hair from the prohibition of corpse uncleanness, based on the subtle point of distinction announced at M. In response, the same distinction that served earlier is reprised, N-O, along with an argument a fortiori. The upshot emerges at S: logic leads in circles, only Scripture can resolve the issue. The exegesis that produces the answer involves the utilization of the same word in two contexts, and the rule that applies in the latter context governs in the former as well, U-V. The interplay of types of argumentation is classic: exegetical, a fortiori, analogical. But the key throughout remains the same: the uncertainty of analogical reasoning, the imperfection of category-formation outside the framework of Scripture.

We have now considered the single most important type of argumentation set forth in Sifré to Numbers (and its companions, Sifra and Sifré to Deuteronomy). Let us now turn to other types of argumentation in the document.

*Fifteen. Sifré to Numbers*

## I:II

1. A. "Command" (Num. 5:2):
   B. The commandment at hand is meant both to be put into effect immediately and also to apply for generations to come.
   C. You maintain that the commandment at hand is meant both to be put into effect immediately and also to apply for generations to come.
   D. But perhaps the commandment is meant to apply only after a time [but not right away, at the moment at which it was given].
   E. [We shall now prove that the formulation encompasses both generations to come and also the generation to whom the commandment is entrusted.] Scripture states, "The Lord said to Moses, 'Command the people of Israel that they put out [of the camp every leper and every one having a discharge, and every one that is unclean through contact with the dead. You shall put out both male and female, putting them outside the camp, that they may not defile their camp, in the midst of which I dwell.'] And the people of Israel did so and drove them outside the camp, as the Lord said to Moses, so the people of Israel did" (Num. 5:1-4). [The verse itself makes explicit the fact that the requirement applied forthwith, not only later on.]
   F. Lo, we have learned that the commandment at hand is meant to be put into effect immediately.
   G. How then do we derive from Scripture the fact that it applies also for generations to come? [We shall now show that the same word used here, command, pertains to generations to come and not only to the generation at hand.]
   H. Scripture states, "Command the children of Israel to bring you pure oil from beaten olives [for the lamp, that a light may be kept burning continually outside the veil of the testimony in the tent of meeting, Aaron shall keep it in order from evening to morning before the Lord continually; it shall be a statute for ever throughout your generations]" (Lev. 24:2).
   I. Lo, we here derive evidence that the commandment at hand is meant both to be put into effect immediately and also to apply for generations to come, [based on the framing of the present commandment].
   J. How, then, do we drive evidence that all of the commandments that are contained in the Torah [apply in the same way]? [We wish now to prove that the language, command, always bears the meaning imputed to it here.]
   K. R. Ishmael maintained, "Since the bulk of the commandments stated in the Torah are presented without further amplification, while in the case of one of them [namely, the one at hand], Scripture has given explicit details, that commandment [that has been singled out] is meant both to be put into effect immediately and also to apply for generations to come. Accordingly, I apply to all of the other commandments in the Torah the same detail, so that in all cases the commandment is meant both to be put into effect immediately and also to apply for generations to come."

The key argument is in two parts. First comes the analogy, based on the formulation of Scripture: the word that is used bears the meaning that is besought. And the framing of matters proves the point. Then, J, we ask whether the language always bears the specified meaning, and, K, we are given a reason. Where Scripture ordinarily does not spell matters out, but, in one instance, does do so, then what it says in the articulated case applies in the comparable, but unarticulated, cases. What is critical to the argument is not only the citation of Scripture but the introduction of an articulated exegetical principle to explain how, under all comparable formulations, the rule is to be derived. So there is nothing arbitrary in the matter, nor does the argument before us rest on the mere formal citation of Scripture. Scripture forms no mere formality, rather a source of vivid argument, when Scripture is correctly interpreted in accord with a prevailing rule.

## XIV:II

1. A. "...the Lord make you an execration and an oath among your people:"
   B. Why is this statement made?
   C. Because it is said, "If a person hears a execration to give evidence as a witness" (Lev. 5:1),
   D. I know only that the law applies to a execration. How do I know that the same rule applies to an oath?
   E. You may reason as follows: in the present case, execration is stated, and elsewhere, the same word occurs. Just as the word execration used here means that an oath is treated as equivalent to an execration, so when the word execration occurs elsewhere, an oath is to be treated as equivalent to an execration.
   F. [Further:] since oaths in general are listed in the Torah without further specification, the Torah has given details in the case of one of them, indicating that it is taken only with the expression of the Holy Name of God beginning with Y H, so I impose that same detail on all oaths that are listed in the Torah, which are to be taken only with the expression of the Holy Name of God beginning with Y H.

The reasoning rests on the analogy established by the use of the same word in two contexts. That establishes a link between one context and the other — a formal link — so that what pertains to the one applies also to the other. This argument is articulated twice, E, F.

## CXVIII:XIII

1. A. "but their flesh shall be yours, as the breast that is waved and as the right thigh are yours:"
   B. Scripture comes along and establishes an analogy between the firstling and the breast and thigh of peace-offerings: just as the breast and thigh of the peace-offerings are to be eaten over a span of two days and the intervening night, so the firstling is to be eaten over a span of two days and one night.
2. A. This question was addressed to sages in the vineyard in Yabneh: "As to a firstling, over how long a span of time is it to be eaten?"
   B. Expounded R. Tarfon and said, "It is for two days and the intervening night."

## Fifteen. Sifré to Numbers

C. Said his disciples to him, "Our lord, instruct us [on the foundations for that ruling]."

D. He said to them, "The firstling falls into the category of Lesser Holy Things, and peace offerings fall into the category of Lesser Holy Things. Just as peace offerings are eaten over a period of two days and the intervening night, so the firstling should be eaten over a period of two days and the intervening night."

E. Now R. Yosé the Galilean was there, having come for the first time to serve sages as a disciple. He said to him, "My lord, a sin offering is a gift to the priest, and a firstling is a gift to the priest. Just as a sin offering is eaten over the span of a day and the following night, so a firstling just be eaten over the span of a day and the following night."

F. He said to him, "My son, I shall derive a lesson for one thing from the corresponding thing, and I shall draw a logical analogy for one thing from a corresponding thing. I shall derive a lesson for one thing, namely, that which falls into the category of Lesser Holy Things, from the corresponding thing, that is, that which falls into the category of Lesser Holy Things, but I shall not derive a lesson concerning something that falls into the category of Lesser Holy Things from something which falls into the category of Most Holy Things."

G. He said to him, "My lord, I shall derive a lesson for one thing from the corresponding thing, and I shall draw a logical analogy for one thing from a corresponding thing. Specifically: I shall draw an analogy from that which is a gift to the priest for that which is a gift to the priest, but I shall not derive a rule for something that is a gift to the priest from something that is a gift to any person."

H. R. Tarfon having been ousted, R. Aqiba leapt forward. He said to him, "My son, here is how I expound the matter: 'but their flesh shall be yours, as the breast that is waved and as the right thigh are yours.' Scripture comes along and establishes an analogy between the firstling and the breast and thigh of peace-offerings: just as the breast and thigh of the peace-offerings are to be eaten over a span of two days and the intervening night, so the firstling is to be eaten over a span of two days and one night."

I. He said to him, "My lord, you draw an analogy to the breast and the thigh of peace-offerings, but I shall draw an analogy to the breast and the thigh of the thank offering. Just as in the case of the breast and the thigh of the thank offering, the meat is eating for a day and the following night alone, so in the case of the firstling, the meat should be eaten for the day and the following night only."

J. He said to him, "My son, thus do I expound the matter: 'but their flesh shall be yours, as the breast that is waved and as the right thigh....' Scripture uses the language, 'shall be yours,' only to serve as a medium for extending the matter through the reference to the verb 'to be' [which is not needed for meaning], so to indicate that the meat is eaten over a period of two days and one night."

K. R. Ishmael says, "Now as to the thank offering, whence do we derive its rule? Is it not from the rule governing peace offerings. Then in

254 *Analysis and Argumentation in Rabbinic Judaism*

  the case of a ruling that is derived by analogy from some other source, do you come along and then derive by analogy a ruling from that item as well! We do not, in fact, derive a rule from a derivative rule. Therefore you have to state matters not in this latter formulation but only as originally set forth, namely: 'but their flesh shall be yours, as the breast that is waved and as the right thigh are yours:' Scripture comes along and establishes an analogy between the firstling and the breast and thigh of peace-offerings: just as the breast and thigh of the peace-offerings are to be eaten over a span of two days and the intervening night, so the firstling is to be eaten over a span of two days and one night."

  L. "Another matter: Scripture states, '...shall be yours...,' only to encompass under the rule the blemished firstling, indicating that it too is a gift to the priest, for we have not heard the rule governing it anywhere else in the entire Torah."

The governing argument is at D, comparing the firstling to the peace offerings, because both are in the category of Lesser Holy Things. Then the rule for the one dictates the procedure of the other. But, E, a different analogy presents itself. The firstling is the gift to the priest, and so is a sin-offering. Hence the rule for the sin offering should apply, not that for peace offerings. Tarfon, F, immediately notes the fallacy of the proposed analogy: the firstling is Lesser Holy Things, and the sin-offering is Most Holy Things. G responds by establishing the indicative trait that establishes the analogy: the specified offerings are gifts to the priest, excluding that which is not. At H a new tack is taken, based on Scripture's own decree. Scripture dictates an analogy between the firstling and the breast and thigh of peace offerings. At I, a different analogy is proposed, to the breast and thigh of the thank offering. Aqiba, J, then moves from arguments concerning the regnant analogy to an exegetical demonstration. At K-L, Ishmael takes over from Aqiba, with a logical consideration: we do not derive a rule from a derived rule. The upshot is the same: logic gives way to scriptural proof.

## XXIV:V
1. A. "...not even the seeds or the skins" (Num. 6:1-4).
  B. Why is this phrase added?
  C. Because it is said, "...he shall eat nothing that is produced by the grapevine," we have a generalization. Then the phrase, "...he shall separate himself from wine and strong drink; he shall drink no vinegar made from wine or strong drink," forms a particularization of the former.
  D. So we have a generalization followed by a particularization, which means that covered by the generalization are only those matters specified in the particularization.
  E. Just as the particular detail is spelled out to encompass the fruit and the refuse of the fruit, so I know only that the fruit and the refuse of the fruit are

*Fifteen. Sifré to Numbers* 255

encompassed, thus encompassing the seeds and the skins, which constitute the fruit and the refuse of the fruit.
F. Or may one argue that just as the produce is a fully formed piece of fruit, so encompassed under the rule is only fully formed fruit.
G. You may argue in this way: What sort of fully ripe fruit have they not included?
H. Lo, you should work the matter out not in accord with the latter, but in accord with the former mode of analysis:
I. Just as the particular detail is spelled out to encompass the fruit and the refuse of the fruit, so I know only that the fruit and the refuse of the fruit are encompassed, thus including the seeds and the skins, which constitute the fruit and the refuse of the fruit.
J. If I have gained the point through reason, what purpose does Scripture serve in specifying, "...not even the seeds or the skins"?
K. It serves to teach you that in the case of a generalization which serves to augment the detailed specification, you may not construct an argument based on the detail in such wise as to exempt it from the encompassing generalization. The exception to that rule would be a case in which Scripture has served to spell out for you the rule at hand, as Scripture has spelled matters out in detail in the case of the Nazirite's law.

At issue now is an exegetical principle. If Scripture presents a generalization followed by a particularization, the upshot is, the traits of the particularization limit the application of the generalization, D. E then spells out the result, which is recapitulated at I. Then J-K ask the obvious question: if logic has yielded the besought result, what need is there fore Scripture's participation? That is then resolved, K. The power of the case should not be missed. There is a general rule of exegesis, governing in all cases. Nothing arbitrary, no appeal to a singular case, serves. What is supplied are the grounds of generalization for the resolution of the particular case at hand.

## LX:II
1. A. "as the Lord commanded Moses:"
   B. There was a half-log of oil for each lamp.
   C. I know only that, as to the candelabrum, the law has treated those that were made in its model to conform to the generative pattern. How do I know that that same principle applies to the incense? [That is, how do I know that the way in which the rite was carried on in the tent of meeting is the way the rite is to be carried on in time to come.]
   D. You may argue in the following way: an act of service is stated in connection with the tent of meeting, as to the candelabrum, and an act of service is stated in connection with the tent of meeting, as to the incense.
   E. If in connection with the candelabrum, the law has treated those that were made in its model so as to conform to the generative pattern, so in connection with the incense, the law has treated those that were made in its model so as to conform to the generative pattern.

### TITLES

*Texts without Boundaries. Protocols of Non-Documentary Writing in the Rabbinic Canon,* Lanham, 2002: University Press of America. Academic Studies in Ancient Judaism series. Volume Two. *Sifra*

*Texts without Boundaries. Protocols of Non-Documentary Writing in the Rabbinic Canon,* Lanham, 2003: University Press of America. Academic Studies in Ancient Judaism series. Volume Three. *Sifré to Numbers.*

*Texts without Boundaries. Protocols of Non-Documentary Writing in the Rabbinic Canon,* Lanham, 2003: University Press of America. Academic Studies in Ancient Judaism series. Volume Four. *Sifré to Deuteronomy.*

*Texts without Boundaries. Protocols of Non-Documentary Writing in the Rabbinic Canon,* Lanham, 2004: University Press of America. Academic Studies in Ancient Judaism series. Volume Five. *Genesis Rabbah.*

*Texts without Boundaries. Protocols of Non-Documentary Writing in the Rabbinic Canon,* Lanham, 2004: University Press of America. Academic Studies in Ancient Judaism series. Volume Six. *Leviticus Rabbah.*

*Texts without Boundaries. Protocols of Non-Documentary Writing in the Rabbinic Canon,* Lanham, 2004: University Press of America. Academic Studies in Ancient Judaism series. Volume Seven. *Pesiqta deRab Kahana.*

*Texts without Boundaries. Protocols of Non-Documentary Writing in the Rabbinic Canon,* Lanham, 2004: University Press of America. Academic Studies in Ancient Judaism series. Volume Eight. *Esther Rabbah and Ruth Rabbah.*

*Texts without Boundaries. Protocols of Non-Documentary Writing in the Rabbinic Canon,* Lanham, 2004: University Press of America. Academic Studies in Ancient Judaism series. Volume Nine. *Song of Songs Rabbah.*

*Texts without Boundaries. Protocols of Non-Documentary Writing in the Rabbinic Canon,* Lanham, 2004: University Press of America. Academic Studies in Ancient Judaism series. Volume Ten. *Lamentations Rabbah.*

*Texts without Boundaries. Protocols of Non-Documentary Writing in the Rabbinic Canon,* Lanham, 2004: University Press of America. Academic Studies in Ancient Judaism series. Volume Eleven. *Mekhilta Attributed to Rabbi Ishmael.*

*Texts without Boundaries. Protocols of Non-Documentary Writing in the Rabbinic Canon,* Lanham, 2004: University Press of America. Academic Studies in Ancient Judaism series. Volume Twelve. *Abot deRabbi Natan.*

F. Lo, the act of service connected with the Day of Atonement will prove the contrary, for even though in its regard an act of service in the tent of meeting is stated, the law has not treated those that were made in its model so as to conform to the generative pattern. That rite therefore proves the case for the incense, that even though an act of service in the tent of meeting is stated in its regard, we should not treat those that were made in its model so as to conform to the generative pattern.

G. No, if you have stated the rule with regard to the act of service on the Day of Atonement, in which regard the requirement that Aaron wear the golden garments is not specified, should we derive a rule concerning which an act of service on the part of Aaron is required, in which the golden garments also are required.

H. Thus we deal with a matter concerning which an act of service, involving Aaron, and involving the golden garments, is at hand. If I draw an analogy, then, to the act of service involving the candelabrum, in which case the law has treated those that were made in its model to conform to the generative pattern, so in the instance of the incense rite, we should treat those that were made in its model to conform to the generative pattern.

I. Lo, the bullock brought on account of an inadvertent sin by the anointed priest will prove the contrary. For in its regard an act of service, done by Aaron in the golden garments, is specified, and yet the law has not treated those that were made in its model to conform to the generative pattern.

J. That case then will prove the matter for the incense rite, for even though an act of service, done by Aaron, in golden garments, is required, nonetheless the law has not treated those that were made in its model to conform to the generative pattern.

K. Now there is a point of distinction, with three specific cases dealt with simultaneously, namely, [1] an act of service, involving [2] the candelabrum, [3] by a priest wearing golden garments, and in this regard, there is a prescription that the rite be carried on continually [so the specifications at the outset govern the act of service later on], and, further, an act of service in the tent of meeting involving the incense rite, done in golden garment, encompasses also a reference to the rite's being done continually.

L. But the act of service on the Day of Atonement cannot be brought in evidence, even though an act of service in the tent of meeting is involved, because the requirement to wear the golden garments is absent,

M. nor should the rite involving the offering of the bullock on account of an inadvertent sin of an anointed priest come under consideration, for even though an act of service in the tent of meeting and in the golden garments is involved, the commandment does not make reference to the rite's being done continually.

N. So shall I draw an analogy from one thing to the next, and argument concerning one thing on the basis of the traits of another in the same classification. [I shall draw an analogy on the basis of the polythetic traits shared among two or more categories, all of which have three traits in common, but I shall not draw an analogy on the basis of something with three definitive traits to something which is not alike in those same three definitive traits, but is alike in only one or two definitive traits.]

*Fifteen. Sifré to Numbers* 257

    O.     If then I draw an analogy to the candelabrum, in which case the law has treated those that were made in its model to conform to the generative pattern, so in regard to the incense rite, we should admit that the law has treated those that were made in its model to conform to the generative pattern.

The argument begins with the assertion of an analogy, as specified at D-E. We have compared an act of service in the tent of meeting with regard to the candelabrum and an act of service in the tent of meeting as to the incense. The rule for the former governs in the case of the latter, by reason of the analogy established by their common venue in the tent of meeting, E. But, by way of breaking down the analogical reasoning, we can show an act of service in the tent of meeting in which the law has not treated those that were made in its model in the same way, F. But, G, we can differentiated that case from the one at hand. Then, H, the issue is stated: which is the governing analogy. But that does not close matters, I, for we have an exception to the analogy just now proposed. We turn out to deal with three analogies and pertinent distinctions, K, and when put together, they can be differentiated from the anomalous case. L-M then differentiate among the generative analogies under discussion, each of which is to be distinguished from the others in some aspect or other. This yields, N-O, an exercise in polythetic classification, invoking not all pertinent indicative traits of classification of each item but only some of them.

## CLIII:VI

1.     A.     "But if her father expresses disapproval to her on the day that he hears of it:"
        B.     I do not know the meaning of the word translated, "express disapproval." When Scripture goes on to state, "But if on the day that her husband comes to hear of it he expresses disapproval," one must conclude that the word translated "express disapprove" must bear the meaning of "release."
        C.     The word-choice further indicates in the case of the husband that the expression of disapproval has the force of nullifying the vow, and Scripture further indicates in the case of the father that Scripture treats silence or hearing, whenever this takes place, as the point at which the vow has been taken, so that at that point he has the power to release the vow.
        D.     How do we know that he may confirm it along the same lines?
        E.     Lo, you may argue as follows: since he has the power to confirm and has the power to annul vows, if I have derived the rule for the matter of annulling the vows that the act of expressing disapproval is the same as the act of nullifying the vow, and the moment of remaining silent or hearing the vow is the point at which the vow is treated as having been made, so in reference to confirming the vow, we should treat the act of expressing disapproval is the same as the act of nullifying the view, and the moment of remaining silent or hearing the view is the point at which the vow is treated as having been made.
        F.     Not at all! If you have stated the rule concerning the release of the vow, which has been treated as distinct from the encompassing rule, it is for that reason that we treat the act of expressing disapproval is the same as the act of nullifying the

view, and the moment of remaining silent or hearing the view is the point at which the vow is treated as having been made.

G. But will you say the same in connection with confirming the vow, in which case the law has not been treated as distinct from the encompassing rule, and it is for that reason that we should not treat the act of expressing disapproval is the same as the act of nullifying the view, and the moment of remaining silent or hearing the view is the point at which the vow is treated as having been made.

H. I have not succeeded. Now I shall construct an argument based on the situation of the husband:

I. Since the husband releases the vows and the father releases the vows, just as in the husband's case, the law has treated the act of remaining silent or hearing the vow as equivalent to the day on which the vow was made when it comes to confirming the vow, so with the father, we should treat the act of remaining silent or hearing the vow as if that were the day on which the vow was taken, so as to confirm the vow.

J. And furthermore it is an argument a fortiori:

K. if in the case of the husband, whose authority does not diminish, the law has treated the act of remaining silent or hearing the vow as the day on which the vow was taken, in the case of the father, whose authority does diminish, surely should be treated so that the act of remaining silent or hearing the vow should be equivalent to the day on which the vow was actually made.

L. Not at all, if you have stated the rule in the case of the husband, who has the power to nullify the vow in the case of a woman past puberty, therefore the law has treated the act of silence or first hearing the vow as equivalent to the day on which the vow was first taken, but will you say the same of the father, who does not have the power to nullify the vow in the case of a girl past puberty? Therefore in his case we should not treat the act of remaining silent or the occasion of first hearing the vow as equivalent to the day on which the vow was made.

M. I have not succeeded in composing an argument based on logic. Therefore it is necessary to appeal to Scripture, when it says, "These are the statutes that the Lord commanded Moses as between a man and his wife and between a father and his daughter while in her youth, within her father's house" (Num. 30:16)— you have no choice but to treat the father as comparable to the husband.

N. Just as in the case of the husband, the law has treated the act of remaining silent or the occasion of first hearing the vow as equivalent to the day on which the vow was taken, so that he may confirm the vow, so in the case of the father we should treat the act of remaining silent or hearing the vow as equivalent to the day on which the vow was made to confirm the vow.

The issue, D, is whether we treat the father's confirming the vow as comparable to his releasing it when it is taken. An analogy is proposed, E, treating the two actions as equivalent. That is because both of them are subject to the father's will. But, F, we can differentiate the two categories. The release of the vow takes place at the point at which the vow is treated as having been made, while confirming the vow is not comparable, G. Then a different tack is taken, H: the situation of the

## Fifteen. Sifré to Numbers

husband. Here we compare the husband's and the father's actions, and deem the rule the same for both, since both have the same power. J-K then offer an argument a fortiori along the same lines. L differentiates between the father and the husband. Then, M-N, Scripture takes over, logic having run its course without success, and Scripture establishes the governing analogy, N.

### III. TYPES OF ARGUMENTATION IN SIFRÉ TO NUMBERS

The sample illustrative of the types of argumentation in Sifré to Numbers that I have chosen leaves no doubt that a single type predominates: the argument built through analogy and contrast to sustain the proposition that *Scripture and not the analogical-contrastive logic alone serves to yield Halakhah: sound comparisons and contrasts for determination of the rule.* That argument, however, is not particular to the Halakhic compositions of the document. The same issue dominates in Aggadic discourse as well. A single example serves to show the ubiquity of the issues of analogical-contrastive thinking, in Aggadic as much as in Halakhic contexts.

## XXXIX:III
1. A. "The Lord said to Moses, Say to Aaron and his sons: Thus shall you bless the people of Israel:"
   B. [This must be done when the priests are] standing.
   C. You maintain that this must be done when the priests are standing.
   D. But perhaps it may be done either standing or not standing?
   E. Scripture states, "And these shall *stand* to bless the people" (Deut. 27:42).
   F. The word "blessing" occurs here and the word "blessing" occurs there. Just as the word "blessing" when it occurs at the later passage involves the priests' standing, so here too the word blessing indicates that the priests must be standing.
   G. R. Nathan says, "It is not necessary to invoke that analogy. For it is said, 'And the Levitical priests shall draw near, for the Lord has chosen them to serve him and to bestow a blessing in the name of the Lord' (Deut. 21:5). The act of bestowing a blessing is compared to the act of service. Just as service is performed only when standing, so bestowing a blessing is bestowed when standing."

## XXXIX:IV
1. A. "The Lord said to Moses, Say to Aaron and his sons: Thus shall you bless the people of Israel:"
   B. It must be done by raising the hands.
   C. You say it must be done by raising the hands.
   D. But perhaps it may be done either by raising the hands or not by raising the hands?
   E. Scripture says, "And Aaron raised his hands toward the people and blessed them" (Lev. 9:22).
   F. Just as Aaron bestowed the blessing by raising his hands, so his sons will bestow the blessing by raising their hands.

    G. R. Jonathan says, "But may one then say that just as that passage occurs in the setting of a blessing bestowed at the new moon, on the occasion of a public offering, and through the medium only of the high priest, so here too the blessing may be bestowed only at the new moon, on the occasion of a public offering, and through the medium only of the high priest!

    H. "Scripture states, 'For the Lord your God has chosen him above all your tribes' (Deut. 18:5). The Scripture compares his sons to him: just as he bestowed the blessing by raising his hands, so his sons will bestow the blessing by raising their hands."

### XXXIX:V

1. A. "The Lord said to Moses, Say to Aaron and his sons: Thus shall you bless the people of Israel:"
   B. It is to be done by expressing the fully spelled out Name of God.
   C. You maintain that it is to be done by expressing the fully spelled out Name of God. But perhaps it may be done with a euphemism for the Name of God?
   D. Scripture says, "So shall they put my name upon the people of Israel" (Num. 6:27).

2. A. "In the sanctuary it is to be done by expressing the fully spelled out Name of God. And in the provinces it is to be done by a euphemism," the words of R. Josiah.
   B. R. Jonathan says, "Lo, Scripture states, 'In every place in which I shall cause my name to be remembered' (Ex. 20:20). This verse of Scripture is out of order, and how should it be read? 'In every place in which I appear before you, there should my Name be mentioned.' And where is it that I appear before you? It is in the chosen house [the Temple]. So you should mention my name [as fully spelled out] only in the chosen house.
   C. "On this basis sages have ruled: 'As to the fully spelled out name of God, it is forbidden to express it in the provinces [but only in the sanctuary].'"

    The argument is precipitated by the proposal that the opposite of the proposition is the rule. This must be…You say that this must be…but perhaps it may be…. Then analogical argument resting on the appearance of the same word in two contexts follows. The word must bear the implications here that it does there. Then the analogy based on a word common to two contexts is shown not to be required, because a different analogy is available: that defined by Scripture in so many words: serving and bestowing a blessing, for XXXIX:III, and so throughout. So the argument concerns whether the generative analogy derives from shared language or shared deeds. But there is no doubt that the matter will be settled by the discovery of the correct comparison: unknown case to known case, unknown rule to known rule, as the context requires.

    Apart from the paramount type of argumentation we have examined, others command attention as well. The most important is the affirmative appeal to Scripture to begin with, not as part of a critique of analogical-contrasting reasoning but as an initial approach. This is done by challenging a proposition and offering the opposite, then invoking Scripture explicitly to prove the challenged proposition: lo we have

## Fifteen. Sifré to Numbers

learned... how then do we derive from Scripture.... What is critical here is the introduction of an exegetical principle that dictates how Scripture is to be read, used for the purposes of the present argument. That principle insists on two matters. First, Scripture does not use language pointlessly or redundantly, and, therefore, an argument resting on the particular implications or traits of a distinctive formulation always serves. Second, the Torah defines for us the rules of generalization and abstraction, explaining how to move from a particular case to an encompassing rule.

What characterizes Sifré to Numbers, by contrast to Leviticus Rabbah, lacking articulated argument, and to Genesis Rabbah, with its parsimonious corpus of argument, is the power not only to prove a point but also to define the logical grounds of proof. I find the best example at CXVIII:XIII. There the unknown is derived from the known by the identification of the proper analogy — and that is said in so many words:

I shall derive a lesson for one thing from the corresponding thing, and I shall draw a logical analogy for one thing from a corresponding thing. I shall derive a lesson for one thing, namely, that which falls into the category of Lesser Holy Things, from the corresponding thing, that is, that which falls into the category of Lesser Holy Things, but I shall not derive a lesson concerning something that falls into the category of Lesser Holy Things from something which falls into the category of Most Holy Things

Then the answer is to the point, the rule of argumentation affirmed, the pertinent data agreed upon, but the correct analogy defined through a shift in the definition of indicative data or quality:

I shall derive a lesson for one thing from the corresponding thing, and I shall draw a logical analogy for one thing from a corresponding thing. Specifically: I shall draw an analogy from that which is a gift to the priest for that which is a gift to the priest, but I shall not derive a rule for something that is a gift to the priest from something that is a gift to any person

What makes the argument dynamic and urgent is the provision of equally-compelling alternatives and the articulation of the basis for choosing one, rather than another, between them. The remainder of the exchange proves equally explicit as to not only the probative considerations but the reasoning that sustains selection of this type of proof, rather than some other, for the present purpose.

The sages of Sifré to Numbers, like their colleagues represented in the companion documents, come to the specificities of Scripture, its stories and its laws, with an interest in generalization and abstraction. Like philosophers, they wish to know the rule that prevails throughout, and they will not accept as adequate demonstration the allegedly self-evident implications of a particular case. Argumentation is critical to their purpose, which is to transform Scripture's narratives and laws into models and paradigms for the social order of holy Israel. And making the probative power of the argument explicit is what renders compelling the compositions of exegesis of Halakhic and Aggadic passages of Numbers alike.

### IV. Conclusion: Types of Argumentation of Rabbinic Judaism: Halakhic and. Aggadic

If I had to identify a single proposition to characterize all types of argumentation we have examined — and hypothetically, all types of Rabbinic argumentation, in all documents — it is a very simple one. Argumentation proceeds in accord with fixed rules of logic and of exegesis of received Scripture. What serves in one setting must govern in all others. Nothing arbitrary or merely exemplary suffices. No case can be settled by appeal to a rule particular to that case. Types of argumentation that are deemed probative here definitively prove the case everywhere else. True, the Aggadic documents are readily differentiated from one another, and the Aggadic sample at hand cannot be confused with the Halakhic counterpart in any way. But when we identify the rules of argumentation and the types of argumentation, we find a set of rules that govern everywhere, and a corpus of types that accommodates both the Halakhic and the (admittedly rather meager) Aggadic exercises of argument.

We began with the question, Do ubiquitous modes of thought — types of analysis, types of argumentation — pervade the entire corpus of the Rabbinic writings of late antiquity and impart coherence to those diverse documents? We may answer that question: general rules of argumentation govern both Halakhic and Aggadic thinking. These rules pertain to analogical-contrastive thinking, translated into exercises of argument, the Halakhic kind involving issues of defining likeness, the Aggadic kind pertaining to problems of selecting the correct parable. It comes down to the same thing. The two kinds of Rabbinic literature, in their types of argumentation, conform to a single set of rules, because they engage in a single mode of thought, that of comparison and contrast. And that mode of thought serves uniformly and consistently throughout: like follows the rule of the like, unlike, the opposite. Where argument enters in, it is in establishing the correct simile, metaphor, or parable, in determining matters of correspondence.

I began this project anticipating one result, but conclude it with the opposite outcome. I expected to show that the Halakhic and the Aggadic documents utilize each its own types of argumentation, respectively. I have shown that, in general terms, a single set of rules of argumentation governs throughout. True, I expected the Halakhic documents to yield a more clearly defined repertoire of types of argumentation, with which to interrogate the Aggadic documents in quest of counterparts and opposites. That is not how matters have turned out. The typology of Halakhic argumentation yielded only dialectical and non-dialectical categories, and the former finds no corresponding type of argument in the Aggadic writings.

So I have realized my original expectation: argumentation in the Halakhic

## Fifteen. Sifré to Numbers

documents is readily differentiated from that in the Aggadic ones. But as matters unfolded — in what remains a probe, not a definitive survey — another result made its appearance: the shared principle of arguing about similarities and differences between and among categories. And, we realize, in both the Aggadic and the Halakhic writing, that shared type of argumentation governs because both Aggadic and Halakhic writing aims at the same result. What is critical is not argument and contention — these are merely strategies of exposition — but what they make possible, which is, the testing of general rules and governing principles, whether of law or of lore, action or attitude, deed or deliberation.

That is, as I said, the reading of Scripture for philosophical and theological purposes: generalization and rationalization. In no other way but the sages' was the Torah to be translated from case to example, from narrative and rule-book into design for the social order — "kingdom of priests and holy people" — that God intended Israel to become. In concrete terms, if we wish to define Rabbinic Judaism, we must find our data in both Halakhic and Aggadic statements, specifically, where these join together in common cause.

STUDIES IN JUDAISM
TITLES IN THE SERIES

S. Daniel Breslauer

*Creating a Judaism Without Religion. A Postmodern Jewish Possibility.* Lanham, November 2001. University Press of America. Academic Studies in Ancient Judaism series.

Jacob Neusner

*Dual Discourse, Single Judaism.* Lanham, February 2001. University Press of America. Academic Studies in Ancient Judaism series.

*The Emergence of Judaism. Jewish Religion in Response to the Critical Issues of the First Six Centuries.* Lanham, April 2000. University Press of America. Academic Studies in Ancient Judaism series.

*The Halakhah and the Aggadah.* Lanham. February 2001. University Press of America. Academic Studies in Ancient Judaism series.

*The Hermeneutics of Rabbinic Category Formations.* Lanham, February 2001. University Press of America. Academic Studies in Ancient Judaism series.

Rivka Ulmer

*Pesiqta Rabbati. A Synoptic Edition of Pesiqta Rabbati Based upon all Extant Manuscripts and the Editio Princeps*, Lanham. January 2002. University Press of America. Academic Studies in Ancient Judaism series. Volume III

Edited by Jacob Neusner and James F. Strange

*Religious Texts and Material Contexts.* Lanham. August 2001. University Press of America. Academic Studies in Ancient Judaism series.

Leslie S. Wilson

*The Serpent Symbol in the Ancient Near East. Nahash and Asherah: Death, Life, and Healing.* Lanham. December 2001, University Press of America. Academic Studies in Ancient Judaism series.

Jacob Neusner

*Talmud Torah. Ways to God's Presence through Learning: An Exercise in Practical Theology.* Lanham, January 2002. University Press of America. Academic Studies in Ancient Judaism series.

Jacob Neusner

*The Aggadic Role in Halakhic Discourses.* Lanham. February 2001. University Press of America. Academic Studies in Ancient Judaism series. Volume I

*The Aggadic Role in Halakhic Discourses.* Lanham. February 2001. University Press of America. Academic Studies in Ancient Judaism series. Volume II

*The Aggadic Role in Halakhic Discourses.* Lanham. February 2001. University Press of America. Academic Studies in Ancient Judaism series. Volume III

*A Theological Commentary to the Midrash.* Lanham. April 2001. University Press of America. Academic Studies in Ancient Judaism series. Volume I. *Pesiqta deRab Kahana.*

*A Theological Commentary to the Midrash.* Lanham. March 2001. University Press of America. Academic Studies in Ancient Judaism series. - Volume II. *Genesis Raba.*

*A Theological Commentary to the Midrash.* Lanham. April 2001. University Press of America. Academic Studies in Ancient Judaism series. Volume III. *Song of Songs Rabbah*

*A Theological Commentary to the Midrash.* Lanham. April 2001. University Press of America. Academic Studies in Ancient Judaism series. Volume IV. *Leviticus Rabbah*

A Theological Commentary to the Midrash. Lanham. June 2001. University Press of America. Academic Studies in Ancient Judaism series. Volume V *Lamentations Rabbati*

*A Theological Commentary to the Midrash.* June 2001. University Press of America. Academic Studies in Ancient Judaism series. Volume VI. *Ruth Rabbah and Esther Rabbah I*

*A Theological Commentary to the Midrash.* June 2001. University Press of America. Academic Studies in Ancient Judaism series. Volume VII. *Sifra*

A Theological Commentary to the Midrash. July 2001. University Press of America. Academic Studies in Ancient Judaism series. Volume VIII. *Sifré to Numbers and Sifré to Deuteronomy*

A Theological Commentary to the Midrash. August 2001. University Press of America. Academic Studies in Ancient Judaism series. Volume IX. *Mekhilta Attributed to Rabbi Ishmael*

*The Unity of Rabbinic Discourse.* January 2001. University Press of America. Academic Studies in Ancient Judaism series. Volume I: *Aggadah in the Halakhah*

*The Unity of Rabbinic Discourse.* February 2001. University Press of America. Academic Studies in Ancient Judaism series. Volume II: *Halakhah in the Aggadah*

*The Unity of Rabbinic Discourse.* February 2001. University Press of America. Academic Studies in Ancient Judaism series. Volume III: *Halakhah and Aggadah in Concert*

**BM
496.5
.N4775
2003**